CANA

W9-BUW-371

St. Lawrence River

Plattsburgh

76°

11

Lake
Champlain

Adirondack Park

Watertown

A d i r o n d a c k

87

Mountains

Lake
George

81

11

Oneida
Lake

Utica

Saratoga Springs

VERMONT

90

Syracuse

Schenectady

NEW YORK

81

Mountains

Susquehanna River

88

ALBANY

90

MASS.

Glen
eny

17

Binghamton

81

11

Delaware River

Catskill Forest
Preserve
C a t s k i l l
M o u n t a i n s

87

Hudson River

CONN.

Kingston

6

Poughkeepsie
NY State
Thruway

72°

nna River

11

Scranton
Pocono
Mountains

TAINS

81

Delaware
Water Gap
Nat. Rec. Area

White
Plains

87

95

Long Island Sound

Yonkers

Long Island

80

Newark

Allentown

Bethlehem

78

New York

URG

Reading

95

TRENTON

Gateway
Nat. Rec. Area

Fire Island
National
Seashore

Long Branch

urnpike

76

NJ TPK

**NEW
JERSEY**

ATLANTIC

caster

Philadelphia

Camden

Cherry
Hill

OCEAN

95

Atlantic City Expwy.

Garden State Pkwy.

Vineland

Atlantic City

DEL.

Delaware Bay

Cape May

NATIONAL ————————
AUDUBON
———————— SOCIETY®
FIELD GUIDE TO THE
Mid-Atlantic
STATES

A Chanticleer Press Edition

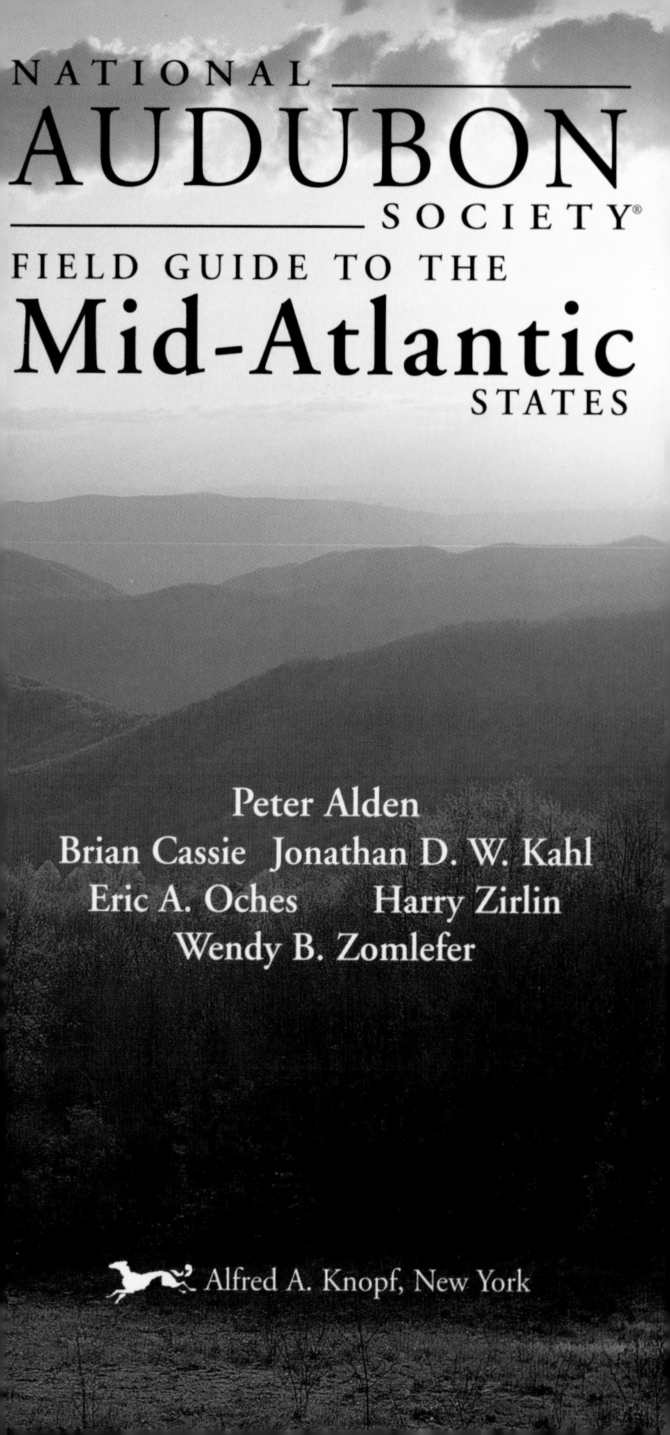

NATIONAL
AUDUBON
SOCIETY®
FIELD GUIDE TO THE
Mid-Atlantic
STATES

Peter Alden

Brian Cassie   Jonathan D. W. Kahl

Eric A. Oches   Harry Zirlin

Wendy B. Zomlefer

Alfred A. Knopf, New York

This is a Borzoi Book.
Published by Alfred A. Knopf, Inc.

Copyright © 1999 by Chanticleer Press, Inc.
All rights reserved under International and Pan-American Copyright Conventions. Published in the United States by Alfred A. Knopf, Inc., New York, and simultaneously in Canada by Random House of Canada Limited, Toronto. Distributed by Random House, Inc., New York.

Prepared and produced by
Chanticleer Press, Inc., New York.

Printed and bound by
Dai Nippon Printing Co., Ltd., Hong Kong.

First Edition
Published April 1999
First Printing

Library of Congress Cataloging-in-Publication Data

National Audubon Society field guide to the Mid-Atlantic states /
   Peter Alden . . . [et al.]. — 1st ed.
     p. cm.
   Includes index.
   ISBN 0-679-44682-6 (hc)
    1. Natural history—Middle Atlantic States—Guidebooks.
  2. Natural areas—Middle Atlantic States—Guidebooks. 3. Parks—
Middle Atlantic States—Guidebooks I. Alden, Peter.
II. National Audubon Society.
QH104.5.M45N38 1999
508.75—dc21   98-38191

Front Cover: Youghiogheny River, Ohiopyle State Park, Pennsylvania
Spine: Higbee Beach, Cape May, New Jersey
Back Cover: Crescent moon and Venus at dawn; Saltmarsh Sabatia; Snow Goose; George Washington National Forest, Virginia
Table of Contents: Plate tectonics illustration; Mill Creek, Delaware Water Gap, Pennsylvania; full moon; palmately compound leaf; horned owl; Niagara Falls, New York
Title Page: Hazeltop Ridge, Shenandoah National Park, Virginia
Pages 8–9: Bluff on the New River, Giles County, Virginia
Pages 74–75: Yellow-rumped Warbler
Pages 370–371: Dolly Sods Wilderness and Scenic Area, Monongahela National Forest, West Virginia

National Audubon Society

The mission of NATIONAL AUDUBON SOCIETY is to conserve and restore natural ecosystems, focusing on birds, other wildlife, and their habitats, for the benefit of humanity and the earth's biological diversity.

One of the largest, most effective environmental organizations, Audubon has 550,000 members, 100 sanctuaries, state offices, and nature centers, and 500-plus chapters in the Americas, plus a professional staff of scientists, lobbyists, lawyers, policy analysts, and educators.

Our award-winning *Audubon* magazine, published six times a year and sent to all members, carries outstanding articles and color photography on wildlife and nature, presenting in-depth reports on critical environmental issues, as well as conservation news and commentary. Audubon also publishes *Audubon Adventures,* a children's newsletter reaching 450,000 students in grades four through six. Through our ecology camps and workshops in Maine, Connecticut, and Wyoming, we offer professional development for educators and activists; through Audubon Expedition Institute in Belfast, Maine, the Society offers unique, traveling undergraduate and graduate degree programs in Environmental Education.

National Audubon Society also sponsors books, field guides, and CD-ROM programs, plus nature travel to exotic places like Antarctica, Africa, Baja California, Patagonia, and the Galápagos Islands.

For information about how you can become an Audubon member, subscribe to *Audubon Adventures,* or to learn more about our camps and workshops, please write or call:

NATIONAL AUDUBON SOCIETY
Membership Dept.
700 Broadway
New York, New York 10003
212-979-3000 or 800-274-4201
http://www.audubon.org

Contents
Part One: Overview

Overview

Natural Highlights

The 180,446 square miles of the Mid-Atlantic region comprise an enormous spectrum of natural delights. One can stare awestruck at New York's Niagara Falls, revel in Pennsylvania's wildflowers, explore for rare plants in New Jersey's Pine Barrens, walk among towering Yellow Poplars in Delaware, canoe a serene Maryland river, hike Virginia's Shenandoah Valley, raft a glorious West Virginia whitewater river, or enjoy the natural environments of these states in any of a thousand other ways. From New York's Mount Marcy and Virginia's Mount Rogers to the expansive beaches and marshlands of the Atlantic shoreline, the Mid-Atlantic region has a superb diversity of natural vistas, habitats, and phenomena.

Migration

Red Knots at Reed's Beach, New Jersey

Nowhere in North America are the annual migrations of birds, butterflies, and dragonflies played out on such a vast scale as in the Mid-Atlantic region. On mountain ridges, Great Lakes shorelines, and coastal peninsulas, birds of prey congregate by the tens of thousands. Shorebirds, swallows, warblers, and other small birds pass through in astronomical numbers, and the waterfowl migration is equally superb. In fall, Monarchs, darner dragonflies, and other showy insects swarm along the Atlantic coast. Presque Isle, Pennsylvania (on the shore of Lake Erie), and Cape May, New Jersey (on the Atlantic coast), offer perhaps the best spring and fall shows, respectively.

Spring Wildflowers

From April in the lowlands to June in the mountains, Mid-Atlantic woodlands offer a breathtaking display of wildflowers in bloom. Every state has regions of vernal wildflower splendor, from acidic bogs and heathlands to limestone-rich hillsides. Many of the richest wildflower communities grow in the fertile soils of the northern hardwood forests, under Sugar Maples and American Beeches. Blue-eyed Mary, Wild Geranium, Virginia Bluebell, and Dutchman's Breeches are but a few of the species that emerge each spring.

Blue Phlox, Shenk's Ferry Glen
Wildflower Preserve, Pennsylvania

Appalachian Mountains

Shenandoah National Park, Virginia

Botanists may look for micro-habitats; herpetologists may turn over rocks looking for rare salamanders; butterfly watchers may hike hillside glades in search of a Diana Fritillary, but most visitors to the Appalachians come for the gorgeous scenery—the tranquil valleys, the splendid coves, the redbuds and dogwoods in spring, the maples and hickories in fall. Shenandoah National Park, more than 96 percent undeveloped, epitomizes the Appalachian landscape.

Gorges, Glens, and Waterfalls

Falling water creates inspiring sights and sounds in the Mid-Atlantic region, which has some of the most memorable gorges, glens, and waterfalls anywhere. Niagara Falls is the most famous, but Taughannock Creek Gorge and Watkins Glen in New York, Great Falls on the Potomac, Pine Creek Gorge Natural Area in Pennsylvania, and the Delaware Water Gap National Recreation Area between Pennsylvania and New Jersey are also choice sites.

Taughannock Creek Gorge, New York

Chesapeake Bay

The huge amounts of nutrients that enter shallow Chesapeake Bay—from the Susquehanna, James, Potomac, Nanticoke, Chester, Choptank, and other rivers, and with the ebb and flow of the tides—make the Chesapeake an unrivaled source of food for all manner of invertebrates and verte-

Blue Crab

brates. Great numbers of ducks and geese, fishes, crabs, shrimps, jellyfishes, and mollusks abound in every convoluted corner of this enormous estuary. Several state and federal wildlife areas ring Chesapeake Bay, but wildlife proliferates seemingly everywhere in the half million wetland acres that surround these waters.

Topography

Mid-Atlantic topography ranges from glacially sculpted landforms in the north, through mountains, plateaus, ridges, and valleys farther south and west, to a broad eastern coastal plain. The highest peaks are Mount Marcy (5,344 feet) in New York's Adirondacks and Mount Rogers (5,729 feet) in Virginia. Most major rivers, including the Hudson, Delaware, Susquehanna, Potomac, James, and Roanoke, flow southeast and east, emptying into the Atlantic Ocean. The Genesee River, the only major north-flowing river, runs from northern Pennsylvania into Lake Ontario. The Allegheny River begins in Pennsylvania, winds into and out of New York, and later joins the Ohio River at Pittsburgh.

Niagara Falls and the Finger Lakes

The water that spills over Niagara Falls, on the U.S.–Canada border in western New York, is outflow from Lakes Superior, Michigan, Huron, and Erie. The Finger Lakes, between Rochester and Syracuse, are 11 parallel troughs carved into already existing valleys by glacial ice. Long, narrow, and deep, the troughs became lakes when a ridge of sediment deposited by a glacier dammed their southern ends 12,000 years ago.

Allegheny Plateau

South and west of the Adirondacks, the Allegheny Plateau—an area of irregularly shaped hills and depressions—extends through southern New York, northern and western Pennsylvania, Ohio, and West Virginia. The plateau region of West Virginia appears mountainous, but the narrow valleys resulted when rivers and streams carved deep into the landscape; the "hilltops," all at about the same elevation, represent the original plateau surface.

Appalachian Ridges and Valleys

To the east of the Allegheny Plateau are the "folded" Appalachians, parallel bands of valleys carved into soft shales, alternating with ridges held up by resistant sandstone and limestone. This zone begins in the lower Hudson River Valley near Kingston, New York, and extends south as the tilted and plunging ridges of central Pennsylvania, through to the Great Valley of Virginia. The valley and ridge formation resulted from plate tectonic collisions and associated folding of thick layers of sediment around 300 million years ago.

Adirondack Mountains

Formed more than a billion years ago, the Adirondack Mountains encompass most of northeastern New York state and include some of the region's oldest rocks. The largest sector, the Highlands Adirondacks, includes the state's tallest mountains; the High Peaks area has more than 40 summits higher than 4,000 feet. Beyond the central peaks, the surface flattens out in three directions—toward the St. Lawrence River to the north, Lake Ontario to the west, and the Mohawk Lowlands to the south; the eastern margin is more abrupt, dropping sharply down into the Champlain Lowlands. The Lowlands Adirondacks, on the range's northwestern side, include a small region of foothills covered with dense forests, swampy wetlands, and winding rivers.

The Piedmont and the Coastal Plain

The piedmont (the word means "foot of the mountain") is a region of gently rolling hills that extends from New York to Alabama east of the Appalachians. It slopes gradually eastward, dropping from an elevation of some 1,300 feet adjacent to the Blue Ridge to about 300 feet at the fall line, the point at which streams and rivers cutting across hard upland rocks plunge down onto the softer sediments of the broad, flat coastal plain. The Mid-Atlantic coastal plain, a region of relatively flat topography between the piedmont and the Atlantic Ocean, is dissected by the Delaware and Chesapeake Bays. The coastal plain narrows northward from Virginia and disappears just south of New York City.

Blue Ridge Mountains

The Blue Ridge is a section of the Appalachians that extends from south-central Pennsylvania across Maryland and Virginia into North Carolina, Georgia, and Alabama. Varying in the Mid-Atlantic region from a 2-mile-wide irregular ridge of mountains to a 10- to 14-mile-wide series of ridges, the Blue Ridge has rugged slopes and summits that range from about 1,200 feet near the Potomac River to Mount Rogers, at 5,729 feet.

Ocean and Coast

New York's Long Island, bulldozed into place by glaciers of the last ice age, is the northernmost limit of the Mid-Atlantic coast. Extending some 435 miles to Virginia's border with North Carolina, the coast is protected by an extensive series of barrier islands, and is interrupted by many estuaries and bays, all of which expand the total shoreline to 10,440 miles. The tidal range is three to five feet; major rivers emptying into the Atlantic Ocean feel the influence of the twice-daily high and low tides as far inland as the fall line. Northern New Jersey has long stretches of mainland beaches, but most of the Mid-Atlantic shoreline is dominated by offshore barrier islands; lagoons and coastal salt marshes between the barriers and the mainland provide a rich habitat for nearshore sea creatures.

Barrier Islands

The barrier islands that dominate the Mid-Atlantic coastline are long, relatively straight ridges of sand lying parallel to the main coast; their formation is favored by the wide, gently sloping continental shelf, abundant sediment, and a relatively

Assateague Island, Maryland

low tidal range. In their natural state, barrier islands have wide sandy beaches, prominent dunes, and back-island mud flats, salt marshes, and lagoons. Waves striking the coast at an angle create currents that carry sediment along the shore, removing or depositing sand, or extending spits in a down-current direction.

Marsh at Deal Island, Maryland

Salt Marshes

Coastal wetlands are flooded and drained by rising and falling tides in protected tidal flats of estuaries and back-barrier lagoons. Rivers emptying into estuaries carry abundant nutrient-rich mineral sediment that supports the growth and expansion of the region's extensive salt marshes. Salt-tolerant plants play an important ecological role in this environment: they build and maintain peat layers by trapping sediment with their roots, and provide habitat, nurseries, and food for fish, fiddler crabs, mussels, and other marsh animals. These wetlands also act as buffers during coastal storms.

Satellite image of Chesapeake Bay

Estuaries

Rivers meet the sea along much of the coast, forming many of the estuaries and bays that occur along 75 percent of the shoreline. Broad, shallow estuaries, including Chesapeake and Delaware Bays, were formed as sea levels rose at the end of the last ice age, about 12,000 years ago, drowning the valleys of rivers draining the Appalachians and the piedmont. As the tides rise and fall, water in the estuaries becomes brackish—a mixture of freshwater inflow from rivers and the ocean's salt water.

Offshore Environment

Warm southern waters are transported north by the Gulf Stream, a 60-mile-wide, 2,000-foot-deep ocean current that begins in the Gulf of Mexico, occasionally bringing with it tropical storms and hurricanes. The continental shelf extends as far as 125 miles out into the ocean, where it reaches a depth of about 200 feet be-

Atlantic Ocean off Mid-Atlantic region (Gulf Stream is pink)

fore the continental slope abruptly drops off to depths of as much as 8,200 feet. The continental shelf off the Mid-Atlantic region has several "canyons" formed when drainage from melting glaciers cut into sediments on the shelf floor.

THE FORMATION OF CHESAPEAKE BAY

The largest coastal estuary in the United States, Chesapeake Bay is a complex of estuaries dominated by the Susquehanna River and including the Potomac, Rappahannock, York, and James Rivers. Covering 2,300 square miles and nearly 187 miles long, the bay ranges from 4 to 30 miles wide and has an average depth of 26 feet. A 56-mile-wide meteor impact crater is buried 1,300 feet below the floor of the lower bay, beneath the town of Cape Charles, Virginia, on the lower Delmarva Peninsula. This impact, which occurred 35 million years ago, may have determined the location of Chesapeake Bay by causing a downwarping of the earth's crust. About 20,000 years ago, during the last ice age, the Susquehanna River drained the piedmont and carved a valley into the soft coastal plain sediments. As the ice melted and sea level rose, the valley filled with water, and Chesapeake Bay gradually took on its modern appearance.

The Sculpting of the Landscape

The topography of the Mid-Atlantic region was shaped by the great tectonic forces of the earth's shifting crustal plates, combined with hundreds of millions of years of erosion by water and wind, and by the waxing and waning of the glaciers of the last 2 million years. Plate tectonic movements forced landmasses together several times in the last 1.2 billion years.

Plate Tectonics

According to the theory of plate tectonics, earth's surface is broken into a dozen major plates that constantly move as a result of convection currents generated by the planet's internal heat. Three types of motion occur along the boundaries of these plates.

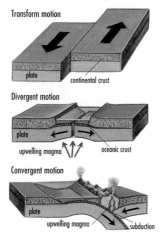

Transform boundaries, or fault lines, where plates are laterally sliding past each other, are the sites of earthquakes. At **divergent** plate boundaries, the plates move away from one another, or rift apart. Magma (molten rock) rises from within the earth and fills the void that was created, solidifying under the ocean as new seafloor or on land as a rift valley. At **convergent** plate boundaries, two plates collide, causing a buckling of the continental crust and forcing one plate beneath the other in a process called subduction, which can result in earthquakes and volcanoes. All the major mountain chains, including the Appalachians, and 80 percent of earth's volcanoes are located along convergent plate boundaries. Convergence events that create mountains are called orogenies.

Transverse Drainage

An interesting drainage pattern has developed across ridges and valleys of the Appalachian Mountains—rivers that cut deep gorges across ridges rather than following them in parallel fashion, as would be expected. Geologists suggest

Delaware River, with Interstate 80 on right

that, as folding and uplift of mountains proceeded, the rivers continued to follow their ancient paths, cutting through the sedimentary cover on the surface, eventually breaching the crests of the new ridges, forming transverse gorges, and connecting adjacent valleys.

Continental Rifting

Hudson River palisades at Alpine, New Jersey

Rifting, the tearing apart of earth's crust, occurred in the Mid-Atlantic piedmont 250 million years ago, the same time period when the Atlantic Ocean began forming between the diverging continents of North America, northwest Africa, and Europe. From New York to Virginia, a major basin developed as large blocks of crust dropped down along faults, and as lava flowed up along fissures extending deep into the crust; the Hudson River palisades are the result of this magma intrusion, which was later brought to the surface by erosion. Rivers flowing from highlands on either side of the rift valley transported vast amounts of sediment that, along with volcanic rocks, filled the basin in layers up to 3 miles thick.

Ancient rift basin (red) of Mid-Atlantic region

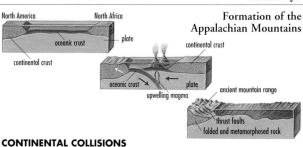

Formation of the Appalachian Mountains

CONTINENTAL COLLISIONS

The folded, faulted, and uplifted Appalachian Mountains formed as a result of three major orogenies, collectively called the Appalachian Orogeny. In the Taconic Orogeny, which formed New York's Taconic Mountains and the New England mountains 450 million years ago, North America and northwest Africa converged, subducting part of eastern North America beneath an offshore volcanic island arc, buckling the continent and uplifting mountains. About 380 million years ago, the Acadian Orogeny refolded and faulted the formations of the Taconic period. The major folding and uplifting of the Appalachian Mountains occurred 300 million years ago during the Alleghenian Orogeny, when ocean bottom crust was subducted beneath eastern Appalachian crust, resulting in the folding and faulting observed in rock outcrops today. During these successive collisions, uplift formed mountain ranges perhaps as high as the Alps or the Himalayas; hundreds of millions of years of water and wind erosion of overlying sediments have produced the gentler topography of the modern Appalachians.

Effects of Glaciers

During the most recent ice age, which ended 10,000 years ago, the Laurentide Ice Sheet, a glacier covering the northeastern United States as far south as Long Island, New York, was a mile thick. As it expanded and retreated, the ice scoured surfaces, sculpted bedrock, and captured eroded debris and deposited it elsewhere. It carved out the basins of the Great Lakes, and created Niagara Falls when it retreated north of the U.S.–Canada border. The landscape of nearly all of New York and northern Pennsylvania retains abundant evidence of glacial action. Glaciers are of two types: Continent-size ice sheets slowly advance outward from a center of accumulation; smaller valley glaciers form in high mountains when accumulated snow compresses into ice and travels downhill.

GLACIAL GORGES

Letchworth Gorge near Rochester, New York

The Laurentide Ice Sheet gouged existing river valleys into deep troughs (gorges). Sediment that acted as a natural dam was often deposited at the terminus of these troughs, forming lakes, including the Finger Lakes of central New York. Erosion destroyed many of the dams, so that today there are many more gorges than lakes. Tributary streams entering the gorges from the sides carved deep canyons, or glens, into the bedrock, and became impressive waterfalls; spectacular examples are Taughannock Falls near Ithaca and Rainbow Falls near Watkins Glen.

ESKERS

As the glacier melted, water flowed like rivers on top of, within, or beneath the ice sheet, carrying large amounts of sediment (sand, gravel, and rocks) that accumulated in cavities in the ice and that were lowered to the ground when the glacier wasted away. One such formation is the esker, a narrow, sinuous ridge of sand and gravel. Found throughout the Adirondacks, eskers are about 50 feet high and up to a few hundred feet wide at the base; they range from a quarter mile to more than 100 miles long.

DRUMLIN FIELDS

The area in New York bounded by Rochester, Syracuse, Lake Ontario, and the Finger Lakes is one of the world's largest and best-developed fields of drumlins—streamlined, asymmetric hills of compacted sediment deposited and molded by the base of an ice sheet. Between 50 and 200 feet high and a few thousand

Drumlin near Livingston, New York

feet long, drumlins typically trail off to a sloping point in the direction the ice flowed, and occur in clusters or fields. The New York drumlin field contains more than 10,000 of these glacially formed hills.

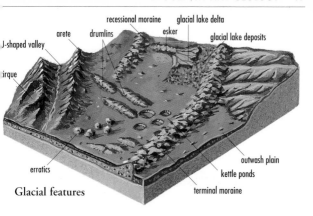

recessional moraine
glacial lake delta
esker
glacial lake deposits
arete
drumlins
cirque
J-shaped valley
erratics
outwash plain
kettle ponds
terminal moraine

Glacial features

KETTLE PONDS

Kettle ponds are sites where blocks of ice broke off from the ice sheet and were buried as meltwater carrying debris built up plains of outwash material around and over them. When the ice blocks melted, the sediment burying them collapsed and the resulting depressions in the sand filled with water, which is replenished by precipitation and groundwater. Kettle ponds dot the landscape of New York and northern Pennsylvania.

Whiteface Mountain, New York

U-SHAPED VALLEYS AND CIRQUES

Valley glaciers high in the Adirondack and Catskill Mountains entered V-shaped valleys and carved out flat floors and steep sides. These U-shaped valleys are often headed by cirques (natural amphitheaters) carved into a mountain peak. Several peaks near Lake Placid, New York—including Whiteface, Lookout, and Esther Mountains—have cirques with headwall cliffs 1,000 feet high.

MORAINES AND OUTWASH PLAINS

When the Laurentide Ice Sheet reached its maximum extent about 21,000 years ago, it covered nearly all of New York, extended southeast across northern Pennsylvania and northern New Jersey, and terminated at Long Island, whose formation is associated with the build-up of extensive ice-shoved ridges of sediments called terminal or end moraines. Long Island's two moraines, the Ronkonkoma and Harbor Hill Moraines, exist along a line that connects to similar ridges that form the spines of Block Island, Nantucket, and Martha's Vineyard to the east and that extend northwest across Pennsylvania to Allegany State Park, New York. South of the Long Island moraines lie outwash plains, formed when meltwater flowed in large volume from the glacier and spread gravel, sand, and mud out into flat, level terrain.

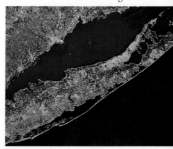

Long Island, New York

Fossils

A fossil is any indication of past plant or animal life, including petrified wood, dinosaur bones, ancient seashells, footprints, and casts in the shape of an animal left in the rock after the organism itself disintegrated. Almost all fossils are discovered in sedimentary rocks, usually in areas that were once covered by water, which explains why many fossils are of aquatic or marine species. The Mid-Atlantic region is underlain by thick layers of sedimentary rocks, including limestone, sandstone, shale, and coal, which preserve a diverse record of past life extending back about 600 million years.

DINOSAUR BONES

The inner coastal plain cuts in a wide, diagonal swath across New Jersey from Raritan Bay to the head of Delaware Bay. This region, underlain by clay and sand deposited between 100 and 50 million years ago, is the site of the earliest major dinosaur discoveries in North America. Beds of marl (loose earthy deposits containing abundant calcium carbonate) mined there as fertilizer in the mid-1800s have yielded many dinosaur fossils. One of these, the famed *Hadrosaurus foulkii,* discovered near Camden in 1858, became the first mounted dinosaur displayed anywhere in the world.

DINOSAUR FOOTPRINTS

Some 250 million years ago, rifting formed a series of basins extending from New York to Virginia. Sediments eroded from the highlands on either side of the great valley filled expansive, shallow lakes on its floor. During dry periods, the margins of these lakes became wide mudflats where dinosaurs left their tracks to be baked in the sun and buried by later floods. Footprints and fossils of several dinosaur species, including the flesh-eating genus *Eubrontes,* which lived 200 million years ago, have been found in shales of ancient lakebed sediments in northern New Jersey and Virginia.

PLANT FOSSILS

Fossil plants preserved in coal beds of West Virginia, Virginia, and Pennsylvania paint a picture of vast tropical swamps that existed 360 to 280 million years ago. *Lepidodendron* and *Sigillaria,* "scale trees" that grew 100 feet high and 3 feet in diameter and that were abundant in the coal swamps, are recognized by their distinctive trunk impressions in coal. Ferns and palm-like plants called cycads are also commonly preserved in the region's coal beds.

SEA SCORPION

An unusual fossil of *Eurypterus remipes,* nicknamed the "sea scorpion," has been found in 400-million-year-old shale and dolomite deposits in upstate New York. The sea scorpion, which grew to 9 feet in length, was one of the few creatures living in its inhospitable supersaline environment, which was probably comparable to today's Dead Sea. Fossil eurypterids have also been found in shales associated with coal beds near Blacksburg, Virginia. The sea scorpion was extinct by about 250 million years ago.

VERTEBRATE FOSSILS

In addition to dinosaur fossils, Mid-Atlantic region coastal plain sediments have yielded abundant remains of other vertebrates, including impressive skeletons of crocodiles, porpoises, sea turtles, walruses, and whales, as well as fossilized sharks' teeth. Vertebrate fossils from ancient saltmarsh deposits near Saltville, Virginia, include the remains of mastodons, bison, caribou, horses, wooly mammoths, muskoxen, and ground sloths.

MARINE FOSSILS

Marine specimens between 300 and 500 million years old are found in limestone formed by expansive seas that covered much of New York, Pennsylvania, West Virginia, and western Virginia. (Limestone forms either from the accumulation of carbonate remains of sea creatures or from the chemical precipitation of calcite from seawater.) Limestone outcroppings in these areas are likely to contain fossils of various types—brachiopods, corals, echinoderms, trilobites, bivalves, cephalopods, and gastropods, among others. Shells of clams, oysters, scallops, and snails found in coastal plain sediments of New Jersey, Maryland, and Virginia are up to 30 million years old and are so well preserved that one could think they were modern.

Minerals

Minerals, the building blocks of rocks, are naturally occurring inorganic, crystalline substances with characteristic chemical compositions and structures that determine their appearance. A mineral may be a single native element, such as copper or gold, or a compound of elements, such as quartz (silicon and oxygen) or calcite (calcium, carbon, and oxygen). Minerals are recognized by such physical properties as hardness (a "scratch test" is noted for several minerals

TALC
Pearly whitish to pale-green color; feels greasy. One of the softest minerals; easily scratched by fingernail. Used in talcum powder. Talc-rich rocks, called soapstones, are found as small, pod-like bodies in piedmont; pre-Columbian people quarried soapstones in Pennsylvania and Washington, D.C., areas to carve as bowls and sculpture. Occurs in Blue Ridge and piedmont metamorphic rocks in New York, Pennsylvania, and Virginia.

CALCITE
Transparent to translucent; white or colorless; sometimes pale gray, yellow, red, green, or blue. Principal mineral in limestone. May form coarsely crystalline veins in places. Key properties: softness (can be scratched with a penny); commonly forms large rhombohedral crystals. Clear crystals or fragments produce a double image of objects viewed through them. Widespread and common in region. "Cave rock" (such as stalactites and dripstone) is commonly all calcite.

FELDSPAR
Very common family of minerals. All are opaque and rather hard when fresh (scratch glass, but not quartz), but weathering rapidly alters them to clay. Two common forms in region. **Microcline:** white to pink; with quartz, a main constituent of all granites. **Plagioclase:** white to dark gray, sometimes iridescent; major mineral in Adirondack anorthosites.

NEW JERSEY'S UNIQUE MINERALS
Franklin, New Jersey, is the site of a billion-year-old lead-zinc deposit with minerals found nowhere else in the United States: *Franklinite* is black, with a dense, metallic luster; it forms small octohedral grains. Franklinite is found with *zincite,* which is rust-red with a greasy luster (like a varnished table), and *willemite,* which is pale yellow-green and often occurs in clusters of short, prismatic crystals. A good place to see them is the Franklin Mineral Museum and Collecting Site, on Evans Road, in Franklin, New Jersey.

below), cleavage or fracture (the planes along which they break), luster (the way the surface reflects light), and crystal structure. Color may be an unreliable identifying feature, since minor impurities can cause significant color variations. However, streak (color left by a mineral scraped against unglazed porcelain) is diagnostic for many softer minerals.

GARNET
Many varieties, but most commonly red. Forms well-developed 10- or 20-sided round crystals, even in rocks. Glassy luster; very hard (similar to quartz). Found in metamorphic rocks of Blue Ridge and piedmont. Common around Gore Mountain, New York.

MICA
A soft, platy mineral, readily broken or peeled into flat, paper-thin sheets. Two kinds are common. **Muscovite:** colorless to white; found with garnet in Appalachian metamorphic rocks, such as schist, and in some granites. **Biotite:** dark brown to black; common as a minor mineral in granites. Shiny, flake-like minerals in rock are usually mica.

QUARTZ
The most common mineral; occurs in many colors and forms. Can be white, gray, red, purple, pink, yellow, green, brown, or black. Usually transparent or milky; glassy luster; breaks like glass. The hardest common mineral. A main constituent in granites, sandstones, and beach sands. Common form: flint (gray to black, microcrystalline quartz), found as pods in limestones. For "Herkimer diamonds" (pictured here), see box.

HERKIMER DIAMONDS
Herkimer County, near Utica in east-central New York, is rich in "Herkimer diamonds," clear quartz crystals with pyramidal ends that resemble diamonds and that grew in cavities in the dolomite-limestone bedrock. See them off the New York State Thruway at Crystal Grove, in St. Johnsville (exit 29) and at Herkimer Diamond Development and Ace of Diamonds Mine, between the villages of Herkimer and Middleville (exit 30).

Rocks

A given rock may be composed of one mineral or may be an aggregate of different minerals. Rocks provide a record of many geologic processes that are impossible to observe directly—for example, the melting of rocks in earth's interior. Clues to the identification of rocks are provided by their appearance and constituent minerals.

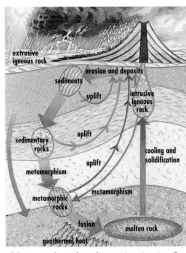

The Rock Cycle

The three basic classes of rocks undergo processes that convert them from one form to another. *Igneous* rocks form through solidification of molten material from earth's interior. Extrusive igneous rock forms on earth's surface through volcanic activity; intrusive igneous rock solidifies below the surface. *Sedimentary* rocks form from consolidation of layers of sediment (fragments of older, weathered rock ranging in size from submicroscopic particles to boulders, and/or organic or chemical matter) deposited at earth's surface. *Metamorphic* rocks form when existing rocks are transformed through heat and/or pressure. Deep within the earth, metamorphic rock is fused into molten rock. As the small arrows on the drawing indicate, the complete cycle can be interrupted (and restarted) at any point. In the Mid-Atlantic region, relatively young sedimentary rocks formed between 5 and 60 million years ago in the coastal plain, while older sedimentary rocks, formed 180 to 250 million years ago, fill New Jersey's rift basin. The piedmont and Blue Ridge have abundant metamorphic rocks and intruded granites. The Allegheny Plateau and areas with valley and ridge topography have mainly older sedimentary rocks, formed between 330 and 600 million years ago in the ocean that preceded the Atlantic.

Bedrock Geology

Bedrock is continuous solid rock either exposed at earth's surface or covered by soil and sediment. In the Mid-Atlantic region, bedrock ranges from igneous granite and metamorphic gneiss and schist over a billion years old in the Adirondacks and parts of the piedmont to younger schists and slates in the Blue Ridge, folded layers in the valley and ridge province, basalts in the ancient rift valleys, and vast areas of horizontal limestone, sandstone, and shale in the Allegheny Plateau and coastal plain regions.

Caves

Luray Caverns, Virginia

Caves form as naturally acidic groundwater slowly dissolves away limestone. The long-term flow of the water through bedrock causes small cracks to grow into shafts and eventually expand into large chambers. The characteristic topography (called "karst") of regions underlain by caves includes sinkholes, springs, natural bridges, disappearing streams, and networks of underground tunnels, with stalactites, stalagmites, columns, and curtains. Impressive caves in the region include Howe Caverns, near Schenectady, New York; Lincoln Cavern, near Huntingdon, Pennsylvania; the Luray Caverns of Virginia; and many others in western Virginia and West Virginia.

LIMESTONE

Sedimentary rock. *Constituent materials:* calcite, either derived from the accumulation of shells of marine organisms or chemically precipitated from seawater. Often contains fossil shells, coral, other shelled sea creatures. *Appearance:* gray or tan; forms hard layers. Very common in western areas of New York, Pennsylvania, and West Virginia.

SANDSTONE

Sedimentary rock. *Appearance:* varies from brownish red in rift valleys to tan in coastal plain sandstone ("brownstone"); color comes from iron oxides that cement together the *constituent minerals:* sand-size quartz and feldspar grains. Features preserved in sandstone provide clues about the environment in which the sediment accumulated.

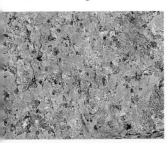

GRANITE

Intrusive igneous rock. *Constituent minerals:* quartz (clear to white), feldspar (pink or white), and dark-colored mica. *Appearance:* speckled pink, white, and gray-black; large, coarse-grained crystals. Seen along Skyline Drive, in Shenandoah National Park, and in Blue Ridge Mountains of Virginia. Also common throughout Virginia piedmont.

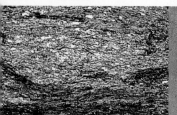

SCHIST

Metamorphic rock common in Appalachians; formed from such other rocks as shale, sandstone, basalt, slate, and granite. *Constituent minerals:* half are platy minerals (those that separate into flat sheets), usually micas (muscovite and biotite); also quartz, feldspar, chlorite, and garnet. *Appearance:* breaks into thin, wavy sheets; can be blue, green, or other colors; medium- to coarse-grained.

SHALE

Fine-grained sedimentary rock. *Constituent minerals:* mix of clay minerals, quartz, mica, and feldspar. *Appearance:* usually grayish to black; often finely layered; splits easily along flat planes. Forms in aquatic environments; often contains fossils. Often found with sandstone and limestone. When metamorphosed, becomes slate, a smooth hard rock that can be red, purple, or green.

GNEISS

Metamorphic rock common in the Appalachians; forms from granites and other rocks rich in quartz and feldspar. *Constituent minerals:* same as in schist, but richer in quartz and feldspars. *Appearance:* prominent mineral banding (interlayered bands of quartz, feldspar, micas, and garnet) and augen (large crystals of feldspar or garnet rimmed by micas, giving the impression of an eye).

BASALT

Igneous rock formed as lava erupts at or near earth's surface. *Constituent minerals:* feldspar and pyroxene. *Appearance:* dark green to black; very fine-grained. **Columnar basalt:** geometrically shaped pillars formed at or near surface. **Pillow basalt:** sac-shaped lumps formed as lava rose through earth's crust and cooled rapidly in water. Found in rift basins of New Jersey and northeastern Virginia.

COAL

A sedimentary "rock" that contains no real minerals. *Constituent materials:* carbon formed from remains of swamp vegetation; originates as peat (vegetable tissue formed by partial decomposition in water of plants). *Appearance:* changes with heat and pressure to a soft, brown fuel called lignite, then to bituminous (or soft) coal, finally to glossy black anthracite (or hard) coal.

Habitats

A habitat is an area of land or water with a substrate and climate that make it an agreeable environment for a predictable collection of plants that in turn support characteristic animals. Some of the factors that influence an area's habitat are availability of water, the shape or contour of the land, elevation, soil and underlying rock types, and climate (temperature, precipitation, exposure, and wind). Across the Mid-Atlantic region, a remarkable variety of habitats has developed over the eons, from a glacial relict alpine habitat in the Adirondacks to the unique heath "balds" of the southern Appalachians and, in the southeast, several habitats that barely extend into the region from the South. The following pages present nine characteristic Mid-Atlantic habitats and important natural communities within each one.

Food Chains and Webs

Primary consumer

In any ecosystem there are three categories of organisms: producers, consumers, and decomposers. Green plants are food producers. Animals are consumers. Herbivores, which consume plant matter directly, are primary consumers. They may be leaf-eating grasshoppers, acorn-eating Blue Jays, or White-tailed Deer browsing on all manner of vegetation. Secondary consumers, or primary carnivores, are those that devour the primary consumers—examples are ladybugs (eat aphids), Rat Snakes (consume birds and rodents), and Red Foxes (feed on Eastern Cottontails). There are also tertiary consumers, or secondary carnivores; a Snowy Egret might eat a fish (a primary carnivore), which feeds on insect larvae (primary consumers). Decomposers are life forms such as bacteria, fungi, and other microorganisms that break down the remains of other organisms, and thus return nutrients to the soil to be used by green plants. The sequence from green plant to secondary carnivore is called the food chain. In

Food producer

any habitat many food chains are intricately interrelated, forming a food web. Deficiency in any one part of a habitat's ecosystem changes the entire system somewhat. If the deficiencies are too great, the entire ecosystem can collapse; in such an event, many species would decline or disappear, and the ecosystem's diversity would be largely eliminated.

Decomposers

Open Inland Water and Waterways

The Mid-Atlantic region has a large number of freshwater lakes, ponds, and rivers. The glaciers carved out thousands of natural lakes and ponds in the northern reaches of the Mid-Atlantic (Adirondack Park alone has 2,200), but nary a handful exist in the southern portions; Virginia has only two natural lakes. The great north–south river valleys, including the Hudson, Susquehanna, and Delaware, are important migratory routes for bird life, from Ospreys to Tundra Swans to Scarlet Tanagers. The region's aquatic environments support a vast range of animals, from Black Bears and salmon to cricket frogs and whirligig beetles.

Susquehanna River, Pennsylvania

Rivers

Rivers are dynamic forces in the natural landscape. Whether they lazily flow with black water or rush headlong in foaming white cascades, they engage the riverbanks and floodplain in a seasonal movement of water, topsoil, and fallen leaves. Beneath the waters, great numbers of gamefishes and other fishes lure sportsmen as well as Northern River Otters and Belted Kingfishers. Most states have given some of their important rivers protective status. Pennsylvania, for example, has designated 13 waterways as state scenic rivers; it also has two national scenic rivers, the Allegheny and the Delaware.

Lakes

The lakes of the Mid-Atlantic area run the gamut from the quiet Baldcypress waters of Lake Drummond in southeastern Virginia to the glistening, crystal depths of central New York's Finger Lakes to sprawling, man-made reservoirs in unglaciated regions to the enormous expanses of Lake Erie and Lake Ontario. Lakes attract recreational activity, but they are also critically important to resident and

Pharaoh Lake, Adirondack Park, New York

migrating wildlife. Freshwater mussels, Chain Pickerel, bass, Common Loons, mergansers, gulls, Ospreys, Bald Eagles—all are dependent on lakes for survival.

Brooks, Streams, and Creeks

Mill Creek at Delaware Water Gap

The flowing waters that pass through Appalachian ravines, piedmont farmlands, and low-lying, coastal pinewoods are a vital element of the ecological landscape. For example, from spring through autumn they recycle and transport nutrients from fallen leaves and the soil that collects in them. The vast numbers of aquatic insects that thrive in these habitats provide food for animals further up the food chain, including snakes, turtles, frogs, fishes, birds, and mammals. In the swift stretches of streams called riffles, immature insects clinging to submerged branches and rocks must possess special streamlining and attachment mechanisms to keep from being carried away. Water striders and Water Boatmen prefer the quiet pools that are also part of a stream's makeup.

Ponds

The definition of a pond is a body of water shallow enough so that sunlight can reach the bottom and rooted plants can grow anywhere across its area. Because of the luxuriant plant growth, a wealth of animal forms is associated with ponds. Among the roots of

Delaware pond with Pickerelweed and White Water-lilies

Pickerelweed and Spatterdock are the hungry naiads of damselflies and dragonflies. Bullfrogs and Green Frogs rest upon water-lily leaves. Red-winged Blackbirds and Marsh Wrens raise their families inches above the pond waters. And bats of several species chase aerial insect prey over cattails on summer evenings.

Freshwater Wetlands

There used to be a lot more wetlands in the Mid-Atlantic region. For many decades our society wrongly assumed that such areas were not "valuable," that fragmenting them with roads or degrading them with pollutants and landfill was a sign of progress. Only recently have conservationists convinced lawmakers that the health of marshes, bogs, and moist meadows has important ecological consequences. Wetlands help keep rivers and lakes clean by filtering out impurities and pollution. Their soils act as sponges during spring flood seasons, absorbing and holding overflow rain and flood water, and later recharging the water table. They also provide food and shelter for myriad plants and animals.

Cranberry Glades Botanical Area, West Virginia

Bogs

Bogs are such distinctive wetlands, in their formation and in the plants and animals that they comprise, that conservationists are trying to save as many as possible. In the Mid-Atlantic region, bogs are most common in northern coniferous areas, where glacial depressions with no outlets for water flow gradually filled with sediment, providing micro-habitats for plants that survive best in nutrient-poor, acidic environments. Other bogs occur below the southern reach of the glaciers, in the New Jersey Pine Barrens and other regions where three conditions occur: a water table intersecting the surface of the land, restricted water flow, and naturally acidic soils. Surrounded by tree species that vary by locale—Tamaracks in northern New York, Red Spruces in West Virginia, Pitch Pines in New Jersey—bog waters are usually tea-colored, the result of tannins from fallen leaves leaching into the water. The presence of carnivorous plants, including three sundews, as well as many species of sphagnum mosses, and several dainty, colorful bog orchids, is one element of many that make bog-trotting fascinating. Note: The possibility of falling through the vegetative mat that covers bog waters is small, but it is wise to explore bogs with a companion.

Freshwater Marshes

Freshwater marshes occur throughout the region, though they are scarce in most of the coastal plain. They develop along the edges of ponds, lakes, and slow-moving streams, and typically have saturated soils and standing water year-round. The vegetation on marsh-

Marsh at Piseco Lake, Adirondack Mountains

lands is overwhelmingly herbaceous, with reeds, grasses, sedges, and rushes in abundance, and few trees. Wildflowers—arrowheads, cattails, water lilies, bur-marigolds—are common, as is the invasive alien Purple Loosestrife, which is overpowering many native species. Another invasive species, the Common Reed, can form enormous beds, especially in brackish-water marshes. Like other wetlands, marshes feature abundant insect life. Mosquitoes are a prime food item for gloriously colored and patterned skimmers, emeralds, gliders, amberwings, and other dragonflies, which can be dazzlingly beautiful in the proper light. A Common Muskrat or two may swim by while you are insect-watching, or perhaps you will flush an American Bittern from its hiding place in the cattails.

Larger Blue Flags

Moist Meadows

Larger Blue Flag irises, standing tall amid meadow grasses and sedges, are one of the glories of early-summer moist meadows. Long Dashes and Indian and Hobomok Skippers visit the irises for nectar in June, while larger butterflies, including Eastern Tiger Swallowtails and Great Spangled Fritillaries, go to Swamp Milkweed and other wildflowers from July through September. Wildflowers tend to be numerous and tall in these wetlands, which feature the two greatest factors governing plant growth—sunshine and water. Swallows can be a conspicuous element of meadow birdlife; several species, including the large Purple Martin and the smaller Tree and Barn Swallows, spend daylight hours hawking mosquitoes, flies, damselflies, and dragonflies over these expanses. Rabbits, moles, mice, shrews, and other small mammals are normally abundant here. Moist meadows, the least wet of our wetlands, often dry out appreciably as summer progresses.

Overleaf: Pitch Pine bog, Wharton State Forest, New Jersey Pine Barrens

Upland and Inland Forests

Not many generations past, virtually all of the eastern woodlands were falling or had fallen to the ax and saw. But the regenerative powers of these forests are strong, and, with protection, they are coming back toward their former prominence. Extensive forests now occur throughout the Mid-Atlantic region—in the Adirondack and Catskill Mountains, Allegheny National Forest and adjacent Allegany State Park; George Washington, Jefferson, and Monongahela National Forests; and Shenandoah National Park. The region's several major forest types, including broadleaf and coniferous species, intermingle in many places.

Pocono Mountains, Pennsylvania

Oak-Hickory Forest

No eastern forest has as large a range as the oak-hickory, which spreads in a great, deep curve around the Appalachian highlands from southeastern New York to southwestern Virginia and then northward through western West Virginia, Pennsylvania, and New York. Much of this forest was once known as oak-chestnut forest, but the American Chestnut was obliterated by a great fungal blight in the first half of the 20th century. Oaks of various species, including Northern Red, Southern Red, Black, and Scarlet, are the dominant trees today, though hickories are also important.

Northern Riverine Forest

Riverine (or riparian) forests grow in the fertile plains alongside rivers throughout the region's broadleaf forests. In New York, northern New Jersey, and much of Pennsylvania, these are known as northern riverine forests. Because of springtime inundation, the understory of these forests tends to have few herbaceous species, though vines can grow rampant. Characteristic American Sycamores,

Delaware Water Gap   Silver Maples, willows, ashes, and Eastern Cottonwoods are often draped with lush vine growth, such as Wild Cucumber and Fox Grape.

Coniferous Forest

Boreas River, Adirondack Mountains, near Minerva, New York

Spruce-fir forests extend from the Adirondacks of northeastern New York south along the high ridges of the Appalachians to Virginia and West Virginia. Northernmost coniferous woodlands are composed of Red and White Spruce, Balsam Fir, and such deciduous species as Paper Birch and American Mountain Ash. The "Appalachian extension" of this forest replaces Balsam Fir with Fraser Fir, and White Spruce drops out in favor of Red Spruce exclusively. The conical shape of these trees helps them shed snow. The thick litter of needles on this forest floor is so acidic that only a small range of specially adapted plants can survive.

Northern Swamp Forest

Swamps are wetlands dominated by tree or shrub growth, or both. New York, New Jersey, and Pennsylvania have vast swamp forests, dominated by Red Maple but including Northern and Atlantic White Cedars. Some 95 percent of wetlands in the Adirondacks are shrub or tree forests. Speckled Alder is abundant in most Red Maple swamps, as are Sweet Pepperbush, Spicebush, and Highbush Blueberry. Herbaceous groundcover includes Jack-in-the-Pulpit, Orange Jewelweed, and Skunk Cabbage.

Northern Hardwood Forest

In much of New York, in northern and central Pennsylvania, and along higher slopes of the Appalachians in western Maryland, West Virginia, and Virginia, the northern hardwood forest of American Beech, Yellow Birch, and Sugar Maple cloaks the countryside. Hemlocks are common in ravines,

Forbes State Forest, Pennsylvania

and Eastern White Pines in sunny areas. This is a forest of spring wildflowers, summer birdsong, and fall foliage. Common Porcupines and Southern Red-backed Voles live here, as do Black-capped Chickadees, Blue-headed Vireos, and White-throated Sparrows.

Lowland and Coastal Forests

The region's eastern lowland forests occur on the Atlantic coastal plain and lower piedmont. Most reach their northern limits in the Mid-Atlantic area and are much more widespread in the South. Some of the best known of these forests—those of Maryland's Pocomoke Swamp, the New Jersey Pine Barrens, and Virginia's Great Dismal Swamp—are well documented in travel guides and local folklore. Many others await chroniclers. Hundreds of species of animals and plants, including rare tree frogs, poisonous snakes, dashing butterflies, and stately hardwoods, reach their northern distributional limits here.

Northern Pine-Oak Forest

On sandy soils in the coastal plain from Long Island south, a pine-oak woodland commonly known as a "pine barren" is the predominant forest type, with many species of oaks and a predominance of Pitch Pines and Virginia Pines. These woodlands have many hidden treasures, such as Whip-poor-wills and Great Horned Owls, as well as abundant blueberry and huckleberry shrubs. Since fires are frequent, the trees that survive best in the thin soils are those adapted to blazes. Both predominant pines have fire-resistant bark and cones that open in response to a fire's heat, releasing seeds when the soil is most conducive to growth.

New Jersey Pine Barrens, Wharton State Forest, New Jersey

Southern Pine-Oak Forest

From southwesternmost New Jersey south through Virginia and beyond, the characteristic woodlands of the sandy coastal plain are those of the southern pine-oak forest. This is a more open forest than its northern counterpart, with far fewer shrubs and much greater grassy cover. The pines are Loblolly and Shortleaf; the oaks are Post, Southern Red, and Live. Common Gray Foxes are residents here, as are Virginia Opossums. Look among the pine boughs for little troops of Brown-headed Nuthatches (pinewood specialists), as well as Eastern Bluebirds, Red-headed Woodpeckers, and Pine and Yellow-throated Warblers.

Bald Cypress Swamp Forest

To best appreciate the splendor of the Bald Cypress swamp forest, found from southern Maryland southward in the coastal plain, take to the ponds, rivers, and streams along and in which this forest grows. Bald Cypress, a specialty tree of the Southeast, is the most

Trusson Pond, Great Cypress Swamp, Lowe, Delaware

common and characteristic species of this wettest of all forests, but others occur, including Red Bay and Water Oak. Expect to find several species of water snakes here, and perhaps a Cottonmouth, at its northern limit in southern Virginia. Prothonotary Warblers and Northern Parulas are diminutive summer residents. Poison Sumac is common here.

Southern Hardwood Swamp Forest

A forest of Black Tupelo, Pawpaw, Sweetgum, and a variety of water-loving oaks, including Overcup, Swamp Chestnut, Water, and Willow, grows on wet coastal plain substrates from Maryland and Virginia southward. Large, red-crested Pileated Woodpeckers tear pieces from dead trunks to get at insects within, male Wood Ducks show off their resplendent plumage and high-pitched calls, Carolina Wrens and Tufted Titmice mob resting screech-owls, and Blue-gray Gnatcatchers call from branches festooned with stringy, gray Spanish Moss.

Southern Riverine Forest

It is not always easy to distinguish the various Mid-Atlantic forest types, which tend to intermingle from north to south and from upland to wetland. The principally deciduous southern riverine forest is known by its great numbers of Green and Carolina Ashes in combination with Sweetgum, Hackberry, cottonwoods, elms, and Black Tupelo, among other trees. It overlaps with the northern riverine forest and occurs from New Jersey and Pennsylvania southward through the region. Common Raccoons live here, though their pawprints are more frequently seen than the creatures themselves.

Potomac River, Langley, Virginia

Appalachian Forests of Virginia and West Virginia

These beautiful forests—called southern or central Appalachian forests—are diverse and span a wide range of elevation. They include most eastern woodland types and even a unique type, the cove forest. Below is a primer on these forests, starting in the lowlands and working up to the peaks. In a few hours' time, visitors who are driving or on foot can travel through all the types, which are not always discrete and often blend into one another. In general, Appalachian forests are humid year-round, with well-drained soils.

American Sycamores

Bottomland Forest

Much of the Appalachian bottomland forest has been cut repeatedly over the last two centuries. If the cutting occurred in the last 60 or 70 years, the streamside woodlands likely will have grown thick with Black, White, and other oaks. If the forest has been spared the ax long enough for the climax species (those that ultimately populate an area left undisturbed) to push up to the canopy, this forest has a rich assortment of broadleaf trees, including American Sycamore, Yellow Poplar, Pignut and Mockernut Hickories, and Black Tupelo. Flowering Dogwood, Witch Hazel, and rhododendrons dominate the understory.

Pine-oak forest, Shenandoah National Park, Virginia

Pine-Oak Forest

This forest, immediately upslope from the bottomlands in areas with sandy soils, shares many wildflowers and shrubs with its lower-elevation neighbor, but the tree mix is noticeably different. White, Black, Chestnut, and Scarlet Oaks mix in the much more open canopy with Pitch, Shortleaf, Eastern White, and Virginia Pines. Mountain Laurel is particularly abundant here.

Oak-Hickory Forest

At elevations similar to those of the pine-oak forest are oak-hickory woodlands, which occupy warm, exposed lower slopes. Acorn- and hickory-loving squirrels, chipmunks, and Wild Turkeys are often seen in this common eastern forest type (see page 34).

Male Scarlet Tanager

Northern Hardwood Forest

Above the oak-, hickory-, and pine-populated lower Appalachian slopes, in the cooler temperatures and well-drained soils of the mid–slopes (about 3,000–4,000 feet), is the spectacular northern hardwood forest—the forest of Sugar Maple and American Beech, trilliums and Wild Geranium, Scarlet Tanager and Ovenbird (see page 35). A main drawing card of the Appalachian woodlands is their fall foliage, and this forest radiates the finest autumn color.

Cove forest, Shenandoah National Park, Virginia

Appalachian Cove Forest

The cove forests, at 4,000 feet or so, are the forgotten forests —remote areas, such as in upper portions of mountain valleys, so far back from the roads that they were left for last to cut and ultimately saved before they were destroyed. Cove forests have grown relatively undisturbed for millennia; richness of wildlife is their hallmark. West Virginia and southwest Virginia mark the northern limit of cove forests, which are more common farther south. White Basswood and Carolina Silverbell are indicator trees for this unique Appalachian woodland type.

Upland Coniferous Forest

Fine Red Spruce, Fraser Fir, and Yellow Birch forests, once widespread in the highest, coolest reaches of this part of the Appalachians, were largely cut to the ground in the 1800s, but protected mountaintops and ridges are now generating significant regrowth. These thick, aromatic woodlands are southerly outposts for the Red Crossbill, Golden-crowned Kinglet, and Northern Saw-whet Owl.

Open Areas

The Mid-Atlantic region has its fair share of open lands—upland areas that are essentially treeless. Many such areas are kept open by the hand of man, including vast acreages of farmland as well as long-distance rights-of-way, including those maintained by railroads and utility companies. Naturally occurring open heathlands are found on mountaintops at the northern and southern reaches of the region, with wholly different animal and plant species inhabiting them. Small areas of natural heathlands also survive on Long Island, with a still different mixture of flora and fauna.

Alpine Regions

Lapland Rosebay

Above the timberline on 11 Adirondack peaks are a total of 85 acres of alpine habitat. As the glaciers retreated northward thousands of years ago, so too the alpine zone in the Adirondacks retreated up the mountain slopes, until today this habitat occurs on only the highest peaks (two are New York's Algonquin Peak and Mount Marcy), the isolated southernmost extensions of alpine habitat. Throughout the long, harsh winter, a deep snow layer protects most alpine flora—Lapland Rosebay, Mountain Sandwort, Alpine Bilberry, Black Crowberry, and other grasses, lichens, mosses, dwarf shrubs, and herbaceous perennials.

Hayfields and Pasture Land

From Appalachian valleys through the piedmont to the coastal plain, hayfields and pastures are part of the Mid-Atlantic landscape. Both habitats are left more or less poison-free by farmers, but their similarities end there. Hayfields provide cover and nutrition for wildlife as diverse as Bobolinks and White-footed Mice, while pastures are often grazed to the point where there is little cover and animal life is restricted to species that can survive among thistles and other herbs that livestock ignore.

Bobolink

Appalachian Balds

Biologists are uncertain about the origin of the balds (heathlands) that occur atop high peaks in the southern Appalachians—for instance, in West Virginia's Iron Mountains. One explanation is that, in areas with thin soils, frequent fires favor shrubby heath growth to the virtual exclusion of trees. The balds are at their best in spring, when blooms of rhododendrons and azaleas paint the mountaintops with glorious shades of purple, pink, white, and orange.

Mountain Laurel in Dolly Sods Wilderness and Scenic Area, West Virginia

Power Lines

A hike along a power line right-of-way often provides easy access to a nice variety of upland and wetland habitats, as the clearings tend to be cut in long straight lines, up, down, over, and through whatever lands lie there. Utility companies maintain the clearings, but the habitats are not continuously altered, so there is almost always abundant shrub growth and frequently extensive herbaceous growth as well. Look here for certain butterflies, Indigo Buntings, Field Sparrows, Eastern Towhees, a variety of warblers, and even Black Bears hunting blueberries.

Old field in Pennsylvania after about twenty years

Abandoned Fields

Dormant seeds by the millions exist in every acre of cultivated land in the Mid-Atlantic region. Set aside the plow for a year and Common Ragweed and Horseweed will bloom in profusion. Within a few years, asters and goldenrods will overspread the area, providing nectar for butterflies, bees, and long-horned beetles. Grasses, Oxeye Daisies, Black-eyed Susans, and other herbaceous species are also pioneers. In perhaps a decade or two, the old field will be home to aspen, pine, birch, and cherry saplings on their way to reclaiming the locale as a forest community.

Cities and Suburbs

One need not live in the countryside to enjoy nature and note its pleasantries and vagaries. Backyards and city parks are fine natural laboratories that attract mammals, birds, reptiles, insects, and arachnids, and harbor grasses, trees, vines, and wildflowers. Tall chimneys on buildings shelter Chimney Swifts, attics serve as nurseries for Little Brown Bats, and boxwood hedges conceal nesting Northern Cardinals.

Gardens

Perennial gardens of wildflowers and cultivated plants are one of the region's best places to study butterflies. Planting flora appropriate for the caterpillars as well as the adult butterflies will make your garden more welcoming to a wide spectrum of swallowtails, sulphurs, azures, fritillaries, admirals, and skippers. Community gardens are great birding areas in the fall, as harvesting gardeners tend to leave behind lots of extra fruits, vegetables, and flowers.

Perennial garden in Virginia

Suburban Backyards

During the National Audubon Society Christmas Bird Counts, when teams of birders scour designated areas looking for avian lifeforms, many participants visit yards that have good plantings and bird feeders, because there are inevitably many birds there, even some that might be otherwise difficult to track down. In warm weather, a good variety of fruiting and cover plants will attract game birds, finches, sparrows, squirrels, and other potential backyard visitors. Nest boxes, including special designs for bats and small owls, can help make a suburban plot more of a wildlife sanctuary.

New York City's Central Park

Urban Parks

Many cities have set aside or developed natural parks. New York's Central Park is a marvel, to be sure, but James River Park in Richmond, Rock Creek Park in Washington, Highland Park in Rochester, and Cylburn Arboretum in Baltimore are all wonderful natural places to get attuned with nature. Birders come to these urban oases in spring and fall to see the migrant songbirds that flock to sizable green spaces as well as to other, smaller parks and arboretums.

Buildings and Bridges

By the mid-1960s, because of rampant DDT use, which affected the ability of the females to produce viable eggs, Peregrine Falcons were completely gone as a breeding bird in the eastern United States. Once DDT was banned, scientists developed programs to help the falcons recover their populations. One of the best approaches has been to erect nesting platforms on building ledges and under bridges. The falcons feel secure, there are plenty of other birds to feed upon, and the nests are closely monitored. To date, the program has been an unqualified success. Three introduced species—House Sparrows, European Starlings, and Rock Doves (Pigeons)—have found bridges and buildings to their liking as well, nesting and roosting by the millions across the region.

Peregrine Falcons, Baltimore, Maryland

Seacoasts

From the rocky headlands of Montauk Point, at the eastern tip of Long Island, to the sandy barrier beaches at Back Bay, Virginia, the Mid-Atlantic coastline presents a fascinating front to the Atlantic Ocean. Montauk is a regional anomaly—the only rocky shoreline in the Mid-Atlantic area. The rest of Long Island and shores to the south are dominated by marshlands, lagoons and estuaries, and numerous barrier islands (the longest are Fire Island and Assateague Island). The near-shore life-forms in the region differ markedly from the cooler-water forms of New England and the truly southern species found from Cape Hatteras southward.

Sunrise at Swan Cove, Chincoteague National Wildlife Refuge, Virginia

Barrier Beaches

Barrier beaches line fewer than 10 percent of the world's coastlines, but in the Mid-Atlantic region they are the predominant coastal feature. Long and narrow, they run parallel to the shore between 1 and 8 miles from the mainland, and are composed of five primary elements: a sandy outer beach, a primary dune system, a leeward interdune swale, a secondary dune ridge, and finally a lagoon shore. It's not known exactly how barrier beaches form, but we do know they are transfigured by every coastal storm. The dunes are held in place by American Beach Grass and other herbaceous species, such as Seaside Goldenrod and Beach Heather. Between the primary and secondary dune ridges grow maritime and shrub forests of Sassafras, American Holly, bayberry, Wax Myrtle, Poison Ivy, and other woody plants and vines; the Sunken Forest on Fire Island is the region's best-known maritime forest. Wildlife is abundant in the thick vegetation; Red Foxes live here with Meadow Voles, Yellow-rumped Warblers, Fowler's Toads, and Eastern Hognose Snakes.

Fire Island National Seashore, New York

Tidal Flats

Gateway National Recreation Area, New Jersey

Coastal tidal flats, sandy or muddy, may seem to lack animal life at low tide because the animals that live here depend on ocean waters for survival; when the tide recedes, they retract below the mud surface or retreat with the tide until its next incoming stage. (When salt water covers a tidal flat, its true nature may be examined with a glass-bottomed viewing box or a mask and snorkel.) Blue, Spider, and Mud Crabs move over the bottom, as do mud snails of several species, and moon snails, whelks, and Atlantic Horseshoe Crabs. Within the substrate are creatures of three feeding types: predators, including many species of marine worms; deposit feeders, again including worms; and suspension feeders, such as scallops, oysters, quahogs, razor clams, and other bivalves. Gulls and shorebirds arrive at low tide to probe the flats for retiring invertebrates.

Salt Marshes

From New Jersey to Virginia, the Mid-Atlantic coastline has some of North America's most extensive salt marshes. The region's rivers carry huge amounts of silt and nutrients, and because Mid-Atlantic topography includes a gentle contour at the ocean's edge

Great Egret

and river waters slow at their mouths, topsoil is deposited along the shore, building up marshes and supplying them with nourishment. Salt marshes have the highest production of organic material—5 to 10 tons per acre per year—of any habitat on earth. Saltmarsh grasses are the primary vegetation of tracts inundated at high tide. Above the tide line grow Sea Rocket and saltmarsh asters. Common Raccoons and White-footed Mice commonly live in coastal marshes, and bird life is a conspicuous feature: egrets, herons, Clapper Rails, terns, and ducks are here at the right seasons. Fiddler crabs share the shorelines with Ribbed Mussels, Salt-marsh Snails, and periwinkles.

Oceans and Bays

Fingers of the Atlantic Ocean extend far up coastal estuaries, and its waters swirl around deep bays and cover submerged offshore substrates, supporting Brown Pelicans and Bottle-nosed Dolphins that drift north for the summer and the flocks of scoters, Buffleheads, Oldsquaws, and other ducks that winter here. The area is critically important for migrating and wintering birds: Delaware Bay was the first site to be protected in the Western Hemisphere Shorebird Reserve Network. Billions of fishes, crustaceans, and mollusks use coastal estuaries and shallows as feeding and nursery grounds.

Estuaries
Chesapeake Bay, Blackwater National Wildlife Refuge, Maryland

An estuary differs from a bay in that it is significantly affected by the mixing of fresh water from rivers and their tributaries with salt water that rushes in from the sea, yet America's largest estuary is called Chesapeake Bay. In common with other estuaries, but on a much grander scale, the Chesapeake has a range of depths, temperatures, and salinities in its various waters. The brackish-water regions, where the rivers meet the Bay proper, are the outstanding nurseries of the Atlantic. Almost all commercial fishes of the Mid-Atlantic use estuaries as nursery grounds, where juvenile fishes can feed in the murky soup of phytoplankton and detritus that is so abundant here. Atlantic Stingray, Summer Flounder, Striped Mullet, Bluefish, White Perch, Atlantic Croaker, American Shad—all have different feeding and reproductive requirements that are met at some season in the estuary. The Blue Crab begins its life in deep water at the mouth of the Bay, gradually gets carried up the estuary as it develops, and reaches sexual maturity and mates in the brackish waters well away from the ocean; the female carries her eggs out to the Bay's mouth to begin the cycle anew.

Offshore Canyons

Greater Shearwater

The Atlantic coastal plain does not end at the shoreline, but extends 50 to 80 miles offshore before dropping steeply down along the continental slope to the continental shelf, which has a depth of about 6,000 feet. Along the edge of the continental slope are deep canyons that extend toward shore and that carry nutrients to the surface on the currents swirling up their sides. Should you find yourself on a charter boat in the waters of the Hudson, Wilmington, or Baltimore Canyon off the New Jersey or Delaware coast or near Poor Man's, Washington, or Norfolk Canyon off the Virginia coast, you will likely see a variety of offshore species. Watch for pilot whales and dolphins, Shortfin Makos, Blue Sharks, Ocean Sunfishes, and such ocean-going seabirds as jaegers, shearwaters, storm-petrels, and Northern Fulmars.

Bays and Inlets

The coast between Cape Cod and Cape Hatteras, including all of the Mid-Atlantic region, is the "embayed section" of the western Atlantic coast. Many deep- and shallow-water bays, inlets, and sounds pro-

Leidy's Comb Jelly

vide excellent habitat for a wide range of fishes, including the Sandbar Shark, Cownose Ray, Black Sea Bass, Striped Bass, Red Drum, Oyster Toadfish, Northern Puffer, and Northern Searobin. Jellyfishes and comb jellies, gelatinous and sometimes opaque, can arrive in great numbers. The small, bioluminescent Leidy's Comb Jelly and Sea Gooseberry have no stinging apparatus and are harmless to humans. But swimmers should be wary of two powerfully armed jellyfishes—the Lion's Mane and the Sea Nettle.

Conservation and Preservation

The 20th century has seen both wholesale loss of wildlife populations and habitats and widespread concern and efforts to preserve what remains. Laws have been enacted to protect migratory birds, national forests, endangered species of flora and fauna, and other vital elements of our environment. In many cases, the work of a small group of citizens or even of one single-minded conservationist has had far-reaching consequences.

Preserving Birds of Prey

Cooper's Hawk

In the early 1900s, gunners positioned themselves each fall along coastal dunes and mountain ridges, and shot every bird of prey that came within range. Thousands upon thousands of raptors were killed by these ill-informed hunters, who believed they were ridding the world of unwanted varmints. At the points of greatest concentration, such as Cape May, New Jersey, and Hawk Mountain, Pennsylvania, the slaughters were enormous. In 1934, Rosalie Edge of the Emergency Conservation Committee in New York City took direct action at Hawk Mountain, purchasing 1,450 acres and hiring a persuasive ornithologist, Maurice Broun, to oversee the world's first sanctuary for birds of prey. Through the pioneering efforts of Edge and Broun, the public came to appreciate the ecological importance and majesty of birds of prey. Hawk Mountain Sanctuary and the Cape May Bird Observatory are now internationally known.

Honey Hollow Environmental Education Center

Preserving Farmlands

The farming practices of early Mid-Atlantic homesteaders left much to be desired. By the 1930s, places such as Honey Hollow, Pennsylvania, had been under the plow for generations, and the land had lost most of its viability. Federal soil conservationists got a message through to the farmers: Adopt new, long-term farming techniques, including planting of trees, contour farming, planting for wildlife, and ongoing soil analysis, and the land would regenerate itself. The landowners in the Honey Hollow watershed set a national precedent by all agreeing to take part in the conservation program. Today Honey Hollow is a National Historic Landmark, a model of conservation and commitment. The area boasts healthy trees, excellent bird and wildflower populations, and productive farmland. (See also page 406.)

Preserving Forests

From the late 1600s to the late 1800s, the great forests of the Mid-Atlantic region fell to the ax and saw at ever-accelerating rates. Chestnut, oak, fir, pine, hickory, cherry, cypress—all succumbed to America's insatiable appetite for wood. By 1850, New York

Monongahela National Forest, West Virginia

led the nation in timber production. In West Virginia, the harvesting of forests for profit was the state's largest business. Only in the last hundred years or so have federal and state governments considered forest preservation a priority. Although there are virtually no virgin tracts remaining, the forest parks and reserves, particularly the enormous holdings in New York's Adirondack and Catskill Parks and those in the region's national forests, are testimony to the scope of the region's relatively recent environmental awareness.

Jamaica Bay, with New York City subway train at right

Preserving Bays

By the mid-1950s, after decades of dredging and filling operations, nearly half of the area of New York's Jamaica Bay had been lost. The bird list for the site stood at fewer than 80 species. But then the New York City Parks Commission and the New York Transit Authority struck a deal: The transit folks could have dredge material they needed for a railroad embankment if they would excavate two large freshwater impoundments for a wildlife sanctuary. The backhoes and tractors went to work, and the Parks Commission hired Herbert S. Johnson as manager of the Jamaica Bay Wildlife Refuge. Johnson, an amateur horticulturist, implemented an extraordinary management program, propagating and planting thousands of native plants and garnering support from everyone who would listen. Under his leadership, the 9,000 acres of Jamaica Bay Wildlife Refuge developed into one of the region's premier nature sanctuaries, where more than 320 species of birds have been observed. Other coastal preserves have followed the precedent set by Jamaica Bay.

Introduced Species and Their Effects on the Land

Over the millennia, regional temperatures fluctuate, animal migratory paths change, species evolve—such changes have shaped and will continue to affect our flora and fauna. It is the nature of life on earth for species to come and go. We humans, however, tend to move species around artificially, sometimes accidentally, sometimes on purpose. Today House Sparrows, European Starlings, and Rock Doves inhabit our cities, and Oxeye Daisies, Common Dandelions, Red Clover, and Honey Bees are now integral parts of the countryside. These introduced species and a thousand more, mostly plants, alter the balance of nature when they become established.

Purple Loosestrife, Montezuma National Wildlife Refuge, New York

Purple Loosestrife

No flowering plant in the Northeast has caused as much concern as the European, marsh-loving Purple Loosestrife. Crowding out other wetland species with its tenacious root system, Purple Loosestrife is changing the face of many freshwater marshes by turning them into biologically unproductive monocultures. The sometimes vast magenta flowerbeds attract bees and butterflies to their blossoms, but offer no sustenance to higher life-forms. Efforts to control the species by pulling it up have been fruitless. Introducing European beetles that feed exclusively on this plant may prove the best defense.

Zebra Mussel

Natives of southern Europe and Asia, Zebra Mussels were accidentally introduced into the Great Lakes in the ballast water of a European tanker in the 1980s. These bivalves—small, prolific breeders that stack up on one another with such exuberance that as many as 1 million may crowd into a square meter of space—crowd out indigenous species and clog water pipes and screens.

Zebra Mussels

American Chestnut with fruit

Chestnut Blight

From New York to Virginia there is today not a single mature American Chestnut where once there were millions. A fungal disease, *Endothia parasitica,* found its way into New York's Zoological Park aboard Chinese Chestnuts in 1904. Once the blight began to spread there was no way to combat it, as the pathogen produces spores that ride the wind; within decades, countless trees were infected. The blight, lethal to all chestnuts, survives in stumps and saplings to affect any trees that may approach maturity; one occasionally sees a small tree in fruit, but its fate is sealed. The great eastern chestnut-oak forests have been replaced by an oak-hickory mix.

Gypsy Moth

Gypsy Moths were accidentally released from a Boston suburban laboratory in the 1860s. By the early 1900s, feeding upon many tree species in the Northeast and with no natural predators, they had spread to eastern New York and New Jersey. By 1981 the species had traveled west through 46 counties in Pennsylvania; that same year they stripped millions of trees and vines in 800,000 acres of New Jersey.

Reintroduced Mammals

Not all the species introduced into the region are aliens. Some of our finest extant mammals—White-tailed Deer, American Beaver, Elk—were original inhabitants of most of the Mid-Atlantic area. Along with the Moose, Gray Wolf, American Bison, and Mountain Lion, they were systematically shot and trapped by European settlers and their descendants until many were extirpated (eliminated) from the region. White-tailed Deer have rallied with hunting restrictions to attain pest proportions in some districts. Away from the coastal plain, beavers are doing well in more secluded areas. Even Elk, which were reintroduced into northern Pennsylvania in 1913 and 1926, have a viable population once again, albeit in a very restricted range in two counties.

American Beaver

Threatened and Endangered Species and Habitats

Wildlife biologists working for federal, state, and private agencies, such as the National Audubon Society, have studied animal and plant populations and have developed a sequence of categories under which threatened species can be listed: Special Concern, Threatened, State Endangered, and Federally Endangered, in order of level of endangerment, plus Extirpated (gone from a defined region) and Extinct. All Mid-Atlantic states are actively working to preserve populations of all extant "listed" flora and fauna and to keep other species from being listed. In Pennsylvania alone, more than 350 species of plants and animals have made these lists. While a great number of species are benefiting from the attention, a few have slipped through the cracks into oblivion.

Bald Eagle

Bald Eagle

The Bald Eagle suffered great losses from pesticide contamination but since the 1960s has been recovering regionally and nationwide. It is no longer officially listed as Federally Endangered, thanks to the efforts of conservationists who worked to ban DDT, implemented programs to reintroduce breeding eagles to their former ranges, and continue to monitor the species. In the Mid-Atlantic region, there are now several hundred breeding pairs, in a population centered on the Chesapeake Bay. Wintering eagles concentrate at the Delaware Water Gap, along the Lower Susquehanna River, and at Catskill reservoirs and other sites.

Mitchell's Satyr

Some butterflies are large, brightly colored, and impossible to overlook. Others, such as the Mitchell's Satyr, are small and delicately but beautifully marked, and live in out-of-the-way places. Mitchell's

Satyrs have been rare, as their only habitat, calcareous wetlands known as fens, have a very limited distribution in the East. In 1974 a petition was made to have the Mitchell's Satyr listed as Federally Endangered. As so often happens with deserving species that are out of the limelight, its petition sat unanswered for 17 years. By the time this butterfly

Mitchell's Satyr

was officially recognized as endangered, it was lost to the Mid-Atlantic region; unscrupulous collectors had wiped out the one remaining colony in New Jersey.

Virginia Roundleaf Birch

Virginia Roundleaf Birch

Like the Mitchell's Satyr, the Virginia Roundleaf Birch (also known as the Ashe Birch) is a relatively small, virtually unknown species. First described scientifically in 1914 from a specimen at 2,800 feet near Sugar Grove Station, Virginia, the species quickly disappeared from view. No one would see it again until the summer of 1975, when a local biology teacher whose passion was the species' rediscovery found 12 Virginia Roundleaf Birches and 16 seedlings. The trees were enclosed behind high fences to protect them, yet in 1983 vandals destroyed all but five of the specimens. Since then, a small number of this rare birch have been planted and survive at secret sites in national forests.

Serpentine Barrens

Some habitats, such as oak-hickory woodlands, are vast. Others, including serpentine barrens, barely survive. Serpentine and associated minerals make for sterile soil conditions; the places where they exist close to the land surface had always been considered worthless, since little of "value" would grow there. Today we realize that serpentine soils harbor an important group of wildflowers, including Serpentine Aster, Moss Phlox, Fringed Gentian, and Lyre-leaved Rock

Fringed Gentian

Cress, plus such butterflies as Silvery Checkerspot, Mottled Duskywing, and Common Roadside Skipper—all local in distribution in the Mid-Atlantic region. Most serpentine barrens are buried under houses and malls; those that remain should be treated as treasures.

Weather

The diverse topographic features within and surrounding the Mid-Atlantic region contribute to a wide range of weather patterns. In winter, ample moisture picked up by air passing over the Great Lakes comes down in northwestern Pennsylvania and upstate New York as copious snowstorms. To the south, the Appalachian Mountains are a partial barrier to storm systems approaching from the Great Lakes and the Midwest. The mountainous terrain throughout

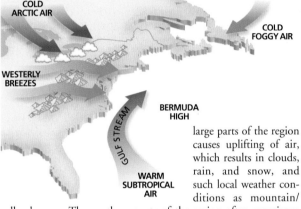

large parts of the region causes uplifting of air, which results in clouds, rain, and snow, and such local weather conditions as mountain/valley breezes. The northern parts of the region often experience cold temperatures and other wintery conditions. Along the eastern coast, the ocean moderates the large seasonal swings in temperature experienced in the region's interior. The Gulf Stream produces a steady supply of warm, moist air—a major component of the storm systems that frequently visit the region. In an average year several nor'easters, so named because northeasterly winds blow onshore from a low off the coast, pound the Mid-Atlantic region.

Tracing a Nor'easter

A nor'easter can drop several inches of rain (or a foot of snow) across much of the Mid-Atlantic region and whip the coastline with gale-force winds (39 mph or higher).

THE STAGE IS SET

All nor'easters feature an arctic high from the north and warm subtropical air from the south, with a front separating them. Before the storm system develops, the front may remain stationary for a while, producing light rain or snow or heavy thunderstorms.

THE STORM BUILDS

As the storm system starts spinning in a counterclockwise direction, a warm front to the east marks the leading edge of northbound warm air. As it rises over the colder, denser air to its north, the gently rising warm air produces

Wind Patterns

Earth's atmosphere is driven into motion as hot tropical air rises and spreads toward the poles and cold polar air sinks and flows toward the equator. Earth's rotation warps this north-south exchange of warm and cold air into vast wind patterns, including the prevailing westerly winds, a broad west-to-east current of air that flows over the United States and southern Canada. Because of these westerlies, most weather approaches the region from the west. Embedded in the prevailing westerlies are a succession of whirls and eddies: systems of high pressure (fair weather) and low pressure (high humidity, cloudiness, storms) that form and dissipate along fronts, the boundaries between warm and cold air masses. Winds blow in a circular pattern around the center of weather systems. In the Northern Hemisphere, they blow counterclockwise in a low-pressure system and clockwise in a high-pressure system. Weather in the Mid-Atlantic region is dominated by alternating influences of high and low pressure; each type of system usually lasts for three to five days before being replaced by a new weather pattern. Airflow along the coast is influenced by both the westerlies and fronts coming in off the ocean.

Bermuda High

During summer and into fall, much of the Mid-Atlantic region experiences hot, humid weather, and the Bermuda High, a massive, semi-permanent high-pressure system covering the tropical portion of the North Atlantic Ocean, is responsible. Persistent southerly winds blowing around the west side of the Bermuda High carry warm, moist air from the tropical Atlantic Ocean and the Gulf of Mexico into the Mid-Atlantic region. The summertime heat and humidity often produce isolated showers and thunderstorms as heat from the sun causes the warm air to rise and condense into clouds. During winter, the Bermuda High weakens and moves to the eastern side of the Atlantic, too distant to directly affect the weather of the Mid-Atlantic states.

steady rain or snow. Meanwhile, west of the center, arctic air plunges south behind a cold front, along which heavier cold air shoves like a wedge beneath the warm and usually moist air. Forced upward, the warm air expands and cools, its moisture condensing into clouds, rain, or snow.

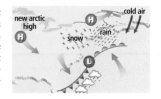

THE END OF THE STORM

After several hours, the center of low pressure passes, generally to the east or northeast, followed by the cold front, which may set off brief showers, squalls, and thunderstorms. In-flowing high pressure brings clearing, colder weather along the coast (with lingering

precipitation and clouds over the mountains and east of the Great Lakes), one or more days of fair skies, and southerly winds ahead of the next storm.

Rain

Annual rainfall ranges from 32 to 48 inches throughout most of the Mid-Atlantic states. Mountainous areas receive more than 48 inches. Rainfall is greatest in summer, much of it coming down during thunderstorms, and varies considerably from year to year. During winter, ice storms can cripple large areas when temperatures that are slightly below freezing cause rain to freeze on contact, covering trees, roads, and power lines with a glaze of heavy ice.

☐ 60 inches or more
☐ 36 to 60 inches
☐ 12 to 36 inches
■ 1 to 12 inches

Snow

Snowfall is highly variable throughout the Mid-Atlantic region. Areas downwind of the Great Lakes, including northwestern Pennsylvania and most of New York, receive more than 60 inches annually, much of it from individual large storms that can drop more than a foot of snow in a single day. Annual snowfall in mountainous areas of West Virginia and southwest Pennsylvania can also exceed 60 inches. Farther east, between 12 and 36 inches of snow fall annually, while coastal areas of Virginia, Maryland, and southern Delaware receive fewer than 12 inches each year.

Floods

Ample rainfall and the region's varied topography occasionally give rise to floods. Heavy spring rains over an extensive late-winter snowpack can overload the ability of streams and rivers to carry excess water. Mountainous areas are particularly susceptible to flooding, as narrow valleys channel water that originates over large tracts of upstream areas. Flooding also may accompany heavy rainfall from severe thunderstorms.

Flood, Cayuga Lake, New York

Record-setting Weather

LOWEST TEMPERATURE –52° F in Old Forge, New York, on February 18, 1979.

HIGHEST TEMPERATURE 112° F in Martinsburg, West Virginia, on July 10, 1936.

GREATEST 24-HOUR RAINFALL 34.5 inches of rain fell in Smethport, Pennsylvania, on July 17, 1942.

MOST SNOW FROM A SINGLE STORM 69 inches buried Watertown, New York, January 18–22, 1940.

CLOUDIEST CITIES Binghamton, New York, is the seventh-cloudiest city in the United States. Beckley and Elkins, both in West Virginia, are tied for eighth.

Tornadoes

While tornadoes occur around the globe, the 48 contiguous U.S. states are especially prone to them; some 700 are reported annually. An average of 21 tornadoes touch down each year in the Mid-Atlantic region—most in Pennsylvania, Virginia, and New York, but occasionally elsewhere in the region, mainly in spring and early summer.

Thunder and Lightning

In a typical year, lightning—an electrical discharge between one part of a cloud and another, between two clouds, or between a cloud and earth—strikes locations in the region more than 500,000 times (often, but less than the Great Plains and Florida), and perhaps ten times as many flashes arc across the sky without touching ground. Thunder, the sound of air expanding explosively away from the intense heat of lightning bolts, is common in late spring, summer, and early fall.

Hurricanes

While a full-strength hurricane (a storm with winds of 74 mph or higher) strikes the region only once every few years, even states as far west as West Virginia run a 5 percent annual risk of getting slammed by a hurricane. Much of the region's rainfall comes from hurricanes and tropical storms (wind speeds between 39 and 73 mph), including those located farther east over the Atlantic Ocean.

Hurricane Bob, 1991

WORST HURRICANE The "Long Island Express" roared up the Mid-Atlantic coastline on September 21, 1938, killing 600 people and causing $3.6 billion in damage.

WORST FLOODING The Johnstown Flood—6 inches of rain caused the Conemaugh River to rise 20–30 feet near Johnstown, Pennsylvania, on May 31, 1889, killing 2,100 people.

WORST ICE STORM From January 8 to 11, 1953, up to 4 inches of ice accumulated in Pennsylvania, New York, and New Jersey, causing 31 deaths, $2.5 million in damage, and a loss of electrical power to more than 100,000 homes.

Seasons

Because weather patterns mainly move from west to east, significant seasonal changes in the central United States are carried east to the Mid-Atlantic region, so, despite being close to the ocean's moderating influence, the region typically experiences large weather changes from season to season. In Pittsburgh, Pennsylvania, high temperatures typically reach 80° F in July but only 35° F in January.

Seasons result from the changing angle of sunlight striking the ground over the course of a year. As the earth moves around its orbit, its 23½-degree tilt on its axis means that for part of the year the Northern Hemisphere is inclined toward the sun and the sun's rays shine on it more directly; for part of the year it is tilted away from the sun and the sun's rays are more oblique. The latitude that receives the greatest heat from the sun is farther north during the summer months (though the earth's surface—land and sea—takes a while to warm up, so that early August is actually hotter than late June). Atmospheric current, such as the prevailing westerlies, in turn shift toward the north. Higher sun angles and longer days in the Arctic during summer warm up the polar air masses, and the northern position of the westerlies keeps the coldest air north of the Mid-Atlantic region.

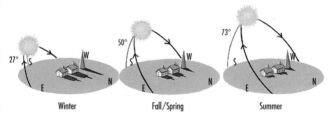

| Winter | Fall/Spring | Summer |

At 40° N latitude (the latitude of Philadelphia, Pennsylvania), the noontime sun at the winter solstice has an altitude above the horizon of only 27°; at the spring and fall equinoxes, its altitude is 50°; and at the summer solstice, the noontime sun rises 73° above the horizon.

Adirondack Park, New York

Spring

Spring officially begins on March 21 or 22, called the spring (or vernal) equinox, when the sun, heading north, appears directly overhead at noon at the equator. In spring, the first incursions of mild air from the tropical Atlantic Ocean and the Gulf of Mexico arrive in the Mid-Atlantic region, but the Arctic can still send bitter-cold air masses south; the clash provides some of the most violent weather of the year. March is often snowy and cold. Sunshine begins to increase in April and May, as do showers and thunderstorms.

Summer

The sun reaches its peak altitudes over the Northern Hemisphere on June 21 or 22, the longest day (that is, daylight period) of the year, known as the summer solstice. As the sun's more direct rays heat the high Arctic, tempering the Mid-Atlantic region's source of cold air, and the Bermuda High reaches inland from the Atlantic Ocean, the region experiences prolonged periods of heat and humidity. Temperatures above 90° F are common. Frequent showers and thunderstorms bring temporary relief from hazy, hot, and humid conditions.

Gateway National Recreation Area, New Jersey

Fall

As it does at the spring equinox, the sun "crosses" the equator again at the fall (autumnal) equinox, on September 21 or 22, heading south. Temperatures begin to drop, with the first frost occurring in New York, Pennsylvania, West Virginia, and western Maryland in late September and along the Virginia and Maryland coastline by November. Cold polar air masses dropping down from the north clash with warm tropical air, creating snowstorms sometimes as early as September in upstate New York, and about a month later in coastal areas.

Monongahela National Forest, West Virginia

Winter

Winter arrives on December 21 or 22, the winter solstice, but low temperatures, chilly rains, and snow often make it feel like winter by early December. In parts of New York, the temperature falls below freezing on more than 150 days each year. In eastern Virginia, freezing temperatures occur on fewer than 90 days annually. Inland and in the north, most precipitation falls as snow, while along the coast, rain or a mixture of sleet and snow is quite common. More than 60 inches of snow fall each year in parts of New York and West Virginia, while coastal areas receive fewer than 12 inches. Late January often brings the season's coldest outbreak, and winter conditions generally persist into March.

Delaware Water Gap

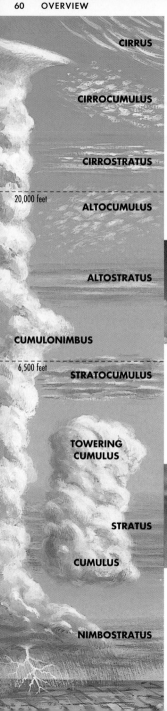

CIRRUS

CIRROCUMULUS

CIRROSTRATUS

20,000 feet

ALTOCUMULUS

ALTOSTRATUS

CUMULONIMBUS

6,500 feet

STRATOCUMULUS

TOWERING
CUMULUS

STRATUS

CUMULUS

NIMBOSTRATUS

Typical Clouds

Clouds form when moist air is cooled, causing water molecules to condense into water droplets or ice crystals. While most types of clouds can be spotted over the Mid-Atlantic region, the ones described here are among the most common. The illustration at left shows the relative common altitudes of the different cloud types; distances are not shown to scale.

CUMULONIMBUS
Tallest of all cloud types; commonly called thunderheads. Lower part composed of water droplets; fuzzy, fibrous top—the "anvil"—made of ice crystals. Produce lightning, thunder, heavy rain, and sometimes hail, high winds, or tornadoes. Most common from May to September.

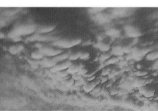

MAMMATUS
Series of pouch-shaped, often gray to pale blue cloud elements hanging downward from middle or upper cloud layer; part of underside of "anvil" blowoff from cumulonimbus. Large expanse of mammatus signals nearby presence of strong thunderstorm. Most common from May to September.

CUMULUS

Water-droplet clouds formed at tops of rising air currents set in motion by uneven heating of ground by sun. Domed tops, like bright white heads of cauliflower. Typical clouds of fine summer days but can occur any time of year. Very common inland and over hilly or mountainous terrain.

TOWERING CUMULUS

Cumulus clouds grow into towering, or swelling, cumulus if atmospheric moisture is sufficient and if it is much warmer at ground level than in the air aloft. Can grow taller and develop into thunderstorms—watch for rapid billowing in the tops.

CIRRUS

High (5 miles or more), thin, wispy clouds made of ice crystals; may be seen in any season, anywhere in the region. Cirrus thickening from west or south may signal approaching rain or snow; however, cirrus often come and go without bringing any lower clouds or rain.

STRATOCUMULUS

Low, flat-based, white to gray water-droplet clouds that usually cover most of the sky and are arranged in rows or patches. Common year-round along the coast and during winter throughout the Mid-Atlantic region.

FOG

Clouds formed at ground level; heavy fog (visibility ¼ mile or less) occurs at least 20 days per year, more than 60 days in mountains. **Advection fog:** forms when humid air overruns cold surfaces, like ocean water. **Radiation fog:** caused by overnight cooling of still air; burns off as sun rises; common in valleys.

STRATUS AND NIMBOSTRATUS

Stratus: low, indistinct, gray water droplet clouds, usually covering sky in summer along coast; may become fog if it occurs close to the ground. **Nimbostratus:** stratus clouds from which precipitation falls; almost always present during periods of steady rain or snow.

Our Solar System

The sun, the nine planets that revolve around it, and their moons make up our solar system. Venus, Mars, Jupiter, and Saturn are easily visible to the naked eye; Mercury is sometimes viewable, and Uranus, Neptune, and Pluto require telescopes. Other objects in our solar system are transient; the large orbits of comets make them only occasional visitors near earth, and meteors flash brightly for only seconds before disappearing.

Sky-observing in the Mid-Atlantic Region

Observation of the night sky in the Mid-Atlantic region is adversely affected by a combination of geography and population. The prevailing westerly airflow tends to become turbulent as it passes over the Appalachians, making for poor viewing of celestial objects in telescopes, and this heavily populated region produces widespread light pollution, particularly in its eastern half. Clear skies may occur at any time of year (about one-fourth of nights are clear), but cold nighttime winter temperatures, especially in Pennsylvania, New Jersey, and New York, tend to make it difficult to stay outside for long. In general, the best viewing conditions occur in summer. The skies are darkest in upstate New York, in the Adirondacks north of Interstate 90; in much of central Pennsylvania; and in the Appalachians to the south of Pennsylvania, including most of West Virginia.

FULL MOON

The full moon rises at sunset and sets at sunrise. It is highest in the sky in December, up to 77–82 degrees above the horizon in the Mid-Atlantic region; in summer, it rises to only about 20–25 degrees. Some lunar features show up best when the moon is full: the dark "seas" (hardened lava flows) and the "rays" of bright material splattered from craters. Craters and mountain ranges are best seen before and after full moon, when the angle of sunlight throws them into relief; look especially near the terminator, the dividing line between the moon's day and night sides. Because the moon is locked in earth's gravitational grip, the same side of the moon always faces us.

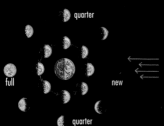

PHASES OF THE MOON

As the moon makes its monthly orbit around earth, the illuminated lunar surface area appears to grow (wax), shrink (wane), and even disappear (at new moon). The center of the illustration shows the phases, with sunlight coming from the right. The outer drawings show how the moon looks from our perspective on earth.

MARS

Every 25 months, when earth is aligned between Mars and the sun, Mars is closest to us and at its brightest and most colorful, appearing orange-red to the naked eye. At this time, called opposition (opposite in the sky from the sun), Mars rises at sunset and remains in the sky all night. Bright, white polar caps and dusky surface markings may be glimpsed through a small telescope at opposition. Mars rivals Jupiter in brightness at opposition, but fades somewhat at other times.

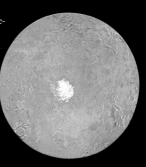

JUPITER

Visible in our morning sky for about five months at a stretch and in our evening sky for five months, Jupiter appears brighter than any star in the night sky at all times. The largest planet in our solar system, it has a diameter of 88,850 miles, 11.2 times that of earth. Jupiter's four largest moons—Io, Europa, Ganymede, and Callisto—can often be spotted with binoculars.

Jupiter (top) and moons

SATURN

Visible most of the year, Saturn appears to the naked eye as a slightly yellowish, moderately bright star. A small telescope reveals its rings, composed mainly of rocky chunks of ice, and the two largest (Titan and Rhea) of its more than 20 known moons.

METEORS

These "shooting stars" are typically chips ranging from sand-grain to marble size that are knocked off asteroids (tiny planets) or blown off comets and burn up as they strike our atmosphere. The strongest annual meteor showers are the Perseids, which peak around August 12, and the Geminids, which peak around December 13.

VENUS

Cloud-shrouded Venus alternates between being our "morning star" and "evening star," depending on where it is in its orbit. This brilliant planet usually outshines everything in the sky except for the sun and moon. As it circles the sun, Venus displays phases, which can be viewed through a small telescope or high-power binoculars.

Venus (left) and the moon

Stars and Deep-sky Objects

As earth orbits the sun in its annual cycle, our planet's night side faces in steadily changing directions, revealing different stars, constellations, and views of our own Milky Way. People in ancient times named constellations after mythological figures and familiar creatures whose shapes they saw outlined by the stars. The best known of these constellations lie along the ecliptic, the imaginary line that traces the apparent path of the sun through the sky. Earth, our moon, and other planets orbit in nearly the same plane, all traveling along a band roughly 16 degrees wide centered on the ecliptic and called the zodiac. (The zodiac is traditionally divided into 12 segments, but 13 constellations actually intersect it.)

Constellations are simply designated regions of the celestial sphere, like countries on a map. Most constellations bear little resemblance to their namesakes. Beyond the approximately 6,000 stars visible to the naked eye lie other fascinating deep-sky objects—star clusters, galaxies, nebulas (gas clouds)—that can be seen, some with the naked eye and others with binoculars or a small telescope.

The Zodiac

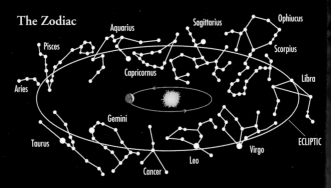

Ophiucus, Sagittarius, Aquarius, Pisces, Aries, Capricornus, Scorpius, Libra, ECLIPTIC, Virgo, Leo, Cancer, Gemini, Taurus

Seasonal Sky Maps

The following pages show star maps for each of the four seasons, drawn at a latitude of 45 degrees north for the specific times and dates given. (If you wish to observe at a different time or date, note that the same stars appear two hours earlier each month, or one hour earlier every two weeks.) The map for each season is divided into four quadrants: northeast, northwest, southeast, and southwest. Start by facing the direction in which you have the clearest view; if your best view is southeastward, use the southeast map. The maps plot the constellations and major stars; the wavy, pale blue areas represent the band of the Milky Way; the zenith, the point directly overhead, is indicated. The key to finding your way around the sky is to locate distinctive constellations or star groups (a few are described at right), and then to use them to find others. The maps do not chart the planets of our solar system, whose positions change continually. Their locations are often listed in newspapers in the weather section.

WINTER: ORION

On winter nights, we look outward through a spiral arm of our disk-shaped galaxy. Many hot, young blue or white stars (such as Sirius, Rigel, and Procyon), along with some older, cooler yellow and reddish stars (Betelgeuse, Capella, and Aldebaran), dominate the sky. New stars are being born in the Orion Nebula, a mixture of young stars, gases, and dust visible to the naked eye or with binoculars as a fuzzy area in Orion's sword, which hangs from his belt.

SPRING: THE DIPPERS

The spring sky features the well-known Big Dipper, part of the constellation Ursa Major, the Great Bear. The two stars at the end of the Big Dipper's bowl point almost directly at Polaris, the North Star, a moderately bright star (part of the Little Dipper, or Ursa Minor) that lies slightly less than 1 degree from

the true north celestial pole. Polaris sits above the horizon at an altitude equal to the observer's latitude. Its altitude for the cities of Buffalo, Rochester, Syracuse, Utica, and Albany, New York, is 43 degrees; for Richmond, Virginia, it is 37 degrees.

SUMMER: MILKY WAY

During the summer months, earth's dark side faces toward the bright center of the Milky Way, making that hazy band of light a dominant feature in the sky. A scan with binoculars through the Milky Way from Cygnus to Sagittarius and Scorpius reveals a dozen or more star clusters and nebulas. High to the northeast, the hot, white stars of the Summer Triangle—Vega, Deneb, and Altair—are usually the first stars visible in the evening.

FALL: ANDROMEDA GALAXY

On autumn evenings, earth's night side faces away from the plane of our galaxy, allowing us to see other, more distant ones. The Andromeda Galaxy can be found northeast of the Great Square of Pegasus, just above the central star on the dimmer northern "leg" of Andromeda. (On the Fall Sky: Southeast map the galaxy is near the first D in Andromeda.) Appearing as an elongated patch of fuzzy light, it is 2.5 million light-years away.

The Winter Sky

The chart is drawn for these times and dates, but can be used at other times during the season.

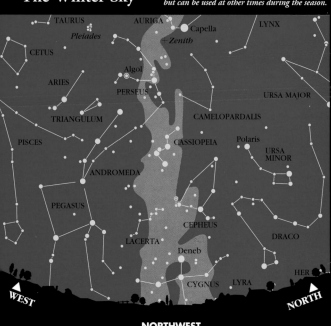

NORTHWEST

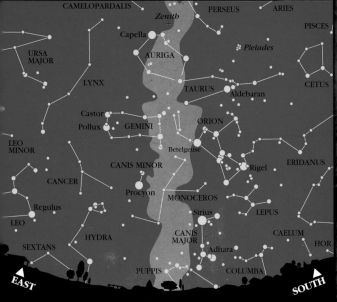

SOUTHEAST

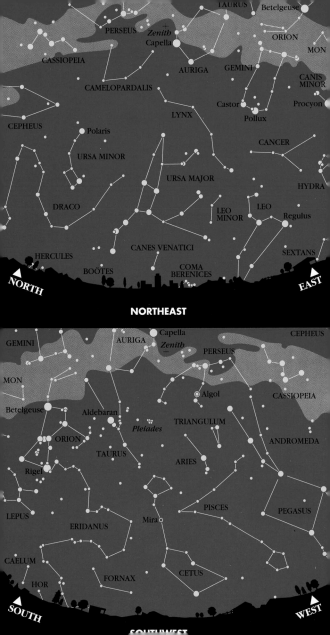

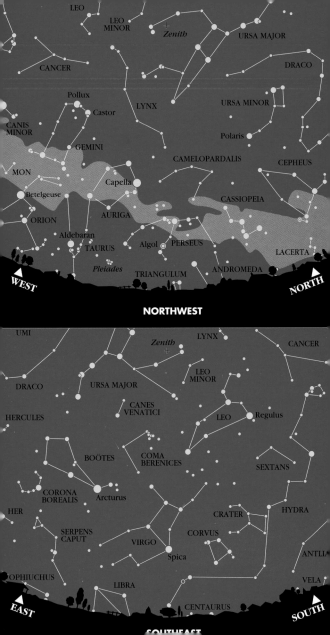

March 1, midnight; April 1, 10 P.M. (11 P.M. DST); May 1, 8 P.M. (9 P.M. DST)

NORTHEAST

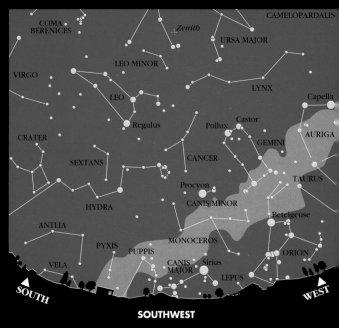

SOUTHWEST

The Summer Sky

The chart is drawn for these times and dates, but can be used at other times during the season.

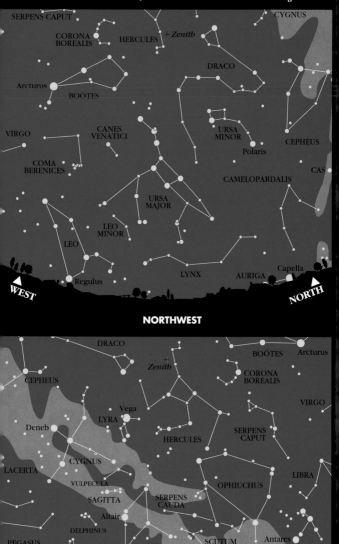

NORTHWEST

SOUTHEAST

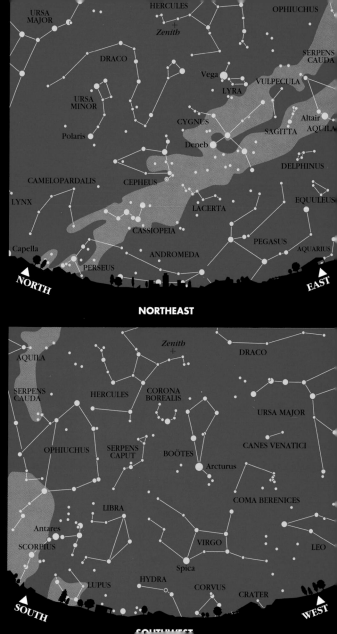

NORTHEAST

SOUTHWEST

NORTHWEST

PEGASUS

EQUULEUS

Zenith

LACERTA

PERSEUS

DELPHINUS

CASSIOPEIA

SAGITTA

Deneb

Altair

CEPHEUS

CAMELOPARDALIS

CYGNUS

VULPECULA

AQUILA

LYRA   Vega

Polaris

URSA
MINOR

OPHIUCHUS

HERCULES

DRACO

CORONA
BOREALIS

URSA MAJOR

SERPENS CAPUT

BOÖTES

WEST

NORTH

SOUTHEAST

CAMELOPARDALIS

LACERTA

CYGNUS

Zenith

CASSIOPEIA

DELPHINUS

ANDROMEDA

PEGASUS

EQUULEUS

Algol

AQUARIUS

PERSEUS

TRIANGULUM

Pleiades

ARIES

PISCES

CAPRICORNUS

TAURUS

PISCIS
AUSTRINUS

Aldebaran

Mira

Fomalhaut

ORION

CETUS

GRUS

ERIDANUS

SCULPTOR

EAST

SOUTH

September 1, midnight (1 A.M. DST); October 1, 10 P.M. (11 P.M. DST); November 1, 8 P.M.; December 1, 6 P.M.

NORTHEAST

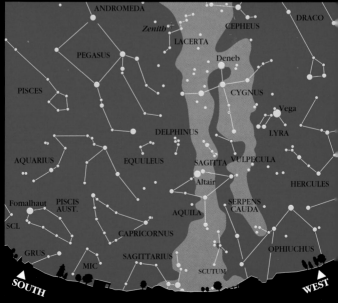

SOUTHWEST

How to Use the Flora and Fauna Section

Part Two of this book presents nearly 1,000 of the most common species found in the Mid-Atlantic states, beginning with mushrooms, algae, lichens, ferns, and other spore plants, and continuing with trees and shrubs, wildflowers, invertebrates (mostly seashore creatures and insects), fishes, amphibians, reptiles, birds, and mammals. Flora species are presented alphabetically by family name. Fauna species are sequenced according to their taxonomy, or scientific classification. The classification and the names of species in this guide are based on authoritative sources when these exist for a given group.

Introductions and Other Essays

Most major sections of Part Two—for example, trees, wildflowers, marine invertebrates, birds—have an introduction, and some groups within the larger sections are also described in brief essays. The introductions should be read along with the species accounts that follow, as they present information that is fundamental for understanding the plants or animals in question. For groups without introductory essays, shared features are sometimes given in the opening sentence of the first species in the sequence.

Names

Each account begins with the common name of the species. Common names can change and may differ in other sources; if a species has a widely used alternate name, that is given within quotation marks, directly below the common name. The scientific species name, shown below the common name, is italicized (alternate scientific names are also sometimes listed). In a few cases (some flowers and invertebrates), organisms are best known on the genus level and are presented as such here. For example, the Periodical Cicadas are presented as a group: the *Magicicada* species. Below the scientific name is the name of the group (class, order, family) with which the species is most commonly associated.

Description

The species accounts are designed to permit identification of species in the field. An account begins with the organism's typical mature or adult size: length (L), height (H), width (W), diameter (D), tail length (T), and/or wingspan (WS). The size is followed by physical characteristics, including color and distinctive markings. We use the abbreviations "imm." (immature) and "juv." (juvenile). The term "morph" describes a distinctive coloration that occurs in some individuals.

Other Information

For every species, the typical habitat is described. Other information may also be given, such as seasonality (bloom times of flowers or periods of activity for mammals) or the need for caution (species

immature (left), adult (right)

Names —

AMERICAN ROBIN
Turdus migratorius
THRUSH FAMILY

Description —

10″. Male breast and sides rufous orange; back and wings brownish gray; head blackish; bill yellow; tail black with tiny white corners; vent white. Female head and back duller grayish. Imm. buffy white below with blackish spots; buffy scaling on back. In spring and summer, eats earthworms, fruits.

Other Information —

In fall and winter, roams in flocks, roosts communally. **VOICE** Song: rising and falling *cheery-up cheery-me*. Calls: *tut tut tut* and *tseep*. **HABITAT** Woods, towns. **RANGE** Mar.–Nov.: entire region. Dec.–Feb.: mainly coastal plain.

that can cause irritation, illness, or injury). Similar species are sometimes described at the end of an account. The range (the area in which the species lives) is not stated if the species occurs throughout the Mid-Atlantic region; the one exception to this rule is the birds, for which the range is always given. The term "local" means that a species occurs in spotty fashion over a large area, but not throughout the entire area. In describing the geographic range of species, we use the abbreviations e (east), w (west), n (north), s (south), c (central), and combinations of these (sc for southcentral). For state names, we use the two-letter postal codes.

Readers should note that color, shape, and size may vary within plant and animal species, depending on environmental conditions and other factors. Bloom, migration, and other times can vary with the weather, latitude, and geography.

Classification of Living Things

Biologists divide living organisms into major groups called kingdoms, the largest of which are the plant and animal kingdoms. Kingdoms are divided into phyla (or divisions, in plants), phyla are divided into classes, classes into orders, orders into families, families into genera (singular: genus), and genera into species. The species, the basic unit of classification, is generally what we have in mind when we talk about a "kind" of plant or animal. The scientific name of a species consists of two words. The first is the genus name; the second is the species name. The scientific name of the Meadow Jumping Mouse is *Zapus hudsonius. Zapus* is the genus name, and *hudsonius* is the species name.

Species are populations or groups of populations that are able to interbreed and produce fertile offspring themselves; they usually are not able to breed successfully or produce fertile offspring with members of other species. Many widespread species have numerous races (subspecies)—populations that are separated from one another geographically; races within a species may differ in appearance and behavior from other populations of that species.

Flora

The flora section of this guide includes flowering and nonflowering plants as well as algae and mushrooms, which are no longer considered part of the plant kingdom. Botanists are developing new classification systems that place most algae outside of the green plants group. Mushrooms are covered here because they are somewhat plant-like in appearance and are often found on plants or plant matter.

In this guide, we begin with mushrooms, followed by algae and lichens. The next group is the nonflowering spore plants such as mosses, clubmosses, horsetails, and ferns. Trees follow, beginning with conifers, then large broadleaf trees, and finally small broadleaf trees and shrubs. Wildflowers, including flowering vines, grasses, and water plants in addition to terrestrial herbaceous plants, end the flora section.

In most of the flora subsections, species are grouped by family. The families are sequenced alphabetically by the English family name. The measurements given in the species accounts are typical mature sizes in the Mid-Atlantic region. Colors, shapes, and sizes may vary within a species depending on environmental conditions. Bloom times vary throughout the region (northern New York can be several weeks behind West Virginia and Virginia) and can also be affected by the weather conditions in a given year. The geographic range is specified only when the species is not found throughout the entire Mid-Atlantic region.

Users of this guide are warned against eating or otherwise consuming any plants or parts of a plant (including fiddleheads or berries or other fruits) or any mushrooms based on the information supplied in this guide.

Mushrooms

The organisms known as fungi—including molds, yeasts, mildews, and mushrooms—range from microscopic forms to mammoth puffballs. Unlike plants, they do not carry out photosynthesis, and thus must obtain food from organic matter, living or dead. The fungi in this book are of the type commonly known as mushrooms.

Mushrooms that grow on the ground typically have a stalk and a cap. The stalks of different species vary in shape, thickness, and density. There is often a skirt-like or bracelet-like ring midway up or near the top of the stalk, and the stalk base is often bulbous or sometimes enclosed by a cup at or just below the surface of the ground. Bracket (or shelf) mushrooms, which grow on trunks or logs, are often unstalked or short-stalked. A mushroom's cap may be smooth, scaly, warty, or shaggy, and its shape may be round, flat, convex (bell- or umbrella-shaped), or concave (cup- or trumpet-shaped). The caps of many species change as they mature, from closed and egg-shaped to open and umbrella-like; the cap color may also change with age.

Fungi reproduce through the release of single-celled bodies called spores. Many mushrooms bear their microscopic, spore-producing structures on the underside of the cap, either on radiating blade-like gills or within tiny tubes that terminate in pores. In others, the spore-producing structures line the inside of a cup-shaped cap or are located in broad wrinkles or open pits on the sides or top of the cap. Puffball mushrooms produce their spores within a ball-shaped body; the spores are released when the mature ball breaks open at the top or disintegrates.

In the accounts that follow, sizes given are typical heights (for stalked species) and cap widths of mature specimens.

CAUTION
Of the many hundreds of mushroom species occurring in the Mid-Atlantic region, at least 10 are deadly poisonous to eat, even in small amounts, and many others cause mild to severe reactions. The brief descriptions and few illustrations in this guide do not provide adequate information for determining the edibility of mushroom species. Inexperienced mushroom-hunters should not eat any species they find in the wild.

FLY AMANITA
"Fly Agaric"
Amanita muscaria var. *formosa*
AMANITA FAMILY
H 6"; W 6". Cap umbrella-shaped, yellow or orange, with flaky white warts. Stalk stout, whitish, usu. with skirt; base bulbous. Gills white. **CAUTION** Deadly poisonous. **SEASON** June–Sept. **HABITAT** Forests, pastures.

DESTROYING ANGEL
Amanita virosa
AMANITA FAMILY
H 6"; W 4". Entirely white. Cap umbrella-shaped, with ragged edges. Stalk tall with tattered skirt, bulbous base. **CAUTION** Deadly poisonous; can be mistaken for edible *Agaricus* species. **SEASON** June–Oct. **HABITAT** Broadleaf forests, pastures.

OLD-MAN-OF-THE-WOODS
Strobilomyces confusus
BOLETUS FAMILY

H 5″; W 6″. Cap umbrella-shaped, pale brown with small brown or black scales, underside with large white or gray pores. Stalk stout, shaggy. Scales, stalk, and pores darker with age. **SEASON** June–Oct. **HABITAT** Broadleaf forests, often under oaks.

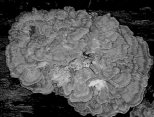

ARTIST'S FUNGUS
Ganoderma applanatum
BRACKET FAMILY

W 11″. Cap flat to convex, semicircular to fan-shaped; grayish brown with concentric zones of brown and gray; hard, stalkless, attached directly to wood. Cap underside white, bruises brown, with pores. **SEASON** Year-round. **HABITAT** Living or dead broadleaf trees.

SULFUR SHELF
"Chicken Mushroom"
Laetiporus (Polyporus) sulphureus
BRACKET FAMILY

W 7″. Cap flat, fan-shaped; orange, with yellow-lobed edge; stalkless, attached directly to wood. Cap underside yellow, with tiny pores. Forms overlapping clusters or rosettes. **SEASON** May–Nov., mainly autumn. **HABITAT** Living or dead trees.

YELLOW-TIPPED CORAL
Ramaria formosa
CORAL FUNGUS FAMILY

H 6″; W 6″. Densely branching; coral-like. Branches pink, pinkish orange, or pinkish tan; branch tips yellow, bruising brownish. Stalk often tapered toward white base. **CAUTION** Poisonous. **SEASON** July–Dec., mainly autumn. **HABITAT** Broadleaf forests.

PIGSKIN POISON PUFFBALL
"Common Earthball"
Scleroderma citrinum
EARTHSTAR FAMILY

H 2″; W 3″. Yellow to tan ball with rind-like skin and darker scales. Spores released by pore at top. Inside white, maturing purplish black. **CAUTION** Poisonous. **SEASON** July–Nov. **HABITAT** On ground or rotten wood in forests or gardens.

PARASOL MUSHROOM
Lepiota procera
LEPIOTA FAMILY

H 12"; W 6". Cap light brown, very scaly, umbrella-shaped. Stalk tall, slender, scaly; has movable bracelet-like ring, swollen base. Gills white to pinkish, with wooly edges. **SEASON** June–Oct. **HABITAT** On ground in pastures, lawns.

GREEN-GILLED LEPIOTA
Chlorophyllum molybdites
LEPIOTA FAMILY

H 8"; W 10". Cap white, scaly; umbrella-shaped, cup-shaped with age. Stalk slender, smooth; has bracelet-like ring. Gills white to pale yellow, green when mature. Often grows in rings and arcs. **CAUTION** Poisonous. **SEASON** June–Oct. **HABITAT** Pastures, lawns.

MEADOW MUSHROOM
Agaricus campestris
MEADOW MUSHROOM FAMILY

H 2½"; W 3". Cap flat, white to gray-ish or gray-brown; smooth or silky-scaled; ragged-edged. Stalk stout, often tapered toward base, with ragged skirt. Gills pink, dark brown when mature. **SEASON** May, Aug.–Sept. **HABITAT** Meadows, pastures.

YELLOW MOREL
Morchella esculenta
MOREL FAMILY

H 3"; W 1½". Cap conical to egg-shaped, honeycombed with deep pits, yellow-brown to grayish, hol-low. Stalk hollow, enlarged at base, whitish. Spores produced in pits on cap. **SEASON** Apr.–May. **HABITAT** Under hardwoods, esp. cottonwoods and in abandoned apple orchards.

HONEY MUSHROOM
Armillaria mellea
TRICHOLOMA FAMILY

H 3"; W 3". Cap convex, cream to rusty, sticky; hairy-scaled, esp. in center. Stalk slender; white above thick cottony ring, brown below. Gills white; become dingy. Forms large clusters, with caps overlapping. **SEASON** Aug.–Nov. **HABITAT** Bases of trees or stumps.

FAIRY RING MUSHROOM
Marasmias oreades
TRICHOLOMA FAMILY
H 3″; W 2″. Cap tan, umbrella-shaped, with central bump; tough and leathery; edges inrolled. Stalk slender, yellowish brown, velvety, often twisted. Gills whitish to pale tan. Grows in rings or arcs. Has a pleasant, almondy odor. **SEASON** May–Oct., after rain. **HABITAT** Pastures, lawns.

OYSTER MUSHROOM
Pleurotus ostreatus
TRICHOLOMA FAMILY
H 1½″; W 5″. Bracket. Cap fan- or funnel-shaped, wavy-edged; white, gray, or brown. Stalk absent or very short, curved, whitish, attached to one side of cap, velvety at base. Gills whitish, extend down stalk. Forms overlapping clusters. **SEASON** May–Nov. **HABITAT** Trunks, logs, stumps of broadleaf trees.

Algae

Algae are a diverse array of organisms ranging from microscopic unicellular forms to large seaweeds. Three groups of algae are included in this guide: red algae, yellow-brown algae, and green algae. (In this section, the species are presented in these large groupings rather than by family or order.) Red algae and yellow-brown algae occur almost exclusively in salt water. Green algae most often live in fresh water but are also found in salt water and on land. In fact, land plants evolved from certain kinds of green algae.

The selected algae in this guide are all sizable marine plants commonly known as seaweeds. Most have stalks, leaf-like structures called fronds (sometimes with air bladders that keep them afloat), and a pad-, disk-, or root-like structure called a holdfast with which they attach to a substrate such as sand, rock, shells, a pier, or some other surface. Some species tend to become detached from the substrate and float freely. In the accounts that follow, sizes given are lengths of mature specimens, unless otherwise noted.

PURPLE LAVER
Porphyra umbilicalis
RED ALGAE
D 12″. Olive green, purple-red, or brown-purple, shiny. Fronds very thin ruffled sheets, roundish and pinched in middle where holdfast is attached. Attached to rocks, pilings, and other seaweeds. Edible. **HABITAT** Rocky shores exposed to waves; intertidal zone.

HOLLOW GREEN ALGAE
Enteromorpha intestinalis
GREEN ALGAE

24". Bright green. Fronds long unbranched inflated tubes. Air bubbles trapped at regular intervals along tube. Attached to rocks, shells, wharfs; sometimes free-floating. **HABITAT** Rocky shores exposed to waves; intertidal zone (tidal pools).

SEA LETTUCE
Ulva lactuca
GREEN ALGAE

D 24". Green, shiny. Fronds thin ruffled sheets; roundish to irreg. in outline; can be clusterd, resembling a head of lettuce. Attached to rocks and pilings; sometimes free-floating. **HABITAT** Oceanside rocks, mudflats, shallow pools.

BLADDER ROCKWEED
Fucus vesiculosus
YELLOW-BROWN ALGAE

D 24". Olive green. Fronds long, flat, rubbery; branched in twos; edges bumpy, often lined with paired oval air bladders. Attached to rocks and piers by small disk-like holdfast. **HABITAT** Rocky shores exposed to waves; intertidal zone.

SOUTHERN KELP
Laminaria agardhii
YELLOW-BROWN ALGAE

8'. Shiny brown. Fronds long, ruffle-edged, and strap-shaped narrowing to short stem above root-like holdfast. Attached to rocks, stones, shells, wharfs, piers. **HABITAT** Rocky shores exposed to waves; intertidal zone to deep water.

ATTACHED GULFWEED
Sargassum filipendula
YELLOW-BROWN ALGAE

3'. Dark brown. Branched stalks and toothed, lance-shaped to linear fronds with prominent midvein and round, stalked air bladders. Attached by large lobed holdfast to natural limestone and jetty rock and shells. **HABITAT** Just below low-tide line to deep offshore waters.

Lichens

A lichen is a remarkable dual organism made up of a fungus and a colony of microscopic green algae or cyanobacteria ("blue-green algae"). Such a relationship—dissimilar organisms living in intimate association—is known as *symbiosis* and may be detrimental to one of the participants (parasitism) or beneficial to both (mutualism). In a lichen, the fungus surrounds the algae and takes up water and minerals that come its way from rainwater, fog, and dust; the algae supply carbohydrates produced by photosynthesis. It is not definitely known whether symbiosis in lichens is mutually beneficial or mildly to wholly parasitic. The balance is probably different in each species.

Lichens occur in a wide range of habitats, including some of the harshest environments on earth, such as deserts and the Arctic (where they serve as the primary food of reindeer and caribou). They can also be found in forests, along roadsides, on buildings and other man-made structures, and on mountaintops. During droughts they dry up and become dormant; they rapidly absorb water when it does become available, springing back to life. Lichens range widely in color, occurring in white, black, gray, and various shades of green, orange, brown, yellow, or red. Their color often varies dramatically with moisture content.

Most lichens grow very slowly, about ⅟₂₅ inch to ½ inch per year, and can have extremely long lifetimes: specimens estimated to be at least 4,000 years old have been found. Many lichens have special structures for vegetative reproduction: tiny fragments that break off easily or powdery spots that release tiny balls of algae wrapped in microscopic fungal threads. In others, the fungal component produces spores on conspicuous fruiting bodies, which may be disclike, cup-like, or globular.

Lichens are an important source of food and nesting material for many mammals and birds. Humans have used lichens as food, medicine, dye, and fiber. Because lichens are sensitive indicators of air quality and ecosystem continuity, they serve as natural tools for monitoring the environment.

In the accounts that follow, sizes given are typical heights (H) or widths (W) of mature specimens.

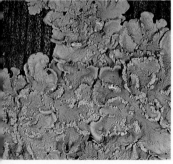

COMMON GREENSHIELD
Flavoparmelia caperata
W 4″. Light greenish-yellow rosettes of undulating, rounded, smooth to wrinkled lobes. Fruiting bodies rare. Reproduces via powdery to granular patches erupting on surface. Underside black (brown at edges) with root-like hairs. **HABITAT** Trunks and branches of trees in open forests; rare on rocks. **Baltimore Greenshield** *(P. baltimorensis),* which has small bumps instead of powdery patches, grows on rocks.

BRITISH SOLDIERS
Cladonia cristatella

H ¾". Tufts of yellowish gray-green, branched near top; erect, somewhat scaly stalks. Fruiting bodies round, scarlet, found on tops of stalks. **HABITAT** On soil, wood, or rotting logs in open areas.

SCRIPT LICHEN
Graphis scripta

W 1". Thin, round, white crusts. Fruiting bodies short, many-branched, with black cracks; most numerous at center. **HABITAT** Branches and trunks of mostly broadleaf trees in shaded forests.

SPECKLED GRAYSHIELD
Punctelia rudecta

W 4". Gray to greenish or bluish-gray patches of undulating, rounded lobes, with small, irreg. white spots and many tiny, cylindrical or lobe-like projections from upper surface. Projections break off for reproduction; fruiting bodies rare. Underside tan, with dense root-like hairs. **HABITAT** Trunks and branches of trees, rocks; in open forests.

GIANT ROCKTRIPE
Umbilicaria mammulata

W 5". Leathery (damp) to crisp (dry), brown disks attached to rock by a single central cord. Upperside smooth, margins somewhat folded or undulating. Underside very dark with dense, black, branched hairs. Fruiting bodies black, disk-like, with concentric grooves; rarely seen. **HABITAT** Large boulders in open forests in mtns.

BUSHY BEARD LICHEN
Usnea strigosa

W 2". Shrubby, pale yellowish to greenish, intricately branching, stringy tufts covered with perpendicular bristles and small bumps. Fruiting bodies disk-like, smooth, sometimes undulating, often more yellow or tan than branches; edged with bristles. Species of *Usnea* have antibiotic properties and have been used medicinally in cultures all over the world. **HABITAT** Branches and twigs of broadleaf trees.

Spore Plants

Spore plants are green land plants such as mosses, clubmosses, horsetails, and ferns (ferns are introduced separately on page 88) that do not reproduce from seeds. Among the earliest evolved land plants still present on earth, these plants do not produce flowers or fruits. The most conspicuous part of their reproduction is the spore, a reproductive cell that divides and eventually develops the structures producing the sperm and egg, which fuse to form a new adult plant.

Mosses are feathery, mat-forming plants typically found in shady, damp to wet habitats. When "fruiting," their spores are released from a lidded capsule often elevated on a wiry brown fertile stalk. Mosses typically absorb water and nutrients directly from the

HAIRCAP MOSS
Polytrichum juniperinum
MOSS CLASS
3". Green carpet of tall erect stalks with stiff, pointed leaves. Fertile stalks reddish, each topped with golden-brown, cylindrical capsule. **HABITAT** Disturbed soil in forests, on bog edges.

PEAT MOSSES
"Sphagnum Mosses"
Sphagnum species
MOSS CLASS
12". Yellow-green to red mats of long spongy stalks with thick, whorled branches covered with tiny, scale-like leaves. **HABITAT** Swamps, bogs, ponds, streams; sometimes floating.

SOUTHERN RUNNING-PINE
Diphasiatrum (Lycopodium) digitatum
CLUBMOSS FAMILY
8". Green, forms colonies. Horizontal stems on soil surface; erect stems with horizontal, flat, fan-shaped branches at regular intervals. Branches covered with tiny, flat, lanceolate leaves. Spore cones yellowish, 3–4 atop 3" branched stalks atop stems. **HABITAT** Dry forests, fields, meadows. **RANGE** NY and south to mtns. of WV, VA.

SHINING FIR-MOSS
Huperzia (Lycopodium) lucidula
CLUBMOSS FAMILY
8". Dark green, forms bristly, loose colonies. Horizontal stems on soil surface, often becoming covered with leaf litter; erect stems forked and densely covered with tiny, needle-like, shiny, evergreen leaves. Sporangia in rows along branches at base of leaves. **HABITAT** Cool moist forests and stream banks.

environment, as they lack a sophisticated vascular system for conducting water and nutrients internally.

Like ferns, conifers, and flowering plants, clubmosses and horsetails have well-developed vascular systems. Clubmosses often look like upright green pipe cleaners or tiny conifers rising from the ground in shady woodlands. When fruiting, spores are produced in tiny sacs, called sporangia, between the leaves. In some species the leaves and sporangia are densely clustered into a long, narrow, cone-like structure. Horsetails have conspicuously jointed stems with whorls of tiny, scale-like leaves and branches at most joints. Sporangia are produced along the edges of umbrella-like structures clustered into a cone-like configuration atop a brownish, whitish, or green stem. In the accounts that follow, the size given is the typical height of a mature specimen.

GROUND PINE
"Tree Clubmoss" "Princess Pine"
Lycopodium obscurum
CLUBMOSS FAMILY

8″. Green, erect, tree-like, with many flat, forking branchlets covered with tiny, needle-like, flattened leaves. Spore cones yellowish, unstalked; several atop upper branches. **HABITAT** Moist open forests, bogs.

SCOURING RUSH
Equisetum hyemale ssp. *affine*
HORSETAIL FAMILY

4′. Clusters of green, jointed, hollow, rough, ridged, usu. unbranched stalks, with ash-gray or brown bands; each topped by sharp-pointed ¾″ spore cone; evergreen. **HABITAT** Streamsides, ditches, seeps, abandoned wet pastures.

FIELD HORSETAIL
"Common Horsetail"
Equisetum arvense
HORSETAIL FAMILY

20″. Stems erect, rough, green, with many rosettes of long ascending branches. Fertile stems pale brown, unbranched, stout; each topped with brown spore cone in spring. **HABITAT** Forests, fields, swampsides.

Ferns

Ferns, the largest group of seedless vascular plants still found on earth, are diverse in habitat and form. In the Mid-Atlantic region they occur mainly in shady forests and near fresh water, but several fern species thrive in open sunny areas. Most ferns grow in soil, often in clumps or clusters; some species grow on rocks or trees, and a few float on water.

Ferns have a stem called a *rhizome* that is typically thin and long and grows along the surface or below the ground. The rhizome bears the roots and leaves, and lives for many years. Fern leaves, called *fronds,* are commonly compound and may be *pinnate* (divided into leaflets), *bipinnate* (subdivided into *subleaflets*), or even *tripinnate* (divided again into segments); they are often lacy or feathery in appearance.

Frond types

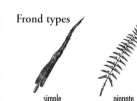

simple   pinnate   bipinnate   tripinnate

Ferns reproduce through the release of spores from tiny sacs called *sporangia,* which commonly occur in clusters *(sori)* on the underside of the frond. The sori may cover the entire frond underside, may form dots or lines, may occur only beneath the frond's curled-under edges, or may be covered by specialized outgrowths of the frond. Fronds that bear sporangia are called fertile fronds; those that do not are called sterile fronds. In some species the sterile and fertile fronds differ in size and shape.

Some ferns are evergreen, but the foliage of most Mid-Atlantic ferns dies back each year with the autumn frosts. Each spring the rhizome gives rise to coiled tender young fronds called *fiddleheads.* Fiddleheads of some ferns are popular delicacies, but identification is difficult: the shoots of some deadly poisonous flowering plants (including various poison hemlocks) can be mistaken for fern fiddleheads, and many fiddleheads are edible at certain stages and poisonous at others. Only local experts should collect fiddleheads for consumption.

segment

sori

Parts of a Fern

leaflet

subleaflet

stalk

fiddlehead

rhizome

In the accounts that follow, sizes given are typical mature heights. For illustrations of leaf shapes, see page 132.

RATTLESNAKE FERN
"Common Grape Fern"
Botrychium virginianum
ADDER'S-TONGUE FAMILY
20". Stalks solitary, slender, smooth. Frond pale bright green, halfway up stalk, divided into 3 triangular, bi- or tripinnate lacy leaflets. Fertile frond atop stalk, bi- or tripinnate with seed-like clusters of sporangia. **HABITAT** Rich soil in moist forests.

HAY-SCENTED FERN
Dennstaedtia punctilobula
BRACKEN FAMILY
24". Stalks hairy. Fronds delicate, sticky-hairy; tripinnate, with about 20 or more pairs of lance-shaped leaflets, each with several ovate to lanceolate subleaflets. Fronds grow in line above creeping rhizome. Sori in cup-like structures along leaflet edges. **HABITAT** Sandy fields, woodland clearings.

BRACKEN
Pteridium aquilinum
BRACKEN FAMILY
3'. Stalks rigid; green, becoming dark brown. Fronds arched, divided into 3 broadly triangular, stalked, bi- or tripinnate leaflets, each with many pinnate subleaflets. Sori in dots on curled-under leaflet edges. Forms large weedy colonies. Highly variable species, found worldwide. **HABITAT** Fields, woodland clearings.

VIRGINIA CHAIN FERN
Woodwardia virginica
CHAIN FERN FAMILY
4'. Stalks erect, shiny; purple-brown and swollen at base, straw-colored above. Fronds leathery, pinnate, with many oblong to lanceolate, deeply lobed leaflets; grow in clusters. Sori form chain-like pattern along veins on frond undersides. **HABITAT** Bogs, swamps, marshes, moist forests.

NORTHERN MAIDENHAIR
Adiantum pedatum
MAIDENHAIR FERN FAMILY

18″. Stalks shiny, purple-black, wiry, forked. Fronds bluish green, bipinnate; fan out in delicate whorls. 5–6 leaflets per forked stalk, each with several fan-shaped to oblong subleaflets with scalloped or incised edges. Sporangia along curled-under, whitish-green leaflet edges. **HABITAT** Forests, moist ground, rock faces; esp. limestone areas.

NEW YORK FERN
Thelypteris noveboracensis
MARSH FERN FAMILY

20″. Stalks slender, straw-colored. Fronds yellow-green, finely hairy beneath, bipinnate, with 20 or more pairs of lanceolate leaflets; subleaflets many, oblong to linear. Fertile fronds larger, narrower, and more erect. Sori few, near leaflet edges, under kidney-shaped flaps. **HABITAT** Sunny clearings in moist forests, thickets.

MARSH FERN
Thelypteris palustris
MARSH FERN FAMILY

3′6″. Stalks slender; green above, black at base. Fronds pinnate, with about 12 lanceolate leaflets, each pinnately divided into several lobes. Sori in rows on frond undersides near midvein, each under a kidney-shaped flap; partly covered by curled-under leaflet edges. **HABITAT** Marshes, ditches, swamps, riversides, wet forests.

COMMON POLYPODY
"Rock Polypody"
Polypodium virginianum
POLYPODY FERN FAMILY

8″. Stalks slender. Fronds pinnate, widest near middle; with 10–20 pairs of linear, wavy-edged, blunt leaflets. Fronds grow in line from creeping rhizome. Sori in 1 row on each side of leaflet midrib. **HABITAT** Rocks and logs in moist forests. **Appalachian Polypody** (*P. appalachianum*) has fronds widest toward base, pointed leaflets.

CINNAMON FERN
Osmunda cinnamomea
ROYAL FERN FAMILY

4'. Stalks covered with cinnamon-brown wooly hairs. Fronds bipinnate with many oblong, pinnate, many-lobed leaflets. Fertile fronds erect, bright green turning cinnamon brown; have club-shaped, seed-like clusters of sporangia; appear before sterile fronds. Rhizome covered with wiry roots. **HABITAT** Moist forests, streamsides, swamps.

INTERRUPTED FERN
Osmunda claytoniana
ROYAL FERN FAMILY

30". Stalks slender, arched. Fronds bipinnate, with 18 or more pairs of lanceolate leaflets and many subleaflets. Fertile fronds interrupted in middle by 4 or more pairs of fertile leaflets with sporangia clustered along edges; middle bare after spring spore season. Rhizome stout, stubbly, creeping. **HABITAT** Moist forests, swamps, roadsides.

ROYAL FERN
Osmunda regalis var. *spectabilis*
ROYAL FERN FAMILY

5'. Stalks erect, reddish. Fronds bipinnate, with 6 or more pairs of leaflets, each with 5–7 oblong subleaflets. Fertile leaflets contracted, covered with sporangia that form conspicuous, rusty brown clusters atop fronds. Rhizome covered with old, withered stalks. **HABITAT** Swamps, marshes, streamsides, moist forests.

EBONY SPLEENWORT
Asplenium platyneuron
SPLEENWORT FAMILY

14". Fertile stalks stiff, erect, brittle, dark brown, shiny; sterile stalks shorter and arching. Fronds tapered at both ends; pinnate, with many pairs of blunt leaflets. Sori oblong, under ragged-edged flaps; in 1 row on each side of leaflet midrib. Sterile fronds shorter, arching outward. **HABITAT** Dry, rocky, open forests.

LADY FERN
Athyrium filix-femina
WOOD FERN FAMILY

4'. Stalks blackish at base, straw-colored above; scaly. Fronds arch outward, bi- or tripinnate, tapered at both ends, with lobed, fine-toothed leaflets. Sori kidney-shaped, under kidney-shaped, hairy flaps. Rhizome often exposed, with old stalks attached. Grows in clusters. **HABITAT** Wet ground.

SPINULOSE WOOD FERN
Dryopteris carthusiana
WOOD FERN FAMILY

30". Stalks tan; densely scaly. Fronds light green, tripinnate, with many pairs of leaflets; subleaflets cut into toothed segments. Sori under kidney-shaped flaps, in 1 row on each side of leaflet midrib. Rhizome thick, scaly, creeping. Used by florists for greenery. **HABITAT** Moist forests, marshes, swamps.

MARGINAL WOOD FERN
Dryopteris marginalis
WOOD FERN FAMILY

2'. Stalks scaly, brittle, brownish, erect. Fronds dark green, arch outward, bipinnate, with many pairs of leaflets; subleaflets blunt-toothed, leathery, evergreen. Sori under kidney-shaped flaps along leaflet edges. Rhizome semi-erect, shaggy, with golden brown scales. **HABITAT** Rocky slopes in moist forests, ravines.

COMMON OAK FERN
Gymnocarpium dryopteris
WOOD FERN FAMILY

10". Stalks slender, brittle, scaly at base. Fronds bright yellow-green; divided into 3 broadly triangular leaflets, lower 2 tripinnate, upper 1 bipinnate. Subleaflets deeply cut into blunt segments. Few sori on each side of leaflet midrib. Resembles a tiny bracken fern. **HABITAT** Rocky slopes in cool forests.

OSTRICH FERN
Matteuccia struthiopteris var.
pensylvanica
WOOD FERN FAMILY
4'. Sterile fronds ostrich-plume-like, bipinnate, with many pairs of leaflets; subleaflets linear. Fertile fronds dark brown, stiff, lyre-shaped; leaflets with sori form dark brown clusters of pod-like structures. **HABITAT** Moist forests, swamps, streamsides.

SENSITIVE FERN
Onoclea sensibilis
WOOD FERN FAMILY
24". Stalks stiff, brittle, straw-colored. Sterile fronds leathery, pinnate, with about 12 pairs of wavy-edged leaflets. Fertile fronds a brown cluster of bead-like, hardened, modified leaflets enclosing sori. Killed by first frost, hence the common name. **HABITAT** Moist forests, swamps, wet meadows.

CHRISTMAS FERN
Polystichum acrostichoides
WOOD FERN FAMILY
21". Stalks stout, very scaly. Fronds leathery, lustrous, pinnate; with many pairs of lanceolate, spiny-toothed leaflets, each with prominent, ear-like projection at base. Sori cover frond underside. Evergreen. Grow in arching clumps. Used in Christmas decorations. **HABITAT** Forests, streamsides, ravines.

RUSTY WOODSIA
"Rusty Cliff Fern"
Woodsia ilvensis
WOOD FERN FAMILY
6". Stalks scaly, rusty-haired, arch outward. Fronds pinnate, with 10–15 pairs of rounded to fan-shaped, lobed leaflets, white- and rusty-hairy below. Sori with radiating hairs along curled-under leaflet edges. **HABITAT** Rock crevices of cliffs and rockslides.

Trees and Shrubs

Trees and shrubs are woody perennial plants. Trees typically have a single trunk and a well-developed crown of foliage; some attain heights of more than 100 feet. Shrubs are usually less than 20 feet tall and often have several woody stems rather than a single trunk. This book covers two major categories of trees and shrubs. Conifers begin on page 95. Broadleaf trees and shrubs begin on page 102.

Individual tree sizes vary according to age and environmental factors. The heights given in the following sections are for average mature individuals in the Mid-Atlantic region; younger trees and those exposed to harsh conditions are smaller; older specimens may attain greater heights in optimal conditions. Trunk diameter, which also varies greatly within a species, is cited only for very large species.

Identifying a Tree

Trees can be identified by three key visual characteristics: crown shape (illustrated below), bark color and texture, and leaf shape and arrangement (illustrated on page 132). Below are common crown shapes for mature conifers and broadleaf trees. These shapes are idealized and simplified for illustrative purposes. The first line of each species account describes the tree's shape in these terms.

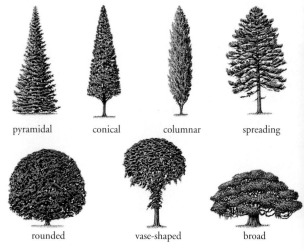

pyramidal   conical   columnar   spreading

rounded   vase-shaped   broad

The roots, trunk, and branches of most trees and shrubs are covered in bark, a protective layer consisting mainly of dead cells. The bark of young trees often differs in color and texture from mature bark. As a tree grows, the bark splits, cracks, and peels. In some trees, such as birches, the bark peels horizontally. In cedars the bark shreds in vertical strips. In many trees the bark may develop furrows, ridges, or fissures, may break up into plates, or may flake off. The species accounts describe mature bark unless otherwise noted.

Beneath the bark is the wood, most of which is dense, dark, dead tissue (heartwood) that provides structural support for the plant.

Between the heartwood and the bark are many pale, thin layers of living tissue (including sapwood) that transport water and minerals, and produce new wood and bark. Concentric rings, each representing a period (often a year) of growth, are visible in cut trunks and branches.

Conifers

Gymnosperms ("naked seeds") are trees and shrubs that produce exposed seeds, usually in cones, rather than seeds that are enclosed in an ovary, as in the angiosperms (flowering plants). Conifers, ginkgos, and cycads are all gymnosperms. The Mid-Atlantic's native gymnosperms are all conifers.

Commonly called "evergreens" and known in the timber industry as "softwoods," conifers are the most numerous and widespread gymnosperms found on earth. Their leaves are needle-like (long and slender) or scale-like (small and overlapping), typically evergreen, and well adapted for drought and freezing temperatures, thanks to a thick waxy coating and other protective features.

A distinctive characteristic of conifers is the cone, a reproductive structure comprised of a central axis with spirally arranged scales bearing pollen or seeds. A single tree usually has both pollen-bearing (male) and seed-bearing (female) cones; male cones are usually carried on lower branches, or lower down on the same branches as females. Male cones appear in spring, shed pollen, and soon fall from the tree. Female cones are larger, more woody, and have scales that protect the seeds until the cones expand to release them; this often occurs in the autumn of the second year after the formation and pollination of the cones. Unless otherwise specified, the cones described in this guide are female.

Most conifer species in the Mid-Atlantic region—pines, larches, hemlocks, spruces, and firs—belong to the pine family. In our area, those commonly known as pines (genus *Pinus*) bear long needles in bundles of two to five; cones vary widely among different species. Other pine family members found in the Mid-Atlantic region have much shorter needles. Larches bear needles in brush-like clusters that are deciduous (shed seasonally) and that turn yellow in autumn; cones are upright, stalked, and round to egg-shaped. Hemlocks bear needles on woody cushions and have small cones at the branch tips. Spruces have rough twigs, hanging cones, and sharp, four-sided needles borne on tiny, raised, woody pegs. The true firs (those of the genus *Abies*) are characterized by upright cones and needles arising from tiny depressions on the branches.

Other conifers in the Mid-Atlantic region include those of the cypress family (such as the Atlantic and Northern White Cedars, the Eastern Red Cedar, and the Common Juniper) and the yew family. Most members of the cypress family have narrow, scale-like leaves covering their branches; their small cones are round, bell-shaped, or (in the junipers) fleshy and berry-like. Yews have needles in two opposite rows and bear seeds not in cones but individually and surrounded by a fleshy, cup-shaped, berry-like structure called an aril.

Typical tree shapes are illustrated on pages 94, and leaf shapes, including the needles and scale-like leaves of conifers, are shown on page 132. Unless otherwise noted in the individual species description, needle or scale color is green, fading to yellowish or brown when shedding, and cone color is brown.

COMMON JUNIPER
Juniperus communis var. *depressa*
CYPRESS FAMILY

H 4'; W 10'. Usu. a spreading shrub; rarely a small tree. Needles ½", sharp, curved, in whorls of 3. Cones tiny, berry-like, bluish. Bark shreddy, red-brown or gray. **HABITAT** Pastures, abandoned fields, rocky slopes.

EASTERN RED CEDAR
Juniperus virginiana
CYPRESS FAMILY

40'. Crown narrow, compact, columnar. Leaves tiny, scale-like, cover twigs. Cones tiny, berry-like, dark blue. Bark thin, shreddy, reddish brown. **HABITAT** Open areas, abandoned fields, roadsides.

BALD CYPRESS
Taxodium distichum
CYPRESS FAMILY

130'. Crown conical to irregularly flat-topped; trunk enlarged at base, often with conical "knees." Needles ¾", bases twisted; in feather-like arrangement. Cones 1½", round. Bark dark reddish brown to light brown, furrowed into thin strips. **HABITAT** Swamps, lakesides, floodplains, riversides. **RANGE** Coastal plain, s DE and south.

NORTHERN WHITE CEDAR
"Eastern Arborvitae"
Thuja occidentalis
CYPRESS FAMILY

45'. Crown narrow, conical; branches short, spreading. Leaves tiny, pointed, flat scales. Cones ½", tulip-shaped, light blue or brown, upright. Bark thin, shreddy, reddish brown. **HABITAT** Swamps and bogs in limestone areas. **RANGE** NY, n NJ, PA and south to mtns. of VA, WV.

BALSAM FIR
Abies balsamea
PINE FAMILY

50'. Crown narrow, pyramidal, pointed. Needles ¾", flat, blunt or notched at tip, curved upward, in 2 rows per twig; aromatic. Cones 3", cylindrical, purplish, upright, on highest branches. Bark thin, smooth, blistered, scaly, brown. Commonly used as Christmas tree. **HABITAT** Moist, boreal forests. **RANGE** NY, n PA; mtns. of WV, n VA.

TAMARACK
"American Larch"
Larix laricina
PINE FAMILY

80'. Crown pyramidal to conical; thin, open. Needles 1", in soft, brush-like clusters. Cones ½", egg-shaped, yellow-brown, upright. Bark scaly, thin, reddish brown. **HABITAT** Bogs, swamps, watersides, upland areas. **RANGE** NY, n NJ, n PA, WV. Widely planted **European Larch** *(L. decidua)* has hairy cones.

NORWAY SPRUCE
Picea abies
PINE FAMILY

80'. Crown pyramidal; branches short and stout, lower ones drooping. Needles ¾", 4-sided, blunt-tipped. Cones 5", cylindrical, slightly pointed, yellow-brown, hang down. Bark scaly, reddish brown. The most widely cultivated spruce in North America. **HABITAT** Cultivated stands, towns.

RED SPRUCE
Picea rubens
PINE FAMILY

65'. Crown pyramidal to conical. Needles ½", mostly sharp. Cones 1½", cylindrical, reddish brown, hang down. Bark thin, scaly, gray to reddish brown. Most common native spruce; forms pure stands in rocky areas. **HABITAT** Rocky forests, mainly mtns. **RANGE** NY, n NJ, ne PA to ne WV, nw VA.

BLACK SPRUCE
Picea mariana
PINE FAMILY

40′. Shrub-like at tree line. Crown irreg., conical; branches short, drooping. Needles ½″, rigid, dark green, on yellow-brown twigs. Cones 1″, egg-shaped, gray, hang down; often clustered at treetop; may remain on tree for years. Bark thin, scaly, gray to black. **HABITAT** Mainly bogs. **RANGE** NY, NJ, ne PA.

SHORTLEAF PINE
Pinus echinata
PINE FAMILY

90′. Crown spreading to rounded. Needles 2½″, in bundles of 2 or 3. Cones 1½″, egg-shaped; each cone scale has small, sharp spine. Bark reddish-brown, with scaly plates. Important lumber tree. **HABITAT** Dry, upland forests and abandoned fields, often in pure stands. **RANGE** s PA and south.

TABLE MOUNTAIN PINE
Pinus pungens
PINE FAMILY

50′. Crown rounded to irreg.; trunk often crooked. Needles 3″, dark blue-green, twisted, in bundles of 2. Cones 4″, round; scales with stout curved spines. Bark dark reddish brown, with irreg. scaly plates. **HABITAT** Dry, rocky mountain slopes and ridges. **RANGE** sc PA and south in Appalachian Mtns.

RED PINE
"Norway Pine"
Pinus resinosa
PINE FAMILY

70′. Crown broad, irreg. or rounded; branches spreading. Needles 6″, in bundles of 2. Cones 2″, egg-shaped, light brown. Bark thick, scaly, with reddish-brown plates. **HABITAT** Well-drained, sandy areas. **RANGE** NY, ne PA, n NJ; mtns. of e WV, VA.

PITCH PINE
Pinus rigida
PINE FAMILY

55′. Crown broad, rounded or irreg. Needles 4″, stout, stiff, in bundles of 3; also in tufts on trunk. Cones 2″, egg-shaped, yellow to brown. Bark thick, brown to gray plates. **HABITAT** Sandy and rocky areas. **RANGE** NY, NJ and south to WV and mtns. of VA.

EASTERN WHITE PINE
"Northern White Pine"
Pinus strobus
PINE FAMILY

H 100′; D 3′6″. Crown broad to irreg.; branches whorled, nearly horizontal. Needles 4″, bluish green, soft, flexible, in bundles of 5. Cones 6″, curved, yellow-brown to gray; scales lack spines. Bark furrowed, scaly, blackish gray. Largest, most common Mid-Atl. conifer. An important lumber tree. **HABITAT** Variable, but prefers moist sandy areas, rocky slopes, swamps. **RANGE** NY and south to WV and mtns. of VA.

LOBLOLLY PINE
Pinus taeda
PINE FAMILY

125′. Crown pyramidal, trunk straight. Needles 8″, in bundles of 2–3, slender, stiff. Cones 4″, egg-shaped; scales with short prickle. Bark scaly plated. Important lumber tree. **HABITAT** Moist soils, abandoned fields, roadsides. **RANGE** s NJ and south along coastal plain.

VIRGINIA PINE
Pinus virginiana
PINE FAMILY

40′. Crown spreading, branches drooping. Needles 2″, in bundles of 2, grayish green. Cones 2″, round; scales with short spines. Bark dark red-brown, with thin, scaly plates. **HABITAT** Dry, rocky forests, often in pure stands. **RANGE** s NY and south to s VA.

EASTERN HEMLOCK
Tsuga canadensis
PINE FAMILY

H 70′; D 30″. Crown pyramidal; branches drooping. Needles ½″, flat, flexible; 2 white stripes below; spread in 2 rows on slender, rough twigs. Cones ¾″, elliptical, brown; hang at twig ends. Bark brown; furrowed in scaly ridges. **HABITAT** Ravines, rocky outcrops, north-facing slopes.

Broadleaf Trees and Shrubs

Trees belonging to the angiosperm (flowering plant) group are called broadleaf trees because their leaves are generally broad and flat, in contrast to the needle-like leaves of most conifers. Whereas the seeds of conifers and other gymnosperms are exposed, those of angiosperms are enclosed in an ovary that ripens into a fruit. The fruit may take the form of a drupe or berry, a hard-cased nut, the paired winged fruit of a maple, or a dried-out seedpod, such as that of a locust.

In warmer regions of North America, many broadleaf species (known in the timber industry as "hardwoods") maintain green leaves year-round, but in the Mid-Atlantic region most flowering trees are deciduous, shedding their leaves for the winter because the leaves cannot survive long periods of freezing weather. A prominent exception is the American Holly, which retains its shiny green leaves all winter.

The individual species descriptions in this guide note leaf color only if it is not green. The term "turn" indicates the fall color of the leaves. The various types of leaf arrangements and shapes mentioned in the species descriptions are illustrated on page 132, between the trees and wildflowers sections. As most broadleaf trees bear their leaves in an alternate arrangement, only exceptions are noted in the species descriptions. Leaf measurements indicate length unless otherwise stated. Leaflet measurements are given for compound leaves.

Illustrations of flower types and parts, and a discussion of flower structure and function, are given on pages 133–135, at the beginning of the wildflowers section. Because the flowers of many trees are inconspicuous, only prominent ones are emphasized in the species accounts. In the Mid-Atlantic region, trees generally flower from early March to mid-May (Virginia, Maryland, Delaware) or mid-April to early June (West Virginia, New Jersey, Pennsylvania, New York). Bloom dates are included only if they differ from these typical ranges. Fruits of broadleaf trees mature in the Mid-Atlantic states mainly from June to October (a week to four months after the flowers). Months of maturation are given only for edible fruit.

To facilitate identification, we have grouped descriptions of large broadleaf trees (which begin on page 101) separately from small broadleaf trees and shrubs (which begin on page 119).

Fall Foliage of the Mid-Atlantic Region

Deciduous trees change color elsewhere in the world, but few other regions can match the Mid-Atlantic in species diversity and the resulting dramatic display of fall color. Maples, Sassafras, hickories, sumacs, and some oaks turn shades of brilliant red, red-purple, orange, and yellow—often with leaves of different colors on a single tree—while birches, aspens, beeches, and willows exhibit golden hues. The map below shows typical fall foliage "peak" periods.

Each color represents a subtle change in leaf chemistry. In late summer, leaves begin forming layers of cells at the leafstalk base that will help the leaf detach and heal the resulting scar on the branch. As these layers grow, the veins of the leaves become clogged. The dominant pigment of the green leaf, chlorophyll, is no longer renewed and disintegrates, revealing the yellow and orange pigments that had been masked by the chlorophyll. Under the right conditions, some species convert colorless compounds into new red, scarlet, and purple pigments. Because these pigments require high light intensity and elevated sugar content for their formation, the colors appear after a period of bright autumn days and cool nights, which prevent accumulated sugar from leaving the dying leaf.

The best autumn leaf colors follow a summer with plentiful rainfall, which promotes the formation of leaf sugars. Leaves remain attached longer in relatively dry, warm autumn weather, while heavy winds, downpours, and early frosts may cause premature leaf drop.

AMERICAN BEECH
Fagus grandifolia
BEECH FAMILY

80′. Crown rounded. Leaves 4″, elliptical, toothed, turn yellow or brown, often last into winter. Bark smooth, light gray. Fruit light brown, prickly, ¾″ burs; split in fall to reveal 2–3 triangular, brown, ½″ beechnuts. Often forms stands. **HABITAT** Upland slopes, well-drained lowlands.

Oaks

Oaks, a large genus *(Quercus)* of the beech family numbering several hundred species, are widely distributed in temperate regions of the Northern Hemisphere. Twenty-two species form a major component of the deciduous hardwood forest in the Mid-Atlantic region. The durable, straight-grained wood of many oak species is valued as timber.

Highly variable in shape, oak leaves may be deeply lobed or unlobed, toothed or untoothed; different shapes sometimes occur on a single tree. Many oak species are evergreen in warmer climates, but nearly all are deciduous in the Mid-Atlantic region. Newly emerged leaves in the spring are often reddish; mature leaves often turn red or yellow in the autumn. Many dead leaves remain attached to the branches until early winter or even throughout winter. Oak flowers are minute, greenish, simple in structure, and unisexual. Flowers of both sexes occur on the same tree. Male flowers are clustered into slender pendulous spikes called catkins, which produce copious pollen. Female flowers occur singly or in short spikes at leaf axils; after fertilization, each tiny pistil develops within one or two years into an acorn with a scaly cap.

WHITE OAK
Quercus alba
BEECH FAMILY

H 90′; D 3′6″. Crown rounded; branches stout, numerous, wide-spreading. Leaves 7″, with 5–9 rounded lobes; bright green above, whitish green below, turn dull red or bronze; often remain attached through winter. Bark scaly, shallowly furrowed, light gray. Acorns 1¼″, oblong; cap shallow, warty. An important lumber tree. **HABITAT** Riversides, sandy areas, dry hillsides. **RANGE** Entire region, ex. Adirondacks.

SWAMP WHITE OAK
Quercus bicolor
BEECH FAMILY

60′. Crown rounded, open; branches mostly drooping. Leaves 6″, with 5–10 rounded lobes per side; shiny above, white-hairy below; turn red or brown. Bark furrowed, gray-brown. Acorns 1¼″, egg-shaped; cap deep. **HABITAT** Streamsides, swamps. **RANGE** NY and south to n VA, e, sw WV.

SCARLET OAK
Quercus coccinea
BEECH FAMILY

70'. Crown rounded, open. Leaves 7", with 7–9 deep, widely spaced lobes with bristly toothed tips; shiny, turn scarlet. Bark furrowed into scaly ridges or plates, dark gray. Acorns 1", egg-shaped, with faint rings; cap deep. **HABITAT** Slopes, ridges. **RANGE** Entire region, ex. n NY.

CHINQUAPIN OAK
Quercus muehlenbergii
BEECH FAMILY

70'. Crown rounded. Leaves 6", with 9–15 sharp teeth per side; turn yellow or red. Bark rough, flaky, light gray. Acorns ¾", egg-shaped, cap deep, thin, hairy. **HABITAT** Dry upland forests, usu. on limestone. **RANGE** s NY, w PA, s NJ, WV and mtns. of VA.

PIN OAK
Quercus palustris
BEECH FAMILY

60'. Crown spreading; dead branchlets project from trunk like pins. Leaves 5", with 5–7 deep, widely spaced lobes with bristly toothed tips; shiny, turn red or brown. Bark rough, dark gray. Acorns ½", roundish; cap shallow, thin, saucer-shaped. **HABITAT** Moist areas, esp. riversides and streamsides. **RANGE** se NY and south to WV, c VA..

WILLOW OAK
Quercus phellos
BEECH FAMILY

80'. Crown rounded. Dead branches project from trunk. Leaves 4", narrowly oblong, without teeth or lobes; turn yellow-brown. Bark furrowed into scaly ridges, light to dark brown. Acorns ½", roundish, cap shallow, thin, hairy. **HABITAT** Moist to wet woodlands, streamsides, swamps. **RANGE** Coastal plain and piedmont, NY City, s NJ, se PA and south.

CHESTNUT OAK
Quercus montana (prinus)
BEECH FAMILY

60'. Crown spreading, irreg. Leaves 6", with 10–16 rounded teeth per side; turn yellow. Bark thick, furrowed, gray. Acorns 1¼", egg-shaped; cap deep, thin, warty. **HABITAT** Well-drained lowlands, rocky ridges. **RANGE** Entire region, ex. n NY, se, w VA.

BLACK OAK
Quercus velutina
BEECH FAMILY

60'. Crown spreading, open. Leaves 7", with bristle-tipped lobes shallower than those of Scarlet Oak; have rusty brown hairs beneath; turn dull red or bronze. Bark blackish, deeply furrowed in long ridges. Acorns ¾", oval; cap deep, rough-scaled, flat-based. **HABITAT** Sandy, rocky, and clay hillsides; uplands. **RANGE** Entire region, ex. nw NY.

NORTHERN RED OAK
Quercus rubra
BEECH FAMILY

65'. Crown rounded; branches stout, spreading. Leaves 7", with 7–11 shallow lobes with bristly toothed tips; dull green, turn dark red. Bark furrowed into scaly ridges, dark gray. Acorns 1", egg-shaped; cap shallow, broad. Often in pure stands. **HABITAT** Hillsides, lowlands.

POST OAK
Quercus stellata
BEECH FAMILY

45'. Crown spreading. Leaves 5"; 5 lobes form cross shape; leathery, hairy, gray-green below; turn brown. Bark scaly, furrowed, light gray. Acorns 1", oval; cap deep. **HABITAT** Floodplains, drier ridges. **RANGE** Coastal plain and piedmont of NY, NJ, PA and south to WV, VA

NORTHERN CATALPA
"Cigar Tree"
Catalpa speciosa
BIGNONIA FAMILY

80'. Crown spreading, open. Leaves 10", heart shaped, hairy below; turn yellow-brown. Bark gray-brown, scaly. Flowers 1½"; white, trumpet-shaped, fringed petals with purple-and-yellow-striped throats; in 10" clusters at branch tips. Seedpods 12", slender, dark brown; split to release seeds. **HABITAT** Rich moist forests. **RANGE** Midwestern native naturalized from e NY and south. **Southern Catalpa** *(Catalpa bignonioides)*, southeastern native naturalized from se NY and south, has smaller, more numerous flowers.

YELLOW BIRCH
Betula alleghaniensis
BIRCH FAMILY

80′. Cylindrical; crown rounded. Leaves 4″, elliptical, toothed; bases often notched; turn bright yellow. Bark when young silver-gray to yellowish, peeling in curly, papery strips; ages reddish brown, scaly plated. Fruit 1″, cone-like, oval, brownish, scaly, upright. **HABITAT** Moist mixed forests, woodland edges, swamps. **RANGE** NY and south to mtns. of e, s WV, VA.

SWEET BIRCH
"Cherry Birch"
Betula lenta
BIRCH FAMILY

60′. Crown broad, rounded. Leaves 4″, ovate to elliptical, long-pointed, toothed; bases unequal; turn bright yellow. Bark smooth, shiny, slaty (young); blackish- or reddish-brown scaly plates (mature). Fruit 1″, cone-like, oblong, brown, upright. Crushed leaves and twigs have strong wintergreen odor. **HABITAT** Forests, north-facing slopes. **RANGE** c NY and south to WV, c, w VA.

PAPER BIRCH
"White Birch"
Betula papyrifera
BIRCH FAMILY

70′. Crown narrow, open. Leaves 3″, ovate, long-pointed, toothed, turn light yellow. Bark when young chalky to creamy white, with thin, horizontal stripes, peels in papery strips to reveal orange inner bark; later brown, furrowed. Fruit 1¾″, cone-like, cylindrical, brown, scaly, hanging. **HABITAT** Upland forests, clear-cut and burned areas. **RANGE** NY, ne PA, n NJ, ne WV, nw VA.

GRAY BIRCH
Betula populifolia
BIRCH FAMILY

30′. Crown open, conical, often bushy; branches droop to ground. Leaves 3″, triangular, toothed, turn yellow. Bark smooth, brownish, becoming grayish white with horizontal lines. Fruit 1″, cone-like, scaly. **HABITAT** Clearings, burned areas, roadsides. **RANGE** NY, e PA, NJ, n DE, n WV, n VA.

AMERICAN HORNBEAM
"Musclewood"
Carpinus caroliniana
BIRCH FAMILY

20'. Crown broad, rounded; trunk fluted, muscular-looking, short, often forked. Leaves 3", elliptical, toothed, parallel-veined, turn orange or scarlet. Bark smooth, gray. Fruit tiny, hairy, greenish nutlets, with 3-pointed, leaf-like scale; in 3" clusters. **HABITAT** Streamsides, wooded ravines. **RANGE** Entire region, ex. n NY.

EASTERN HOP HORNBEAM
"Ironwood"
Ostrya virginiana
BIRCH FAMILY

25'. Crown rounded; trunk fluted, muscular-looking; branches slender, spreading. Leaves 3½", ovate or elliptical, toothed, turn yellow. Bark scaly, furrowed in wide ridges, gray-brown. Fruit many tiny nutlets in papery, light brown sacs, in hanging, hop- or cone-like, 2" clusters. **HABITAT** Moist, upland forests.

FLOWERING DOGWOOD
Cornus florida
DOGWOOD FAMILY

25'. Crown spreading. Leaves 4", opposite, elliptical; veins curved; turn red. Bark small squarish plates, reddish brown. Flowers tiny, white to cream; in dense head encircled by 4 white, 2" petal-like bracts (leaves from which flowers arise) with pink notches. Fruit ½", berry-like, bright red, in clusters of 3–4. **HABITAT** Broadleaf forests, yards. **RANGE** s NY and south.

BLACK TUPELO
"Blackgum"
Nyssa sylvatica
DOGWOOD FAMILY

70'. Crown dense, conical; branches nearly horizontal. Leaves 6", elliptical to obovate, glossy, turn bright red. Bark plated, deeply furrowed, gray to dark brown. Fruit ½", berry-like, deep blue. Tupelo honey is produced from this tree. **HABITAT** Floodplains. **RANGE** Entire region, ex. n NY.

COMMON PERSIMMON
Diospyros virginiana
EBONY FAMILY

65'. Crown broad, rounded; trunk short; branches stout, spreading; thicket-forming. Leaves 6", lanceolate to broadly elliptical, leathery; turn yellow. Bark brown to blackish, roughly square-plated. Flowers tiny, greenish yellow. Berries 1½", orange; edible, ripe Aug.–Oct. **HABITAT** Pinelands, moist forests, fields. **RANGE** se NY to s PA and south.

AMERICAN ELM
Ulmus americana
ELM FAMILY

90'. Crown vase-shaped; trunk forks into many upwardly angled branches that droop at ends. Leaves 5", asymmetrical, elliptical, toothed, turn yellow. Bark gray, furrowed into interlocking ridges. Dutch Elm disease, spread by beetles, killed most trees from 1930 to 1960. **HABITAT** Floodplains, woodland edges.

NORTHERN HACKBERRY
Celtis occidentalis
ELM FAMILY

35'. Crown rounded; branches often bushy "witches' brooms" deformed by mites and fungi. Leaves 3", ovate, toothed; bases asymmetrical; turn yellow. Bark gray, smooth with corky ridges (young), or scaly (mature). Fruit ⅜", cherry-like, red to purple. **HABITAT** Bottomlands, ridges.

AMERICAN HOLLY
Ilex opaca
HOLLY FAMILY

40'. Crown narrow, pyramidal to rounded, dense; branches short. Leaves 3", elliptical, spiny-toothed, stiff, shiny, leathery, evergreen. Bark smooth to warty, light gray. Flowers ¼" wide, white, with 4 petals, in short clusters. Fruit ⅜", berry-like, red; lasts into winter. **HABITAT** Coastal plains. **RANGE** se NY; NJ to se PA and south.

SASSAFRAS
Sassafras albidum
LAUREL FAMILY

40'. Tree or thicket-forming shrub; crown spreading. Leaves 5", 1-, 2-, or 3-lobed; turn red, orange, yellow (various colors on same tree). Bark thick, furrowed, gray-brown. Fruit ½", oval, berry-like, shiny, dark blue on thick red stem; clustered. **HABITAT** Moist, sandy woodland openings and edges. **RANGE** Entire region, ex. n NY.

AMERICAN BASSWOOD
Tilia americana
LINDEN FAMILY

80'. Crown dense, rounded; branches often drooping. Leaves 5", broadly ovate or rounded, coarsely toothed; bases asymmetrical; turn yellow. Bark thick, tough, gray, furrowed. Flowers yellowish, ½" wide, with 5 petals; hang in clusters on long stalk from bracts (leaves from which flowers arise); sweetly fragrant. Fruit ½", nut-like. **HABITAT** Moist valleys and uplands, towns. **RANGE** NY, n NJ, PA, WV, w VA.

CUCUMBER TREE
Magnolia acuminata
MAGNOLIA FAMILY

80′. Crown pyramidal. Leaves 6″, elliptical; shiny, dark green above; paler, soft-hairy below; turn yellow or reddish. Bark brown, scaly, with shallow furrows. Flowers 2½″, cup- to bell-shaped, yellow-green. Fruit 2″, cone- or cucumber-shaped, seeds bright red. **HABITAT** Rich, moist forests on low mtn. slopes. **RANGE** w NY, w PA and south to w VA.

SWEET BAY MAGNOLIA
Magnolia virginiana
MAGNOLIA FAMILY

25′ (can grow much taller). Crown narrow, rounded. Leaves 6″, oblong, thick; shiny above, whitish below; turn brown. Bark smooth, gray, aromatic. Flowers 2½″, white, cup-shaped, with 9–12 petals; fragrant. Fruit 1½″, cone-like, seeds bright red. **HABITAT** Coastal plains, swamps, riversides, pondsides. **RANGE** Coastal plain and piedmont, NY and south.

YELLOW POPLAR
"Tulip Tree"
Liriodendron tulipifera
MAGNOLIA FAMILY

100′. Crown rounded; trunk tall, straight. Leaves 5″, with 4 pointed lobes, basal pair wider and straight-based; long-stalked; turn yellow. Bark thick, gray with white furrows. Flowers 2″, large, tulip-shaped; 6 rounded green petals, orange at base; solitary at branch tips. Fruit cone-like, made up of winged seeds. **HABITAT** Wooded wetlands, slopes, gardens. **RANGE** s NY and south.

Maples

Maples are part of a large family of trees (and occasionally shrubs) native to the temperate zone of the Northern Hemisphere. They are a major component of the deciduous hardwood forest that covers vast areas of North America. Nine maple species occur in the Mid-Atlantic region, where they are essential to the brilliance of the fall foliage. Maples have considerable economic value as cultivated ornamental trees, as timber, and as the source of maple syrup.

Maples are characterized by their distinctive leaves, flowers, and fruit. The leaves are deciduous; those of most Mid-Atlantic species are palmately lobed (hand-shaped). Maple flowers——typically small and yellow, greenish, or reddish—are arranged along the branches in variously shaped bunches (fascicles). Most distinctive is the flat, boomerang-shaped maple fruit (the samara), commonly known as a key, which is composed of two winged portions linked together at their bases. When it detaches from the tree, the key twirls in the air like a helicopter propeller. The precise shape of the key and the spread of the V-shaped angle between the wings distinguish each maple species.

BOX ELDER
"Ashleaf Maple"
Acer negundo
MAPLE FAMILY

65'. Crown broad, irreg.; trunk often crooked; branches wide-spreading, twigs white-coated. Leaves 5", opposite, pinnately compound, with 3–5 ovate or elliptical, toothed, 4" leaflets. Bark light brown to gray, furrowed. Key 1½", spreading less than 45 degrees, red-brown. **HABITAT** Moist forests, streamsides, floodplains.

NORWAY MAPLE
Acer platanoides
MAPLE FAMILY

60'. Crown rounded, dense. Leaves 6", opposite, 5-lobed, sharply and irregularly toothed; sap milky; turn bright yellow. Red-leaved form (pictured) rare. Bark narrowly furrowed, ridged, gray or brown. Key 2"; wings at 160-degree angle. Introduced from Europe; invasive. **HABITAT** Towns, roadsides.

RED MAPLE
Acer rubrum
MAPLE FAMILY

70′. Crown narrow or rounded, compact. Leaves 3½″, opposite, 3- to 5-lobed, irregularly toothed, whitish-hairy below, red-stalked; turn red, some orange or yellow. Bark furrowed, scaly, gray. Key 1″, reddish; wings at 60-degree angle. Often first tree to show fall color, in late Aug. **HABITAT** Swamps, streamsides; slopes in mixed forests.

SUGAR MAPLE
"Rock Maple"
Acer saccharum
MAPLE FAMILY

80′. Crown rounded, dense. Leaves 5″, opposite, with deep, long-pointed, few-toothed lobes; multicolored in fall (red, orange, yellow). Bark smooth and gray-brown, becoming deeply furrowed, gray. Key 1¼″; wings at 60-degree angle. **HABITAT** Valleys, mtns., forests, field edges. **RANGE** Entire region, ex. coastal plain.

SILVER MAPLE
Acer saccharinum
MAPLE FAMILY

70′. Crown spreading, open, irreg.; trunk short, stout, forked. Leaves 5″, opposite, with 5 deep, pointed lobes (middle one often 3-lobed), toothed, silvery white below; stalk reddish; turn pale yellow. Bark gray, furrowed in long shaggy ridges. Key 2″; wings at 90-degree angle. **HABITAT** Watersides, swamps, bottomlands. **RANGE** Entire region, ex. coastal plain.

RED MULBERRY
Morus rubra
MULBERRY FAMILY

65′. Crown rounded; trunk stout; branches spreading. Leaves 4″, heart-shaped, toothed, white-hairy below. Bark reddish brown, ridged, fissured. Flowers tiny, greenish; males in pendulous 2″ spikes, females in thick 1″ spikes; bloom Apr.–June. Fruit 1¼″, blackberry-like, red to dark purple; edible, ripe July–Aug. **HABITAT** Rich moist forests, floodplains, thickets, towns. **RANGE** Entire region, ex. n NY and n PA.

WHITE ASH
Fraxinus americana
OLIVE FAMILY

70′. Crown rounded or conical, dense. Leaves 10″, opposite, pinnately compound, with usu. 7 ovate or elliptical, toothed leaflets, each 4″, whitish below; turn purplish or yellow. Bark gray, deeply furrowed into forking ridges. Fruit 1½″, single-winged key; in hanging clusters. **HABITAT** Valleys, streamsides, moist, rich, upland slopes.

GREEN ASH
Fraxinus pennsylvanica
OLIVE FAMILY

60′. Crown rounded or irreg., dense. Leaves 8″, shiny, opposite, pinnately compound, with usu. 7 lanceolate, short-stalked, shiny leaflets, each 4″; turn yellow. Bark furrowed, gray. Fruit 2″, very narrow, 1-winged key; in dense hanging clusters. Widespread native species. **HABITAT** Streamsides, swamps; widely planted as ornamental.

HONEY LOCUST
Gleditsia triacanthos
PEA FAMILY

80′. Crown broad, open, flat; trunk, branches have bunches of long branched spines. Leaves 8″, pinnately or bipinnately compound, with many oblong 1″ leaflets; turn yellow. Bark deeply furrowed, gray-brown. Flowers ½″ yellowish bells in short clusters. Fruit 16″, black, twisted pods; shed unopened. **HABITAT** Towns, gardens, streamsides, waste areas. **RANGE** s PA to WV, VA; thornless variety planted elsewhere.

BLACK LOCUST
Robinia pseudoacacia
PEA FAMILY

50′. Crown rounded, irreg., open; trunk crooked, spiny. Leaves 10″, pinnately compound, with 7–19 oval leaflets, each 1½″; fold at night; turn yellow. Bark light gray, deeply furrowed into forking ridges. Flowers fragrant, white, ¾″ pea-flowers in 8″ drooping clusters. Fruit 4″, brown or black, flat, hanging pods. **HABITAT** Sandy, rocky areas; open areas; forests. **RANGE** c PA to WV and w VA; naturalized and invasive elsewhere.

AILANTHUS
"Tree of Heaven"
Ailanthus altissima
QUASSIA FAMILY

60′. Crown spreading, rounded, open. Leaves 24″, pinnately compound, with 13–25 lanceolate 4″ leaflets with toothed, uneven bases; turn yellow. Bark rough, furrowed, light brown. Flowers tiny, yellow, in 8″ branched clusters; often fetid. Fruit 1½″, pinkish pods in clusters. Can grow from cracks in concrete. Introduced from Asia; invasive. **HABITAT** Towns. **RANGE** Entire region, ex. n NY.

DOWNY SERVICEBERRY
"Shadbush"
Amelanchier arborea
ROSE FAMILY

30'. Crown rounded. Leaves 2½", ovate or elliptical, finely toothed, turn yellow to red. Bark furrowed, gray. Flowers 1¼", white, with 5 narrow petals; clustered at branch ends. Fruit ½", pink-red to purple-red, berry-like. **HABITAT** Riversides, moist slopes.

COCKSPUR HAWTHORN
Crataegus crus-galli
ROSE FAMILY

25'. Thicket-forming. Crown broad; trunk short, stout; branches densely tangled, with very long thorns. Leaves 2½", obovate, toothed near tips, turn orange and red. Bark scaly, gray or brown. Flowers ½", white, 5-petaled, clustered. Fruit ½", berry-like, oval, red. One of many Mid-Atl. hawthorns. **HABITAT** Abandoned fields, pastures.

SWEET CRAB APPLE
Malus (Pyrus) coronaria
ROSE FAMILY

25'. Crown broad, open; trunk short; branches stout; twigs with short spines. Leaves 3", ovate, toothed, turn yellow. Bark furrowed, scaly, red-brown. Flowers 2", white or pink, with 5 rounded petals; in small clusters covering outer branches. Apples 1", yellow-green, edible, ripe Aug.–Sept. **HABITAT** Woodland edges, gardens.

APPLE
Malus pumila (Pyrus malus)
ROSE FAMILY

30'. Crown broad, rounded; trunk short; branches stout. Leaves 3", ovate, wavy-edged, toothed, gray-hairy below, turn yellow. Bark scaly, flaky, gray. Flowers 2", pinkish-white, with 5 rounded petals. Apples 3", yellow or red, edible, ripe Sept.–Oct. Introduced from Eurasia. **HABITAT** Roadsides, woodland edges, fields; widely planted as fruit and ornamental tree.

BLACK CHERRY
Prunus serotina
ROSE FAMILY

40'. Crown rounded. Leaves 5", elliptical, toothed, with curled edges, tapered tip; turn yellow and/or red. Bark scaly, dark gray to black. Flowers ½", with 5 white rounded petals; in 5" clusters. Cherries ½", dark red to blackish; flesh edible but bitter, ripe Aug. **CAUTION** Seeds and wilted leaves poisonous. **HABITAT** Moist, rich broadleaf or mixed forests, abandoned fields, woodland edges.

AMERICAN MOUNTAIN ASH
Sorbus americana
ROSE FAMILY

25'. Crown spreading. Leaves 7", pinnately compound, with 11–17 lanceolate, finely toothed leaflets, each 3"; turn yellow. Bark thin, smooth, gray, with short horizontal lines. Flowers tiny, white; in dense, flat, 5" clusters. Fruit berry-like, tiny, red, in clusters of 100 or more. **HABITAT** Swampsides, mtns. **RANGE** NY, mtns. of PA, e WV, w VA.

AMERICAN SYCAMORE
Platanus occidentalis
SYCAMORE FAMILY

H 90'; D 3'6" or more. Crown very broad, open, spreading; trunk massive, with enlarged base. Leaves 6", incl. long stalk; broadly ovate, maple-like, with 3–5 pointed lobes, toothed; turn brown. Bark smooth; silvery-white base overlaid with peeling patches of darker gray and brown. Fruit 1" brown balls; each hang from long stalks. Among Mid-Atl.'s largest broadleaf trees. **HABITAT** Streamsides, lakesides, floodplains. **RANGE** Entire region, ex. n NY.

PIGNUT HICKORY
Carya glabra
WALNUT FAMILY

60'. Crown spreading, irreg. Leaves 8", pinnately compound, with 5 pointed, finely toothed, lanceolate 5" leaflets; turn yellow. Bark light gray, rough, furrowed in forking ridges. Flowers tiny, greenish; males in slender, drooping catkins. Fruit 2", thin, pear-shaped, green to dark brown husks; contain thick-shelled nuts. **HABITAT** Upland forests. **RANGE** Entire region, ex. n NY.

SHAGBARK HICKORY
Carya ovata
WALNUT FAMILY

60'. Crown narrow, irreg. Leaves 11", pinnately compound, with 5 elliptical to ovate, pointed, finely toothed leaflets, each 5"; turn golden. Bark long curling strips; looks rough and shaggy; light gray. Fruit 2½", roundish, thick, green to brown or black husks; contain edible nuts; ripe Oct. **HABITAT** Bottomlands, rocky hillsides in mixed forests,

BUTTERNUT HICKORY
Juglans cinerea
WALNUT FAMILY

100'. Crown spreading. Leaves 15", pinnately compound, with 11–17 lanceolate, toothed, 3" leaflets; 1 stalked end leaflet; turn yellow. Bark light gray-brown, with diamond-shaped furrows. Female flowers tiny, greenish-yellow; males in slender, 3" drooping catkins. Fruit egg-shaped, 2", light brown, sticky; 1–5 in cluster; eggshaped nutshell with edible kernel; ripe Oct.–Nov. **HABITAT** Floodplains, mixed hardwood forests.

BLACK WALNUT
Juglans nigra
WALNUT FAMILY

125'. Crown spreading. Leaves 15", pinnately compound, with 15–23 sharp-toothed, lanceolate leaflets (end leaflet small or absent; turn yellow). Bark smooth reddish brown when young, maturing dark gray with deep furrows. Female flowers tiny; males in 3" hairy catkins. Fruit round, 2½", green or dark brown husk, single or in pairs; contains furrowed nutshell with edible kernel. **HABITAT** Mixed hardwood forests, floodplains.

WEEPING WILLOW
Salix babylonica
WILLOW FAMILY

40'. Crown open, rounded to irreg.; trunk short, broad; branches slender, very long, drooping, yellow-green. Leaves 4", narrowly lanceolate, with long-pointed tips, finely toothed; turn yellow. Bark dark gray, rough, deeply furrowed. Introduced from Eurasia. **HABITAT** Watersides, roadsides.

BLACK WILLOW
Salix nigra
WILLOW FAMILY

75'. Crown narrow or irreg.; has 2–5 leaning trunks; branches up-right; new twigs reddish. Leaves 4", narrowly lanceolate, finely toothed, often curve to one side, shiny; turn light yellow. Bark dark brown or blackish, furrowed into scaly ridges. Mid-Atl.'s largest willow. **HABITAT** Watersides.

EASTERN COTTONWOOD
Populus deltoides
WILLOW FAMILY
90′. Crown open, spreading; trunk massive, forked. Leaves 5″, incl. long stalk; triangular, with straight base, pointed tip; toothed, shiny; turn yellow. Bark thick, rough, deeply furrowed, light gray. Fruit ½″, light brown, elliptical capsules, arranged in 8″ catkins; release cottony seeds in late spring. **HABITAT** Riversides, floodplains, sandbars in rivers. **RANGE** Local throughout.

BIGTOOTH ASPEN
Populus grandidentata
WILLOW FAMILY
50′. Crown narrow, rounded. Leaves 3½″, ovate, with coarse, curved teeth; stalks long, slender, flat; turn yellow or reddish with yellow veins. Bark furrowed, brown. Fruit 2½″ catkins of tiny, narrow, conical, green capsules; release many cottony seeds. **HABITAT** Sandy uplands, streamsides, abandoned fields, burned areas. **RANGE** Entire region, ex. se VA.

QUAKING ASPEN
Populus tremuloides
WILLOW FAMILY
50′. Crown narrow, rounded. Leaves 2½″, nearly round, with tiny point, finely toothed; stalks slender, flat; turn golden-yellow. Bark yellowish to dark gray, usu. thin, smooth, with warty patches (furrowed on large trunks). Fruit tiny, narrow green capsules in drooping 4″ catkins; release cottony seeds. Leaves "quake" in slightest breeze. **HABITAT** Woodland edges, burned and clear-cut areas. **RANGE** NY and south to PA and e WV, n VA.

Small Broadleaf Trees and Shrubs

To facilitate identification, we have separated most small broadleaf trees and shrubs from the large broadleaf trees. The species in this section generally reach an average mature height of 20 feet or less.

Although there is no scientific difference between trees and shrubs, trees typically have a single woody trunk and a well-developed crown of foliage, whereas shrubs usually have several woody stems growing in a clump. Many of the Mid-Atlantic region's small trees and shrubs have beautiful and conspicuous spring flowers and/or colorful late-summer or autumn fruits. Flower and leaf arrangements and shapes are illustrated on pages 132–133. The majority of species covered here are deciduous; evergreens are noted as such.

PAWPAW
Asimina triloba
ANNONA FAMILY

20′. Small tree with open crown, or large shrub. Leaves 9″, elliptical, light green above, paler below. Bark dark brown, smooth. Flowers 1″, maroon, bell-shaped; bloom Apr.–May, before leaves. Fruit 4″, oblong, light green to yellow, fleshy; pulp edible, ripe Aug.–Oct. **HABITAT** Rich, moist forests and floodplains. **RANGE** w NY and south.

GROUNDSEL TREE
"Sea Myrtle"
Baccharis halimifolia
ASTER FAMILY

13′. Many-branched shrub with resinous stems. Leaves 2½″, obovate to oblanceolate, dull gray-green, evergreen. Flowers tiny, bell-shaped; in brushy, yellowish or whitish, ½″ heads; bloom Aug.–Dec. **HABITAT** Open forests, marshes, disturbed areas, beaches. **RANGE** Coastal plain, NY and south.

COMMON BARBERRY
Berberis vulgaris
BARBERRY FAMILY

8′. Loosely branched shrub. Leaves 2″, elliptical, bristly toothed, lower veins prominent; bunched at nodes. Branches and twigs gray; with spines single or in clusters of 2–3. Flowers ¼″, yellow, in 2″ hanging clusters at branch tips; bloom May–June. Berries ¼″, red, oval. Invasive. **HABITAT** Deciduous forests and thickets, roadsides. **Japanese Barberry** *(B. thunbergii)* is smaller (3′) and denser; spines single; leaves spoon-shaped, untoothed; flowers and fruits bunched on branches.

AMERICAN CHESTNUT
Castanea dentata
BEECH FAMILY

20′. Formerly large, abundant; wiped out by disease; now found in Mid-Atl. only as sprouts from bases of long-dead trees; rarely live long enough to fruit. Leaves 7″, oblong, toothed; turn yellow. Bark smooth. **HABITAT** Mainly hillsides in mixed hardwood forests. **RANGE** Entire region, ex. n NY and sc VA.

ALLEGHENY CHINQUAPIN
Castanea pumila
BEECH FAMILY

50′. Shrub to small tree; crown rounded; trunk(s) short; branches slender. Leaves 6″, elliptical, toothed, leathery; yellow-green above; whitish green, velvety below. Bark gray to light reddish brown, shallowly furrowed. Flowers tiny, whitish; in 6″, upright catkins. Fruit 1¼″, spiny, round, green to brown bur; splits to release shiny, brown, egg-shaped, edible nut (resembles a small chestnut); ripe Aug.–Oct. **HABITAT** Dry forests, disturbed areas. **RANGE** s PA, s NJ, to VA, e, s WV.

BEAR OAK
"Scrub Oak"
Quercus ilicifolia
BEECH FAMILY

15′. Small rounded tree or much-branched shrub. Leaves 3″, usu. with 5 shallow lobes with bristly toothed tips; turn yellow-brown. Bark furrowed, scaly, gray. Acorns ½″, egg-shaped, vertically striped; cap deep. **HABITAT** Sandy barrens, rocky ridges. **RANGE** e NY and south to mtns. of VA, e WV.

SMOOTH ALDER
Alnus serrulata
BIRCH FAMILY

10′. Large thicket-forming shrub or small tree. Leaves 3″, elliptical, doubly-toothed. Bark brown, smooth. Male flowers tiny, in drooping 1″ catkins; bloom Mar.–May. Fruit cone-like, ½″, erect. **HABITAT** Streamsides, swamps. **Speckled Alder** *(A. incana)* has white-speckled, dark brown bark, single-toothed leaves, and drooping cones.

STRAWBERRY BUSH
Euonymus americanus
BITTERSWEET FAMILY

5′. Erect to sprawling shrub, with stiff, 4-sided, green stems. Leaves 3″, opposite, ovate to elliptical; turn red. Flowers ⅜″, yellow-green, flat, in leaf axils; bloom May–June. Fruits ½″, round-lobed, warty, pink to red, open to reveal orange seeds. **HABITAT** Rich, moist to dry broadleaf forests. **RANGE** se NY to s VA.

EUROPEAN BUCKTHORN
Rhamnus cathartica
BUCKTHORN FAMILY

15′. Large shrub or small tree with irreg. crown. Twigs thorn-tipped. Leaves 2″, opposite, some alternate, elliptical. Flowers tiny, greenish-yellow, in small clusters along branches; bloom May–June. Berries ¼″, black. Invasive. **HABITAT** Abandoned fields, pastures, edges of broadleaf forests.

JAPANESE KNOTWEED
Polygonum cuspidatum
BUCKWHEAT FAMILY

8′. Arching, thicket-forming shrub. Leaves 5″, ovate. Stems bamboo-like, turn orange in fall, die back in winter. Flowers tiny, white, in 5″ slender spikes in upper leaf axils; bloom Aug. Fruit tiny, white, papery, with wings. Invasive. **HABITAT** Streamsides, roadsides, yards.

WINGED SUMAC
"Shining Sumac"
Rhus copallina
CASHEW FAMILY

10′. Shrub or small tree with stout spreading branches. Leaves 10″, pinnately compound, with 7–23 shiny, lanceolate leaflets, each 2½″ and on winged axis; turn crimson. Bark smooth, light gray-brown. Flowers tiny, greenish white; in 3″ conical clusters atop branches; bloom July–Aug. Fruit berry-like, tiny, reddish, hairy, in 3″ conical clusters. **HABITAT** Dry forests, clearings, roadsides. **RANGE** Entire region, ex. n NY.

STAGHORN SUMAC
"Velvet Sumac"
Rhus hirta (typhina)
CASHEW FAMILY

18′. Tall shrub or small tree with upright branches; crown open, flat, irreg. Leaves to 18″, pinnately compound, with 11–31 lanceolate, toothed, 4″ leaflets; turn red. Bark smooth or scaly, dark brown; twigs velvety. Flowers tiny, yellowish green; in dense, 6″, upright clusters; bloom June–July. Fruit berry-like, tiny, red, velvety; in 6″ upright oval clusters at branch tips; last into winter. **HABITAT** Abandoned fields, woodland edges, roadsides. **RANGE** Entire region, ex. se VA.

SMOOTH SUMAC
Rhus glabra
CASHEW FAMILY

10′. Large shrub or small tree; crown open, flat. Leaves 12″, pinnately compound, with 11–31 lanceolate, toothed, 3″ leaflets; turn red or orange. Bark smooth, brown; twigs gray or red. Flowers tiny, yellow-green, in 7″ clusters; bloom June–July. Fruit tiny, red, hairy, sticky; in 8″ upright, conical clusters. **HABITAT** Old fields, woodland edges, roadsides. **RANGE** Entire region, ex. n NY.

RED OSIER DOGWOOD
Cornus sericea (stolonifera)
DOGWOOD FAMILY

8′. Thicket-forming shrub; red branches conspicuous in winter. Leaves 3″, opposite, elliptical or ovate, toothless, with curved sunken veins; turn reddish. Bark smooth, glossy, reddish. Flowers tiny, white, in upright, flattish, 2″ clusters. **HABITAT** Streamsides, moist forests. **RANGE** NY, n NJ, PA; local in mtns. south.

GRAY DOGWOOD
Cornus racemosa
DOGWOOD FAMILY

9′. Rounded shrub; forms large clumps. Leaves 3″, opposite, elliptical, with curved veins; turn maroon. Bark scaly, gray-brown. Flowers tiny, white, red-stalked, in 2″ conical clusters; bloom May–June. Fruit berry-like, tiny, white, red-stalked. **HABITAT** Streamsides, woodland edges, roadsides.

DEVIL'S WALKING STICK
"Hercules'-club"
Aralia spinosa
GINSENG FAMILY

25′. Spiny shrub or small tree with open, umbrella-like crown. Leaves 20″, bi- or tripinnately compound, with many ovate, toothed, 3″ leaflets. Bark furrowed, brown. Flowers tiny, white, in round bunches arranged in large branched clusters. Fruit ⅓″, berry-like, black. **HABITAT** Moist to wet forests. **RANGE** s NY and south.

BLACK HUCKLEBERRY
Gaylussacia baccata
HEATH FAMILY

2′. Many-branched, rounded, thicket-forming shrub. Leaves 1½″, elliptical, covered with small yellow resin dots; turn red. Flowers tiny, narrow, red bells in small clusters along branch tips; bloom May–June. Berries tiny, black. **HABITAT** Dry, rocky or sandy forests and barrens.

MALE-BERRY
Lyonia ligustrina
HEATH FAMILY

12'. Large many-stemmed shrub. Leaves 3", lanceolate to obovate with small teeth. Flowers tiny, white, ball-like, in broad, branching terminal clusters; bloom June–July. **HABITAT** Swamps, wet thickets. **RANGE** s NY and south.

MOUNTAIN LAUREL
Kalmia latifolia
HEATH FAMILY

10'. Many-stemmed, rounded evergreen shrub or small tree with crooked trunk. Leaves 3"; alternate, opposite, or in threes along twigs; crowded at tips; elliptical, thick, stiff. Bark shreddy, rusty. Flowers ¾", white or pink, with red dots; bowl-shaped; stamens pop out when touched; in upright branched clusters. **HABITAT** Mixed forests, heaths.

SHEEP LAUREL
"Lambkill"
Kalmia angustifolia
HEATH FAMILY

30". Rounded evergreen shrub. Leaves 2", mostly in whorls of 3 oblong; lower ones hang down. Bark smooth, brown. Flowers ½", deep pink, saucer-shaped, in round clusters; stamens pop out when touched; bloom May–Aug. **HABITAT** Bogs, shrubby swamps, pastures. **RANGE** e NY, e PA, NJ and south to e VA.

GREAT LAUREL
"Rosebay"
Rhododendron maximum
HEATH FAMILY

20'. Large, thicket-forming, evergreen shrub; crown rounded; trunk short, crooked. Leaves 6", alternate along twigs, crowded at tips, oblong, thick. Bark scaly, thin, red-brown. Flowers 1½", white or pink, waxy, in upright clusters; bloom June–July. **HABITAT** Moist forests, streamsides in hills, swamps. **RANGE** s NY, n NJ, PA to WV and mtns. of VA.

PINKSTER FLOWER
"Pink Azalea"
Rhododendron periclymenoides
HEATH FAMILY

6'. Open, rounded, shrub. Leaves 3", alternate along twigs, crowded at tips, oblong, hairy-edged; turn yellow. Bark smooth, brown. Flowers 2", usu. pink, with long curved stamens; clustered at twig tips; bloom Apr.–May. **HABITAT** Swamps, bogs, woodland clearings. **RANGE** s NY and south.

WHITE SWAMP AZALEA
"Clammy Azalea"
Rhododendron viscosum
HEATH FAMILY

6'. Many-branched, rounded shrub. Leaves 2", alternate along twigs, crowded at tips, obovate. Twigs hairy, grayish. Flowers 2", white, trumpet-shaped, sticky, fragrant; clustered at branch tips; bloom June–Aug. **HABITAT** Swamps, pondsides. **RANGE** e NY, NJ, e, s PA and south.

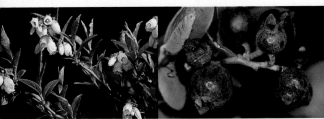

LOWBUSH BLUEBERRY
Vaccinium angustifolium
HEATH FAMILY

16". Small rounded shrub; forms thickets. Leaves ¾", oblong, turn red. Flowers tiny, white to pink bells; in clusters; bloom May–June. Berries ½", waxy blue, edible; ripe July–Aug. **HABITAT** Mtn. slopes, lowland barrens. **RANGE** NY, NJ, PA to mtns. of e WV, VA.

HIGHBUSH BLUEBERRY
Vaccinium corymbosum
HEATH FAMILY

10'. Large, rounded, many-stemmed shrub. Leaves 2¼", elliptical, hairy below, turn bronze or red. Flowers ¼" white bells in short clusters; bloom May–June. Berries ½", dark blue dusted whitish, edible; ripe June–Aug. **HABITAT** Shrubby swamps, meadows, dry hillsides.

WINTERBERRY HOLLY
"Black Alder"
Ilex verticillata
HOLLY FAMILY

7'. Rounded shrub or small tree with short, low-branching trunk. Leaves 2", oblong, finely toothed, not spiny; turn brown to black. Bark smooth, gray. Flowers tiny, each with 4–6 petals; in small, ½" clusters. Fruit berry-like, tiny, bright red, in rows along leaf axils, conspicuous into winter. Deciduous, unlike other hollies. **HABITAT** Swamps, damp thickets, pondsides.

ELDERBERRY
"Black Elderberry"
Sambucus canadensis
HONEYSUCKLE FAMILY

12'. Tall shrub with spreading branches. Leaves 7", opposite, pinnately compound, with 5–11 oblong, toothed leaflets, each 4"; turn greenish yellow. Bark smooth with raised dots, light gray-green. Flowers tiny, white; in 8" flat-topped clusters; bloom June–July. Fruit berry-like, tiny, purplish black, in flat clusters; used for jelly, wine; ripe July–Sept. **HABITAT** Moist broadleaf forests, fields, roadsides.

MAPLELEAF VIBURNUM
Viburnum acerifolium
HONEYSUCKLE FAMILY

4'. Low shrub. Leaves 3½", opposite, 3-lobed, toothed; turn purplish pink. Bark warty, gray or dull brown. Flowers tiny, white, in 2" round clusters; bloom May–July. Fruit berry-like, tiny, glossy black, in 3" clusters on upright stalks. **HABITAT** Broadleaf forests.

HOBBLEBUSH VIBURNUM
"Witch-hobble"
Viburnum lantanoides
HONEYSUCKLE FAMILY

6'. Shrub; branches bend to ground and take root. Leaves 8", opposite, rounded, short-pointed, fine-toothed; turn orange or red. Stems smooth, brown. Flowers white, in 6" clusters; outer ones 1", inner ones tiny. Fruit berry-like, tiny, red to black. **HABITAT** Cool forests to 3,000'. **RANGE** NY, n NJ, PA and south to mtns. of e WV, VA.

NORTHERN ARROWWOOD
Viburnum dentatum var. lucidulum
HONEYSUCKLE FAMILY

7'. Much-branched, thicket-forming shrub with many shoots from base. Leaves 3", opposite, ovate, coarsely toothed; turn shiny red. Bark smooth, gray. Flowers tiny, white, each with 5 petals; in upright 3", flat-topped clusters; bloom May–July. Fruit berry-like, tiny, dark blue, in 3½", flat-topped clusters of 30 or more at branch tips. **HABITAT** Moist low areas. **RANGE** NY, NJ, PA and south to mtns. of e WV, VA.

SPICEBUSH
Lindera benzoin
LAUREL FAMILY

9'. Rounded shrub; branches spreading to upright. Leaves 4", oblong, turn yellow. Bark smooth, greenish brown. Flowers tiny, yellow, in clusters along twigs; bloom Apr. Fruit ½", berry-like, oval, red, single to groups of 5. Most parts spicy-fragrant. **HABITAT** Swamps, moist forests. **RANGE** s NY and south.

BUTTONBUSH
Cephalanthus occidentalis
MADDER FAMILY

12′. Spreading, multi-stemmed shrub; branches many, crooked, leaning. Leaves 5″, opposite, in whorls of 3, ovate or elliptical. Bark scaly, gray-brown. Flowers tiny, white, densely compacted into 1½″ pincushion-like balls; bloom June–Aug. Fruit 1″ rough brown balls of tiny nutlets. **HABITAT** Swamps, streamsides, pondsides.

STRIPED MAPLE
Acer pensylvanicum
MAPLE FAMILY

25′. Shrub to small tree. Crown open, irreg.; trunk has vertical whitish stripes. Leaves 6″, with 3 pointed, finely toothed lobes; paler below; turn yellow. Bark smooth or rough, greenish brown, striped. Key 1¼″; wings at 140-degree angle. **HABITAT** Cool, moist, upland forests. **RANGE** West of coastal plain and piedmont, NY and south.

EASTERN REDBUD
Cercis canadensis
PEA FAMILY

25′. Shrubby tree; crown low, spreading, flat to rounded. Bark reddish brown, scaly. Leaves 5″, heart-shaped, with pointed tip; turn yellow. Bark brown, scaly, ridged. Flowers ½″, magenta, pea-flowers in small clusters; bloom Apr.–May (before leaves), covering the bare branches. Fruit 4″, flat, oblong, brown, hanging pods. Popular ornamental. **HABITAT** Moist forests, yards. **RANGE** NJ, s PA and south.

BEACH PLUM
Prunus maritima
ROSE FAMILY

6′. Rounded shrub; branches many, upright. Leaves 2″, elliptical, finely toothed; turn yellow. Bark smooth, blackish. Flowers ½″, white, with 5 petals; line branches in clusters of 2 or 3; bloom early June. Plums 1″, round, purple with a white bloom, edible; ripe Sept.–Oct. **HABITAT** Coastal dunes. **RANGE** Coastal plain, NY and south to MD.

PIN CHERRY
"Fire Cherry"
Prunus pensylvanica
ROSE FAMILY

20′. Crown narrow, rounded, open. Leaves 4″, lanceolate, fine-toothed, turn yellow. Bark papery, red-brown to gray, with horizontal lines. Flowers ½″, with 5 white, rounded petals; clustered. Cherries tiny, red; flesh sour, edible; ripe July–Aug. **HABITAT** Clearings. **RANGE** NY, NJ, PA to e WV, w VA.

COMMON CHOKECHERRY
Prunus virginiana
ROSE FAMILY

18′. Thicket-forming shrub or small tree. Leaves 2½″, elliptical, fine-toothed; turn yellow. Bark smooth to scaly, gray-brown. Flowers ½″, white, 5-petaled, in 4″ clusters; bloom May. Cherries ½″, red to blue-black, in grape-like clusters; edible, tart; ripe July–Aug. **HABITAT** Hilly streamsides, clearings, roadsides. **RANGE** NY, NJ, PA to e WV, w VA.

MULTIFLORA ROSE
Rosa multiflora
ROSE FAMILY

10′. Dense, rounded shrub; stems long, arching. Leaves 5″, pinnately compound, with 7–11 ovate, toothed, 1½″ leaflets; have fringed appendages; turn yellow. Bark smooth, gray to reddish. Thorns sparse, curved, flattened. Flowers 1″, white, 5-petaled, fragrant, at stem ends; bloom June–July. Fruit many, ¼″, round, scarlet rose hips. Introduced from Asia; invasive. **HABITAT** Fields, roadsides. **RANGE** Entire region, ex. n NY.

CAROLINA ROSE
"Pasture Rose"
Rosa carolina
ROSE FAMILY

3′. Low, thicket-forming, multi-branched shrub. Leaves 4″, pinnately compound, with 3–7 toothed, 1½″ leaflets; turn yellow. Bark brown, covered with needle-like prickles. Flowers 3″, light to dark pink, 5-petaled; bloom May–Oct. Fruit few, ½″, round, red rose hips. **HABITAT** Pastures, roadsides, dunes, dry woodland edges.

SWAMP ROSE
Rosa palustris
ROSE FAMILY

5'6". Multi-branched shrub. Leaves 4½", pinnately compound, with 5–7 elliptical, fine-toothed, 1½" leaflets; turn yellow. Stems smooth, green. Thorns sparse, strong, paired at leaf nodes. Flowers 2¼", pale rose-pink, 5-petaled; bloom June–Aug. Fruit few, ½", ovate, scarlet, bristly rose hips. **HABITAT** Swamps, marshes, woodland watersides.

PURPLE-FLOWERING RASPBERRY
Rubus odoratus
ROSE FAMILY

6'. Multi-branched shrub. Leaves 6", palmately 5-lobed, toothed. Bark thin, peeling. Flowers 2", deep pink, 5-petaled; bloom June–Aug. Young branches with sticky hairs. Fruit ½", red; edible; ripe July–Sept. **HABITAT** Shaded woodland edges and roadsides. **RANGE** NY, NJ, and south to mtns. of VA, WV.

HIGHBUSH BLACKBERRY
"Common Blackberry"
Rubus allegheniensis
ROSE FAMILY

8'. Thicket-forming, thorny bramble with upright, arched stems. Leaves 5", palmately compound, with 3 or 5 toothed, 2" leaflets; turn orange. Flowers 1", white, 5-petaled; bloom May–July. Fruit ¾", black when ripe (Aug.); edible. **HABITAT** Clearings. **RANGE** NY, NJ, and south to mtns. of VA, WV.

SWEET FERN
Comptonia peregrina
WAX-MYRTLE FAMILY

3'. Low-growing shrub; branches fern-like. Leaves 5", linear, with 10–20 rounded lobes per side; turn brown. Stems reddish, smooth. Fruit ¾", green bristly bur; each encloses 1–4 edible nutlets; ripe July–Aug. Leaves very aromatic. **HABITAT** Sandy clearings, pastures, disturbed forests barrens.

NORTHERN BAYBERRY
Myrica pensylvanica
WAX-MYRTLE FAMILY

6'. Dense, rounded shrub. Leaves 3", obovate; fragrant; turn bronze. Stems smooth, with irreg. resinous bumps, gray-brown. Fruit tiny, silvery, wax-covered; in grape-like clusters lining stems below leaves. **HABITAT** Dry, sandy areas. **RANGE** w, s NY, NJ, e PA to se VA; scattered inland.

SWEET PEPPERBUSH
Clethra alnifolia
WHITE ALDER FAMILY

6′. Tall, multi-branched, leafy shrub. Leaves 2½″, obovate, coarsely toothed on outer half. Stems smooth, flaky, gray-brown. Flowers ⅓″, white, with 5 petals, 10 long stamens; in 8″ upright spikes; strongly scented; bloom late July–Sept. **HABITAT** Coastal wetlands; swamps. **RANGE** Coastal plain; NY and south.

PUSSY WILLOW
Salix discolor
WILLOW FAMILY

10′. Multi-stemmed shrub or small tree with open, rounded crown. Leaves 3″, lanceolate, silvery below; turn yellow. Bark smooth to scaly, gray; twigs smooth, brown. Flowers tiny, clustered into 2″, hairy, silvery catkins; bloom late Feb.–Apr., long before leaves. Fruit ½″ capsules; contain downy seeds; ripen in spring, before leaves. **HABITAT** Meadows, bogs, riversides. **RANGE** NY, NJ, PA; scattered elsewhere.

WITCH HAZEL
Hamamelis virginiana
WITCH HAZEL FAMILY

15′. Scraggly shrub or small tree with broad, open crown and multiple trunks. Leaves 4″, obovate, with uneven bases, scallop-toothed; turn yellow. Bark smooth or scaly, gray. Flowers 1″, yellow, with narrow, ribbon-like petals; bloom Oct.–Nov. Fruit ½″, light brown, egg-shaped capsules; eject black seeds as far as 20′. **HABITAT** Forests, streamsides.

Leaf Shapes

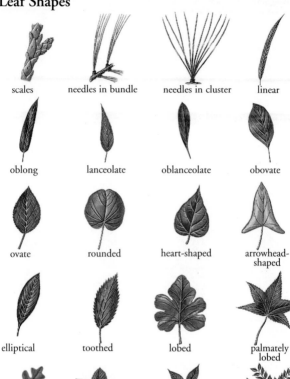

scales | needles in bundle | needles in cluster | linear

oblong | lanceolate | oblanceolate | obovate

ovate | rounded | heart-shaped | arrowhead-shaped

elliptical | toothed | lobed | palmately lobed

pinnately lobed | palmately compound | pinnately compound | bipinnately compound

Leaf Arrangements

axil | alternate | opposite | whorled

basal | clasping | sheathing

Flower Types

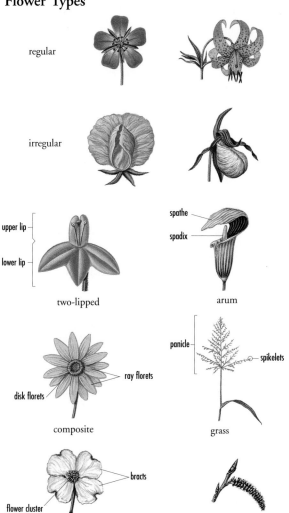

regular

irregular

upper lip
lower lip
two-lipped

spathe
spadix
arum

disk florets
ray florets
composite

panicle
spikelets
grass

bracts
flower cluster
bracts and flower cluster

catkin

Flower Cluster Types

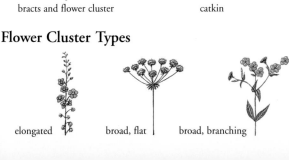

elongated

broad, flat

broad, branching

Wildflowers

The Mid-Atlantic region has more than 3,000 species of flowering plants in more than 100 families. This section covers a selection of common wildflowers, including vines and grasses. For the purposes of this field guide, wildflowers are defined as relatively small, non-cultivated flowering plants that die back after each growing season.

The wildflowers included here are mainly herbaceous (non-woody); some are woody but too small to be placed with the shrubs; a few have a woody base with herbaceous stems. These plants come in many forms. Many have a single, delicate, unbranched, erect stem terminated by a single flower or flower cluster. Some have robust stems, others are many-branched and shrubby. In some, the stems trail along the ground, sometimes spreading by runners. Those known as "vines" have long, slender, often flexible stems that either trail on the ground or climb, sometimes with tendrils to hold them in place. Plants of the grass family have erect, jointed stems and blade-like leaves; some other plants, such as rushes and sedges, are described as grass-like because they have narrow leaves and slender stems. Some plants are aquatic, adapted to life in or along water.

Wildflowers are most often identified by their flowers. The flowers or flower clusters may be borne in the leaf axils along the main stem or on branches off the stem. Modified leaves called *bracts* are often situated at the base of the flower or cluster. Flowers are typically composed of four sets of parts. The outermost set in a flower is the green, leaf-like *sepals* (known collectively as the *calyx*) that protect the often colorful second set—the *petals*. The next set is the *stamens,* the "male" part of the flower, each consisting of pollen sacs *(anthers)* typically on a stalk *(filament)*. The innermost set is the "female" part, with one or more *pistils,* each of which typically has a swollen base— the *ovary* (containing the ovules that after fertilization become the seeds)—and a stalk *(style)* topped by the pollen-collecting *stigma*. The fruit develops from the ovary, forming a cover for the seed or seeds. The form of the fruit varies from species to species.

Although many plants have flowers with both stamens and pistils, some species have unisexual flowers that may occur on the same or separate plants. Many wind-pollinated species, such as ragweeds and

Parts of a Flower

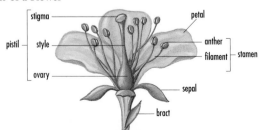

grasses, have reduced flowers that often lack petals and/or sepals. These flowers tend to be inconspicuous, unlike flowers that need to attract insects for pollination. Seed dispersal is often aided by animals: migrating birds and other animals eat fruit or seeds and disperse seeds in their droppings; fruits that are bur-like or covered with sticky hairs attach to animals on contact and later fall off or are shed with fur. Plants such as dandelions bear tiny fruits that have parachute-like tops and are carried by the wind far from the parent plant.

Flowers of a few representative types are illustrated on page 133. The buttercup and the lily are *regular* flowers: their parts radiate in a wheel-like (radially symmetrical) fashion. For purposes of this guide, pea and orchid flowers are considered *irregular:* they can be divided evenly along only one plane (bilateral symmetry). Many plants in the lobelia, mint, and snapdragon families have tubular, *two-lipped* flowers. The tiny flowers of arums are clustered on a club-like *spadix,* which is usually enfolded by a leaf-like *spathe.* The *composite* "flower" of the aster is actually a head of many flowers: tiny tubular *disk florets* form a disk in the center, encircled by petal-like *ray florets.* (Dandelions and hawkweeds have flower heads made up of all ray florets; true thistles have all disk florets.) The entire flower head is generally cupped by a set of numerous green bracts. Grasses have tiny, reduced florets enclosed in scale-like bracts; these are organized in overlapping arrangements called *spikelets,* which typically form a larger *spike,* if each spikelet attaches directly to the main stem, or a *panicle,* if spikelets share branched stalks from the main stem. Dogwood "flowers" consist of a dense head of tiny flowers encircled by several large, petal-like *bracts.* The tiny unisexual flowers of oaks and many other species of trees and shrubs are clustered into slender spikes called *catkins.* Many plants bear flowers in clusters along or atop the stems or branches. Flower clusters take many forms, such as small round bunches, elongated spikes, feathery plumes, and broad, flat-topped or branching arrangements.

In the accounts that follow, sizes given are typical heights of mature specimens.

BEAR-GRASS YUCCA
"Spanish Bayonet"
Yucca filamentosa
AGAVE FAMILY

8'. Basal rosette of stiff, fraying, spine-tipped, evergreen leaves encircles tall stem topped by loose spray of creamy white, bell-shaped, 2" flowers. **BLOOMS** Apr.–Sept. **HABITAT** Beaches, fields, dry open forests. **RANGE** Coastal plain, s NJ and south; escaped farther north to s PA, n NJ.

BROADLEAF ARROWHEAD
Sagittaria latifolia
ARROWHEAD FAMILY

3′6″. Flowers ¾″, white, 3 petals around green button with yellow stamens; in whorls of 3 on tall stalk. Leaves 12″, usu. arrowhead-shaped. Roots bear edible tubers that rise to surface in fall. **BLOOMS** June–Sept. **HABITAT** Shallow water, ditches.

JACK-IN-THE-PULPIT
Arisaema triphyllum
ARUM FAMILY

24″. Spathe ("pulpit") hood-like, green, often maroon-striped; curves over fleshy, finger-like spadix ("jack"). Leaves large, 3-parted, tall-stalked; 1–2 per plant. Berries shiny red, clustered. **CAUTION** Eating berries causes mouth irritation; touching roots can blister skin. **BLOOMS** May–June. **HABITAT** Shady forests.

GOLDEN CLUB
Orontium aquaticum
ARUM FAMILY

16″. Flowers tiny, golden yellow, condensed atop fleshy 4″ spikes. Leaves ovate to elliptical, bluish, emergent or floating. Berries blue-green, inflated. **BLOOMS** Apr.–June. **HABITAT** Shallow streams, ponds, swamps, bogs. **RANGE** Hudson River Valley, se NY and Long Island, s and e PA and south.

ARROW ARUM
Peltandra virginica
ARUM FAMILY

24″. Colony-forming. Erect, wavy-edged, 6″ spathe curls around pale yellow, rod-like, tapering spadix. Leaves large (18″), arrowhead-shaped, fleshy, prominently veined, long-stalked. Berries greenish or blackish; clustered. **BLOOMS** May–July. **HABITAT** Marshes, pondsides; esp. common along waterways.

SKUNK CABBAGE
Symplocarpus foetidus
ARUM FAMILY

24″. Shell-like 6″ spathe, mottled brownish purple and green; encloses knob-like spadix covered with tiny flowers. Leaves very large, cabbage-like, veined; unfurl from tight roll after flowering. Smells like decaying meat; attracts pollinating insects. **BLOOMS** Feb.–Apr. **HABITAT** Swampy forests.

YARROW
Achillea millefolium
ASTER FAMILY

24″. Gray-green, leafy, usu. hairy stems topped with tiny white or pink flowers in dense, flat, 3″ clusters. Leaves very finely dissected, fern-like, gray-green, stalkless, soft; pleasantly aromatic when crushed. Formerly used for a wide variety of medicinal purposes. Introduced from Europe. **BLOOMS** June–Sept. **HABITAT** Fields, roadsides.

WHITE SNAKEROOT
Eupatorium rugosum (Ageratina altissima)
ASTER FAMILY

3′. Solitary or clustered, firm, smooth, branching stems bear tiny, white, rayless flowers in flat, fuzzy, 2″ clusters. Leaves ovate, sharp-toothed. Fruit tiny, seed-like, with white bristles. **CAUTION** Cows eating this plant give toxic (potentially fatal) milk. **BLOOMS** July–Oct. **HABITAT** Shady forests.

COMMON RAGWEED
"Hayfever Weed"
Ambrosia artemisiifolia
ASTER FAMILY

3′. Coarse, hairy, branched stems bear tiny, inconspicuous greenish male flowers in open, dangling clusters of 3½″ spikes. Female flowers in inconspicuous clusters. Leaves light green, deeply bipinnately dissected into many lobes, each 4″. Wind-borne pollen among primary causes of hay fever. **BLOOMS** July–Sept. **HABITAT** Fields, disturbed areas, roadsides.

Plants That Cause Allergies

An allergy is a sensitivity in certain individuals to ordinarily harmless substances. "Allergy plants" include those that produce airborne pollen, which causes hay fever in susceptible individuals (reportedly at least 10 to 20 percent of the population). The cold-like symptoms include respiratory irritation, sneezing, and eye inflammation and may lead to more serious conditions such as ear infections and asthma.

Allergy plants typically have inconspicuous flowers that produce copious pollen. They include various grasses and trees (such as pines and oaks), as well as the most common agents of hay fever in the United States: the infamous ragweeds (*Ambrosia* species). The amount of pollen in the air generally peaks three times during the year, depending on the plant species in bloom: early spring (mainly early-flowering trees), midsummer (mainly grasses, some other herbaceous plants, and a few late-flowering trees), and fall (ragweeds and a few other plants).

Some plants are unfairly blamed for allergies. For example, the conspicuous, insect-pollinated goldenrods (*Solidago* species) are not responsible for late-summer to autumn allergies; ragweed is probably the culprit.

PEARLY EVERLASTING
Anaphalis margaritacea
ASTER FAMILY

24″. Slender erect stems end in flat clusters of tiny globular flowers, each made up of many petal-like, papery white bracts around yellow center. Leaves linear, wooly underneath. **BLOOMS** July–Sept. **HABITAT** Woodland clearings, fields, roadsides.

FIELD PUSSYTOES
Antennaria neglecta
ASTER FAMILY
10″. Forms dense colonies. Flowers in small, fuzzy, white heads clustered atop erect stem. Basal leaves obovate with 1 main vein, wooly; stem leaves tiny. **BLOOMS** Apr.–June. **HABITAT** Dry open areas. Range NY, NJ, e PA to w VA, WV.

COMMON BURDOCK
Arctium minus
ASTER FAMILY
4′. Bushy. Flowers ¾″, thistle-like, pink or purple; surrounded by hook-tipped bracts. Upper leaves ovate, lower leaves heart-shaped; wooly below. Prickly fruit heads catch on fur, clothing. **BLOOMS** July–Oct. **HABITAT** Fields, disturbed areas.

DUSTY MILLER
Artemisia stelleriana
ASTER FAMILY
24″. Mat-forming. Tiny yellow flowers bloom atop erect spikes. Leaves white-wooly, broadly rounded, deeply multi-lobed. Introduced from Asia. **BLOOMS** May–Sept. **HABITAT** Beaches, coastal dunes.

HEARTLEAF ASTER
Aster cordifolius
ASTER FAMILY
3′. Flowers ½″, with blue to purple rays around reddish center; in branched clusters atop stem. Leaves heart-shaped, toothed. **BLOOMS** Aug.–Oct. **HABITAT** Woodland edges and clearings.

WHITE WOOD ASTER
Aster divaricatus
ASTER FAMILY
2′. Colony-forming. Flowers 1″, with white rays around yellow center; in flat, branched clusters atop stem. Leaves 5″, heart-shaped, toothed. **BLOOMS** July–Oct. **HABITAT** Dry forests and clearings. **RANGE** Entire region, ex. se VA.

CALICO ASTER
Aster lateriflorus
ASTER FAMILY
4'. Shrubby. Flowers tiny, daisy-like, with white to pale purple rays around yellow to reddish-purple center; dozens borne on one side of each branch. Leaves lanceolate, toothed. **BLOOMS** Aug.–Sept. **HABITAT** Fields, beaches, dry open forests.

NEW ENGLAND ASTER
Aster novae-angliae
ASTER FAMILY
5'. Flowers 1", with many pale blue or violet rays around yellow or bronze center; many clustered at branch ends. Stems hairy. Leaves lanceolate, crowded, clasping. **BLOOMS** Aug.–Oct. **HABITAT** Meadows, moist road-sides. **RANGE** NY and south to WV and mtns. of VA.

PURPLE-STEMMED ASTER
"Bristly Aster" "Swamp Aster"
Aster puniceus
ASTER FAMILY
6'. Flowers 1½", with many light violet to bluish rays around yellow disk; few per branch. Stems and leaves usu. rough. **BLOOMS** Aug.–Oct. **HABITAT** Swamps, wet thickets.

NODDING BUR MARIGOLD
Bidens cernua
ASTER FAMILY
3'. Flowers 1¼", with 6–8 yellow rays around darker bulbous center; sometimes rayless; nod with age. Leaves lanceolate, toothed, stalkless. Barbed, seed-like fruits stick to fur, clothing. **BLOOMS** Aug.–Sept. **HABITAT** Pond-sides, backwaters, moist meadows.

SPOTTED KNAPWEED
Centaurea maculosa
ASTER FAMILY
3'. Flowers 1", thistle-like, lavender, with forked outer rays and black-tipped bracts. Stems hairy, wiry, many-branched. Leaves deeply cut. Introduced from Europe. **BLOOMS** July–Aug. **HABITAT** Fields, road-sides, disturbed areas.

OXEYE DAISY
Chrysanthemum leucanthemum
ASTER FAMILY
24″. Flowers 2″, composed of white rays around yellow disk; solitary on erect stem. Leaves dark green; coarsely lobed; many lobed. The familiar field daisy. **BLOOMS** June–July. **HABITAT** Fields.

CHICORY
Cichorium intybus
ASTER FAMILY
3′. Flowers 1½″ wide, stalkless, with bright blue, toothed rays; close at midday. Basal leaves dandelion-like; stem leaves linear, clasping. Introduced from Europe. **BLOOMS** July–Sept. **HABITAT** Fields, roadsides.

CANADA THISTLE
Cirsium arvense
ASTER FAMILY
4′. Many fringy, rounded, 1″, pale purple-pink flowers atop smooth, much-branched stems. Leaves lanceolate, deeply cut, spiny. Introduced from Europe. **BLOOMS** June–Sept. **HABITAT** Fields, roadsides.

FIELD THISTLE
Cirsium discolor
ASTER FAMILY
5′. Flowers 1½″, purple; heads solitary at ends of branches. Leaves oblong, narrowly lobed with spiny teeth, white-wooly below. **BLOOMS** July–Oct. **HABITAT** Open forests, fields, waste areas.

BULL THISTLE
Cirsium horridulum
ASTER FAMILY
5′. Extremely prickly. Flowers 2½″, cream to yellow (rarely purple), urn-shaped, surrounded by spiny bracts. Stems stocky, spiny, cottony-hairy. Leaves pinnately lobed, spiny-toothed and spiny-tipped, clasping. **BLOOMS** July–Sept. **HABITAT** Fields, meadows, disturbed areas, edges of salt marshes. **RANGE** Coastal plain of NY and south.

LANCELEAF COREOPSIS
"Tickseed"
Coreopsis lanceolata
ASTER FAMILY
20". Colony-forming. Flowers 2½", yellow, with rays toothed at tips; long-stalked. Leaves linear, sometimes lobed at bases. Native west of region; planted here and escaped. **BLOOMS** June–July. **HABITAT** Sandy fields, roadsides.

DAISY FLEABANE
Erigeron annuus
ASTER FAMILY

4'. Hairy, leafy, branching stems bear dense clusters of ¾" flowers, with many short white, pink, or purple rays tightly packed around yellow disk. Leaves lanceolate, toothed. **BLOOMS** June–Sept. **HABITAT** Fields, disturbed areas. **Philadelphia Fleabane** (*E. philadelphicus*), 3', has 1" flowers and hairy leaves, oblong or ovate, upper ones clasping; blooms May–Aug.

HYSSOP-LEAF BONESET
Eupatorium hyssopifolium
ASTER FAMILY
3'. Flowers tiny, white, in flat clusters atop stem. Leaves linear, in whorls of 3–4, with bundles of smaller leaves in axils. **BLOOMS** Aug.–Oct. **HABITAT** Open sandy areas, roadsides. **RANGE** Coastal plain of NY and south and west through PA to piedmont of VA.

BONESET
Eupatorium perfoliatum
ASTER FAMILY

4'. Thick hairy stems seemingly grow through leaves. Flowers tiny, fuzzy, white, in dense flat clusters. Leaves lanceolate, wrinkly, toothed, united at base to surround stem. **BLOOMS** July–Sept. **HABITAT** Moist meadows.

LANCELEAF GOLDENROD
Euthamia graminifolia
ASTER FAMILY
3'. Flat clusters of tiny yellow flowers at branch ends. Stems smooth or downy. Leaves linear, pointed, parallel-veined. Fragrant. **BLOOMS** July–Oct. **HABITAT** Fields, roadsides, saltmarsh edges.

SPOTTED JOE-PYE-WEED
Eupatorium maculatum
ASTER FAMILY

4'. Sturdy, hairy, purple or purple-spotted stems end with tiny, pink-purple flowers in flat, fuzzy 5" clusters. Leaves lanceolate, toothed, whorled. **BLOOMS** July–Sept. **HABITAT** Moist meadows, thickets.

WOODLAND SUNFLOWER
Helianthus strumosus
ASTER FAMILY

4'. Flowers 3", yellow rays around yellow disk. Leaves shallowly toothed, rough above, hairy below; short-stalked on smooth stems. **BLOOMS** July–Sept. **HABITAT** Open woods, clearings.

JERUSALEM ARTICHOKE
Helianthus tuberosa
ASTER FAMILY

8'. Flowers 3", several yellow rays around yellow disk. Stems rough, hairy. Leaves ovate, thick, rough; lower ones opposite. Tuber edible; ripe Sept.–Nov. **BLOOMS** Aug.–Oct. **HABITAT** Fields, roadsides, clearings.

CAMPHORWEED
Heterotheca subaxillaris
ASTER FAMILY

3'. Shrubby. Flowers ¾", yellow rays surrounding yellow disk; in open clusters atop branches. Leaves ovate, upper ones clasping, lower ones stalked. **BLOOMS** Aug.–Oct. **HABITAT** Dry, sandy clearings, roadsides. **RANGE** Coastal plain of NY and south.

ORANGE HAWKWEED
"Devil's Paintbrush"
Hieracium aurantiacum
ASTER FAMILY

15". Single stem bears ¾", orange, dandelion-like flowers with toothed rays; buds surrounded by black, hairy bracts. Leaves hairy, elliptical, in rosette at stem base. **BLOOMS** June–Aug. **HABITAT** Fields, roadsides. **Yellow Hawkweed** (*H. caespitosum* or *pratense*), 24", with yellow flowers on hairy stalks and large, oblong, hairy leaves; blooms May–Sept.

WILD LETTUCE
Lactuca canadensis
ASTER FAMILY

7'. Tall, branched stem "bleeds" white juice when leaf is picked. Flower heads tiny, dandelion-like, pale yellow; in long clusters. Leaves deeply lobed, toothed. **BLOOMS** July–Sept. **HABITAT** Woodland edges, roadsides, disturbed areas.

SALTMARSH FLEABANE
Pluchea odorata
ASTER FAMILY

3'. Erect, camphor-scented. Flowers tiny, cup-like, pink-purple; in flat 2" clusters. Leaves variable, often ovate and slightly toothed. **BLOOMS** Aug.–Sept. **HABITAT** Saltmarsh edges. **RANGE** Coastal areas, NY and south.

RATTLESNAKE ROOT
Prenanthes alba
ASTER FAMILY

3'. Flowers ½" long, white, bell-shaped in 3–4 drooping clusters atop stem. Stems slender, purple, with whitish coating and milky sap. Leaves arrowhead-shaped, variously lobed. **BLOOMS** Aug.–Sept. **HABITAT** Moist forests.

BLACK-EYED SUSAN
Rudbeckia hirta
ASTER FAMILY

3'. Flowers 3", long, yellow, daisy-like rays around brown central cone; solitary on slender, rough, hairy stems. Leaves lanceolate to ovate, hairy; lower ones toothed; in rosette at stem base. **CAUTION** Stem and leaves very bristly, may irritate skin. **BLOOMS** June–Sept. **HABITAT** Fields, roadsides.

GOLDEN RAGWORT
Senecio aureus
ASTER FAMILY

24". Flowers ¾", daisy-like, yellow; in branched, flat clusters on smooth, branching stems. Basal leaves heart-shaped; stem leaves finely cut. **BLOOMS** May–July. **HABITAT** Swamps, moist forests, meadows.

BLUE-STEMMED GOLDENROD
Solidago caesia
ASTER FAMILY

3'. Arching or horizontal stems. Small tufts of tiny yellow flowers scattered along stems. Stems smooth, purplish, unbranched, white-powdered. Leaves elliptical, toothed, stalkless. One of more than a dozen goldenrods found in region. **BLOOMS** Aug.–Oct. **HABITAT** Forests, thickets.

CANADA GOLDENROD
"Common Goldenrod"
Solidago canadensis
ASTER FAMILY

4'. Plume-like, pyramidal clusters of tiny yellow flowers at curved branch ends. Stems hairy at top. Leaves lanceolate, sharp-toothed, 3-veined, crowded. **BLOOMS** Aug.–Oct. **HABITAT** Meadows, fields, roadsides, open forests.

EARLY GOLDENROD
Solidago juncea
ASTER FAMILY

38. Plume-like, pyramidal clusters of tiny yellow flowers at branch ends. Stems smooth. Basal leaves broadly elliptical, tapered, toothed; stem leaves narrowly elliptical, with tiny leaves in axils. **BLOOMS** July–Sept. **HABITAT** Dry woodland clearings, fields, roadsides.

ROUGH-STEMMED GOLDENROD
Solidago rugosa
ASTER FAMILY

5'. Plume-like clusters of tiny yellow flowers on upper side of branches. Stems rough-hairy. Leaves broadly elliptical, tapered, wrinkled, deep-toothed, hairy. **BLOOMS** July–Oct. **HABITAT** Fields, roadsides, forest edges.

SEASIDE GOLDENROD
Solidago sempervirens
ASTER FAMILY

4'. Club- or plume-like clusters of tiny yellow flowers on arched branches. Stems smooth, thick. Leaves fleshy, lanceolate to oblong, untoothed, smooth, clasping. **BLOOMS** Aug.–Oct. **HABITAT** Coastal marshes, sand dunes.

PRICKLY SOW-THISTLE
Sonchus asper
ASTER FAMILY

4'. Flowers 2", dandelion-like, yellow. Stems smooth, angled. Leaves prickly-edged, lanceolate, with downward-curled basal lobes, clasping. Introduced from Europe. **BLOOMS** July–Sept. **HABITAT** Open disturbed areas.

COMMON DANDELION
Taraxacum officinale
ASTER FAMILY

10". Flowers 1½", yellow, 1 per stem; each ripens into fluffy, white, globular ball of seed-like fruits. Stems hollow, milky-juiced. Leaves deeply and irregularly toothed, in rosette at stem base. Introduced from Eurasia. The common lawn weed. **BLOOMS** Apr.–Sept. **HABITAT** Lawns, fields.

YELLOW GOATSBEARD
Tragopogon pratensis
ASTER FAMILY

24". Flowers 2½", yellow, dandelion-like, with green, long-pointed bracts; close at midday; 1 per stem; each ripens into very large ball of seed-like fruits. Stems smooth, milky-juiced. Leaves grass-like, clasping. Introduced from Europe. **BLOOMS** June–Aug. **HABITAT** Fields.

COLTSFOOT
Tussilago farfara
ASTER FAMILY

8". Clump-forming. Each scaly stalk has single yellow, 1", dandelion-like flower. Leaves large, heart-shaped, toothed, whitish below, upright; appear after flowers. Among Mid-Atl.'s earliest blooming wildflowers. Introduced from Europe. **BLOOMS** Mar.–May. **HABITAT** Moist areas, roadsides.

NEW YORK IRONWEED
Vernonia noveboracensis
ASTER FAMILY

5'. Tall erect stems, branched toward top, with open clusters of tiny, fringed, deep lavender or violet flowers at branch ends. Leaves lanceolate, finely toothed. **BLOOMS** Aug.–Oct. **HABITAT** Moist areas. **RANGE** se NY, NJ, PA and south.

MAY-APPLE
Podophyllum peltatum
BARBERRY FAMILY
12″. Flower 1½″, creamy white, nodding in fork of leafstalks. 2 leaves, each 12″ wide, deeply palmately lobed with notched tips. Fruits oval, lemon-yellow; edible, used for jams and jellies; ripe Aug. Emerging leaves look like unfurling umbrellas. **BLOOMS** Apr.–June. **HABITAT** Rich forests.

HAREBELL
"Bluebell"
Campanula rotundifolia
BELLFLOWER FAMILY
15″. Flowers ¾″, violet-blue, 5-lobed bells; nod on thread-like stalks. Stems wiry. Leaves mostly narrow, grass-like. **BLOOMS** June–Aug. **HABITAT** Dry forests, rocky meadows, cliffs, beaches. **RANGE** NY, n NJ, e PA to WV and mtns. of sw VA.

CARDINAL FLOWER
Lobelia cardinalis
BELLFLOWER FAMILY
4′. Leafy erect stems bear slender spikes of showy scarlet flowers, each 1½″, tubular, 2-lipped; upper lip 2-lobed, lower lip 3-lobed; stamens united into projecting tube. Leaves lanceolate, toothed. Name refers to bright red robes worn by Roman Catholic cardinals. **BLOOMS** July–Sept. **HABITAT** Wooded streamsides, moist meadows.

INDIAN TOBACCO
Lobelia inflata
BELLFLOWER FAMILY
3′. Flowers tiny, pale blue-violet, 2-lipped, with long-pointed, green sepals; each base becomes inflated seedpod. Stems hairy. Leaves ovate, toothed. **CAUTION** Poisonous. **BLOOMS** July–Sept. **HABITAT** Fields, roadsides.

GREAT LOBELIA
Lobelia siphilitica
BELLFLOWER FAMILY
3′. Flowers 1″, bright blue, white-striped, 2-lipped, in long clusters at stem ends. Leaves ovate, toothed. **BLOOMS** Aug.–Sept. **HABITAT** Meadows, swamps, lowland forests.

VENUS' LOOKING-GLASS
Triodanis (Specularia) perfoliata
BELLFLOWER FAMILY

2'. Stems solitary, erect. Flowers ¾", 5 blue petals with yellow eye; in leaf axils. Leaves small, heart-shaped, clasping stem. **BLOOMS** May–Aug. **HABITAT** Woodland clearings, fields, disturbed areas.

TRUMPET VINE
"Trumpet Creeper"
Campsis radicans
BIGNONIA FAMILY

H/L variable. Woody vine; climbs via aerial roots. Hanging clusters of 3" trumpet-shaped flowers; dull orange-red outside, yellowish and red-streaked inside. Stems have pale, shreddy bark. Leaves pinnately compound. **BLOOMS** Apr.–Sept. **HABITAT** Thickets, moist forests. **RANGE** PA, NJ and south; escaped sparingly to NY.

WILD GINGER
Asarum canadense
BIRTHWORT FAMILY

9". Single, 1½", brownish flower, with 3 long-pointed lobes; close to ground. Leaves (1 pair) heart-shaped, dark, leathery, hairy. **BLOOMS** Apr.–June. **HABITAT** Forests.

AMERICAN BITTERSWEET
Celastrus scandens
BITTERSWEET FAMILY

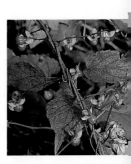

H/L variable. Climbing woody vine. Leaves ovate to elliptical, long-pointed, toothed. Flowers tiny, green. Fruit orange, in 3" clusters at branch tips; break open to reveal bright red seed covers. **BLOOMS** May–June. **HABITAT** Broadleaf forest edges, roadside thickets. Invasive **Oriental Bittersweet** *(C. orbiculatus)* has rounded leaves and smaller fruit clusters along stem.

HORNED BLADDERWORT
Utricularia cornuta
BLADDERWORT FAMILY

4". Aquatic, carnivorous. Flowers ¾", yellow, 2-lipped, with ½" pointed spur. Leaves basal, finely divided, with tiny bladders that catch minute insects and aquatic organisms. **BLOOMS** May–Aug. **HABITAT** Submerged in mud or shallow water.

WATER SMARTWEED
Polygonum amphibium
BUCKWHEAT FAMILY

3'. Floating or erect, single, leafy stem. Flowers tiny, rose-pink, in 2½" spike. Leaves lanceolate. **BLOOMS** June–Oct. **HABITAT** Lakes, marshes, streams.

COMMON SMARTWEED
Polygonum hydropiper
BUCKWHEAT FAMILY

2'. Flowers tiny, green, in narrow arching 3" spikes from leaf axils. Stems sometimes reddish. Leaves lanceolate, from knot-like stem joints. Introduced from Europe. **BLOOMS** June–Oct. **HABITAT** Moist or wet clearings, pondsides.

CURLY DOCK
Rumex crispus
BUCKWHEAT FAMILY

4'. Flowers tiny, greenish, in dense branching 1" clusters. Stem single, erect. Leaves 8", oblong or lanceolate, wavy-edged. Bears hundreds of small, reddish-brown, winged seedpods. Introduced from Europe. **BLOOMS** June–Sept. **HABITAT** Fields, roadsides.

WHITE BANEBERRY
"Doll's Eyes"
Actaea pachypoda
BUTTERCUP FAMILY

24". Flowers tiny, white, clustered atop stems. Leaflets ovate, toothed. Berries white with black dot, thick red stalks. **CAUTION** Berries very poisonous. **BLOOMS** May–June. **HABITAT** Rich forests, thickets. **Red Baneberry** *(A. rubra)* is a bushier plant, with cherry-red berries on wiry stalks; grows from NY south to n NJ, WV, w VA.

WOOD ANEMONE
Anemone quinquefolia
BUTTERCUP FAMILY

8". Single, white, 1" flower, usu. with 5 petal-like sepals, often pink below. Stem slender. Single whorl of 3 leaves, each with 3 toothed leaflets. Forms sizable stands. **BLOOMS** Apr.–June. **HABITAT** Open forests, woodland edges. **RANGE** Entire region, ex. se VA.

RUE ANEMONE
Anemonella thalictroides
BUTTERCUP FAMILY

8″. 2–3 white to pink-tinged, 1″ flowers, each with 5–10 petal-like sepals. Stems slender. Leaves just beneath flowers 3-lobed, whorled; lower leaves more rounded. **BLOOMS** Apr.–May. **HABITAT** Forests. **RANGE** Entire region, ex. n NY.

WILD COLUMBINE
Aquilegia canadensis
BUTTERCUP FAMILY

18″. Flowers 1½″, drooping, red and yellow bells; shaped like lanterns, with long, red, upward-projecting spurs. Leaves light green, long-stalked, divided and subdivided into 3s. **BLOOMS** May–June. **HABITAT** Rocky forests, ledges.

MARSH MARIGOLD
"Cowslip"
Caltha palustris
BUTTERCUP FAMILY

24″. Flowers 1½″, buttercup-like, shiny, bright yellow. Leaves heart-shaped, shallow-toothed, glossy, succulent. **BLOOMS** Apr.–June. **HABITAT** Streams, swamps, wet meadows, ditches.

EASTERN VIRGIN'S BOWER
"Wild Clematis"
Clematis virginiana
BUTTERCUP FAMILY

L variable. Climbing vine. Flowers ¾″, with 4 white petal-like sepals; in stalked rounded clusters from leaf axils. Leaves with 3 ovate, toothed leaflets. Fruit white, plume-like, in ball-shaped clusters. **BLOOMS** July–Sept. **HABITAT** Woodland edges, streamsides, roadsides.

ROUNDLEAF HEPATICA
Hepatica nobilis var. *obtusa*
BUTTERCUP FAMILY

5″. Flowers 1″, white, pink, lavender, or blue; 5–9 petal-like sepals; 1 per hairy stalk. Leaves rounded, 3-lobed; persist through winter. **BLOOMS** Mar.–June. **HABITAT** Forests.

COMMON BUTTERCUP
"Tall Buttercup"
Ranunculus acris
BUTTERCUP FAMILY
2'. Flowers 1", golden, with 5 glossy, overlapping petals. Stem erect, hairy, branching. Basal leaves deeply palmately divided. **BLOOMS** May–Aug. **HABITAT** Disturbed open areas, meadows.

EARLY MEADOW RUE
Thalictrum dioicum
BUTTERCUP FAMILY
2'. Flowers ¼", green with showy yellow anthers; in drooping branched clusters atop stems; male and female flowers on separate plants. Leaves compound, long-stalked, with 3–5 small, rounded, shallowly lobed leaflets. **BLOOMS** April–May. **HABITAT** Moist forests.

TALL MEADOW RUE
Thalictrum pubescens (polygamum)
BUTTERCUP FAMILY
5'. Tall, feathery. Flowers ⅜", white, bushy, clustered in plumes. Leaves bluish to olive, divided into many roundish, 3-lobed leaflets. **BLOOMS** June–Aug. **HABITAT** Wet meadows, swamps.

PRICKLY PEARS
Opuntia species
CACTUS FAMILY
10". Flowers 3", yellow, waxy. Stems flat, fleshy, bristle-tufted pads. Fruit reddish or purplish. Mid-Atl.'s only cactus. **CAUTION** Prickly. **BLOOMS** May–July. **HABITAT** Dunes, sandy or rocky clearings. **RANGE** se NY, e PA, NJ and south.

WATER HEMLOCK
Cicuta maculata
CARROT FAMILY
5'. Dome-shaped, loose, 4" clusters of many tiny white flowers. Stems smooth, sturdy, branched, magenta-streaked. Leaves doubly or triply divided into toothed, pointed leaflets. **CAUTION** All parts deadly poisonous. **BLOOMS** June–Aug. **HABITAT** Moist fields, swamps, thickets.

QUEEN ANNE'S LACE
"Wild Carrot"
Daucus carota
CARROT FAMILY
4'. Flat, lacy, 4" clusters of tiny white flowers, with purple floret at center and 3-pronged bracts below. Stems usu. hairy. Leaves very finely cut. Introduced from Europe. **CAUTION** Poisonous; may irritate skin. **BLOOMS** June–Sept. **HABITAT** Fields, roadsides.

WILD PARSNIP
Pastinacea sativa
CARROT FAMILY

5′. Flat 2″ clusters of tiny yellow flowers. Stems ridged. Leaves pinnately compound, with 5–15 ovate, toothed or lobed leaflets. Introduced from Europe. **BLOOMS** June–Oct. **HABITAT** Fields, roadsides.

GOLDEN ALEXANDERS
Zizia aurea
CARROT FAMILY

24″. Flat 2″ clusters of tiny, bright yellow flowers. Leaves 3-parted, redivided into several narrow, toothed, pointed leaflets. **BLOOMS** Apr.–June. **HABITAT** Meadows, moist forests, roadsides.

Poisonous Plants

Poisonous plants are those that contain potentially harmful substances in high enough concentrations to cause injury if touched or swallowed. Determining whether a plant species is "poison" or "food" requires expertise. The information in this guide is not to be used to identify plants for edible or medicinal purposes.

Sensitivity to a toxin varies with a person's age, weight, physical condition, and individual susceptibility. Children are most vulnerable because of their curiosity and small size. Toxicity can vary in a plant according to season, the plant's different parts, and its stage of growth; plants can also absorb toxic substances, such as herbicides, pesticides, and pollutants from the water, air, and soil. The tasty-looking berry-like red seeds of yews, so often planted around schools, are highly toxic. Among the potentially deadly plants in the Mid-Atlantic region are Water Hemlock and White Snakeroot.

Physical contact with plants that contain irritating resinous compounds causes rashes in many individuals. In the Mid-Atlantic, the main offender is the widespread Poison Ivy. The sap of several other plants, such as Celandine, can also cause dermatitis. Stinging Nettle is covered with hypodermic-like stinging hairs that actually inject pain-inducing substances when touched.

POISON IVY
Toxicodendron (Rhus) radicans
CASHEW FAMILY

L/H variable. Climbing vine or erect or trailing shrub. Old stems covered with fibrous roots. Flowers tiny, in greenish 3″ clusters. Leaves often palmately compound, with 3 ovate toothed or small-lobed leaflets; dull or shiny; often red. Fruit berry-like, tiny, white. **CAUTION** Causes severe skin inflammation; fruit poisonous to eat. **BLOOMS** May–June. **HABITAT** Forests, thickets, trailsides.

BROADLEAF CATTAIL
Typha latifolia
CATTAIL FAMILY
9′. Tall, stiff stem ends in slender, yellowish, 4″ spike (male flowers), with 6″ green (when flowering) or brown (when fruiting) cylinder (female flowers) just below. Leaves tall, blade-like, sheathing. **BLOOMS** May–July. **HABITAT** Watersides, ditches, marshes.

SPREADING DOGBANE
Apocynum androsaemifolium
DOGBANE FAMILY

3′. Bushy. Flowers ⅜″, pink, bell-like, striped inside, fragrant; dangle from curved stalks. Stems milky-juiced. Leaves smooth, ovate, blue-green. Seedpods long, slender, paired. **BLOOMS** June–Aug. **HABITAT** Fields, roadsides, disturbed areas.

COMMON PERIWINKLE
"Running Myrtle"
Vinca minor
DOGBANE FAMILY
6″. Creeping evergreen. Flowers 1″, pinwheel-like, purplish blue with whitish star in center. Leaves ovate, shiny, dark green, paired. Introduced from Europe. **BLOOMS** Apr.–May. **HABITAT** Gardens, roadsides, forests.

BUNCHBERRY
Cornus canadensis
DOGWOOD FAMILY

6″. Flowers white, 1½″, each made up of 4 petal-like bracts around greenish flower head; atop erect stems from creeping rootstock. Leaves ovate, in 1 whorl. Fruit berry-like, red, in tight cluster. **BLOOMS** May–June. **HABITAT** Forests, bogs.

DUCKWEEDS
Lemna and *Spirodela* species
DUCKWEED FAMILY
Green specks floating on water. Flowers minute, rare. Leaves tiny, round, flat, each with 1 *(Lemna)* or 2 *(Spirodela)* thin 1″ roots below. Among the simplest and smallest flowering plants. Eaten by ducks. **HABITAT** Ponds, quiet rivers, backwaters.

FIREWEED
Epilobium angustifolium
EVENING-PRIMROSE FAMILY

5′. Tall single stem terminates in spike-like flower cluster, with drooping buds at tip. Flowers 1″, deep pink, 4 roundish petals. Leaves linear. Slender, upward-angled seedpods below flowers release silky-haired seeds. **BLOOMS** June–Aug. **HABITAT** Clearings, roadsides, burned areas. **RANGE** Mtns. of NY, NJ, PA, south to VA, WV.

COMMON EVENING PRIMROSE
Oenothera biennis
EVENING-PRIMROSE FAMILY

5′. Flowers 1″, yellow, with 4 roundish petals around X-shaped stigma; lemon-scented; close at midday. Stems rough-hairy. Leaves lanceolate, toothed. **BLOOMS** June–Sept. **HABITAT** Open areas.

VIPER'S BUGLOSS
"Blueweed"
Echium vulgare
FORGET-ME-NOT FAMILY

30″. Hairy. Flowers ¾″, blue, tubular, with 5 lobes; stamens reddish, projecting. Leaves oblong or lanceolate. Introduced from Europe. **CAUTION** May irritate skin. **BLOOMS** June–Aug. **HABITAT** Fields, roadsides.

VIRGINIA BLUEBELL
Mertensia virginica
FORGET-ME-NOT FAMILY

20″. Carpet-forming. Flowers ½″, pink in bud, turning blue; corolla tubular with bell-shaped tips; in nodding bunches at stem ends. Leaves ovate, fleshy; upper ones clasping, lower ones stalked. **BLOOMS** March–May. **HABITAT** Floodplains, forests. **RANGE** c and w NY, PA and south.

TRUE FORGET-ME-NOT
Myosotis scorpioides
FORGET-ME-NOT FAMILY

15″. Sprawling. Flowers tiny, light blue with golden eye, in 2″ clusters at ends of small coiled branches. Stems hairy. Leaves oblong, blunt, hairy, stalkless. Introduced from Europe. **BLOOMS** June–Sept. **HABITAT** Watersides, ditches.

BOTTLE GENTIAN
Gentiana clausa
GENTIAN FAMILY

24″. Flowers 1″, blue-violet, with closed petal lobes; in dense clusters atop stems and in upper leaf axils. Leaves oblong; pointed. **BLOOMS** Aug.–Oct. **HABITAT** Moist meadows, streamsides. **RANGE** NY and south to MD, WV, and mtns. of VA.

FRINGED GENTIAN
Gentianopsis crinita
GENTIAN FAMILY

24″. Flowers violet-blue, with 4 fringed, flaring petal lobes; calyx has unequal pointed lobes; 1 atop each branch; open in sun, close at night. Leaves ovate to lanceolate. **BLOOMS** Aug.–Oct. **HABITAT** Watersides, moist meadows.

SALTMARSH SABATIA
"Marsh Pink"
Sabatia stellaris
GENTIAN FAMILY
18". Flowers 1", with 5 pink petals, yellow eye; sepals hidden by petals. Leaves opposite, narrowly oblong. **BLOOMS** July–Oct. **HABITAT** Salt and brackish marshes. **RANGE** Coastal plain of NY and south.

WILD GERANIUM
Geranium maculatum
GERANIUM FAMILY
20". Flowers 1¼", rose-pink, 5-petaled; in loose clusters at branch ends. Leaves toothed, deeply cut into 5 lobes. **BLOOMS** May–June. **HABITAT** Fields, open forests.

WILD SARSAPARILLA
Aralia nudicaulis
GINSENG FAMILY
12". Hemispherical, 2" clusters of tiny greenish-white flowers under leafy umbrella. Single leaf divided into 3 groups of ovate, toothed leaflets. **BLOOMS** May–July. **HABITAT** Upland forests.

WILD CUCUMBER
"Balsam Apple"
Echinocystis lobata
GOURD FAMILY

L variable. Climbing vine, with tendrils and clusters of greenish-white flowers. Leaves palmately lobed. Berries 1½", fleshy, green, prickly; become dry, papery, with 2 large holes at top. **BLOOMS** July–Sept. **HABITAT** Watersides, woodland edges.

VIRGINIA CREEPER
Parthenocissus quinquefolia
GRAPE FAMILY
L variable. Woody climbing vine. Flowers tiny, yellowish green, clustered. Leaves divided into 3–5 palmately lobed, toothed leaflets; turn red. Berries purple-black. **BLOOMS** June–Aug. **HABITAT** Forests, watersides, thickets, stone walls.

WILD GRAPES
Vitis species
GRAPE FAMILY

L/H variable. Climbing woody vines, with large palmately lobed or toothed leaves, twining tendrils, and shreddy bark. Flowers greenish, inconspicuous. Grapes purple to black-purple. **BLOOMS** May–July. **HABITAT** Thickets, woodland edges.

LITTLE BLUESTEM
Schizachyrium (Andropogon) scoparius
GRASS FAMILY

3′. Clumps of branched, brownish stems. Flowers in feathery, white, 2″ spikes atop branches; above leaves. Leaves 10″, flat or folded. **BLOOMS** Aug.–Oct. **HABITAT** Dry sandy fields and woodland clearings.

SMOOTH BROME GRASS
Bromus inermis
GRASS FAMILY

3′. Erect stems from long rhizomes. Flowers in many narrow 1″ spikelets in 1 open, shiny, brown panicle atop stem. Leaves 10″, flat. Important forage crop. Introduced from Eurasia. **BLOOMS** May–June. **HABITAT** Fields, roadsides. **RANGE** NY and south to MD, WV.

ORCHARD GRASS
Dactylis glomerata
GRASS FAMILY

3′. Clumping. Flowers in beige, open, 6″ panicles of flat compact clusters. Leaf blades 6″, sheaths rough. Introduced from Europe. **BLOOMS** May–Sept. **HABITAT** Fields, roadsides, disturbed areas.

PURPLE LOVEGRASS
Eragrostis spectabilis
GRASS FAMILY

12″. Erect clumps. Flowers in many tiny purple spikelets in open, 8″ panicle that breaks off after flowering and tumbles in wind. Leaves 6″, flat or folded; sheaths hairy. In bloom large stands look like pink mist. **BLOOMS** Aug.–Oct. **HABITAT** Sandy fields, woodland clearings, roadsides.

SWITCHGRASS
Panicum virgatum
GRASS FAMILY

6′. Erect, many-stemmed, leafy clumps. Spikelets solitary at ends of many-branched, open, 12″ panicles. Leaves 18″, flat; sheaths smooth. Stems persist through winter. **BLOOMS** July–Oct. **HABITAT** Sandy soils of woodland clearings, fields, roadsides, streamsides, brackish marshes.

REED CANARY GRASS
Phalaris arundinacea
GRASS FAMILY

4′. Robust, bamboo-like, colony-forming. Spikelets in purplish, compact to spreading, 6″ panicles. Stems stout, from pinkish rhizomes. Leaves 8″, rough. Planted for streambank stabilization, but becomes invasive. **BLOOMS** June–July. **HABITAT** Ditches, ponds, intermittently flooded ground. **RANGE** Entire region, ex. e VA.

TIMOTHY
Phleum pratense
GRASS FAMILY

30″. Thickly clumped grass. Flowering spikes dense, slender, yellowish, 4″ cylinders. Stems bulbous just above root crown. Leaves 7″, flat. Introduced from Europe. Top U.S. hay crop. Hay fever allergen. **BLOOMS** June–Aug. **HABITAT** Roadsides, fields.

COMMON REED
"Phragmites"
Phragmites australis (communis)
GRASS FAMILY

12′. Flowers in spikelets in 12″, reddish (turning silver), tufted panicles. Leaves 12″, sharp, bluish. Often forms pure stands. Invasive, replaces other marsh plants. **BLOOMS** Aug.–Sept. **HABITAT** Brackish and freshwater marshes, ditches.

SALTMARSH CORDGRASS
Spartina alterniflora
GRASS FAMILY

8′. Flowers in 8″, beige panicles of upright spikelets. Leaves 12″, flat, with bases sheathing round stems. Forms large colonies; invasive. **BLOOMS** July–Sept. **HABITAT** Salt marshes. **RANGE** Coastal plain of NY and south. **Saltmeadow Cordgrass** *(S. patens)*, 3′, has 12″ brownish panicles of angled spikelets and in-rolled leaf edges; forms colonies; often flattened by wind.

ROUNDLEAF GREENBRIER
Smilax rotundifolia
GREENBRIER FAMILY

L variable. Prickly, woody, climbing vine. Flowers tiny, greenish, in small clusters. Leaves ovate, leathery; veins meet at leaf point. Berries blue-black. **BLOOMS** May–June. **HABITAT** Waterside thickets

BEARBERRY
Arctostaphylos uva-ursi
HEATH FAMILY

8″. Trailing evergreen shrub. Flowers tiny white to pink bells, clustered at branch ends. Leaves small, glossy, leathery, paddle-shaped. Berries red. **BLOOMS** May–June. **HABITAT** Exposed rocky and sandy areas. **RANGE** NY to DE, occ. in mtns. to n VA.

SPOTTED WINTERGREEN
Chimaphila maculata
HEATH FAMILY

10″. Flowers ¾″, white or pink, waxy, with 5 curled-back petals around knobby pistil; fragrant. Leaves lanceolate, toothed; have white midvein; mostly whorled, evergreen. **BLOOMS** June–July. **HABITAT** Dry forests. **Pipsissewa** *(C. umbellata)* has less pointed leaves; blooms later (July–Aug.).

TRAILING ARBUTUS
"Mayflower"
Epigaea repens
HEATH FAMILY

10″. Flowers tiny, pink to white, tubular, 5-lobed, clustered. Stems woody, hairy, trailing. Leaves ovate, leathery, evergreen. **BLOOMS** Apr.–May. **HABITAT** Sandy or rocky woodland clearings, roadsides.

WINTERGREEN
"Checkerberry"
Gaultheria procumbens
HEATH FAMILY

6″. Leathery-leaved, semiwoody, evergreen. Flowers tiny, waxy, white, 5-lobed bells. Leaves ovate, slightly toothed, minty-scented. Berries scarlet; may persist through winter. Forms colonies via creeping, underground stem. **BLOOMS** Apr.–May. **HABITAT** Moist or dry upland forests.

INDIAN-PIPE
Monotropa uniflora
HEATH FAMILY

7″. Entire plant waxy, whitish. Flower ¾″, bell-shaped, sometimes salmon-pink, with 4–5 petals, nodding; atop thick, translucent stem. Leaves scale-like. Turns black when picked or bruised. Saprophytic: gets nourishment from decayed organic matter. **BLOOMS** June–Sept. **HABITAT** Forests.

SHINLEAF
Pyrola elliptica
HEATH FAMILY

10″. Elongated clusters of waxy, white, nodding, fragrant flowers, each ½″, with 5 thin petals around curved protruding style. Leaves dark olive, broad, oblong, basal, evergreen, red-stalked. **BLOOMS** June–Aug. **HABITAT** Forests. **RANGE** NY and south to DE, w to WV and mtns. of VA.

JAPANESE HONEYSUCKLE
Lonicera japonica
HONEYSUCKLE FAMILY

L variable. Twining vine forms impenetrable thickets. Fragrant tubular flowers 1½", 2-lipped, with long stamens; white petals turn yellow. Paired leaves ovate, hairy. Berries black. Introduced from Asia, invasive. **BLOOMS** April–July. **HABITAT** Woodland edges, disturbed areas, roadsides. **RANGE** se NY, e PA and NJ south.

TRUMPET HONEYSUCKLE
"Coral Honeysuckle"
Lonicera sempervirens
HONEYSUCKLE FAMILY

L variable. Climbing or trailing woody vine. Flowers 2", tubular, 5-lobed, red outside, yellow inside. Stems slender. Leaves elliptical to obovate, semievergreen. Berries tiny, red. Pollinated by hummingbirds. **BLOOMS** Apr.–Sept. **HABITAT** Woodlands, thickets, fences. **RANGE** Entire region, ex. n NY.

LARGER BLUE FLAG
Iris versicolor
IRIS FAMILY

30". Flowers violet-blue, 1 or more per sturdy stalk, each 3", with petal-like parts in 3s: sepals large, dark-veined, yellow-based; petals narrower, erect; styles 2-lobed, arched over sepals. Leaves sword-like, pale to grayish; rise from basal cluster. **BLOOMS** May–July. **HABITAT** Watersides, marshes, swamps.

BLUE-EYED GRASS
Sisyrinchium angustifolium
IRIS FAMILY

15". Flowers ½", blue with yellow eye; 3 petals, 3 petal-like sepals, all tipped with thorn-like point; atop long, flat, twisted, usu. branching stalks. Leaves grass-like, linear. **BLOOMS** May–July. **HABITAT** Moist meadows, shores.

SEA LAVENDER
"Marsh Rosemary"
Limonium carolinianum (nashii)
LEADWORT FAMILY

24". Tiny, pale purple flowers along one side of diffuse wiry, curved branchlets. Leaves broadly lanceolate, basal. Appears as a lavendar mist over coastal marshes. Grossly overcollected; do not pick. **BLOOMS** July–Sept. **HABITAT** Saltmarsh edges. **RANGE** Coastal plain of NY and south.

WILD GARLIC
Allium canadense
LILY FAMILY

15″. Flowers few, ½″, 6-petaled, white to pink, on 1″ stalks above dense cluster of bulblets. Leaves 10″, basal, linear, flat. Bulbs edible May–June. **BLOOMS** May–July. **HABITAT** Open woodlands, fields, meadows.

TROUT LILY
"Dogtooth Violet"
Erythronium americanum
LILY FAMILY

10″. Colony-forming. Flowers 1″, yellow inside, bronzy outside, solitary; nodding atop brownish stalk; 6 petals, all curled back; 6 stamens with brownish, reddish, or yellowish anthers. Leaves elliptical, mottled brownish, sheathe flower stalks. **BLOOMS** Apr.–May. **HABITAT** Moist forests and meadows.

ORANGE DAY-LILY
Hemerocallis fulva
LILY FAMILY

3′. Leafless stalk rises from sword-like basal leaves, bears several tawny orange, upward-facing, funnel-shaped flowers with erect, net-veined petals. Flowers 3½″; each lasts 1 day. Leaves 24″, narrow, pointed, channeled. Introduced as a garden plant; escaped cultivation. **BLOOMS** June–Aug. **HABITAT** Roadsides, meadows.

CANADA LILY
Lilium canadense
LILY FAMILY

4′. Flowers 3″, yellow to orange, dark-spotted, nodding, 1 or more per stem. Leaves lanceolate, prickly-veined underneath, whorled. **BLOOMS** June–Aug. **HABITAT** Forests, moist meadows. **RANGE** NY and south to n DE, MD, WV, and mtns. of VA.

TURK'S-CAP LILY
Lilium superbum
LILY FAMILY

5′. Flowers 2½″, nodding, orange, with reddish-brown spots, curled-back petals, dangling brown anthers. Leaves lanceolate, whorled. **BLOOMS** July–Sept. **HABITAT** Forests, moist meadows. **RANGE** s NY and south.

CANADA MAYFLOWER
"Wild Lily-of-the-Valley"
Maianthemum canadense
LILY FAMILY

5". Forms carpet-like colonies. Flowers tiny, white, star-like, in conical clusters. Leaves heart-shaped. Berries white, ripen to red. **BLOOMS** May–June. **HABITAT** Upland forests. **RANGE** NY and south to n DE, MD, WV, and mtns. of VA.

HAIRY SOLOMON'S SEAL
Polygonatum pubescens
LILY FAMILY

24". Flowers ½", bell-like, greenish white; dangle from leaf axils. Stems arched. Leaves ovate, stalkless, pale green, parallel-veined; hairy below. **BLOOMS** May–June. **HABITAT** Forests. **RANGE** NY and south to n DE, MD, WV, and mtns. of VA.

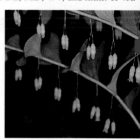

FALSE SOLOMON'S SEAL
Maianthemum (Smilacina) racemosum
LILY FAMILY

30". Flowers tiny, white, fragrant; in pyramidal clusters atop angled, unbranched, arched stems. Leaves elliptical, parallel-veined. Berries speckled green, ripen to red. **BLOOMS** May–July. **HABITAT** Forests.

PURPLE TRILLIUM
Trillium erectum
LILY FAMILY

12". Single 2½", foul-smelling flower, with 3 purple-red petals alternating with 3 green, pointed sepals. Leaves large, diamond-shaped, dark green, net-veined; in whorl of 3. **BLOOMS** Apr.–June. **HABITAT** Wooded hills. **RANGE** NY and south to n DE, MD, WV, and mtns. of VA.

LARGE-FLOWERED TRILLIUM
Trillium grandiflorum
LILY FAMILY

18". Single 4" flower, with 3 waxy, white or pink, wavy-edged petals. Single whorl of 3 broadly ovate or diamond-shaped leaves. Berries red. **BLOOMS** May–June. **HABITAT** Moist forests. **RANGE** NY to w PA and south to mtns. of VA.

TOAD SHADE
Trillium sessile
LILY FAMILY

8". Stalkless, deep maroon flowers with 1½" erect petals; 1 per plant, arising from 3 ovate whorled leaves; have decayed-meat odor. Leaves dark green, dotted with light green spots above. **BLOOMS** April–May. **HABITAT** Rich forests. **RANGE** w NY, w PA and south to w MD, VA, WV.

SESSILE BELLWORT
"Wild Oats"
Uvularia sessilifolia
LILY FAMILY

9". 1 or 2 creamy yellow, narrow, nodding, 1" bell-shaped flowers at tips of angled stems. Leaves oblong, unstalked, whitish underneath. **BLOOMS** Apr.–June. **HABITAT** Forests, thickets.

FALSE HELLEBORE
Veratrum viride
LILY FAMILY

6'. Tall, erect stems with large terminal cluster of ¾" yellow-green flowers. Leaves 10", elliptical, pleated, clasping. **BLOOMS** May–July. **HABITAT** Moist forests, swamps.

PURPLE LOOSESTRIFE
Lythrum salicaria
LOOSESTRIFE FAMILY

5'. Erect, branching stems with 12" spikes of lavender flowers above opposite or whorled, un-stalked leaves. Flowers petals wrinkled. Leaves lanceolate or linear; lower ones downy, clasping. Covers acres of wetlands; invasive. **BLOOMS** July–Sept. **HABITAT** Marshes, pondsides, ditches.

SWAMP LOOSESTRIFE
"Water Willow"
Decodon verticillatus
LOOSESTRIFE FAMILY

7'. Flowers ½", bright pink, with 5–7 wedge-shaped, wrinked petals, in tufts. Stems arched, in-tertwining. Leaves lanceolate, in pairs or whorls. **BLOOMS** July–Aug. **HABITAT** Swamps, watersides.

CLEAVERS
"Bedstraw" "Goosegrass"
Galium aparine
MADDER FAMILY

3'. Mat-forming. Flowers tiny, with 4 white petals; in groups of 3 on stalks from leaf axils. Stems and fruits with downward-hooked prickles that stick to animal fur and clothing. Leaves linear, in whorls of 8. **BLOOMS** May–July. **HABITAT** Moist woodlands.

BLUETS
Hedyotis caerulea
MADDER FAMILY
6″. Patch-forming. Flowers ½″, pale blue with golden eye, tubular, 4-lobed. Basal leaves oblong, in tufts; stem leaves tiny. **BLOOMS** Apr.–June. **HABITAT** Forest clearings, fields.

SWAMP ROSE MALLOW
Hibiscus moscheutos
MALLOW FAMILY
6′. Flowers 7″, hollyhock-like, pink with yellowish column of stamens; musk-scented. Leaves ovate, toothed; white-fuzzy below. **BLOOMS** July–Sept. **HABITAT** Marshes, streamsides. **RANGE** NY and south; mainly coastal and piedmont.

MUSK MALLOW
Malva moschata
MALLOW FAMILY
18″. Flowers 1½″, pink or white, with notched, wedge-shaped petals around pink column of stamens; musk-scented. Leaves intricately cut into very narrow lobes. **BLOOMS** July–Sept. **HABITAT** Fields, roadsides. **RANGE** NY and south to n and w VA.

VIRGINIA MEADOW BEAUTY
Rhexia virginica
MEADOW BEAUTY FAMILY
18″. Flowers 1″, bright pink, with 4 rounded, slightly heart-shaped petals and 8 conspicuous, curly yellow stamens; clustered at branch ends. Stems 4-sided, with wing-like angles. Leaves ovate, rounded at bases, toothed, strongly veined. Fruit urn-shaped with 4 points. **BLOOMS** July–Sept. **HABITAT** Sandy meadows, bogs, pondsides. **RANGE** e NY, e and s PA, NJ and south.

SWAMP MILKWEED
Asclepias incarnata
MILKWEED FAMILY
3′6″. Flowers tiny, deep pink or rose-purple, in 3″ clusters at branch ends. Stems branched, milky-juiced. Leaves narrow, lanceolate. Seedpods long, pointed. **BLOOMS** June–Aug. **HABITAT** Watersides, moist meadows, swamps.

COMMON MILKWEED
Asclepias syriaca
MILKWEED FAMILY

4′4″. Flowers ½″, purplish or pink, in rounded 2″ clusters at leaf axils. Leaves broad-oblong, pale green, downy gray below; with milky juice. Seedpods long, pointed, warty; release silky-hairy seeds. **BLOOMS** June–Aug. **HABITAT** Fields, roadsides.

BUTTERFLY WEED
"Orange Milkweed"
Asclepias tuberosa
MILKWEED FAMILY

18″. Hairy. Flowers ¼″, orange, in 2″ clusters at branch ends. Leaves oblong, with watery juice. Seedpods narrow, hairy, erect. **BLOOMS** June–Sept. **HABITAT** Dry, open, sandy areas. **RANGE** Entire region, ex. n NY.

ORANGE MILKWORT
"Yellow Milkwort"
Polygala lutea
MILKWORT FAMILY

16″. Flowers tiny, bright orange (dry to pale yellow), in dense, cylindrical, 1″ heads. Leaves spoon-shaped to obovate. **BLOOMS** Apr.–Sept. **HABITAT** Wet pinelands, savannas, wet ditches, roadsides. **RANGE** Coastal plain of NY and south.

PURPLE MILKWORT
"Field Milkwort"
Polygala sanguinea
MILKWORT FAMILY

10″. Flowers tiny, pink-violet to white or light green, in ½″ oblong clusters atop stems. Leaves linear. **BLOOMS** June–Oct. **HABITAT** Woodland openings, moist fields and meadows.

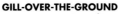

WILD BASIL
Clinopodium vulgare
MINT FAMILY

15″. Flowers ½″, rose-purple, 2-lipped, in rounded wooly clusters in leaf axils and atop 4-sided, hairy stems. Leaves opposite, ovate, mostly untoothed. **BLOOMS** June–Aug. **HABITAT** Thickets, woodland edges.

GILL-OVER-THE-GROUND
"Ground Ivy"
Glechoma hederacea
MINT FAMILY

6″. Flowers ¾″, blue-violet, tubular, in leaf axils of upright branches. Stems creeping, 4-sided. Leaves opposite, roundish, scalloped, evergreen. Introduced from Eurasia. **BLOOMS** Apr.–June. **HABITAT** Lawns, disturbed areas, moist woodland clearings.

MOTHERWORT
Leonurus cardiaca
MINT FAMILY

3'. Flowers ½", pale violet, 2-lipped, upper lip hairy; in whorled clusters around stem in leaf axils. Stems 4-sided. Leaves opposite, with 3 coarsely toothed, pointed lobes. **BLOOMS** June–Aug. **HABITAT** Disturbed areas, roadsides.

WILD MINT
Mentha arvensis
MINT FAMILY

24". Flowers tiny, lilac or white, tubular, 4-lobed, in clusters at leaf bases; encircle weak, hairy, 4-sided stems. Leaves opposite, ovate; aromatic. **BLOOMS** July–Sept. **HABITAT** Moist areas, streamsides.

WILD BERGAMOT
Monarda fistulosa
MINT FAMILY

4'. Flowers 1", lavender, tubular, 2-lipped, in rounded clusters atop 4-sided stems. Leaves grayish green, opposite, lanceolate, toothed. **BLOOMS** July–Aug. **HABITAT** Forest clearings, fields.

SELF-HEAL
"Heal-all"
Prunella vulgaris
MINT FAMILY

12". Flowers ½", violet or pink, 2-lipped, with hood-like upper lip and fringed lower lip; in oblong heads atop 4-sided stems. Leaves opposite, ovate. **BLOOMS** June–Sept. **HABITAT** Fields, roadsides.

VIRGINIA MOUNTAIN MINT
Pycnanthemum virginianum
MINT FAMILY

3'. Erect stems branch toward tops. Flowers tiny, white, 2-lipped, above white hairy bracts; in 2" round heads atop branches. Stems 4-sided. Leaves narrowly lanceolate, opposite. Entire plant fragrant when crushed. **BLOOMS** July–Sept. **HABITAT** Moist woodland clearings, meadows, fields.

MARSH SKULLCAP
Scutellaria galericulata
MINT FAMILY
20″. Flowers 1″, bluish lavender, 2-lipped, with upper lip hooded, lower lip 3-lobed; in upper leaf axils. Stems 4-sided. Leaves lanceolate, toothed. **BLOOMS** July–Aug. **HABITAT** Moist meadows, swamps, watersides. **RANGE** NY and south to DE, west to WV.

BLUE CURLS
Trichostema dichotomum
MINT FAMILY
20″. Sticky. Flowers ¾″, blue to blue-purple, 2-lipped, with upper lip 4-lobed, lower lip longer, white at base; stamens blue, long-curled. Stems hairy. Leaves lanceolate. **BLOOMS** Aug.–Sept. **HABITAT** Sandy and dry rocky areas. **RANGE** c, e NY and south to WV, w and se VA.

HEDGE BINDWEED
Calystegia sepium
MORNING GLORY FAMILY
L variable. Smooth, twining vine. Flowers 3″, funnel-shaped, 5-lobed, pink to white, with one white stripe per lobe. Leaves arrowhead-shaped. **BLOOMS** June–Sept. **HABITAT** Watersides, thickets, disturbed areas.

COMMON MORNING GLORY
Ipomoea purpurea
MORNING GLORY FAMILY
L variable. Twining vine. Flowers 2″, blue to red-purple, funnel-shaped; single to clusters of 5, in leaf axils. Leaves heart-shaped. Introduced from tropical America; escaped from gardens. **BLOOMS** July–Sept. **HABITAT** Fields, roadsides.

GARLIC MUSTARD
Alliaria officinalis
MUSTARD FAMILY
3′. Flowers ¼″, white, in terminal clusters. Leaves broadly heart-shaped, toothed; strong garlic odor when crushed. Introduced from Europe. Invasive. Forms dense stands. **BLOOMS** May–June. **HABITAT** Moist forests, thickets, streamsides, trailsides. **RANGE** Entire region, ex. n NY.

COMMON WINTER CRESS
Barbarea vulgaris
MUSTARD FAMILY

18″. Flowers tiny, bright yellow; cross-shaped; in many elongated 2½″ clusters. Lower leaves pinnately lobed, with terminal lobe largest, rounded; upper ones lobed, clasping. Seedpods beaked. Introduced from Eurasia. **BLOOMS** Apr.–June. **HABITAT** Open areas, moist roadsides.

DAME'S ROCKET
Hesperis matronalis
MUSTARD FAMILY

3′. Flowers 1″, purple, white, or pink, cross-shaped, 4-petaled, clustered at stem end. Leaves lanceolate, toothed. Seedpods long, pointed. Introduced from Europe. Often confused with *Phlox* species. **BLOOMS** May–July. **HABITAT** Fields, woodland clearings, roadsides.

FALSE NETTLE
"Bog Hemp"
Boehmeria cylindrica
NETTLE FAMILY

4′. Minute greenish flowers clustered into compact 4″ spikes. Stems hairy. Leaves ovate, toothed, short-hairy. Lacks stinging hairs of true nettle. **BLOOMS** Apr.–Nov. **HABITAT** Wet forests, thickets, ditches; marshes, swamps, streamsides, canals.

STINGING NETTLE
Urtica dioica
NETTLE FAMILY

6′. Covered with stinging hairs. Flowers inconspicuous, in hanging narrow clusters under upper leaves. Stems 4-sided. Leaves ovate, coarsely toothed, elm-like. **CAUTION** Do not touch; hairs cause pain. **BLOOMS** July–Sept. **HABITAT** Wetlands, woodland edges.

BITTERSWEET NIGHTSHADE
Solanum dulcamara
NIGHTSHADE FAMILY

L variable. Climbing vine. Flowers ½″, with 5 violet petals curled back from yellow central "beak"; in loose clusters. Leaves 3-parted. Berries egg-shaped, shiny green, ripen to bright red. Introduced from Eurasia. **CAUTION** Berries poisonous. **BLOOMS** June–Sept. **HABITAT** Thickets, woodland edges.

GRASS PINK
Calopogon tuberosus
ORCHID FAMILY

15". 2–10 fragrant flowers open sequentially up tall stalk. Flowers 1½", pink, with uppermost petal yellow-bearded (bearded petal or "lip" bottommost in many other orchids). Single grasslike leaf near base of stem. **BLOOMS** June–July. **HABITAT** Bogs, moist meadows.

PINK LADY'S SLIPPER
"Moccasin Flower"
Cypripedium acaule
ORCHID FAMILY

12". Colony-forming. Leafless stalk bears solitary flower with prominent pouch. Flower has distinctive inflated lip petal, 2½" long, pink with red veins (occ. pure white), deeply creased; sepals and side petals greenish brown, spreading. Leaves 7", ovate, ribbed, dark above, silvery-hairy below; basal, opposite. **BLOOMS** May–June. **HABITAT** Forests, esp. under pines; bogs, rocky areas, sand dunes.

HELLEBORINE
Epipactis helleborine
ORCHID FAMILY

3'. Flowers ½", greenish, tinged with purple; lower lip forms sac with pointed, under-turned tip; clustered in 3" terminal spike. Leaves broadly lanceolate, parallel-veined, clasping. Introduced from Europe; the only nonnative orchid growing wild in region. **BLOOMS** July–Sept. **HABITAT** Forests, thickets, roadsides. **RANGE** NY, n NJ, and scattered south to WV, mtns. of VA.

ROSE POGONIA
Pogonia ophioglossoides
ORCHID FAMILY

18". Slender stem bears 1 sheathing leaf midway up; topped by 1¾", solitary, rose-pink flower. Lip petal crested, fringed; 3 sepals form propeller shape; 2 ovate lateral petals overarch lip; 1 large bract below flower. Leaf 4", ovate to broadly lanceolate. This and other wetland orchids suffer from of habitat degradation and overcollection. **BLOOMS** May–July. **HABITAT** Bogs, meadows, moist open forests.

NODDING LADIES' TRESSES
Spiranthes cernua
ORCHID FAMILY

18″. Flowers ½″, creamy white, nodding; arranged in double spiral on seemingly twisted, slender spike; side petals and upper sepal unite to form hood over wavy-edged lower lip; fragrant. Basal leaves long, lanceolate; stem leaves small, scale-like. **BLOOMS** Aug.–Sept. **HABITAT** Moist meadows, thickets, riversides.

WILD INDIGO
Baptisia tinctoria
PEA FAMILY

30″. Bushy. Loose elongated clusters of ½″ yellow pea-flowers at branch ends. Leaves sparse, grayish to bluish, divided into 3 ovate to wedge-shaped leaflets. **BLOOMS** May–Sept. **HABITAT** Dry fields, sandy woodland clearings. **RANGE** e NY, PA and south.

PARTRIDGE PEA
Chamaecrista (Cassia) fasciculata
PEA FAMILY

3′. Flowers 1½″, butterfly-like, with 5 unequal yellow petals with red spots at base. Stems erect to arching. Leaves pinnately compound, with many bristle-tipped leaflets. **BLOOMS** Apr.–Oct. **HABITAT** Pinelands, woodland clearings, disturbed areas. **RANGE** se to w NY, s PA and south.

CROWN VETCH
Coronilla varia
PEA FAMILY

18″. Sprawling or upcurved stems bear clover-like, pink-and-white 1″ flower clusters and many ovate paired leaflets. Introduced from Europe for erosion control; invasive. **BLOOMS** June–Sept. **HABITAT** Roadsides, fields, woodland edges.

PANICLED TICK TREFOIL
Desmodium paniculatum
PEA FAMILY

3′. Tiny, pink to purple pea-flowers in 3″ branched clusters atop stems. Leaves compound with 3 slender, lanceolate leaflets; terminal leaflet stalked. Fruit a 3–6 segmented pod with hooked hairs that cling to clothing. **BLOOMS** July–Aug. **HABITAT** Woodland edges, fields, roadsides.

BEACH PEA
Lathyrus japonicus
PEA FAMILY

20″. Trailing vine often reaching tide line. Pink-lavender ¾″ pea-flowers in long-stalked clusters. Stems stout, angled. Leaves pinnately compound, with 6–12 thick, fleshy, ovate leaflets; tendrils at ends, large arrowhead-shaped appendages at bases. Fruit an elongated veiny pod. **BLOOMS** May–Aug. **HABITAT** Beaches. **RANGE** Coastal plain and Great Lakes shores of NY and south.

EVERLASTING PEA
Lathyrus latifolius
PEA FAMILY

L variable. Climbing or trailing. Pink to purple 1″ pea-flowers in 2″ stalked clusters at leaf axils. Stems have leaf-like wings tapering to 2 ovate leaflets; end in tendrils. Introduced from Europe; escaped from cultivation. **BLOOMS** June–Sept. **HABITAT** Fields, roadsides. **RANGE** Coastal plain and Great Lakes shores of NY, PA, and NJ.

SLENDER BUSH CLOVER
Lespedeza virginica
PEA FAMILY

24″. Upright, bushy. Tiny purple pea-flowers in clusters in leaf axils and at stem ends. Leaves compound with 3 slender, lanceolate leaflets. Fruit a 1-seeded pod. **BLOOMS** Aug.–Sept. **HABITAT** Dry forests.

BIRD'S-FOOT TREFOIL
Lotus corniculatus
PEA FAMILY

15″. Creeper. Flat clusters of yellow ½″ pea-flowers at ends of low or prostrate stems. Leaves clover-like, with 2 small leaf-like appendages at bases of leafstalks. Introduced from Europe as forage crop. **BLOOMS** June–Sept. **HABITAT** Meadows, roadsides.

WILD LUPINE
Lupinus perennis
PEA FAMILY

20″. Upright elongated clusters of purple-blue ½″ pea-flowers atop erect stems. Leaves palmately divided into 7–11 lanceolate leaflets. Fruit a hairy pod. **BLOOMS** May–July. **HABITAT** Dry forests, fields, barrens.

WHITE SWEET CLOVER
Melilotus alba
PEA FAMILY

8'. Bushy. Tiny white pea-flowers; fragrant when crushed; in slender, cylindrical 4" clusters from leaf axils. Leaves pinnately compound, with 3 lanceolate, toothed leaflets. **BLOOMS** June–Sept. **HABITAT** Open areas. **Yellow Sweet Clover** *(M. officinalis)* is yellow-flowered, shorter (4'), and more loosely branched; blooms May–Sept. Both species introduced from Eurasia; cultivated as pasture crops, valued as honey plants, but invasive.

YELLOW HOP CLOVER
Trifolium aureum
PEA FAMILY

12". Tiny, yellow, tubular flowers in elongated, ½" heads. Leaves compound with 3 oblong leaflets, each tipped with short bristle. Introduced from Eurasia. **BLOOMS** May–Sept. **HABITAT** Fields, roadsides, lawns.

RED CLOVER
Trifolium pratense
PEA FAMILY

20". Dense, rounded 1" heads of tiny, red to magenta, tubular flowers. Stems erect, hairy. Leaves compound with 3 ovate leaflets, each marked with a pale V. Introduced from Europe. **BLOOMS** June–Oct. **HABITAT** Open areas.

WHITE CLOVER
Trifolium repens
PEA FAMILY

10". Flowers white, pinkish, or brownish; tubular; in somewhat spherical, ¾", stalked heads. Stems creeping. Leaves compound with 3 ovate leaflets; long-stalked. Introduced from Eurasia. **BLOOMS** May–Oct. **HABITAT** Lawns, open areas.

COW VETCH
Vicia cracca
PEA FAMILY

3'. Vine. Flowers ½", pink or lavender to blue-violet, tubular; crowded on long, 1-sided spikes. Leaves pinnately compound, with 8–12 pairs of oblong leaflets on stalks tipped with paired tendrils. **BLOOMS** June–Aug. **HABITAT** Fields, roadsides.

WILD BLUE PHLOX
Phlox divaricata
PHLOX FAMILY

18". Flowers ¾", blue to purple, 5 petals united to form slender tube at base; in loose cluster atop stem. Leaves lanceolate, opposite, clasping. **BLOOMS** April–June. **HABITAT** Rich forests and woodland edges.

PICKERELWEED
Pontederia cordata
PICKERELWEED FAMILY

3'6". Flowers ⅜", violet-blue, 2-lipped, with yellow 2-lobed spot on upper lip of each; clustered in spikes. Stems mostly under water. Leaves large, heart-shaped. **BLOOMS** July–Aug. **HABITAT** Shallow freshwater wetlands.

DEPTFORD PINK
Dianthus armeria
PINK FAMILY

20". Flowers ½", deep pink, with 5 jagged-edged, white-dotted petals, atop slender stems. Leaves narrow, erect, needle-like. Introduced from Europe. **BLOOMS** June–Aug. **HABITAT** Dry fields, roadsides.

RAGGED ROBIN
Lychnis flos-cuculi
PINK FAMILY

30". Flowers ½", pink or white, raggedy, on delicate, branched stalks. Stems thin, sticky above, hairy below. Leaves lanceolate; smaller ones higher on stem. **BLOOMS** May–July. **HABITAT** Fields, moist meadows. **RANGE** NY, NJ, PA.

BOUNCING BET
"Soapwort"
Saponaria officinalis
PINK FAMILY

24". Flowers 1", white or pinkish, with 5 scalloped petals; clustered atop thin branches; fragrant. Stems thick-jointed. Leaves lanceolate, parallel-veined, clasping. **BLOOMS** July–Sept. **HABITAT** Open areas, roadsides.

WHITE CAMPION
Silene latifolia
PINK FAMILY

3'. Flowers 1", white or pinkish, with 5 deeply notched petals. Female flowers sweet-scented, with 5 curved pistils protruding from center; inflated sticky calyx, 5 curved teeth. Males on separate plants; have slender, 10-veined calyx, 10 stamens. Stems hairy, sticky, many-branched. Leaves ovate or lanceolate, hairy, opposite. Blooms at night; attracts moths. Introduced from Europe. **BLOOMS** May–Sept. **HABITAT** Open areas, roadsides.

STARRY CAMPION
Silene stellata
PINK FAMILY

24″. Flowers ¾″, white, 5 distinct fringed petals with protruding stamens. Leaves lanceolate, in whorls of 4. Can occur in masses. **BLOOMS** June–Aug. **HABITAT** Rich forests and woodland openings.

COMMON CHICKWEED
Stellaria media
PINK FAMILY

8″. Flowers tiny, white, with 5 bisected petals and 5 longer green sepals. Stems weak, branched, trailing, with a hairy line. Leaves ovate; lower ones stalked, upper ones unstalked. **BLOOMS** Mar.–Oct. **HABITAT** Lawns, gardens.

NORTHERN PITCHER PLANT
Sarracenia purpurea
PITCHER PLANT FAMILY

20″. Distinctive, vase-like leaves usu. contain water. Flowers 3″, purplish red, with 5 petals, 4–5 petal-like sepals, and expanded pistil with umbrella-shaped style; nodding, long-stalked. Leaves large, red-veined, curved to form hollow tube with flared lips and downward-pointing bristles. Carnivorous: insects lured by leaf color become trapped inside by hairs and eventually drown in water; plant absorbs nutrients as insects decompose. **BLOOMS** June–July. **HABITAT** Bogs. **RANGE** NY and south to e VA.

ENGLISH PLANTAIN
Plantago lanceolata
PLANTAIN FAMILY

18″. Grooved stalks above leaf rosettes bear spherical or cylindrical, greenish-white to brownish heads of tiny, spirally arranged, papery flowers. Leaves lanceolate, ribbed. Introduced from Eurasia. **BLOOMS** May–Oct. **HABITAT** Lawns, open areas.

POKEWEED
Phytolacca americana
POKEWEED FAMILY

8′. Bushy. Flowers tiny, white, in long clusters; pistil green, button-like. Leaves very large, ovate. Berries purple-black; in drooping clusters on pink stalks. **CAUTION** Berries and root poisonous. **BLOOMS** July–Aug. **HABITAT** Woodland edges, fields, disturbed areas.

CELANDINE
Chelidonium majus
POPPY FAMILY

20″. Loose clusters of yellow, 4-petaled, ¾″ flowers on fragile stems. Leaves lobed, scalloped. Introduced from Eurasia. **CAUTION** All parts toxic; yellow stem-juice irritates skin. **BLOOMS** May–July. **HABITAT** Woodland edges, roadsides, yards.

DUTCHMAN'S BREECHES
Dicentra cucullaria
POPPY FAMILY

10″. Flowers ¾″, pantaloon-shaped, white with yellow tips, waxy; fragrant; dangle in clusters from arched leafless stalk. Leaves grayish, fern-like; divided into many deeply cut leaflets. **BLOOMS** Apr.–May. **HABITAT** Rich forests, ledges. **RANGE** West of coastal plain.

BLOODROOT
Sanguinaria canadensis
POPPY FAMILY

6″ when blooming; taller later. Single 1½″ flower per stalk, with 8–10 white petals around golden center. Stems underground; have red juice. Single leaf deeply lobed, toothed, pale grayish or bluish; often embraces flower stalk. **BLOOMS** Apr.–May. **HABITAT** Rich forests.

MONEYWORT
Lysimachia nummularia
PRIMROSE FAMILY

L variable. Creeping, mat-forming. Flowers 1″, yellow, usu. 5-petaled; on long stalks in pairs at leaf axils. Leaves ovate, opposite. Introduced from Europe; escaped. **BLOOMS** June–Aug. **HABITAT** Moist soils, yards.

WHORLED LOOSESTRIFE
Lysimachia quadrifolia
PRIMROSE FAMILY

20″. Leaves and flowers in whorls of 4–5. Flowers ½″, with 5 yellow petals that are dark red at bases and encircle protruding style. Leaves lanceolate. **BLOOMS** June–Aug. **HABITAT** Open forests, moist meadows.

SWAMP CANDLES
Lysimachia terrestris
PRIMROSE FAMILY

3′. Erect stem topped with 4″ flower spike. Flowers ½″, yellow, star-like; with 5 petals, each with 2 red dots at base. Leaves lanceolate, opposite. **BLOOMS** June–Aug. **HABITAT** Marshes, watersides.

STARFLOWER
Trientalis borealis
PRIMROSE FAMILY

8″. Flowers ½″, white, with 5–9 petals, stamens with golden anthers; paired on thread-like stalks atop stem. Leaves lanceolate, shiny, in whorls. **BLOOMS** May–June. **HABITAT** Moist forests. **RANGE** NY, NJ and southwest to mtns. of VA, WV.

SPRING BEAUTY
Claytonia virginica
PURSLANE FAMILY

10″. Flowers ¾″, pink or whitish, striped with dark pink, with 5 petals and 5 yellow stamens with pink anthers. Leaves dark green, linear, usu. 1 pair midway up stem. **BLOOMS** Apr.–May. **HABITAT** Moist forests, fields.

BEACH HEATHER
"False Heather"
Hudsonia tomentosa
ROCK-ROSE FAMILY

7″. Semiwoody mats. Flowers tiny, sulfur-yellow, 5-petaled, clustered atop short twigs. Leaves tiny, scale-like, gray, wooly; evergreen. **BLOOMS** May–July. **HABITAT** Seaside dunes, lakeshores. **RANGE** Coastal plain; large lakes of NY and south.

COMMON STRAWBERRY
Fragaria virginiana
ROSE FAMILY

5″. Creeper. Flowers 1″, white with 5 petals; on stems not taller than leaves. Leaves long-stalked, compound, with 3 toothed ovate leaflets. Fruit red, round, juicy, edible; ripe July–Aug. **BLOOMS** May–July. **HABITAT** Fields, woodland edges.

WHITE AVENS
Geum canadense
ROSE FAMILY

24″. Flowers ½″, white, with 5 petals. Basal leaves and middle stem leaves divided into 3–5 oblong, toothed leaflets; upper leaves elliptical, toothed. **BLOOMS** May–June. **HABITAT** Dry or moist forests.

COMMON CINQUEFOIL
Potentilla simplex
ROSE FAMILY

12". Creeper. Flowers ½", yellow, on long erect stems from leaf axils. Leaves palmately compound with 5 oblanceolate, toothed leaflets. **BLOOMS** April–June. **HABITAT** Dry or moist fields, open forests.

CANADIAN BURNET
Sanguisorba canadensis
ROSE FAMILY

4'. Flowers tiny, white, lack true petals; sepals petal-like, shorter than long white stamens; giving dense slender 6" flower spike a fringed appearance. Leaves toothed, pinnately compound with 7–15 leaflets. **BLOOMS** July–Sept. **HABITAT** Marshes, wet meadows. **RANGE** NY, NJ, PA, and scattered south to mtns. of VA, WV.

MEADOWSWEET
Spiraea latifolia
ROSE FAMILY

4'. Thicket-forming woody shrub. Flowers tiny, white or pale pink, fuzzy, with many long stamens; clustered into pyramidal spires atop reddish twigs. Leaves narrowly ovate, coarsely toothed, pale below. **BLOOMS** June–Sept. **HABITAT** Moist fields, marshes. **RANGE** NY, NJ, e PA and south to mtns. of WV, VA.

COMMON ST.-JOHN'S-WORT
Hypericum perforatum
ST.-JOHN'S-WORT FAMILY

20". Flowers 1", bright yellow, have 5 petals with black-dotted edges and many stamens; in broad branched clusters. Leaves ovate, with tiny translucent dots. **BLOOMS** June–Aug. **HABITAT** Roadsides, waste areas.

MARSH ST.-JOHN'S-WORT
Triadenum virginicum
ST.-JOHN'S-WORT FAMILY

24". Flowers ½", pink, in small clusters at ends of purplish stems. Leaves oblong, rounded, opposite, dotted with oily glands. **BLOOMS** July–Aug. **HABITAT** Bogs, marshes, wet shores. **RANGE** NY, NJ, e PA to e piedmont and n mtns. of VA.

EARLY SAXIFRAGE
Saxifraga virginiensis
SAXIFRAGE FAMILY

6". Flowers ¼", white, tubular with 5 petals; in branched clusters atop stems. Stems hairy, leafless; rising from basal rosette of toothed, ovate leaves. One of the earliest blooming spring wildflowers. **BLOOMS** March–May. **HABITAT** Open forests, rocky ledges.

EASTERN FOAMFLOWER
Tiarella cordifolia
SAXIFRAGE FAMILY
12″. Flowers ¼″, white, 5 petals with long extended stamens; in elongated cluster. Leaves heart-shaped, palmately 5–7 lobed, toothed, hairy. **BLOOMS** April–June. **HABITAT** Shade of rich forests.

HUMMOCK SEDGE
Carex stricta
SEDGE FAMILY
24″. Forms gumdrop-shaped, tan hummocks. Flowers in 2–6 narrow, 2″ spikes atop stems, above leaves. Stems 3-sided, rough. Leaves 12″; sheaths have net-like fibers below. Can occur in large stands. **BLOOMS** July–Sept. **HABITAT** Freshwater marshes, open wetlands.

MARSH BULRUSH
Scirpus cyperinus
SEDGE FAMILY
5′. Erect stalks in clumps. Flowers in tiny, clustered, wooly spikelets in open rounded panicles atop stems. Leaves 30″, narrow, rough-edged. **BLOOMS** Aug.–Oct. **HABITAT** Marshes, bogs, wet meadows.

PURPLE GERARDIA
Agalinis purpurea
SNAPDRAGON FAMILY
20″. Flowers 1″, pink-purple, bell-shaped with 5 irregular lobes; paired in leaf axils. Leaves linear, rough, opposite. **BLOOMS** Aug.–Sept. **HABITAT** Moist clearings, sandy bogs. **RANGE** Coastal plain of NY and south through piedmont of PA to VA, WV.

WHITE TURTLEHEAD
Chelone glabra
SNAPDRAGON FAMILY

24″. Flowers 1″, white to light pink, 2-lipped, with hooded upper lip; in clusters atop stems. Leaves lanceolate, sharp-toothed, opposite. **BLOOMS** Aug.–Oct. **HABITAT** Moist clearings, streamsides.

BLUE TOADFLAX
Linaria canadensis
SNAPDRAGON FAMILY

24″. Flowers ½″, light blue-violet, with 2 lobed lips, lower one has white-centered hump, thin spur; along slender stem. Leaves linear; basal ones on trailing stems in rosette. **BLOOMS** May–Sept. **HABITAT** Sandy fields, rocky areas.

HAIRY BEARDTONGUE
Penstemon hirsutus
SNAPDRAGON FAMILY

24″. Flowers 1″, pink to violet, trumpet-shaped, 2-lipped; lower lip hairy, often yellow; in few-flowered, stalked clusters atop stems. Stems hairy. Leaves lanceolate, opposite. **BLOOMS** May–July. **HABITAT** Dry forests, fields. **RANGE** NY, NJ, PA and south to ne VA.

WOOD BETONY
"Lousewort"
Pedicularis canadensis
SNAPDRAGON FAMILY

10″. Flowers ¾″, yellow to red, tubular, 2-lipped, with hooded upper lip arching over 3-lobed lower lip; on dense spikes atop stems. Leaves lanceolate, fern-like, deeply toothed, hairy; in basal rosette. **BLOOMS** Apr.–June. **HABITAT** Open forests, fields.

COMMON MULLEIN
Verbascum thapsus
SNAPDRAGON FAMILY

7′. Stem and leaves wooly. Flowers 1″, yellow, 5-petaled; in long, tightly packed, spike-like cluster. Basal leaves very large, thick, oblong; form rosette. Introduced from Europe. **BLOOMS** June–Sept. **HABITAT** Roadsides, disturbed areas.

COMMON SPEEDWELL
Veronica officinalis
SNAPDRAGON FAMILY

8". Prostrate, mat-forming. Flowers tiny, pale lavender or blue, with 4–5 roundish petals; clustered in erect spikes from leaf axils. Leaves ovate, toothed, downy, opposite. Introduced from Europe. **BLOOMS** May–July. **HABITAT** Dry fields, lawns, open forests.

COMMON MONKEYFLOWER
"Square-stemmed Monkeyflower"
Mimulus ringens
SNAPDRAGON FAMILY

30". Flowers 1", blue-purple, with 2 lobed lips, lower one larger, yellow-based; paired on stalks. Stems 4-sided. Leaves oblong to lanceolate, toothed, opposite, clasping. **BLOOMS** July–Aug. **HABITAT** Watersides, moist meadows.

BUTTER-AND-EGGS
Linaria vulgaris
SNAPDRAGON FAMILY

24". Flowers 1", pale yellow, with 2 lobed lips, lower one has orange "yolk" (hump) and long spur; in terminal clusters. Leaves grayish, linear. Introduced from Europe. **BLOOMS** June–Sept. **HABITAT** Fields, roadsides, disturbed areas.

CULVER'S ROOT
Veronicastrum virginica
SNAPDRAGON FAMILY

5'. Flowers tiny, white, tubular; many in long slender racemes. Leaves ovate-lanceolate, toothed; upper ones whorled in groups of 5–7, lower ones opposite. **BLOOMS** June–Aug. **HABITAT** Forests, meadows. **RANGE** Entire region, west of coastal plain.

ASIATIC DAYFLOWER
Commelina communis
SPIDERWORT FAMILY

30″. Colony-forming creeper; reclining stems have upright leafy branches, each topped with 1 flower protruding from enfolding leaf. Flowers 1″, with 2 rounded, deep blue petals above 1 smaller white petal; 6 protruding stamens with yellow anthers. Leaves fleshy, lanceolate, sheathing. Introduced from Asia. **BLOOMS** July–Sept. **HABITAT** Watersides, forests, waste areas.

WOODS STONECROP
"Wild Stonecrop"
Sedum ternatum
STONECROP FAMILY

6″. Creeper. Flowers tiny, white, star-shaped; on upright, usu. 3-branched, curved stalks. Leaves oblanceolate, light green, fleshy, in whorls of 3. **BLOOMS** May–June. **HABITAT** Rocks, moist woodland soils.

ROUNDLEAF SUNDEW
Drosera rotundifolia
SUNDEW FAMILY

8″. Leafless stalk bears elongated, 1-sided, curved cluster of tiny white to pink-tinged flowers. Leaves round, reddish, in basal rosette; covered with sticky hairs that trap insects, which plant then digests. **BLOOMS** June–Aug. **HABITAT** Bogs, swamps, seeps.

TEASEL
Dipsacus fullonum ssp. *sylvestris*
TEASEL FAMILY

5′. Flowers tiny, lavender, in spiny, egg-shaped, thistle-like, 3″ clusters with long spiny bracts surrounding bases. Leaves lanceolate, toothed, opposite, upper ones fused at bases around stems. **BLOOMS** July–Sept. **HABITAT** Meadows, disturbed areas.

ORANGE JEWELWEED
"Spotted Touch-me-not"
Impatiens capensis
TOUCH-ME-NOT FAMILY

6′. Flowers 1″, irregular, golden orange with reddish-brown splotches; extend backward into spurred sacs; dangle from succulent, translucent stems. Leaves ovate, pale below. Fruit a swollen capsule; bursts at touch when ripe. **BLOOMS** July–Sept. **HABITAT** Shady marshes, moist forests. **Yellow Jewelweed** (*I. pallida*) has pale yellow flowers.

BLUE VERVAIN
Verbena hastata
VERBENA FAMILY
6'. Branching, 4-sided stems bear candelabra-like groups of pointed spikes of tiny, blue-violet flowers. Leaves lanceolate, toothed. Flowers bloom a few at a time. **BLOOMS** July–Aug. **HABITAT** Watersides, moist fields, meadows.

SWEET WHITE VIOLET
Viola blanda
VIOLET FAMILY

4'. Flowers ½", white, with 5 petals, upper 2 twisted, lower 1 purple-veined; fragrant; on separate, reddish stalks from heart-shaped, sharply pointed, shiny leaves. **BLOOMS** May. **HABITAT** Moist, usu. coniferous forests. **RANGE** NY, n NJ, PA and south to mtns. of VA, WV.

COMMON BLUE VIOLET
Viola sororia
VIOLET FAMILY
8". Flowers ½", usu. blue or violet (sometimes white), with 5 petals, lowest petal spurred; on separate stalks from heart-shaped, scalloped leaves. **BLOOMS** Apr.–June. **HABITAT** Moist forests, fields.

BIRD'S-FOOT VIOLET
Viola pedata
VIOLET FAMILY
8". Flowers 1½", deep lilac-violet, lowest petal veined; stamens with orange anthers; larger than most violets. Leaves finely cut; on separate stalks from flowers. **BLOOMS** May–June. **HABITAT** Dry, sandy fields; clearings. **RANGE** Coastal plain of NY, NJ and southwest through piedmont of PA to VA, WV.

COMMON YELLOW VIOLET
Viola pubescens
VIOLET FAMILY

12″. Softly hairy to smooth. Flowers ¾″, yellow, with 5 petals, lower 3 purple-veined; stalked together with heart-shaped, scalloped leaves. **BLOOMS** Apr.–June. **HABITAT** Broadleaf forests.

VIRGINIA WATERLEAF
Hydrophyllum virginianum
WATERLEAF FAMILY

24″. Flowers ½″, white to lavender to blue-violet, urn-shaped with 5 stamens extending beyond 5 petals. Leaves 6″, pinnately compound, with 5–7 toothed, ovate leaflets, often white-spotted. **BLOOMS** May–June. **HABITAT** Moist forests, wet meadows. **RANGE** Entire region west of coastal plain.

YELLOW POND LILIES
"Spatterdocks" "Cow-lilies"
Nuphar species
WATER-LILY FAMILY

Flowers and leaves float on or emerge from water; stand high on long stalks when water level drops. Flowers 2″, yellow, tight balls opening into cup-shape with 6 thick waxy petals and many stamens around cylindrical pistil. Leaves 12″, heart-shaped, wrinkled. Fruit greenish to reddish, urn-shaped. **BLOOMS** May–Sept. **HABITAT** Ponds, lakes, backwaters.

WHITE WATER-LILY
"Fragrant Water-lily"
Nymphaea odorata
WATER-LILY FAMILY

Floats on water. Flowers 5″, white (occ. pinkish), with 20–30 long tapering petals that decrease in size toward center and many yellow stamens. Leaves 8″, round, notched to center, often purple below, with spongy, underwater stalks. **BLOOMS** June–Aug. **HABITAT** Ponds, lakes, backwaters.

YELLOW WOOD SORRELS
Oxalis species
WOOD SORREL FAMILY

10″. Spreading. Flowers ½″, yellow, 5-petaled, in small clusters. Stems hairy, often many-branched. Leaves long-stalked, with 3 clover-like, heart-shaped leaflets. **BLOOMS** May–Sept. **HABITAT** Towns, open and disturbed areas.

Invertebrates

Biologists divide the animal kingdom into two broad groupings—vertebrates, animals with backbones, and invertebrates, those without. While this distinction seems apt, perhaps because we are vertebrates ourselves, it is really one of mere convenience. Vertebrates are but a small subphylum of the animal kingdom, and invertebrates comprise the vast majority of animal life forms that inhabit water, air, and land. Invertebrates have thrived on earth for more than a billion years, with species evolving and disappearing through the eons; they include a fascinating spectrum of phyla with extraordinarily diverse life styles and evolutionary developments. This guide describes selected species from seven phyla found in marine, freshwater, and terrestrial environments:

Phylum Cnidaria	Jellyfishes and sea anemones
Phylum Ctenophora	Comb jellies
Phylum Rhynchocoela	Unsegmented worms
Phylum Annelida	Segmented worms and leeches
Phylum Mollusca	Chitons, gastropods, bivalves, and cephalopods
Phylum Arthropoda	Crustaceans, horseshoe crabs, centipedes, millipedes, arachnids, and insects
Phylum Echinodermata	Sea stars, sea urchins, and sea cucumbers

There are two basic invertebrate body structures. *Radially symmetrical* invertebrates, such as cnidarians and echinoderms, have a circular body plan with a central mouth cavity and a nervous system that encircles the mouth. *Bilateral* invertebrates have virtually identical left and right sides like vertebrates, with paired nerve cords that run along the belly, not the back, and a brain (in species with a head). All invertebrates are cold-blooded, and most become dormant or die when temperatures become too high or low.

In this guide, marine invertebrates are covered first, followed by freshwater and land invertebrates. Many of the groups covered are described in more detail in separate introductions.

Plant or Animal?

Some marine invertebrates, such as sea anemones, are often mistaken for plants, but several key features place them in the animal kingdom. Plant cell walls, made of cellulose, are thick and strong, while those of animals are thin and weak. Plants have no nervous system, and therefore react slowly; almost all animals have a nervous system and can react quickly. Through the process called photosynthesis, most plants manufacture their own food from inorganic raw materials, while animals obtain energy by ingesting and metabolizing plants and/or other animals. Plants grow throughout their lives, while most animals stop growing at maturity (a few types, such as fish and snakes, keep growing but at a very slow rate). Finally, most plants are sedentary, while most animals move about. A sea anemone may be as immobile as a seaweed, but it qualifies as an animal on the basis of the above and other characteristics, such as the nature of its reproductive organs and its developmental pattern.

Marine Invertebrates

Mid-Atlantic marine environments are home to a wide variety of clinging, digging, swimming, and scuttling invertebrates. This text covers representatives of classes from seven invertebrate phyla. Members of other invertebrate marine phyla are generally small or difficult to see.

In the phylum Cnidaria are the gelatinous sea anemones and jellyfishes. All are radially symmetrical and many are quite beautiful, a trait that belies their fierce habits; most possess tentacles armed with stinging cells that ensnare and paralyze animals within their reach. Most Mid-Atlantic species are harmless to humans, although some, like the Lion's Mane, can be extremely dangerous. Comb jellies, of the phylum Ctenophora, are small to minute jellyfish-like animals without stinging organs; they are so transparent that they are almost invisible in the water. Unsegmented worms, of the phylum Rhynchocoela, are generally slender, flattened, and brightly colored. The phylum Annelida, or segmented worms, is divided into four classes. The most conspicuous annelids in Mid-Atlantic waters are the bristle worms of the class Polychaeta. These worms have visible external segments covered with bundles of bristles that aid them in swimming, crawling, or digging; they are found in a wide range of habitats, from intertidal to abyssal depths. The phylum Mollusca, including many of the most familiar marine invertebrates, is discussed on page 186. Species of the phylum Arthropoda usually are identified by their rigid exoskeleton and jointed legs. Of the five marine arthropod classes, we cover two: horseshoe crabs (class Merostomata) and crustaceans (class Crustacea). The horseshoe crabs that ply our inshore waters are members of the ancient genus *Limulus,* which dates back 175 million years; they are crabs in name only, having more in common with spiders. Crustaceans, like barnacles, shrimps, crabs, and lobsters, live primarily in sunlit waters. Their forms are so diverse that their single common characteristic is paired antennae. Crabs and lobsters are discussed on page 191. Animals of the phylum Echinodermata, discussed on page 194, include sea stars, sea urchins, and sea cucumbers.

The following accounts give typical adult lengths or heights, unless otherwise noted. Many species can survive in a wide range of water depths, which are noted; the term *intertidal zone* refers to the area between the high- and low-tide lines.

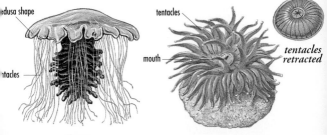

Jellyfish   Anemone, *tentacles out*

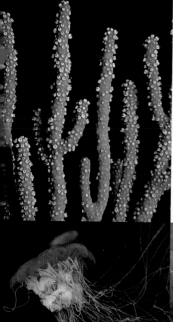

WHIP CORAL
"Sea Whip"
Leptogorgia virgulata
CORAL AND SEA ANEMONE CLASS

2'. Body thin, whip-like, often branched; stems rigid, with horny core; purplish (bays) or yellowish (ocean). Filter-feeds with tiny polyps covering stem. **HABITAT** Shallow water; attaches to piers, rocks. **RANGE** s NJ to e VA, incl. Ches. Bay.

LION'S MANE
Cyanea capillata
JELLYFISH CLASS

W 8". Body a smooth, saucer-shaped, yellowish-orange to reddish-brown bell. 150 long, yellowish tentacles. In Arctic, can grow to 8' wide, with tentacles to 60' long. **CAUTION** Highly toxic; causes severe burns, blisters; can be fatal. **HABITAT** Ocean surface, bays; enters s Ches. Bay Dec.–May.

MOON JELLYFISH
Aurelia aurita
JELLYFISH CLASS

W 8". Body saucer-shaped with 8 shallow marginal lobes; translucent, whitish; fringed with many short white tentacles. Horseshoe-shaped or round gonads near center: yellow, pink, or bluish in adults; white when imm. **CAUTION** Sting causes mild, itchy rash. **HABITAT** Ocean surface, bays; often washes ashore.

SEA NETTLE
Chrysaora quinquecirrha
JELLYFISH CLASS

W 8". Body umbrella-shaped, lobed, covered with tiny warts; pinkish with red stripes (ocean), or milky white (bays); yellowish tentacles to 3'. Bay form smaller. **CAUTION** Mildly toxic; causes rash. **HABITAT** Ocean surface, bays. **SEASON** Year-round; most common Apr.–Oct.

LEIDY'S COMB JELLY
Mnemiopsis leidyi
COMB JELLY PHYLUM

4″. Body oval, translucent, with 2 long lobes and 8 rows of comb-like luminescent ridges. 2 short tentacles between lobes; 4 ribbon-like structures near mouth. **HABITAT** Shallow ocean and brackish water, incl. Ches. Bay north to Baltimore.

MILKY RIBBON WORM
Cerebratulus lacteus
ANOPLA WORM CLASS

3′. Head hard, cylindrical; body flexible, ribbon-like, lacks appendages. Whitish or yellowish pink; breeding male bright red, female browner. Swims; burrows in sand, mud, under rocks. **HABITAT** Shallow ocean water, bays.

CLAM WORM
Nereis virens
POLYCHAETE WORM CLASS

8″. Body tapers toward rear. Iridescent bluish or greenish brown, with red, gold, or white spots; paler below. 200 segments; leaf-like side appendages. Head has 8 tentacles. Swift swimmer; preys on invertebrates, carrion, algae. **HABITAT** Mud, sand, or vegetated ocean bottoms; estuaries.

LUG WORM
Arenicola cristata
POLYCHAETE WORM CLASS

10″. Body elongated, thicker toward front, tapered at both ends; blackish green, with tiny hooks and gill tufts on forward ⅔ of body. Lives in U-shaped burrow; mud pellets visible near flat tube entrance. Feeds by filtering sand for organic matter. **HABITAT** Shallow ocean and brackish water, mudflats.

PLUMED WORM
Diopatra cuprea
POLYCHAETE WORM CLASS

10″. Body elongated; iridescent reddish or brown; 30–40 pairs red plume-like gills behind head; 7 antennae. Lives in leathery tube to 3′ long, with chimney-like entrance; tubes often found washed ashore. **CAUTION** Bites. **HABITAT** Intertidal zone to 270′ deep; mudflats.

Marine Mollusks

Mollusks, of the phylum Mollusca, are amazingly numerous and diverse, with Mid-Atlantic species ranging in size from the microscopic Atom Snail to the deep-water 55-foot Giant Squid. Worldwide, seven classes of mollusks inhabit land, freshwater, and marine environments; four are commonly found in inshore Mid-Atlantic marine waters. Chitons have eight-valved shells held together by a tough outer membrane (called a girdle); they crawl about on rocks and pilings, scraping up algae and microscopic animals. Gastropods, including snails and their relatives, usually have a single calcium carbonate shell, whorled to the right; they feed on marine plants and animals, scraping food with their tiny teeth as they crawl or swim about. Bivalves, which include clams and oysters, have two separate shells called valves, from which protrude two siphons and a muscular foot; they filter-feed on microscopic plant and animal life. Normally, bivalves attach to a hard substrate or burrow into sand, mud, clay, or wood, although some species, such as scallops, can also swim. Cephalopods, the most advanced mollusks, are shell-less, with highly developed eyes and long tentacled arms; they move by swimming and water propulsion and feed by grabbing and eating crabs, fish, and other mollusks.

Gastropods and bivalves can be easily observed at most coastal locations. Chitons are harder to find and must be specially searched for on or under rocks and inside dead whelk shells. Cephalopods are generally found only in subtidal waters. The Mid-Atlantic's inshore molluscan habitats include sand- and mudflats, peat banks, coastal rocks, tidepools, and wooden structures, such as piers, pilings, and crab traps. When exploring, remember to think small—many species measure less than an inch at maturity. Rocky tidepools are home to limpets, periwinkles, dogwinkles, and mussels; shallow flats support moon snails, whelks, scallops, and oysters.

Shell-collecting is a popular and enjoyable hobby. Very high tides and storm waves often bring up harder to find shells of deepwater species, so plan your trips accordingly. Recreational shellfishing is also popular but more tightly regulated—most towns and counties in the Mid-Atlantic require a license. Environmental and seasonal conditions sometimes make local populations unsafe to eat, so always check with authorities before harvesting.

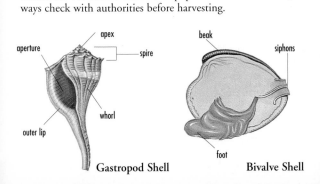

Gastropod Shell   **Bivalve Shell**

COMMON EASTERN CHITON
"Bee Chiton"
Chaetopleura apiculata
CHITON CLASS

¾". Body flattened, oval; 8 leathery ridged shells whitish, gray, or brownish; surrounding girdle narrow, mottled brown and cream. Clings to rocks with muscular foot. **HABITAT** Low-tide line to 90′ deep; on rocks, shells, hard surfaces, and in rock crevices.

MARSH PERIWINKLE
Littorina irrorata
GASTROPOD CLASS

1". Shell conical, thick, with pointed apex, 4–5 whorls. Grayish white with spiraling streaks of reddish brown. Inner lip yellow-orange; outer lip thick, fairly sharp, whitish with black dots. **HABITAT** Clings to stems of saltmarsh grasses at low tide. **RANGE** NJ and south.

COMMON PERIWINKLE
Littorina littorea
GASTROPOD CLASS

1". Shell thick, conical, with blunt apex, 6–7 whorls. Adult smooth, young finely ridged. Grayish to black, with thick, black outer lip, white inner lip. Feeds on seaweeds, algae. Abundant. Edible. **HABITAT** Intertidal zone; on rocks, sand.

COMMON SLIPPER SNAIL
Crepidula fornicata
GASTROPOD CLASS

1½". Shell oval, curved to fit attachment site; apex turned to one side. Mottled white and brown. Flat white shelf below partially covers opening. Rarely moves. **HABITAT** Intertidal zone to 40′ deep; attaches to hard objects.

SALT-MARSH SNAIL
Melampus bidentatus
GASTROPOD CLASS

½". Shell oval, thin, smooth, with low cone-shaped spire. Pale yellow or whitish, sometimes with brown bands or streaks. Opening long, narrow; inner lip white. Glides over mud; climbs grasses. Breathes with lungs. **HABITAT** Above low-tide line; salt marshes, coasts.

NORTHERN MOON SNAIL
Lunatia heros
GASTROPOD CLASS

3″. Shell nearly round, with low spire; 5 convex whorls. Whitish gray-brown; inside white. Opening large, oval, sometimes with tan or purple spots. Large foot leaves wide trail; when feeding, foot envelopes clam or other mollusk, while snail drills into shell. HABITAT Low-tide line to 1,200′ deep; mud, sand bottoms.

ATLANTIC OYSTER DRILL
Urosalpinx cinerea
GASTROPOD CLASS

1″. Shell spindle-shaped; 5–6 whorls with 9–12 vertical folds; spire high. Gray or pale yellow, sometimes with brown bands; inside purple. Opening flared, wide, oval. Feeds on young oysters by drilling hole into shell and sucking out meat. HABITAT Intertidal zone to 50′ deep; rocks, pilings, oyster beds; brackish water.

KNOBBED WHELK
Busycon carica
GASTROPOD CLASS

7″. Shell pear-shaped, with knobbed whorls; low conical spire; long spout-like canal. Yellowish gray. Raids lobster and crab traps. Egg cases resemble coins on a string; often found on beaches. Edible. HABITAT Intertidal zone to 15′ deep; sandy bottoms.

MOTTLED DOG WHELK
Nassarius vibex
GASTROPOD CLASS

½″. Shell thick, spindle-shaped, with pointed apex, high spire; surface rough, corrugated. Grayish with darker bands. Opening oval; lips thick. Feeds on dead fish and by filtering organic particles from mud or sand. HABITAT Below low-tide line in shallow water; salt marshes, bays.

RIBBED MUSSEL
Geukensia (Ischadium) demissa
BIVALVE CLASS

3″. Shell thin, elongated, fan-shaped, glossy. Many strong radial ribs. Yellowish brown (imm.) to brownish black (adult). Burrows halfway into mud or peat; fastens to pilings. Can tolerate high water temperatures and high salinities. HABITAT Intertidal zone; salt marshes, bays.

BLUE MUSSEL
"Edible Mussel"
Mytilus edulis
BIVALVE CLASS

3". Shell thin, shiny; front beaked; rear rounded or fan-shaped. Blue-black to black; inside bluish white. Forms large colonies; attaches to objects using strong, hair-like threads called "byssus." Edible. **HABITAT** Intertidal zone; rocks, pilings, hard objects.

ATLANTIC BAY SCALLOP
"Blue-eyed Scallop"
Argopecten (Aequipecten) irradians
BIVALVE CLASS

2½". Shell nearly round, with straight edge at hinge; 17–21 radiating ribs. Gray, brown, or reddish; interspaces paler. Dozens of blue eyes along margin. Swims. Edible. In MD, VA: ribs squared, right valve white. **HABITAT** Low-tide line to 60' deep; shallow bays, eelgrass beds.

COMMON JINGLE SHELL
Anomia simplex
BIVALVE CLASS

1½". Shell thin, roundish, smooth. Translucent gold, silver, or orange. Lower shell fragile; upper shell rounder, stouter. Attachment muscle uses hole on lower shell. Several strung shells will jingle in breeze. **HABITAT** Low-tide line to 30' deep; on rocks, shells, wood.

EASTERN OYSTER
Crassostrea virginica
BIVALVE CLASS

6". Shell thick, irregularly oval or elongated, with coarse ridges; upper shell flattened, lower deeper. Grayish white. Free-swimming larvae settle on hard surfaces. Edible. **HABITAT** Intertidal zone to 40' deep; brackish bays, estuaries; attaches to solid objects.

NORTHERN QUAHOG
Mercenaria mercenaria
BIVALVE CLASS

4". Shell thick, almost round, raised, with many fine concentric lines. Grayish or buffy; inside stained purple. Edible; smallest are called cherrystones, midsize are called littlenecks, largest used in chowder. **HABITAT** Intertidal zone to 50' deep; burrows in sand, mud.

COMMON RAZOR CLAM
Ensis directus
BIVALVE CLASS

7". Shell long, thin, flattish; sharp edges, square ends; resembles a straight-edged razor. White, with yellowish-brown "skin." Strong foot lets animal descend rapidly into burrow or sand. Edible. **HABITAT** Sandy intertidal flats, shallow water.

ATLANTIC SURF CLAM
Spisula solidissima
BIVALVE CLASS

7". Shell thick, rounded triangle. Yellowish white, with dark brown "skin." Burrows into sand. Dropped on hard surfaces by gulls to break open. Edible. Important commercially. **HABITAT** Low-tide line to 100' deep; sand, mud, gravel bottoms.

SOFT-SHELLED CLAM
"Steamer Clam"
Mya arenaria
BIVALVE CLASS

4". Shell thin, oval, rounded in front; gap between valves. Whitish with thin grayish "skin." Burrows in sand; at low tides, siphons shoot up jets of water when disturbed. Edible; important commercially. **HABITAT** Intertidal zone to 30' deep; mud, sand, brackish water.

ATLANTIC LONG-FINNED SQUID
Loligo pealei
CEPHALOPOD CLASS

20". Shell-less; body cylindrical, tapers toward rear; milky white, with tiny reddish-purple spots. Head has 2 large eyes, 8 arms ½ body length, 2 tentacles ⅔ body length. Triangular fin on each side at rear. Active at night. Edible. **HABITAT** Ocean surface to 600' deep.

COMMON ATLANTIC OCTOPUS
Octopus vulgaris
CEPHALOPOD CLASS

6'. Body globe-shaped, smooth; color changeable: pink, brown, or gray. 8 thick arms with suckers. Head broad with 2 high eyes; tubular siphon below; tough, parrot-like beak. Hides by day in crevices and under rocks. **HABITAT** Shallow rocky areas.

NORTHERN ROCK BARNACLE
Balanus balanoides
CRUSTACEAN CLASS

¾″. Shell conical; elongated when crowded in colonies; whitish. 4 plates protect 6 pairs of retractable, feathery feeding appendages. **CAUTION** Plates extremely sharp. **HABITAT** Shallow ocean water; on rocks, pilings, boats.

HORNED KRILL SHRIMP
Meganyctiphanes norvegica
CRUSTACEAN CLASS

1″. Exoskeleton transparent; stomach contents visible. 4 antennae; 2 black eyes; 10 forked legs; flat "tail fan." Occurs in vast schools, sometimes making water appear pink. **HABITAT** Open ocean to 1,000′ deep.

SAND SHRIMP
Crangon septemspinosa
CRUSTACEAN CLASS

2″. Exoskeleton thin, flattened on top, transparent; pale green, gray, or buff; with many irregular blackish spots. Beak short. 1st pair of legs heavy, with backward-pointing claws; 2nd, 3rd slender. "Tail fan" often blackish. **HABITAT** Eelgrass, tidepools, sand to 300′ deep.

ATLANTIC HORSESHOE CRAB
Limulus polyphemus
HORSESHOE CRAB CLASS

Female 20″; male 15″. Not a true crab. Carapace horseshoe-shaped, turtle-like, greenish brown; abdomen triangular with spiny edges; tail long, spiked; eyes bulbous, unstalked. Mouth surrounded by 5 pairs of walking legs; pincers in front. In spring, lays eggs on beach at high tide. **HABITAT** Mud, sand bottoms to 75′ deep; beaches. **RANGE** Throughout; in May, abundant in Delaware Bay.

Crabs and Lobsters

Crabs and lobsters, of the order Decapoda, fall into two categories: short-tailed decapods, or true crabs, and long-tailed decapods. As the name implies, all have ten legs. True crabs have a large cephalothorax, or forebody, and a small abdomen tucked beneath their shells. They can move well in all directions but usually walk sideways. Some, such as Blue Crabs and Lady Crabs, have paddle-like hindlegs for swimming. Others, such as male fiddler crabs, have a greatly enlarged pincer. Most species are scavengers, although some feed on living animals; fiddlers are generally plant-eaters. Long-tailed decapods, such as lobsters and hermit crabs, are named for their elongated abdomens, or "tails." Hermit crabs protect their soft abdomens by hiding in empty gastropod shells. They are fascinating to observe as they carry their homes about, switching shells as they grow or as their domestic tastes change. Take care when handling crabs and lobsters; some are aggressive, and all can pinch. Crab measurements refer to the carapace—the shell part that extends over the head and thorax, but not the abdomen.

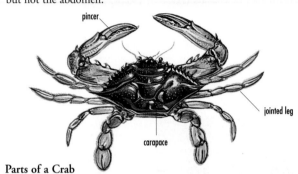

Parts of a Crab

NORTHERN LOBSTER
Homarus americanus
CRUSTACEAN CLASS

L 12–36″. Head and thorax cylindrical, with large pincers; tail (abdomen) somewhat flattened. Greenish brown above, sometimes orangish or blue, paler below; appendages and pointed beak red-tipped. One pair of antennae short, one very long; 2 stalked eyes. 3 pairs of pincers; 1st pair greatly enlarged, unequal: one (usu. left) heavier, blunt, with rounded teeth, used as crusher to open hard objects like snails or clams; other (usu. right) less heavy, sharper, more pointed, used as cutter. Sheds exoskeleton yearly. A few live to 100 years and weigh up to 45 lb.; avg. wt. 1–3 lb. Edible. **HABITAT** 10–2,000′ deep; rocky, sandy bottoms. **RANGE** Throughout; most common off Long Is. and NJ; in winter: imm. south to VA.

ATLANTIC MOLE CRAB
Emerita talpoida
CRUSTACEAN CLASS

L 1″. Carapace oval, convex; sandy yellow to white. Abdomen and legs tightly clasped below carapace. 4 antennae; 1 pair feathery, strains water of breaking waves for plankton. Burrows in sand. **HABITAT** Intertidal zone; open, sandy, wave-swept beaches.

COMMON SPIDER CRAB
Libinia emarginata
CRUSTACEAN CLASS

L 3½″. Carapace round, spiny, with tapering beak; brown or dull yellow. Row of spines down back. Legs round; male's pincer legs to 6″ long. Often covered with algae. **HABITAT** Intertidal zone to 400′ deep; bays, ocean bottoms.

LONG-CLAWED HERMIT CRAB
Pagurus longicarpus
CRUSTACEAN CLASS

L ½″. Lives in gastropod shell. Body oblong, with long soft abdomen; gray, green, or buff. Right pincer larger than left; 5th pair of walking legs turned up. **HABITAT** Beaches and ocean bottoms to 150′ deep.

LADY CRAB
Ovalipes ocellatus
CRUSTACEAN CLASS

W 2¼″. Carapace fan-shaped, slightly wider than long; light gray with purple spots. Pincers large, sharp; 5th pair of legs paddle-like. Aggressive. **HABITAT** Sand, mud, rock bottoms to 150′ deep. **RANGE** Summer: coast, s Ches. Bay; winter: deeper waters.

BLUE CRAB
Callinectes (Cancer) sapidus
CRUSTACEAN CLASS

W 6″. Carapace, smooth, bluish green. Long spine at sides; 8 short red spines along front. Pincers blue (male) or red (female); legs blue. Edible; important commercially. **HABITAT** Summer: shores, estuaries, occ. fresh water; winter: moves deeper, to 120′.

GREEN CRAB
Carcinus maenas
CRUSTACEAN CLASS

W 2″. Carapace fan-shaped; above, green with blackish mottling; below, male and imm. yellow or greenish, female orange. Pincers large; 5th pair of legs pointed. Introduced from Europe. **HABITAT** Salt marshes, tidepools, rocks, jetties. **RANGE** NY, NJ.

ATLANTIC ROCK CRAB
Cancer irroratus
CRUSTACEAN CLASS
W 4½". Carapace oval; yellow, heavily red-spotted; front edge has rounded bumps, grooves. Pincers short, stout, bent downward. Legs short, hairy at edges. Steals bait from lobster traps. Edible. **HABITAT** Intertidal zone to 2,600' deep; rocks, gravel.

SAND FIDDLER
Uca pugilator
CRUSTACEAN CLASS
W ¾". Carapace squarish; male purplish with blackish markings; female darker, more subdued. 1 male pincer greatly enlarged. Lives in 2' burrow; plugs entrance with mud at high tide or when threatened. **HABITAT** Salt marshes, mudflats, calm beaches.

Echinoderms

In the Mid-Atlantic, the phylum Echinodermata is represented by sea stars, sea urchins, and sea cucumbers. *Echinoderm* means "spiny skin," and all species in this phylum are covered with spines or bumps of varying lengths. They are radially symmetrical and possess a unique water vascular system consisting of internal canals that pump fluids through the body. These canals end on the undersurface in tube feet, slender appendages that expand and contract to allow the animal to move and direct food to its centralized mouth (on the head in sea cucumbers). Sea stars, named for their star-like shape, have varying numbers of arms radiating from a central disk; they feed mainly on mollusks and other echinoderms. Sea urchins, including sand dollars, feed on plankton, algae, and tiny organic particles in sand. The spines of the elongated sea cucumbers are actually embedded in the skin, which is outwardly smooth; these animals feed almost exclusively on plankton. Measurements in the accounts are of diameters, including arms and spines, unless otherwise noted.

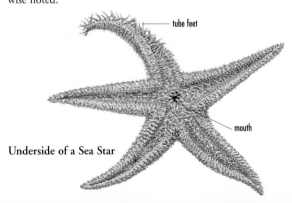

Underside of a Sea Star

COMMON SEA STAR
Asterias forbesi
SEA STAR CLASS

7″. Disk large; 5 long, blunt-tipped arms. Tan, brown, orange, olive, or pink. Covered with short blunt spines. Feeds chiefly on bivalves; pulls open shell, then everts stomach between valves, secreting juices that kill prey. **HABITAT** Low-tide line to 160′ deep; in oceans and bays; on rock, gravel, sand bottoms.

PURPLE SEA URCHIN
Arbacia punctulata
SEA URCHIN CLASS

1½″. Body round; blackish. Covered with thick, grooved, blunt-tipped, purplish-brown or reddish-gray spines to 1″ long. Feeds on mollusks, algae, dead animals. **HABITAT** Intertidal zone to 750′ deep; rock, shell, sea-grass bottoms.

GREEN SEA URCHIN
Strongylocentrotus droebachiensis
SEA URCHIN CLASS

3″. Body round, cactus-like, with hundreds of thin, sharp 1″ greenish spines. Spineless ball-shaped brownish-green bodies wash ashore. Roe edible. **CAUTION** Painful if stepped on. **HABITAT** Rocky shores, kelp beds, bays to 3,800′ deep. **RANGE** NY, NJ.

COMMON SAND DOLLAR
Echinarachnius parma
SEA URCHIN CLASS

3″. Body round, flat, disk-like, with tiny dull spines. Purplish brown; white when washed ashore. 5 radial furrows branch from mouth on underside. **HABITAT** Low-tide line to 5,000′ deep; sand, mud bottoms. **RANGE** NY and south to e shore of VA.

HAIRY SEA CUCUMBER
Thyone (Sclerodactyla) briareus
SEA CUCUMBER CLASS

4″. Body cucumber-shaped; brown, black, green, or purple; covered with hair-like tube feet. 10 bushy tentacles surround mouth. Buries itself in sand, with both ends exposed. **HABITAT** Low-tide line to 20′ deep; mud and sand bottoms.

Freshwater and Land Invertebrates

Tens of thousands of invertebrate species thrive in Mid-Atlantic freshwater and terrestrial environments. Ponds and meadows are home to literally millions of invertebrates per acre, and even sheer rock faces and acidic bogs support a varied assortment. The most commonly seen Mid-Atlantic invertebrates belong to three phyla.

Land and freshwater members of the phylum Mollusca are the generally small, drab species of slugs, snails, and clams. They are both aquatic, living amid vegetation or in bottom sediment, and terrestrial, found in leaf litter and under leaves, boards, and rocks. Some of these terrestrial species, such as slugs, are among our most annoying garden pests. The phylum Annelida includes leeches and earthworms. There are terrestrial leeches in parts of the world, but in the Mid-Atlantic leeches occur only in certain freshwater environments. They are so quick to sense the presence of a warm body that naturalists need no sophisticated equipment to find them—they merely wade into the water and wait! Earthworms can occur at an average of 1,000 pounds per acre; they help fertilize and oxygenate soil by pulling vegetation underground. The phylum Arthropoda comprises the largest number of freshwater and land invertebrates, with five classes sampled here: crustaceans, millipedes, centipedes, arachnids, and insects. Crustaceans include the freshwater crayfishes and the terrestrial pillbugs and sowbugs, commonly found under rocks and rotting logs. Terrestrial millipedes and centipedes look like worms with legs—two pairs per segment for vegetarian millipedes and one pair per segment for predatory centipedes. Arachnids—spiders, daddy-long-legs (harvestmen), and ticks—are discussed on page 198. Insects, introduced on page 201, are comprised of many well-known invertebrate orders, including dragonflies, grasshoppers, beetles, flies, butterflies, and ants, wasps, and bees (see their separate introductions within the section).

FRESHWATER LEECH
Macrobdella decora
LEECH CLASS
2¼″. Body broad, flattened. Brownish green, with black and red spots above. Good swimmer; undulates in water. Front and rear suckers attach to fish, frogs, turtles, mammals; front sucker draws blood. **HABITAT** Lakes, marshes, slow rivers.

EARTHWORMS
"Night Crawlers"
Lumbricus and other genera
EARTHWORM CLASS
To 8″. Body soft, cylindrical, with dozens of segments; purplish orange. Aerates damp soil; feeds on decaying organic matter. Common on surface after heavy rains. **HABITAT** In soil of woods, meadows, lawns.

LEOPARD SLUG
"Garden Slug"
Limax maximus
GASTROPOD CLASS

4". A shell-less mollusk. Gray with blackish spots. Head has 2 long, 2 short tentacles. A garden pest; feeds on flowers, leaves, berries. Chiefly nocturnal but active on rainy days. **HABITAT** Gardens, woods.

ZEBRA MUSSEL
Dreissena polymorpha
BIVALVE CLASS

2". Shell triangular. Pale gray or tan, with brown wavy stripes. Introduced to Great Lakes from Europe in 1988. Crowds out native freshwater mollusks; damages water distribution systems. **HABITAT** Lakes, rivers. **RANGE** n NY; spreading south.

BURROWING CRAYFISH
Cambarus diogenes
CRUSTACEAN CLASS

5". Resembles a lobster, but with smaller pincers. Olive-brown, tinged with bright orange-red. Constructs burrow with chimney-like entrance. Nocturnal. **HABITAT** Streams, ponds, bays. **RANGE** PA to VA, incl. n Ches. Bay.

PILLBUGS/SOWBUGS
"Woodlice"
Armadillidium and *Porcellia* species
CRUSTACEAN CLASS

½". Body convex, oval, with black, gray, or brown shrimp-like plates, 7 pairs short legs, 2 short antennae. Feeds on fungi, decaying plant matter. Pillbugs roll into a ball when disturbed. **HABITAT** Under rocks, logs, leaves; in damp basements.

MILLIPEDES
Spirobolus and other genera
MILLIPEDE CLASS

2½". Body segmented, cylindrical, blackish; 30–200 legs; rounded anterior; short antennae. Slow-moving; rolls into spiral ball when threatened, releasing foul-smelling secretion to repel predators. **HABITAT** Meadows, woods.

CENTIPEDES
Scolopendra and other genera
CENTIPEDE CLASS

3". Body segmented, flattened, black or reddish brown. 24–40 legs; long antennae; pincer-like rear appendages. Fast-moving, aggressive; venom paralyzes insects, spiders. **CAUTION** Bites. **HABITAT** Woods; under bark, logs, rocks.

Spiders and Kin

The class Arachnida includes spiders, harvestmen, ticks, and chiggers. These generally dreaded invertebrates are much maligned; in fact, most species are harmless to humans, many are beneficial to the environment, and all have habits worthy of the naturalist's attention.

Spiders have two body parts and eight legs. Most also have eight simple eyes, the arrangement of which differs from family to family. On jumping spiders, which hunt without benefit of a web, two eyes are tremendously enlarged, a trait that enables them to accurately judge distances to their prey. All spiders extrude three or four types of silk from spinnerets on their undersides: one to

8 eyes

Head of spider

make cocoons for their eggs; another, much finer, for lowering themselves; sturdy strands to construct radial web lines; and finally, the sticky silk they use to entrap prey.

Spiders hunt by stalking, ambushing, or ensnaring their victims, then subduing or killing them with a poisonous bite. Their venom acts as a powerful digestive fluid, which liquefies their prey so they can suck it up. Most spiders are venomous, but most are entirely harmless to humans, and indeed retreat quickly when we arrive on the scene. Spiders are not parasitic on humans or domesticated animals, nor do they transmit any diseases to humans. They can be incredibly abundant, especially in meadows, where hundreds of thousands can inhabit a single acre. Their hearty appetites help to control the insect population.

In addition to spiders, there are many other arachnids among us. Daddy-long-legs, also called harvestmen, are nonvenomous and have one body part and very long, fragile legs. They are normally solitary, but in winter they may huddle together in masses. Ticks and chiggers are parasites with little foreclaws that grasp on to passing animals, including humans. To feed, they bury their heads under the skin and draw blood. Some tick species are carriers of serious diseases, including Lyme disease (see box, page 200).

The accounts below give typical lengths of females, not including legs; the rarely seen males are often much smaller.

BLACK WIDOW SPIDER
Latrodectus mactans
ARACHNID CLASS

⅜". Body black, glossy. Female abdomen bulbous, with red hourglass pattern below; male much smaller, with red and white sides. Builds irregular web with funnel-like exit. **CAUTION** Very poisonous (mainly female bites). **HABITAT** Woodpiles, debris, crawl spaces. **SEASON** Mar.–Nov.

AMERICAN HOUSE SPIDER
Achaearanea tepidariorum
ARACHNID CLASS

¼". Body pale brown; large abdomen mottled black and gray on sides. Male's legs orange; female's banded black and yellow. Builds irregular web in corners of ceilings and windows. **HABITAT** Buildings. **SEASON** Year-round.

BLACK-AND-YELLOW GARDEN SPIDER
Argiope aurantia
ARACHNID CLASS

1". Head/thorax has silvery hair. Abdomen egg-shaped; black with yellowish markings. Legs banded yellow or reddish and black. Web with thick zigzag pattern in center. **HABITAT** Gardens, meadows. **SEASON** Summer–fall.

CAROLINA WOLF SPIDER
Lycosa carolinensis
ARACHNID CLASS

1¼". Body as long as wide; gray-brown, sometimes with central abdominal stripe; well camouflaged. Legs long, hairy. Eyes large. Does not spin web; hunts at night in leaves, rocks, grass; female carries egg sac. **HABITAT** Meadows, woods. **SEASON** May–Sept.

GOLDENROD CRAB SPIDER
Misumena vatia
ARACHNID CLASS

⅜". Female yellow or white; abdomen with red streaks. Male head/thorax dark reddish brown with two white spots; abdomen white, with 2 red streaks. Legs thick, pale. Waits in goldenrods, daisies, snatching insects. **HABITAT** Gardens, meadows. **SEASON** June–Oct.

DARING JUMPING SPIDER
Phidippus audax
ARACHNID CLASS

½". Like a tiny tarantula. Black, hairy; abdomen has whitish crossband, whitish spots. Legs short, stout. Large eyes provide excellent vision. Makes spectacular leaps, pouncing on prey. **HABITAT** Tree trunks, fallen limbs, leaf litter, windowsills. **SEASON** Apr.–Oct.

SIX-SPOTTED FISHING SPIDER
Dolomedes triton
ARACHNID CLASS

¾". Body dark brown, with silvery white stripes along edges, white-spotted abdomen; below, 6 black spots between leg bases. Legs very long. Feeds on insects, sometimes fish or tadpoles. **HABITAT** Sluggish streams, pond edges. **SEASON** Apr.–Oct.

DADDY-LONG-LEGS
Leiobunum and other genera
ARACHNID CLASS
⅜". Head/thorax and abdomen joined in single body; yellowish brown, with dark stripes. Legs long, fragile, arching; 2nd pair longest, used like antennae. Feeds on tiny spiders, insects, mites, plant juices. **HABITAT** Tree trunks, buildings. **SEASON** Mar.–Nov.

AMERICAN DOG TICK
"Eastern Wood Tick"
Dermacentor variabilis
ARACHNID CLASS
⅜". Body oval. Female reddish brown, with silvery shield near small orange head. Male gray, with reddish-brown spots. **CAUTION** If bitten, remove tick head to prevent infection. **HABITAT** Brush, tall grass. **SEASON** Year-round.

DEER TICK
Ixodes dammini
ARACHNID CLASS
1/16". Body oval, flattened; light brown (larva, nymph) to reddish brown (adult). Nymph minute, size of poppy seed. **CAUTION** Can transmit Lyme disease, a serious illness (see box below). **HABITAT** Brushy fields, open woods. **SEASON** Year-round.

Deer Ticks and Lyme Disease
Ticks of the genus *Ixodes* are carriers of Lyme disease, a dangerous illness that can be difficult to treat. In the Mid-Atlantic region, the Deer Tick carries the responsible spirochete (spiral-shaped bacterium), *Borrelia burgdorferi*. Both nymphs, active April through July, and adults, active on warm days from August through April, can be infectious. Deer Ticks are tiny and their nymphs are almost microscopic. They inhabit woods and fields, especially where deer are numerous. To avoid infection, it helps to wear light-colored pants tucked into socks and to carefully check clothing and skin after outings. Initial symptoms of Lyme disease vary, but about 75 to 80 percent of all victims develop a circular, expanding red rash around the tick bite, which can appear up to 35 days after the bite. Other symptoms include stiff neck, headache, dizziness, fever, sore throat, muscle aches, joint pain, and general weakness. Should these symptoms develop, consult a physician promptly, as antibiotics are most effective in early stages of infection. Untreated Lyme disease can be difficult to cure and may cause chronic arthritis, memory loss, and severe headaches.

CHIGGERS
Trombicula species
ARACHNID CLASS
Body minute, almost microscopic; reddish. Sucks mammalian blood, including humans'. **CAUTION** Bite causes intense itching that can last for weeks. **HABITAT** Grassy fields, wet meadows. **SEASON** Apr.–Sept. **RANGE** Long Is.; c NJ and south.

Insects

Insects (class Insecta) bring out many feelings: they fascinate children with their forms and colors; they bewilder naturalists with their ecological intricacies; they cause rational adults to cringe at their mere presence. Their vast repertory of environmental adaptations is overwhelming, as are their sheer numbers and staying power. Try as we might (and we have tried mightily), we have not succeeded in exterminating any Mid-Atlantic insect pests. Perhaps instead we should spend more time observing their beauty and variety.

All insects have three main body parts—head, thorax, and abdomen—to which various other organs are attached. The head has a pair of antennae, which may be narrow, feathery, pointed, short, or long (sometimes much longer than the body). The eyes are compound and the mouthparts are adapted to chewing, biting, piercing, sucking, and/or licking. Insect wings (usually four) and legs (six) attach at the thorax. The abdomen, usually the largest section, houses the reproductive and other internal organs.

A remarkable aspect of invertebrate life is the transformation from egg to adult, known as metamorphosis. In complete metamorphosis, which includes a pupal stage and is unique to insects, the adult females lay eggs from which the larvae are hatched. The larva feeds and grows, molting its skin several times, until it prepares for its immobile pupal state by hiding or camouflaging itself. Within the pupa, larval organs dissolve and adult organs develop. In incomplete metamorphosis, there is no pupal stage, and insects such as dragonflies, grasshoppers, and bugs gradually develop from hatched nymphs into adults.

It is impossible to overstate the importance of insects to the ecological health of the planet. In the Mid-Atlantic and other temperate regions, insects pollinate approximately 80 percent of the flowering plants. They are a vital link in every ecosystem.

This book introduces representative species or genera of insects from many orders in a sequence from primitive to more advanced. We have placed the large butterfly and moth section last, although traditionally they precede the ants, bees, and wasps. For many insects there is no commonly accepted English name at the species level. Descriptions and seasonal information refer to adult forms unless otherwise noted. Measurements are of typical adult body lengths, except in the butterfly accounts, in which wingspan measurements are given.

SILVERFISH
Lepisma saccharina
BRISTLETAIL ORDER
½". Body flattened, wingless, covered with silver scales; tapers to 3-pronged tail. Antennae thread-like; eyes small, compound. Fast runner. Feeds on glue, starch, dried cereal, paper. **HABITAT** Buildings. **SEASON** Year-round.

MAYFLIES
Isonychia and other genera
MAYFLY ORDER
¾". Body gray, brown, or yellowish; tube-shaped, with trailing tail filaments as long as abdomen. 4 transparent wings. Nymph aquatic; adults often emerge in vast swarms that persist a day or two. **HABITAT** Streams, ponds, lakes, rivers. **SEASON** May–Sept.

Dragonflies

Dragonflies are large predatory insects, many of which specialize in killing mosquitoes. The order is 300 million years old and comprises two major groups—dragonflies and damselflies. Both have movable heads and large compound eyes that in dragonflies nearly cover the head and in damselflies bulge out from the sides. Their legs are attached to the thorax just behind their heads, a feature that makes walking all but impossible but greatly facilitates their ability to grasp and hold prey while tearing into it with sharp mouthparts. They have four powerful wings that move independently, allowing for both forward and backward flight. At rest, the wings are held horizontally by dragonflies and together over the abdomen by damselflies. Nymphs, called naiads, live among the vegetation and muck in ponds and streams and feed on mosquito larvae, other insects, tadpoles, and small fish. Many of the Mid-Atlantic's 170 or so colorful species of dragonflies and damselflies have captured the interest of bird and butterfly enthusiasts. Some have been found to be migratory, gathering in swarms at many of the same coastal sites where migrating birds and Monarchs abound. In the accounts that follow, all species not noted as damselflies are dragonflies. The size given is the typical adult body length (not the wingspan).

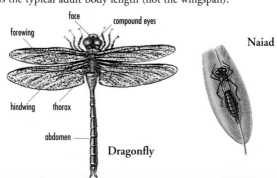

Dragonfly

Naiad

EBONY JEWELWING
"Black-winged Damselfly"
Calopteryx maculata
DRAGONFLY ORDER

1¾". Damselfly. Male metallic green; wings black. Female dull brown; wings smoky with glistening spot near tip. Naiad pale brown with darker markings. **HABITAT** Wooded streams, rivers. **SEASON** May–Aug.

COMMON SPREADWING
Lestes disjunctus
DRAGONFLY ORDER

1⅝". Damselfly. Thorax brownish; abdomen long, blackish, with bluish-white tip. Eyes and face blue; pale green shoulder stripe. Wings transparent, short; held half open (unlike most damselflies). **HABITAT** Ponds, marshes. **SEASON** May–Sept.

BLUETS
Enallagma species
DRAGONFLY ORDER

1¼". Damselflies. Body usually bright blue or violet, with black stripes on thorax. Wings clear. **HABITAT** Ponds, marshy areas. **SEASON** May–Oct.

EASTERN FORKTAIL
Ischnura verticalis
DRAGONFLY ORDER

1". Damselfly. Male thorax black with 2 lime-green stripes; abdomen black, blue-tipped. Female blue-gray or orange. Wings clear. A common damselfly. **HABITAT** Ponds, streams, rivers. **SEASON** Mid-May–Sept.

COMMON GREEN DARNER
Anax junius
DRAGONFLY ORDER

3". Thorax green; abdomen blue (male) or purplish brown (female). Wings clear; older female's tinged with amber. Flies over fields in large numbers in late summer; seldom perches. **HABITAT** Ponds, streams, fields. **SEASON** May–Oct.; migrates in fall.

COMET DARNER
Anax longipes
DRAGONFLY ORDER

3¼". Thorax green. Male has bright red abdomen, green eyes; female has red-brown abdomen, blue eyes. Wings transparent. Uncommon and beautiful. **HABITAT** Shallow grassy ponds. **SEASON** Mar.–Nov.

SWAMP DARNER
Epiaeschna heros
DRAGONFLY ORDER

3¼″. Body large, dark brown; lime-green stripes (thorax) and bands (abdomen). Eyes blue. Wings transparent. Flies high; eats large insects like bees, dragonflies. **HABITAT** Shady ponds, slow streams, swampy areas. **SEASON** Apr.–Nov.; most common June–Aug.

DRAGONHUNTER
Hagenius brevistylus
DRAGONFLY ORDER

3¼″. Thorax and abdomen black with bold yellow stripes. Head green, small, contrasts with swollen thorax; eyes green. Wings transparent. Preys on other dragonflies. **HABITAT** Streams, rivers. **SEASON** May–Oct.

STREAM CRUISER
Didymops transversa
DRAGONFLY ORDER

2¼″. Thorax brown; pale yellow diagonal band on each side. Abdomen brown with conspicuous yellow banding. Eyes brown (imm.) or shining green (adult). Flies low, sometimes hovers among weeds. **HABITAT** Streamsides, riversides, dirt roads near water. **SEASON** Apr.–early June.

PRINCE BASKETTAIL
Epitheca princeps
DRAGONFLY ORDER

3″. Body slender, brown. Eyes red-brown (imm., female) or green (male). Wings clear, with dark brown markings at base, center, tip. Flies high, but swarms at any level. Southern form larger, more boldly marked. **HABITAT** Near rivers, streams, lakes. **SEASON** June–Aug.

CALICO PENNANT
Celithemis elisa
DRAGONFLY ORDER

1¼″. Thorax red; abdomen black with red (male) or yellow (female) markings on top. Wings spotted; hindwing base amber. **HABITAT** Marshy ponds, fields. **SEASON** Mid-June–late Aug.

HALLOWEEN PENNANT
Celithemis eponina
DRAGONFLY ORDER

1½". Thorax reddish brown; abdomen blackish with yellow or orange markings on top. Wings yellow-orange with large, dark brown spots. Often perches atop prominent vegetation. **HABITAT** Fields, marshes. **SEASON** June–late Aug.

EASTERN PONDHAWK
Erythemis simplicicollis
DRAGONFLY ORDER

1¾". Female (called "Green Jacket") and imm. bright green with dark markings on abdomen. Male face green; thorax and abdomen pale blue. Wings clear. Often rests on ground. **HABITAT** Ponds, nearby fields. **SEASON** Mid-June–early Sept.

SPANGLED SKIMMER
Libellula cyanea
DRAGONFLY ORDER

1¾". Female and imm. dark brown with yellowish markings on abdomen sides and top of thorax. Male thorax and abdomen slaty blue. Wings clear with bright white markings set back from tip. **HABITAT** Woodland edges, marshy areas. **SEASON** June–Sept.

WIDOW SKIMMER
Libellula luctuosa
DRAGONFLY ORDER

1¾". Thorax dark brown with yellow stripe; abdomen dark brown with yellowish (imm., female) or blue (male) side markings. Inner half of wings black. **HABITAT** Ponds, marshes. **SEASON** Mid-June–early Sept.

COMMON WHITETAIL
Libellula lydia
DRAGONFLY ORDER

1¾". Body chunky. Male abdomen pale bluish white; wings have broad black band. Female brown with yellowish markings on abdomen sides; 3 dark spots on wings. **HABITAT** Ponds, grassy swamps, pathways, gardens. **SEASON** June–early Sept.

TWELVE-SPOTTED SKIMMER
Libellula pulchella
DRAGONFLY ORDER

2″. Head/thorax light brown; abdomen gray-brown to whitish. White and black spots on wings. Female and imm. differ from Common Whitetail in larger size, lack of obvious yellow on abdomen. **HABITAT** Ponds, marshes. **SEASON** Mid-June–Sept.

PAINTED SKIMMER
Libellula semifasciata
DRAGONFLY ORDER

1½″. Thorax brown with 2 pale stripes on each side; abdomen ochre with blackish tip. Eyes red. Wings clear, with conspicuous banding. **HABITAT** Ponds, marshy areas, wet meadows. **SEASON** May–June.

BLUE DASHER
Pachydiplax longipennis
DRAGONFLY ORDER

1½″. Male thorax striped black and yellow; abdomen blue with black tip. Female and imm. duller. Wings mostly clear. Common near quiet waters. **HABITAT** Ponds, marshes, sluggish streams. **SEASON** Late June–early Sept.

WANDERING GLIDER
"Globetrotter"
Pantala flavescens
DRAGONFLY ORDER

2″. Thorax light brown; abdomen has golden-yellow sides. Eyes reddish. Wings clear. Flies almost constantly, often above trees; widespread. Breeds in rain puddles. **HABITAT** Fields, open areas, sometimes ponds. **SEASON** Late June–Sept.

EASTERN AMBERWING
Perithemis tenera
DRAGONFLY ORDER

1″. Body short, stocky; yellowish brown with 2 greenish stripes on thorax. Wings amber, female's with variable dark spots. Flies low over water or perches on vegetation. **HABITAT** Ponds. **SEASON** Late June–Aug.

RUBY MEADOWHAWK
Sympetrum rubicundulum
DRAGONFLY ORDER

1¼". Head and thorax brown. Male abdomen scarlet with black side markings; female abdomen ochre. Legs black. Wings clear. **HABITAT** Pond edges, wet fields, gardens. **SEASON** Aug.–Nov.

YELLOW-LEGGED MEADOWHAWK
Sympetrum vicinum
DRAGONFLY ORDER

1¼". Thorax reddish brown; abdomen reddish orange. Legs yellowish. Wings clear. Common late in season. **HABITAT** Fields, ponds. **SEASON** Late July–Oct.

CAROLINA SADDLEBAGS
Tramea carolina
DRAGONFLY ORDER

2". Thorax brown; abdomen red with black tip. Face violet (male) or blue and orange (female). Wings clear; large red-brown band covers basal fourth of broad hindwings. **HABITAT** Ponds. **SEASON** Apr.–Oct.

BLACK SADDLEBAGS
Tramea lacerata
DRAGONFLY ORDER

2". Body purplish blue; abdomen with yellow spots above. Wings clear, with black "saddlebag" bands covering basal fourth of each hindwing. **HABITAT** Near slow-moving or still, fresh water. **SEASON** Apr.–Oct.

EUROPEAN EARWIG
Forficula auricularia
EARWIG ORDER

⅝". Body brownish to black; legs yellowish. Pincers at abdomen tip curved (male) or straight (female). Eats flowers, fruit, garbage, insect larvae. Female guards eggs, feeds nymphs. **HABITAT** Logs, leaf litter, sheds. **SEASON** Apr.–Oct.

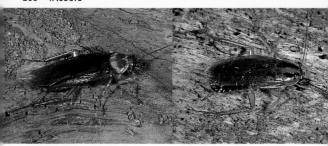

AMERICAN COCKROACH
"Waterbug"
Periplaneta americana
COCKROACH ORDER

2". Body reddish brown; large, pale yellow head shield; long antennas. Yellow stripe on front margin of forewings. Legs dark. Largest cockroach in Mid-Atlantic. **HABITAT** Warm buildings. **SEASON** Year-round.

GERMAN COCKROACH
Blattella germanica
COCKROACH ORDER

⅝". Body brown; 2 blackish stripes on pale yellow-brown shield behind head. With adhesive pads on pale legs, can climb vertical smooth surfaces. Introduced from Eurasia; pest in all N. Amer. cities. **HABITAT** Buildings. **SEASON** Year-round.

EASTERN SUBTERRANEAN TERMITE
Reticulitermes flavipes
TERMITE ORDER

¼". Reproductive black or brown; 4 membranous wings held flat. Worker and soldier lack eyes, wings; whitish or yellowish. Eats rotting wood; damages buildings. **HABITAT** Rotting wood. **SEASON** Year-round.

CHINESE MANTIS
Tenodera aridifolia
MANTID ORDER

3". Body tan to pale green; forewings tan, edged green. Head triangular, mobile. Forelegs close like a jackknife to grasp prey; other legs long, thin, used to climb and walk. Introduced from China. **HABITAT** Meadows, gardens. **SEASON** June–Aug.

NORTHERN WALKINGSTICK
Diapheromera femorata
WALKINGSTICK ORDER

3¾". Body greatly elongated, sticklike, wingless; brown to greenish brown. Head tiny; legs thin. Superbly camouflaged. Active at night; eats leaves, plant juices. Eggs white with black stripe. **HABITAT** Broadleaf woods. **SEASON** Apr.–Oct.

Grasshoppers and Kin

Members of the order Orthoptera are beloved for their musical abilities and despised for their voracious appetites. All species have mouthparts designed to bite and chew, and straight, membranous wings. Grasshoppers and crickets have greatly developed hindlegs for jumping. Female grasshoppers and locusts have short ovipositors for digging, while crickets and katydids have long ovipositors, straight in crickets and sickle-shaped in katydids; they lay eggs in soil or tree vegetation. While no insects have true voices, orthopterans manage to make themselves heard in a variety of distinctive ways; most melodies are produced by males trying to attract mates. Crickets and katydids raise their wings and rub together specialized parts to produce their well-known calls. Most crickets are "right-winged," rubbing their right wings over their left, while katydids are "left-winged." Grasshoppers rub their hindlegs and wings together, and also make rattling, in-flight sounds by vibrating their forewings against their hindwings.

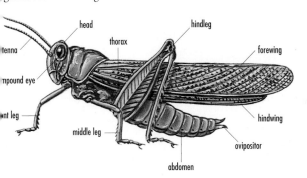

head · hindleg · thorax · forewing · antenna · compound eye · front leg · middle leg · hindwing · ovipositor · abdomen

Parts of a Grasshopper

DIFFERENTIAL GRASSHOPPER
Melanoplus differentialis
GRASSHOPPER ORDER
1⅛". Body grayish yellow, glossy. Antennae yellow or red. Hindlegs with distinct black herringbone pattern. Wings transparent with whitish veins. **HABITAT** Grassy areas, croplands. **SEASON** June–Aug.

CAROLINA LOCUST
Dissosteira carolina
GRASSHOPPER ORDER
2". Body cinnamon-brown, incl. eyes. Hindwings black with broad, light yellow border (visible in flight). Flies with purring, fluttering sound. **HABITAT** Roadsides, meadows. **SEASON** June–Sept.

RED-LEGGED LOCUST
Melanoplus femur-rubrum
GRASSHOPPER ORDER

1". Body dark brown, sometimes greenish. Hind femur herringbone-patterned; hind tibia bright red to yellow with black spines. Wings dusky; male's wings at rest project beyond abdomen tip. Eats grasses, weeds, field crops. **HABITAT** Fields. **SEASON** July–Oct.

TRUE KATYDID
Pterophylla camellifolia
GRASSHOPPER ORDER

2". Body triangular in cross section, with ridge above. Thorax shield and wings resemble yellowish-green, net-veined leaf. Both sexes make 2-part *katy-DID* and 3-part *katy-DIDN'T* calls from treetops to ground at night. **HABITAT** Broadleaf and mixed woods, esp. oaks. **SEASON** July–Sept.

FORK-TAILED BUSH KATYDID
Scudderia furcata
GRASSHOPPER ORDER

1½". Body leaf-green. Hindlegs, antennae long, thin. Wings, long, narrow, extend past abdomen. Female has stout upcurved ovipositor; male has forked "tail." Call: 1–2 strong rasping pulses close together, with pauses in between. Nocturnal. **HABITAT** Meadows, marshes, woods. **SEASON** Summer.

FIELD CRICKET
Gryllus pennsylvanicus
GRASSHOPPER ORDER

1". Body black, with spiky abdominal appendages. Antennae black, as long as body. Hindlegs strong, spiny. Wings short, dusky. Gives series of ½-second triple chirps, or when courting, a continuous, high-pitched trill. Often enters houses in fall, attracted there by warmth. **HABITAT** Fields, houses. **SEASON** June–Oct.

SNOWY TREE CRICKET
Oecanthus fultoni
GRASSHOPPER ORDER

⅝". Body delicate, pale green; hindlegs and antennae long, thin. Wings clear; male's forewings paddle-shaped, held over back; female's narrow, curved around body. Many males together make series of rhythmic trills night or day. Adult eats aphids, caterpillars. **HABITAT** Trees, shrubs. **SEASON** July–Sept.

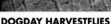

PERIODICAL CICADAS
Magicicada species
CICADA ORDER

1″. Body black, robust; eyes large, red; wings clear, orange-veined. Nymph feeds on sap in tree roots for 17 years (emergence years vary geographically). Adult lives about 1 month. Call a loud, rising and falling, staccato whine. **HABITAT** Broadleaf woods. **SEASON** June–July.

DOGDAY HARVESTFLIES
Tibicen species
CICADA ORDER

1⅛″. Body black and green. Wings clear, tinged with green at base. Nymph lives underground for 3 years, sucking root juices; new generation every year. Call a booming staccato trill. **HABITAT** Coniferous and mixed woods. **SEASON** Late July–Sept.

SCARLET-AND-GREEN LEAFHOPPER
Graphocephala coccinea
CICADA ORDER

⅜″. Body bullet-shaped, with pointed head; brownish, with distinct scarlet and green striping on forewings. Feeds on plant juices, incl. cultivated plants. **HABITAT** Fields, gardens. **SEASON** Apr.–Oct.; several generations.

MEADOW SPITTLEBUG
Philaenus spumarius
CICADA ORDER

⅜″. Adult, called froghopper, hops about on leaves like tiny frog. Body long, pear-shaped; antennae and wings very short. Gray, green, yellow, or brown. Nymph, called spittlebug, oval, clear yellowish, scarcely pigmented; emits bubbly protective froth. **HABITAT** Brushy meadows, roadsides. **SEASON** May–Sept.

EASTERN DOBSONFLY
Corydalus cornutus
NERVEWING ORDER

2″. Body elongated, with large head; brown. Wings long, veined, translucent, grayish. Male's mandibles forceps-like, ½ body length; female's shorter, but can bite strongly. Adult short-lived. Larva (hellgrammite) an aquatic predator. **HABITAT** Woods near streams; attracted to lights. **SEASON** June–July.

GREEN LACEWINGS
Chrysopa species
NERVEWING ORDER
⅝″. Body elongated, pale green. Head narrow; eyes large, coppery; antennae long, thread-like. Wings clear, veined; at least ¼ longer than body; fold together over back. Adult and larva eat destructive aphids. **HABITAT** Gardens, meadows, woodland edges. **SEASON** May–Sept.

ANTLIONS
Myrmeleon species
NERVEWING ORDER
1½″. Body soft, with long abdomen; gray-green. Antennae knobbed. Wings clear, narrow; poor flier. Larva (⅝″), called Doodlebug, builds funnel in sand, seizes sliding ants with powerful jaws. **HABITAT** Adult: woodland edges; larva: sandy areas. **SEASON** Summer.

ZEBRA CADDISFLY
Macrostemum zebratum
CADDISFLY ORDER
¾″. Body green with black ribbing, becoming black with yellow ribbing. Antennae long, black. Legs yellow. Wings ginger with black markings. **HABITAT** Warm trout rivers.

WATER BOATMEN
Corixa species
TRUE BUG ORDER
½″. Body long, oval, gray-brown. Wings gray-brown, veined. Forelegs short, scoop-like; other legs paddle-shaped, used for rowing. Aquatic; can fly. Eats algae in birdbaths. **HABITAT** Ponds, rivers, small patches of water. **SEASON** May–Sept.

COMMON WATER STRIDER
Gerris remigis
TRUE BUG ORDER
⅝″. Body dark, slender. Middle and hindlegs very long, slender. Skates over water using surface tension. Feeds on mosquito larvae and insects that fall in water. **HABITAT** Quiet, fresh water. **SEASON** May–Oct.

SMALL MILKWEED BUG
Lygaeus kalmii
TRUE BUG ORDER
½″. Body oval, black; red band behind head. Forewings have large, bright red X. Toxic to predators. Lays eggs on milkweeds; immune to plant's toxins. **HABITAT** Meadows with milkweeds. **SEASON** May–Oct.

GREEN STINK BUG
Acrosternum hilare
TRUE BUG ORDER

¾". Body shield-shaped, compact; green, with yellow-orange edges. Head small; antennae banded. Eats fruits, vegetables. Emits foul-smelling fluid when disturbed. **HABITAT** Orchards, gardens, field crops. **SEASON** Summer.

Beetles

There are more species of beetles (order Coleoptera) than any other group of animals on earth. Not all are called beetles: fireflies are included in this order, for example. Beetles' forewings are hardened dense sheaths known as *elytra,* which meet in a straight line down the back. Their hindwings underneath function as the organs of flight. Beetle legs and antennae vary from long and straight to stout and angled. Both adults and larvae, known as grubs, have mouthparts adapted for biting and chewing. They are vegetarians, predators, scavengers, and in a few instances parasites. Some, like lady beetles, are highly prized by gardeners because they eat aphids and other garden pests, while others, including the introduced Japanese Beetle, are nuisances at best. Beetles range in size from microscopic organisms to some of the largest insects in the world.

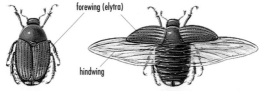

forewing (elytra)

hindwing

BROWN TIGER BEETLE
Cicindela repanda
BEETLE ORDER

½". Body elongated. Brownish bronze with creamy pattern above; metallic green below. Legs and antennae long, slender. Runs and flies fast; seizes prey insects with powerful jaws. Very alert; elusive. Bites. **HABITAT** Open sand and gravel areas, often near water. **SEASON** Apr.–Oct.

SIX-SPOTTED GREEN TIGER BEETLE
Cicindela sexguttata
BEETLE ORDER

⅝". Body elongated; bright metallic green; antennae long, clubbed. Forewings have 6 or more white spots along rear edge. Legs brilliant green, some with purplish sheen. Eats spiders, insects. **CAUTION** Bites. **HABITAT** Sandy areas in fields; woodland paths. **SEASON** Apr.–Aug.

EUROPEAN CATERPILLAR HUNTER
Calosoma sycophanta
BEETLE ORDER

1⅛″. Body robust. Thorax shield circular, dark blue. Forewings iridescent golden-green, grooved. Ground beetle introduced from Eurasia to eat Gypsy Moth caterpillars; climbs trees to reach them. **HABITAT** Woods, gardens. **SEASON** May–Oct.

LARGE WHIRLIGIG BEETLES
Dineutus species
BEETLE ORDER

½″. Body oval, flat; black, often with bronzy sheen. Forewings have shallow grooves. Hindlegs short, paddle-like. Gathers in groups that swim in circles. Eats aquatic insects and insects that fall into the water. **HABITAT** Surfaces of ponds, streams. **SEASON** June–Oct.

MAY BEETLES
"June Bugs"
Phyllophaga species
BEETLE ORDER

1⅜″. Body bulky. Thorax shield chestnut. Forewings lighter brown, without grooves; hindwings well developed. Antennae end in right angles. Attracted by lights; slow, noisy, buzzing flight. **HABITAT** Broadleaf woods, fields. **SEASON** May–Aug.

JAPANESE BEETLE
Popillia japonica
BEETLE ORDER

½″. Body rotund. Metallic green; forewings mostly brownish or reddish orange. Abdomen ringed with white hair tufts. Adults infest flowers, fruit, vines, shrubs; white grubs eat lawn roots; can become serious garden pests. **HABITAT** Gardens, yards, open woods. **SEASON** May–Sept.

LONG-HORNED PINE SAWYERS
Monochamus species
BEETLE ORDER

1¼″. Body cylindrical; black or reddish brown, mottled with gray or white. Male's antennae extremely long. Active day and night; attracted to lights. **HABITAT** Coniferous and mixed woods. **SEASON** June–Sept. **RANGE** Throughout; some species, like *M. carolina*, only south of NJ.

PENNSYLVANIA FIREFLY

"Lightning Bug"
Photuris pennsylvanicus
BEETLE ORDER

½". Body long, flattened. Head and thorax shield have black spot ringed with orange. Forewings brown or gray, edged with yellow. Flashes yellow-green light every 2–3 seconds when courting. Eggs, larvae, pupae also luminous. HABITAT Fields, gardens, open woods. SEASON June–Aug.

TWO-SPOTTED LADY BEETLE

Adalia bipunctata
BEETLE ORDER

¼". Body oval, rounded. Head, thorax black with yellow marks. Forewings reddish orange with 1 black spot on each. Larva velvety, black with yellow and white spots. Adult and larva feed on aphids. Overwinters in houses and under bark. HABITAT Fields, gardens. SEASON May–Oct.

CONVERGENT LADY BEETLE

Hippodamia convergens
BEETLE ORDER

¼". Body oval, rounded. Head, thorax black, with converging white stripes on thorax. Forewings reddish orange, usu. with 13 black spots. Larva velvety, black with orange spots. Adult and larva feed on destructive aphids. HABITAT Woods, meadows, gardens. SEASON May–Oct.

MARGINED BURYING BEETLE

Nicrophorus marginatus
BEETLE ORDER

1". Body cylindrical; black, glossy, with 2 orange bands across short forewings. Antennae clubbed. Adult buries small animals for larvae to feed on. Nocturnal. Sometimes seen near lights or under dead unburied animals. HABITAT Woods, fields. SEASON Mar.–Nov.

RED MILKWEED BEETLE

Tetraopes tetrophthalmus
BEETLE ORDER

½". Body long, cylindrical; bright red above with large black dots. Antennae gray-beaded; legs mostly gray. Makes grating sounds by rubbing rough areas on thorax. Immune to milkweed poison; adult and larva poisonous to birds. HABITAT Meadows with milkweeds. SEASON Summer.

Flies and Mosquitoes

Flies and mosquitoes, some of humankind's least favorite insects, are nonetheless worthy of a second glance. All species have two wings and mouthparts formed for sucking, or for piercing and sucking combined. The legless and wingless larvae undergo complete metamorphosis, and can be either terrestrial (maggots) or aquatic (called by various names). Adults fly with a wingbeat frequency often of hundreds of beats per second. This incredible speed produces the familiar in-flight buzzing sounds. Flies feed on decomposing matter, nectar, and sometimes blood. Mosquitoes' lower lips form a proboscis with six knife-sharp organs, some smooth and some sawtoothed, that cut into skin. Only the females feed on blood.

CRANE FLIES
Tipula species
FLY ORDER

2½". Body mosquito-like; long, delicate, gray to gold. Legs very long, slender, fragile. Wings clear, veined; held at 60-degree angle from body. Feeds on plants; does not bite humans. **HABITAT** Watersides; may enter houses. **SEASON** May–Sept.

PHANTOM CRANE FLY
Bittacomorpha clavipes
FLY ORDER

½". Body long, very thin, black. Legs long, delicate, with black and white bands. Wings clear, black-veined. Drifts slowly in the air, with legs extended, seeming to appear and disappear. **HABITAT** Streamsides, woods. **SEASON** May–Sept.

MOSQUITOES
Aedes and *Culex* species
FLY ORDER

¼". Body slender, delicate; brown or black, with silvery white scales forming streaks on thorax. Male's antennae feathery, female's thread-like. Wings transparent. Female sucks blood; male feeds on plant juices. **HABITAT** Forests with tree holes, marshes, backyards. **SEASON** Mar.–Oct.

BLACK FLIES
Simulium species
FLY ORDER

⅛". Body humpbacked; head pointed down; blackish. Antennae thick. Wings clear. Larvae pupate in cocoons that coat rocks in streams. Female sucks bird and mammal blood. Abundant in north woods in early summer. **HABITAT** Woods, watersides. **SEASON** Late May–July.

DEER FLY
Chrysops callidus
FLY ORDER

½″. Body flattish; head small. Thorax black; abdomen striped golden. Wings veined, with black patches. Circles targets silently, giving quick nasty bite on landing, often on head. Only female bites; male feeds mostly on flower nectar. **HABITAT** Woods and meadows near water. **SEASON** June–July.

AMERICAN HORSE FLY
Tabanus americanus
FLY ORDER

1″. Body very large, wide, hairy; brown-black. Antennae reddish brown. Eyes large, green; legs reddish. Wings dusky, dark near base. Anticoagulant in female's saliva causes bite wound to continue bleeding. **HABITAT** Watersides, farms. **SEASON** May–Sept.

HOUSE FLY
Musca domestica
FLY ORDER

¼″. Body gray with black stripes. Eyes large, red-brown; legs hairy. Wings clear. Egg hatches in 10–24 hours; matures to adult in 10 days; male lives 15 days, female 26. Sucks liquid sugars from garbage; spreads disease. **HABITAT** Buildings, farms. **SEASON** Year-round.

BEARDED ROBBER FLY
Efferia pogonias
FLY ORDER

½″. Thorax bulbous, brown. Abdomen long, thin; male's gray with silvery white tip, female's light gray with 2 black spots. Head has white beard-like bristles. Wings smoky gray, translucent. **HABITAT** Fields, meadows. **SEASON** Aug.–Sept. **RANGE** MD to VA and south.

GREEN BOTTLE FLIES
Phaenicia and other genera
FLY ORDER

½″. Body stout; metallic blue-green with gold highlights, black markings. Black hairs cover thorax. Antennae and legs black. Eyes red. Wings clear, with brown veins. Eats carrion and decaying organic matter. **HABITAT** Near manure and garbage. **SEASON** May–Sept.

Ants, Wasps, and Bees

The insects of the order Hymenoptera include horntails and narrow-waisted bees, wasps, and ants. Hymenopterans have two pairs of membranous, transparent wings, mouthparts modified to chew and lick, and in adult females, an ovipositor. All species undergo complete metamorphosis.

Adult horntails resemble typical wasps except for their cylindrical bodies. The narrow-waists are divided into two broad groupings. The first, parasitic wasps, include the large and varied assemblage of nonstinging ichneumon wasps, which live as parasites during their larval stage. Some ichneumons are greatly feared by humans for their astonishingly long ovipositors, which in fact are used not for stinging but to probe about in woody vegetation for suitable insects on which to lay eggs. The second group of narrow-waists are the stinging insects, with ovipositors that have been modified into stinging organs. Included here are vespid wasps (such as hornets, yellow jackets, and potter wasps), bees, and many ants.

Ants and some wasps and bees are highly social creatures, but some species in this order live solitary lives. The nests constructed by ants, wasps, and bees vary in complexity from the Eastern Sand Wasp's single-cell hole in the ground to the Honey Bee's elaborate comb structure. Many ant species excavate in soil or wood, building multi-chambered homes mostly hidden from sight. The Mid-Atlantic hosts hundreds of ant species. Yellow jackets and some hornets build similar homes. Unlike ants, though, they build separate six-sided chambers for each of their young, made of a papery material that consists of wood or bark and adult saliva. Bald-faced Hornets often construct their nests in open situations, while Honey Bees utilize man-made hives or hollow trees or logs. The Honey Bees' two-sided, vertically hanging beeswax combs can contain more than 50,000 cells.

Bees and flowering plants have developed a great many interdependencies over the eons as they have evolved together. We would lose too many of our flowers and fruits were we to let our bees be poisoned out of existence. We would also lose some of the greatest known examples of animal industry.

The following species accounts give typical body lengths of the commonly seen workers; queens are usually larger.

PIGEON HORNTAIL
Tremex columba
ANT, WASP, AND BEE ORDER

1½". Cylindrical. Head and body orange; abdomen long, with black and yellow bars; horny plate at end. Wings blackish to yellowish. Female has long, yellowish ovipositor (not stinger), used to drill and deposit eggs deep into wood. Larva eats wood, adult drinks nectar. **HABITAT** Woods. **SEASON** May–Sept.

BLACK CARPENTER ANT
Camponotus pennsylvanicus
ANT, WASP, AND BEE ORDER

½". Black; large part of abdomen has long brownish hairs. Antennae elbowed. Constructs intricate tunnel systems in wood; does not eat it, but can cause structural damage in buildings. **CAUTION** Bites. **HABITAT** Dying trees, logs, wooden structures. **SEASON** Mar.–Nov.

MOUND ANTS
Formica species
ANT, WASP, AND BEE ORDER

⅛". Body red, brown, or black; narrow, 1-segmented waist. Milks aphids and sometimes caterpillars for honeydew; some species are closely associated with caterpillars of certain blue or hairstreak butterflies. **CAUTION** Bites, but is not aggressive. **HABITAT** Open areas. **SEASON** Mar.–Nov.

COW KILLER
"Velvet Ant"
Dasymutilla occidentalis
ANT, WASP, AND BEE ORDER

⅞". Wasp. Body covered with short hairs; above red with narrow black band; below black. Male wings brownish; female wingless. **CAUTION** Female stings. **HABITAT** Sandy areas in meadows, woodland edges. **SEASON** July–Sept. **RANGE** Throughout; more common southward.

SHORT-TAILED ICHNEUMONS
Ophion species
ANT, WASP, AND BEE ORDER

⅝". Body elongated; light yellowish to reddish brown. Abdomen long, compressed; legs and antennae long, pale. Wings clear. Feeds on flower nectar. Female ovipositor short; deposits egg into living caterpillar; larva pupates inside cocoon. **HABITAT** Woods, brushy fields. **SEASON** Mar.–Sept.

PAPER WASPS
Polistes species
ANT, WASP, AND BEE ORDER

¾". Body slender, with 1-segmented waist; reddish brown to black, occ. with yellow rings on abdomen. Wings translucent, smoky. Builds hanging nest in sheds, barns. Queen hibernates in logs, stone walls. **CAUTION** Stings; aggressive if disturbed. **HABITAT** Open areas. **SEASON** Mar.–Nov.

BLACK-AND-YELLOW MUD DAUBER
Sceliphron caementarium
ANT, WASP, AND BEE ORDER
1″. Wasp. Body slender, with long, narrow waist; black with yellow markings on thorax and top of abdomen. Legs yellow. Builds tubular mud nest under eaves, overhangs. **CAUTION** Stings; not aggressive. **HABITAT** Fields, gardens. **SEASON** June–Sept.

EASTERN YELLOW JACKET
Vespula maculifrons
ANT, WASP, AND BEE ORDER
⅝″. Body stout with narrow waist; black, with thin yellow bands on thorax and abdomen. Wings dusky. Nests under log or stone, or in crevice. Raids picnic food and trash cans. **CAUTION** Stings repeatedly if bothered. **HABITAT** Fields, gardens, urban areas. **SEASON** May–Oct.

BALD-FACED HORNET
Vespula maculata
ANT, WASP, AND BEE ORDER
¾″. Body rotund; black, with yellowish-white spots on short head, base of wings, waist, and abdomen tip. Builds football-size paper nest under branch or overhang. **CAUTION** Stings nest visitors. **HABITAT** Woodland edges. **SEASON** May–Sept.

EASTERN CARPENTER BEE
Xylocopa virginica
ANT, WASP, AND BEE ORDER
1″. Body robust, metallic blue-black; darker and less hairy than American Bumble Bee. Wings dark brown, translucent. Female burrows deep into wood of trees or houses to make egg chambers. **CAUTION** Stings, but rarely. **HABITAT** Woodland edges, houses. **SEASON** May–Aug.

HONEY BEE
Apis mellifera
ANT, WASP, AND BEE ORDER
⅝″. Body rounded. Thorax hairy, reddish brown and black; abdomen banded black and golden. Wings dusky. Makes honey; pollinates crops; nests in tree holes. Introduced from Eurasia. **CAUTION** Stings, but is not aggressive; if stung, remove stinger immediately. **HABITAT** Fields, orchards. **SEASON** Apr.–Oct.

AMERICAN BUMBLE BEE
Bombus pennsylvanicus
ANT, WASP, AND BEE ORDER
⅞". Body robust, hairy; banded with black and yellow. Wings smoky. Busily pollinates flowers. Queen overwinters and nests underground. **CAUTION** Stings, but is not aggressive. **HABITAT** Fields. **SEASON** May–Sept.

Butterflies and Moths

The order Lepidoptera comprises the familiar groups of moths and butterflies. *Lepidoptera* means "scale-winged" and refers to the minute scales that cover the four wings of all butterfly and moth species. All lepidopterans share the same generalized life cycle—egg to larva to pupa to adult. Eggs are laid singly, or in rows, stacks, or masses, depending on the species. The emergent larva, usually referred to as a caterpillar, feeds on plant life and grows through several stages, or instars, shedding its skin each time.

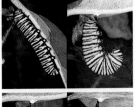

When fully grown, the caterpillar prepares to pupate by spinning a silken cocoon (moth) or finding a secure hiding place (butterfly). Then the caterpillar sheds its last larval skin, revealing the pupa, an outer shell with no head or feet within which the wings and other adult features fully develop. Finally, the pupal skin breaks open and the winged moth or butterfly emerges. The time required for this process varies. Many species have only one emergence of adults per year; others have two or three. Most Mid-Atlantic lepidopterans live out their lives within the region, although a few species, like the world-famous Monarch, migrate south in the fall. The thousands of species that stay behind survive the winter as eggs, larvae, or pupae, although a few overwinter as adults.

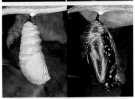

Metamorphosis of a Monarch

Several key differences distinguish moths and butterflies. Moths' antennae are either feather-like or wiry and lack the clubbed tip of butterflies' antennae. Moths rest with their wings outstretched, folded, or at an angle above the body; butterflies rest with their wings outstretched or held together vertically, like a sail. Moths can fly day and night, while butterflies fly only by day. Color and size are poor general distinguishing features between the two groups.

When trying to identify a species, pay attention to the wing colors, shape, and pattern. Most of the characteristic wing markings on moths are found on the uppersides. In butterflies, look on the uppersides of those species that rest with outstretched wings and on the undersides of those that rest with their wings folded up.

Butterflies drink nectar from many species of wildflowers and shrubs. Among the best wild nectar plants in the Mid-Atlantic are milkweeds, dogbanes, asters, Buttonbush, New Jersey Tea, and Joe-Pye-weed. Garden flowers that attract butterflies and moths include Butterfly Bush, Gayfeather, Phlox, Bee Balm, and Coreopsis. Nocturnal moths are also drawn to lights. Each larva, or caterpillar, species has its own select food plants (as opposed to those visited by adults for nectar), and the accounts list many of these. Descriptions are given for those caterpillars most frequently encountered. Measurements are of typical wingspans for adults, from tip to tip.

PIPEVINE SWALLOWTAIL
Battus philenor
SWALLOWTAIL FAMILY

3⅛". Forewings black above, with creamy spots along borders; iridescent blue on hindwings. Below, outer hindwings blue, with large orange spots. Female duller. Caterpillar dark with red tubercules. **HABITAT** Fields, open woods, gardens. **FOOD PLANTS** Pipevines. **SEASON** Apr.–Sept. **RANGE** Entire region, ex. n NY.

ZEBRA SWALLOWTAIL
Eurytides marcellus
SWALLOWTAIL FAMILY

3". Black above, with white or pale greenish stripes; hindwings have red and blue spots near tail. Below, hindwings have red stripe. Caterpillar green with yellow bands or blackish with orange and white bands. **HABITAT** Woodlands, streams. **FOOD PLANTS** Pawpaw trees. **SEASON** Apr.–Sept. **RANGE** WV to DE and south.

BLACK SWALLOWTAIL
Papilio polyxenes
SWALLOWTAIL FAMILY

3¼". Black to blue-black above, with median row of yellow spots (male's larger, forming band), yellow spots along rear edges; hindwings have tail, blue spots (larger on female), bright orange black-centered eyespot. Below, hindwings have orange spots. Caterpillar pale green with black bands broken by yellow or red-orange spots. **HABITAT** Fields, gardens. **FOOD PLANTS** Carrot family. **SEASON** Apr.–Oct.

EASTERN TIGER SWALLOWTAIL
Papilio glaucus
SWALLOWTAIL FAMILY

4⅜″. Males and many females yellow above; forewings have bold black stripes; yellow dashes on black trailing edge; hindwings have orange and blue spots. Below, yellow with narrow black lines; blue and orange spots along outer margins. Southern females tend to be mostly black above, with blue on hindwings and vague tiger striping below. Caterpillar green with black and orange eyespots. **HABITAT** Open woods, fields, gardens. **FOOD PLANTS** Cherry and tulip trees, lilacs. **SEASON** Apr.–Sept. **RANGE** Entire region, ex. n NY, where replaced by nearly identical **Canadian Tiger Swallowtail** (*P. canadensis*).

SPICEBUSH SWALLOWTAIL
Papilio troilus
SWALLOWTAIL FAMILY

4″. Forewings black above, with large light spots; hindwings washed greenish blue, with greenish-blue spots along margins; orange spots near tail. Below, hindwings have orange spots. **HABITAT** Open woods. **FOOD PLANTS** Sassafras trees, Spicebush. **SEASON** Apr.–Sept. **RANGE** Entire region, ex. n NY.

CABBAGE WHITE
Pieris rapae
WHITE AND SULPHUR FAMILY

1⅝″. Very common. White above; forewing tips slaty, with 1 (male) or 2 (female) black spots; hindwings have 1 black spot. Below, yellowish white. Caterpillar green with lengthwise yellow stripes. **HABITAT** Fields, gardens, waste lots. **FOOD PLANTS** Mustard family, incl. cabbages. **SEASON** Mar.–Nov.

FALCATE ORANGETIP
Anthocharis midea
WHITE AND SULPHUR FAMILY

1⅜″. White above; forewings with hooked (falcate) tip; male has orange patches at wingtips. Below, hindwings marbled with black. **HABITAT** Broadleaf and pine woods, openings. **FOOD PLANTS** Mustard family, incl. cresses. **SEASON** Apr.–May.

ORANGE SULPHUR
Colias eurytheme
WHITE AND SULPHUR FAMILY

2″. Orange-yellow above, with black edges, yellow-spotted on female. **HABITAT** Fields. **FOOD PLANTS** Pea family, incl. alfalfas, clovers, vetches. **SEASON** Apr.–Nov. **Clouded Sulphur** (*C. philodice*) lemon yellow, not orangy.

CLOUDLESS SULPHUR
Phoebis sennae
WHITE AND SULPHUR FAMILY

2½". Male clear yellow above; below, yellow with tiny brown dots. Female yellow above and below; black spot on forewings, black spots along margins. Migratory. **HABITAT** Open areas, gardens, beaches. **FOOD PLANTS** Sennas. **SEASON** June–Nov. **RANGE** s WV, VA, coastal plain north of VA.

AMERICAN COPPER
Lycaena phlaeas
GOSSAMER-WING FAMILY

1". Forewings orange above, with black spots, dark gray-brown outer edge; hindwings gray-brown with orange rear edge. Below, forewings orange and light gray; hindwings light gray, with fine black dots, narrow orange line. **HABITAT** Fields, openings. **FOOD PLANTS** Docks, esp. Sheep Sorrel. **SEASON** Apr.–Nov. **RANGE** Entire region, ex. se VA.

BANDED HAIRSTREAK
Satyrium calanus
GOSSAMER-WING FAMILY

1⅛". Brown above; hindwings have 1 long, 1 short tail. Below, brown with broken dark bands outlined with white; hindwings have large blue spot near tail, row of orange spots along rear margin. **HABITAT** Woodlands and edges, brushy fields. **FOOD PLANTS** Oaks, hickories. **SEASON** June–Aug.

CORAL HAIRSTREAK
Satyrium titus
GOSSAMER-WING FAMILY

1⅛". Brown above; tail-less. Below, paler brown, with row of coral red spots along rear border of hindwings; sometimes has scattered rows of black, white-ringed spots. **HABITAT** Brushy fields and edges. **FOOD PLANTS** Wild cherry and plum trees. **SEASON** June–Aug.

EASTERN PINE ELFIN
Callophrys niphon
GOSSAMER-WING FAMILY

1". Brown above. Below, pale and reddish brown, with striking mix of short, thin, black and white bands. Wing margins checkered, giving scalloped appearance. **HABITAT** Pine-oak woods. **FOOD PLANTS** Pines. **SEASON** Apr.–June. **RANGE** Entire region, ex. w PA and w WV.

GRAY HAIRSTREAK
Strymon melinus
GOSSAMER-WING FAMILY

1⅛". Dark gray above; hindwings have orange spot, tails. Below, lighter gray, with distinct black and white line; orange patches near tail. Often rests with wings partly open. **HABITAT** Fields, gardens, shores. **FOOD PLANTS** Varied. **SEASON** Apr.–Nov.

EASTERN TAILED-BLUE
Everes comyntas
GOSSAMER-WING FAMILY

⅞". Dark gray-blue (female) to bright blue (male) above, edged in slate and white; hindwings have orange spot near tiny tail. Below, pale gray (male) or pale brown (female), with tiny sparse black dots; large orange spots near tail. Flight low, weak. **HABITAT** Disturbed open areas, incl. fields, gardens. **FOOD PLANTS** Pea family. **SEASON** Apr.–Nov.

SPRING AZURE
Celastrina ladon
GOSSAMER-WING FAMILY

1". Male entirely pale blue above; female with black border. Below, grayish white with black checkered borders, irregular small dark spots. Widespread and common in early spring. **HABITAT** Woodland openings. **FOOD PLANTS** Dogwoods, viburnums. **SEASON** Mar.–May; similar azure species fly Apr.–Sept.

AMERICAN SNOUT
Libytheana carinenta
BRUSHFOOT FAMILY

1¾". Brown above, with orange patches; white spots on squared forewing tips. Below, hindwings grayish. Extremely long palpi form "snout." **HABITAT** Woodland edges, clearings. **FOOD PLANTS** Hackberry. **SEASON** June–Sept. **RANGE** Entire region, ex. n PA.

GREAT SPANGLED FRITILLARY
Speyeria cybele
BRUSHFOOT FAMILY

2½". Orange above, with black marks; brownish near body. Below, shades of orange-brown; forewings have black marks; hindwings have silvery-white spots, wide cream band. **HABITAT** Fields and edges, gardens. **FOOD PLANTS** Violet family. **SEASON** June–Sept.

MEADOW FRITILLARY
Boloria bellona
BRUSHFOOT FAMILY

1½". Orange above, with blackish-brown bands and spots. Below, hindwings orange-brown at base, outer half mottled grayish. **HABITAT** Open meadows. **FOOD PLANTS** Violet family. **SEASON** Apr.–Oct. **RANGE** Piedmont and higher elevs. **Silver-bordered Fritillary** *(B. selene)* has black margins above, silver spots below.

PEARL CRESCENT
Phyciodes tharos
BRUSHFOOT FAMILY

1¼". Orange above, with black borders, complex markings. Below, hindwings tan to bright orange-yellow with fine black lines and silvery areas. **HABITAT** Fields, waste lots. **FOOD PLANTS** Asters. **SEASON** Apr.–Nov. **RANGE** Entire region, ex. n NY. **Northern Crescent** *(P. selenis)* almost identical; occurs in n NY.

BALTIMORE CHECKERSPOT
Euphydryas phaeton
BRUSHFOOT FAMILY

2". Black above, with tiny white spots and few orange spots, orange trailing edges. Below, black and white checkerboard pattern, with 2 orange bands. Caterpillar largely orange with black spines. **HABITAT** Meadows. **FOOD PLANTS** Turtlehead, plantains. **SEASON** June–July. **RANGE** Piedmont and higher elevs.

QUESTION MARK
Polygonia interrogationis
BRUSHFOOT FAMILY

2½". Forewing tips squared (falcate); orange above, with large black spots; hindwings orange (fall) to very dark (summer), with violet edges; pointed tail. Below, mottled brownish and violet; silver "question mark" on hindwings. **HABITAT** Open woods and edges. **FOOD PLANTS** Elms, nettles, Hackberry. **SEASON** Mar.–Nov.

EASTERN COMMA
Polygonia comma
BRUSHFOOT FAMILY

2". Orange above, with large blackish spots and borders; jagged edges; hindwings orange (fall) to very dark (summer); rounded tails. Below, mottled shades of brown; hooked silver "comma" on hindwings. **HABITAT** Woodland openings, edges. **FOOD PLANTS** Hop vines, elms, nettles. **SEASON** Mar.–Nov.; hibernates.

MOURNING CLOAK
Nymphalis antiopa
BRUSHFOOT FAMILY

3⅛″. Dark purplish brown above, with creamy edges beyond blue-spotted black borders. Below, blackish brown with pale borders. Flies early through leafless woods. Caterpillar black with red spots, black spines. **HABITAT** Woods, parks, fields. **FOOD PLANTS** Willows, elms. **SEASON** Feb.–Dec.; hibernates.

AMERICAN LADY
Vanessa virginiensis
BRUSHFOOT FAMILY

2″. Orange above; outer forewings black with white markings; hindwings with linked row of blue-centered eyespots. Below, lacy brown, black, light gray, and pink; hindwings have 2 large eyespots. Migratory. Caterpillar variable, spiny. **HABITAT** Fields, gardens. **FOOD PLANTS** Everlastings. **SEASON** May–Nov.

PAINTED LADY
Vanessa cardui
BRUSHFOOT FAMILY

2″. Orange above; forewing tips black with white spots; hindwings have black spots at trailing edge. Below, forewings lacy brown and pink; hindwings have row of black-centered spots. Migratory; pop. plentiful to virtually absent, depending on year. **HABITAT** Open areas. **FOOD PLANTS** Varied, incl. thistles. **SEASON** Apr.–Nov.

RED ADMIRAL
Vanessa atalanta
BRUSHFOOT FAMILY

2″. Brownish black above, with wide orange semicircular band; forewings have large white spots near tip. Below, mottled brown and black; forewings have red bar, white-spotted tip; hindwings have blue patch. Migratory. **HABITAT** Meadows, woodland edges, gardens. **FOOD PLANTS** Nettles. **SEASON** Apr.–Dec.

COMMON BUCKEYE
Junonia coenia
BRUSHFOOT FAMILY

2¼″. Tawny brown above, with orange and white bands; bold eyespots: 1 on forewings, 2 on hindwings. Below, forewings similar; hindwings with small eyespots. Migratory; esp. from south in late summer. **HABITAT** Fields, shores. **FOOD PLANTS** Gerardias, plantains, Toadflax. **SEASON** May–Nov. **RANGE** Entire region, ex. n NY.

RED-SPOTTED PURPLE
Limenitis arthemis astyanax
BRUSHFOOT FAMILY

3″. Iridescent dark blue above, edged with light blue bands; forewing tips have red spots. Below, slaty-blue with orange spots at base and margins. Caterpillar mottled dark and cream. **HABITAT** Woodland openings and edges. **FOOD PLANTS** Cherry and aspen trees. **SEASON** May–Sept.

VICEROY
Limenitis archippus
BRUSHFOOT FAMILY

2¾″. Orange above, with blackish veins and margins; narrow black line crossing hindwings above and below. Below, similarly patterned. Resembles Monarch, which is distasteful to predators. Glides with wings horizontal. Caterpillar mottled dark and cream. **HABITAT** Brushy (usu. moist) meadows. **FOOD PLANTS** Willows, aspens. **SEASON** May–Oct.

HACKBERRY EMPEROR
Asterocampa celtis
BRUSHFOOT FAMILY

2″. Brown above; forewings pointed, outer half blackish with white spots, one orange-ringed black eyespot; hindwings lighter with black eyespots along orange-brown margin. Below, marbled brownish-gray with black eyespots. Often lands on humans. **HABITAT** Woodlands, clearings. **FOOD PLANTS** Hackberry. **SEASON** June–Sept. **RANGE** Entire region, ex. NY.

APPALACHIAN BROWN
Satyrodes appalachia
BRUSHFOOT FAMILY

1¾″. Brown above, with black eyespots along margins, smaller and less numerous on forewings. Below, brown with prominent black-, yellow-, and white-ringed eyespots. **HABITAT** Swamps, moist woodland edges. **FOOD PLANTS** Sedges. **SEASON** June–Sept. **RANGE** c NY and south; locally in w PA, w WV, and s VA.

LITTLE WOOD-SATYR
Megisto cymela
BRUSHFOOT FAMILY

1¾″. Pale dull brown above and below; each wing has 2 evenly spaced black spots, circled with yellow, visible above and below. Below, wings crossed by darker brown lines. **HABITAT** Woodlands and edges, meadows. **FOOD PLANTS** Grasses. **SEASON** May–Aug. **RANGE** Entire region, ex. n NY.

COMMON WOOD-NYMPH
Cercyonis pegala
BRUSHFOOT FAMILY

2⅜". Dark brown above; forewings have prominent yellow patch encircling 2 black eyespots. Below, similar but paler, with net-like, blackish lines. **HABITAT** Brushy fields, brackish marshes. **FOOD PLANTS** Grasses. **SEASON** June–Sept.; 1 brood.

MONARCH
Danaus plexippus
BRUSHFOOT FAMILY

3¾". Orange above, with black veins, orange- and white-spotted blackish margins; male has black spot on vein of hindwing. Below, yellow-orange. Head and body black with white spots. Glides with wings held at an angle. Caterpillar banded black, white, and yellow. Adult and caterpillar are poisonous to predators. Eastern Monarchs migrate south in fall to overwinter in fir trees in mtns. of c Mexico. In spring, 1 or 2 generations breed as they fly east, and 1 or 2 more generations breed before the next fall migration. **HABITAT** Fields, shores. **FOOD PLANTS** Milkweed family. **SEASON** May–Nov.

SILVER-SPOTTED SKIPPER
Epargyreus clarus
SKIPPER FAMILY

2". Chocolate-brown above, with golden patches on forewings. Below, hindwings have silver patch. Territorial; aggressively chases other butterflies away. Caterpillar green; head black with 2 orange spots. **HABITAT** Fields, gardens. **FOOD PLANTS** Pea family, esp. locust trees. **SEASON** Apr.–Oct. **RANGE** Entire region, ex. NY mtns.

NORTHERN CLOUDYWING
Thorybes pylades
SKIPPER FAMILY

1½". Patternless brown above; trailing edges buffy; forewings have few random dull white spots. Below, hindwings have darker brown mottling. **HABITAT** Fields, woodland edges. **FOOD PLANTS** Pea family. **SEASON** May–July.

JUVENAL'S DUSKYWING
Erynnis juvenalis
SKIPPER FAMILY

1½". Dark brown above (female slightly lighter); male has 4 small buffy-white spots in cluster on leading edge of forewings; female has many buffy spots. Usu. seen with wings spread. **HABITAT** Oak woods and edges, pine barrens. **FOOD PLANTS** Oaks. **SEASON** Apr.–June. **RANGE** Entire region, ex. n NY.

COMMON CHECKERED-SKIPPER
Pyrgus communis
SKIPPER FAMILY

1". Dark brown with variable white checkered pattern above; bluish hairy scales on body and wing bases; checkered fringes. Below, white with rusty-brown pattern. Male aggressively defends territory. **HABITAT** Weedy fields, disturbed areas. **FOOD PLANTS** Mallow family. **SEASON** May–Nov. **RANGE** c NY and south.

LEAST SKIPPER
Ancyloxypha numitor
SKIPPER FAMILY

¾". Above, forewings dark brown; hindwings orangish with wide black margin. Below, forewings dark brown with orangish markings; hindwings clear yellow-orange. Notably tiny; weak flier. **HABITAT** Marshes, pond edges, moist meadows. **FOOD PLANTS** Grasses. **SEASON** May–Oct. **RANGE** Entire region, ex. NY.

EUROPEAN SKIPPER
Thymelicus lineola
SKIPPER FAMILY

⅞". Orange above, with dark veins, narrow dark borders, and white fringes. Below, unmarked orange. Can be abundant. Introduced from Europe in this century; spreading. **HABITAT** Fields. **FOOD PLANTS** Timothy Grass. **SEASON** June–July. **RANGE** Entire region, ex. se VA.

ZABULON SKIPPER
Poanes zabulon
SKIPPER FAMILY

1¼". Male yellow-orange above, with dark brown edges; below, hindwings often yellow-orange, with orange-brown spots and borders. Female dark brown; below, frosted borders and white leading edge to hindwings. **HABITAT** Open woods, fields. **FOOD PLANTS** Grasses. **SEASON** May–Oct. **RANGE** East and south of c PA; lower Hudson Valley, NY.

PECK'S SKIPPER
Polites peckius
SKIPPER FAMILY

⅞". Forewings brownish above, with orange markings. Below, hindwings have large yellow patches. **HABITAT** Fields, yards. **FOOD PLANTS** Grasses. **SEASON** May–Oct. **RANGE** Entire region, ex. se VA.

EASTERN TENT CATERPILLAR MOTH
Malacosoma americanum
TENT CATERPILLAR MOTH FAMILY

1½". Wings brown; forewings have 2 white bands. Caterpillar blackish; orange and blue side stripes, white line above; in May, many construct communal tents in cherry and apple trees; can denude trees. **HABITAT** Young broadleaf trees. **FOOD PLANTS** Apple and cherry trees. **SEASON** June–Aug.

LUNA MOTH
Actias luna
GIANT SILKWORM MOTH FAMILY

4". Body and wings pale green, each wing with eyespot; forewings and outer curve of hindwings edged purple, all else edged yellow-white; very long tail. Nocturnal. Caterpillar green with yellow stripes, spiny points. **HABITAT** Broadleaf woods. **FOOD PLANTS** Many trees, incl. hickories, beeches. **SEASON** Apr.–Aug.

POLYPHEMUS MOTH
Antheraea polyphemus
GIANT SILKWORM MOTH FAMILY

4½". Body and wings pale orange-brown, with eyespots: yellow on forewings, larger yellow and black on hindwings; narrow black and white line near trailing edges. Nocturnal. Caterpillar bright green with yellow bands, red bumps. **HABITAT** Broadleaf woods. **FOOD PLANTS** Many trees, incl. oaks, maples, birches. **SEASON** May–July.

IO MOTH
Automeris io
GIANT SILKWORM MOTH FAMILY

2½". Forewings yellow (male) or reddish brown (female); hindwings yellow with prominent eyespot, narrow black and rusty bands. Body yellow-brown, cylindrical. Nocturnal. Caterpillar green with reddish and white side stripes, branching black spines; stings. **HABITAT** Open woods and edges. **FOOD PLANTS** Many and varied. **SEASON** May–July.

CECROPIA MOTH
Hyalophora cecropia
GIANT SILKWORM MOTH FAMILY

5¼". Wings gray-brown, with lighter margins, half-moon eyespots, wavy red and white bands. Body reddish, with white collar; abdomen ringed white. Nocturnal. Caterpillar bluish green with red, yellow, and blue knobs. Largest moth north of Mexico. **HABITAT** Woods and edges, fields. **FOOD PLANTS** Many trees, incl. apples. **SEASON** May–July.

TOMATO HORNWORM HAWK MOTH
Manduca quinquemaculata
SPHINX MOTH FAMILY

4". Wings narrow, pointed, gray-brown. Body very large, tapered, with 5–6 pairs of yellow spots on abdomen. Caterpillar bright green with wavy yellow lines; green and black rear horn. **HABITAT** Gardens. **FOOD PLANTS** Tomato, tobacco, and potato plants. **SEASON** May–Oct.

WHITE-LINED SPHINX
Hyles lineata
SPHINX MOTH FAMILY

3". Wings long, narrow. Forewings brown with white veins, tan stripe; hindwings rose, edged with brown. Body brown; thorax has 6 white stripes; abdomen has black and white bars. Active day and night. Caterpillar bright green with yellow head, orange or yellow rear horn. **HABITAT** Meadows, gardens, roadsides. **FOOD PLANTS** Many low-growing plants. **SEASON** Apr.–Oct.

HUMMINGBIRD CLEARWING MOTH
Hemaris thysbe
SPHINX MOTH FAMILY

1¾". Wings brownish with clear, translucent patches. Body spindle-shaped; orange and olive; long, flexible proboscis. Hovers by day at flowers like a hummingbird. Caterpillar yellowish green with darker lines, reddish-brown spots on abdomen; yellow tail horn. **HABITAT** Woodland edges, fields, gardens. **FOOD PLANTS** Hawthorn and cherry trees, honeysuckles. **SEASON** Apr.–Sept.

VIRGIN TIGER MOTH
Grammia virgo
TIGER MOTH FAMILY

2½". Forewings and thorax black, with complex network of bold white veining and white margins. Hindwings and abdomen pink with black splotches. Nocturnal. Caterpillar blackish, covered with stiff hairs. **HABITAT** Fields, woodland edges. **FOOD PLANTS** Lettuces, clovers, goosefoot family, incl. Lambs Quarters. **SEASON** June–Aug.

WOOLLY BEAR CATERPILLAR MOTH
Pyrrharctia isabella
TIGER MOTH FAMILY

1¾". Forewings orange-yellow, with rows of small black spots; hindwings lighter. Body rusty orange. Nocturnal. Caterpillar distinctive, hairy, reddish brown and black; often crosses roads, paths by day in Sept., Oct. **HABITAT** Shrubby fields, roadsides. **FOOD PLANTS** Dandelions, plantains, low-growing weeds, and many others. **SEASON** Apr.–Aug.

FALL WEBWORM MOTH
Hyphantria cunea
TIGER MOTH FAMILY

1⅜". Wings ghostly white; forewings have varying amounts of black spots. Body white. Caterpillar variably colored, with long light hairs; in late summer makes large gray webs near branch tips; conspicuous in fall. **HABITAT** Broadleaf and mixed woodlands. **FOOD PLANTS** Many broadleaf trees. **SEASON** Apr.–Aug.

caterpillar (top left), adult (top right), web (bottom)

VIRGINIA CTENUCHID MOTH
Ctenucha virginica
CTENUCHID MOTH FAMILY

1⅝". Butterfly-like. Wings dark brown, with narrow white trailing edges. Body metallic blue-green; head orange. Flies by day. Caterpillar brown, with clumps of blackish or creamy hairs; head red. HABITAT Moist meadows. FOOD PLANTS Grasses, sedges, irises. SEASON May–July. RANGE NJ and north.

GYPSY MOTH
Lymantria dispar
TUSSOCK MOTH FAMILY

Female 2"; male ¾". Female wings and body creamy white with blackish wavy lines; flightless. Male pale brown, mottled; flies erratically. Female lays brownish-yellow egg masses on shady sides of trees, buildings. Caterpillar very hairy, feeds in trees by day, often on ground at night. Introduced from Eurasia to MA in 1869; major pest and nuisance; defoliates vast forests, where you can hear excrement drop from trees. Diseases and natural predators reduce numbers after several summers of infestation. HABITAT Woods, esp. oak. FOOD PLANTS Mainly broadleaf trees. SEASON July–Aug.

ILIA UNDERWING
Catocala ilia
OWLET MOTH FAMILY

3". Forewings mottled dark gray to blackish, with white markings near front edge; hindwings black with pinkish-red base, wavy transverse band. Body grayish-brown. Rests on tree by day, with forewings hiding brilliant hindwings. Nocturnal. Caterpillar mottled gray above; bright pink below; tapered at both ends. HABITAT Oak woods. FOOD PLANTS Oaks. SEASON June–Sept.

EIGHT-SPOTTED FORESTER
Alypia octomaculata
OWLET MOTH FAMILY

1⅛". Wings black; forewings each have 2 yellow spots; hindwings each have 2 white spots. Body hairy, black with yellow shoulders; forelegs have bright orange hair-like scales. Flies by day. Caterpillar banded black, white, and orange. HABITAT Woodland edges, brushy fields. FOOD PLANTS Grapes, Virginia Creeper. SEASON Apr.–June.

Vertebrates

There are approximately 43,000 vertebrate species on earth. The evolution of a variety of anatomical structures has made them extraordinarily successful for half a billion years. Today vertebrates are one of the most widespread groups of animals, inhabiting every corner of the globe, from ocean depths to mountaintops, deserts, and polar regions.

Vertebrata is one of three subphyla of the phylum Chordata. All members of Chordata possess an internal stiffening rod called a notochord during their embryonic development. The sac-like marine sea squirts, salps, and their relatives (members of the subphylum Urochordata, the most primitive of the Chordata) lose the notochord completely as they develop, and in the file-shaped marine lancelets (of the subphylum Cephalochordata), the notochord remains an unsegmented rod. In vertebrates, the notochord is replaced during the animal's development by a series of cartilaginous or bony disks, known as vertebrae, that run along the back.

The evolution of the vertebrates stemmed from an invertebrate sea squirt–like animal, passed through a "missing link" invertebrate-to-vertebrate stage with the lancelets, and reached the beginnings of the vertebrate stage some 500 million years ago (mya) with the appearance of the first jawless fishes. During the following 350 million years, the various classes of vertebrates evolved. The ancestors of modern fishes developed from their jawless ancestors about 400 mya; 100 million years further into vertebrate development, amphibians evolved from fishes crawling about in search of water during the droughts of the Devonian period. Reptiles first appeared about 250 mya and flourished because of their ability to reproduce on land. Mammals and birds, warm-blooded and able to successfully live in places too cold for amphibians and reptiles, spread across the world's environments, mammals beginning about 170 mya and birds about 150 mya.

Today's vertebrates share a number of characteristics that separate them from the estimated 50 million or so invertebrate species with which they share the earth. Virtually all vertebrates are bilaterally symmetrical; that is, their left and right sides are essentially mirror images of one another. A strong but flexible backbone, composed of vertebrae, protects the spinal cord and serves as the main structural component of the internal skeletal frame and the segmented muscles that attach to it. Vertebrates are well-coordinated runners, jumpers, swimmers, and/or fliers because of this unique combination of skeletal and muscular development. Other shared characteristics of nearly all vertebrates include one pair of bony jaws (with or without teeth), one or two pairs of appendages, a ventrally located heart (protected by a rib cage), and blood contained in vessels.

The subphylum Vertebrata includes several classes: three classes of living fishes, the amphibians, the reptiles, the birds, and the mammals.

Fishes

Living fishes fall into three major groups: the primitive hagfishes and lampreys, the cartilaginous fishes (sharks, skates, and rays), and the bony fishes. Aquatic, mostly cold-blooded vertebrates with fins and internal gills, fish are typically streamlined and have muscular tails. Most move through the water by weaving movements of their bodies and tail fins, using their other fins to control their direction. The skin of a fish is coated with a slimy secretion that decreases friction with the water; this secretion, along with the scales that cover most fish, provides their bodies with a nearly waterproof covering. The gills are located in passages that lead from the throat usually to a pair of openings on the side, just behind the head. With rare exceptions, fish breathe by taking water in through the mouth and forcing it past the gills and out through the gill openings; the thin-walled gills capture oxygen from the water and emit carbon dioxide.

The body shapes of fishes vary from cylindrical eels and elongated, spindle-shaped mackerels (rounded in the middle, with tapered ends) to vertically compressed (flattened) sunfishes to horizontally compressed skates and rays. Body colors can vary within a species due to season, sex, age, individual variation, and water temperature, and the color normally fades or otherwise changes after death. Most fishes have one or more dorsal (back) fins that may be spiny or soft (a few fishes, such as trout and salmon, have an additional fleshy fin behind the dorsal fins called an adipose fin); a tail (caudal) fin, usually with an upper and a lower lobe; and an anal fin, just in front of the tail along the edge of the ventral (belly) side. They also have a pair of pectoral fins, usually on the sides behind the head, and a pair of pelvic fins, generally under the middle of the body. Some fishes lack one or more of these fins.

The mouths and snouts of fishes may be disk-shaped, pointed, tubular, or spear-like; depending on the species, the upper jaw (the snout) projects beyond the lower, the two parts of the jaw are of equal length, or the lower jaw projects beyond the upper. Some species have sensory barbels, whisker-like projections of the skin, usually on the lower jaw, that detect objects, especially in muddy or murky water. Most fish are covered with scales, but some species lack scales altogether, and some lack scales on the head or other areas; in other species, scales have been modified into bony plates. Some fishes have a conspicuous lateral line, a sensory organ beneath the skin that responds to vibrations in the water and often looks like a thin stripe along the side; others have no lateral line, while a few have branching lateral lines.

Some fish species are solitary, some live in small groups, and others are found mainly in enormous schools in which members respond as a unit to stimuli while feeding or migrating.

Lengths given (from the tip of the snout to the tip of the tail) are for typical adults, although, as fish continue to grow throughout their lives, larger individuals may be seen. The icon ![icon] denotes fishes that can be found in both salt and fresh water (see box, page 248).

Hagfishes and Lampreys

The primitive hagfishes and lampreys are jawless and eel-like in appearance; their skeletons are formed of cartilage. They lack scales and the paired pelvic and pectoral fins of the more advanced fishes. Hagfishes (often called slime eels) are carrion-feeders that use a circular mouth, which contains teeth, for biting. All hagfishes live in salt water; they are rare in waters off the Mid-Atlantic coast. Adult lampreys are parasitic, using the mouth as a suction disk to hold on to prey, whose blood they suck as they are carried along by the host fish; larval lamprey are filter feeders. Marine lampreys return to fresh water to breed, while other lamprey species live their entire lives in freshwater brooks and rivers.

Sea Lamprey (left) with prey

SEA LAMPREY
Petromyzon marinus
LAMPREY FAMILY

24–30″. Eel-like, scaleless. Mottled brown above, yellowish on sides, white below. 2 dorsal fins wavy-edged; tail fin small, diamond-shaped. Row of 7 gill openings on each side. Mouth round, with many rasp-like teeth. Attaches to large fish, sucks blood, kills host over many days. Invaded Great Lakes via Welland Canal in 1833; has killed off most Lake Trout and other fisheries. **HABITAT** Breeds in streams; spends most of life in ocean to 1,600′ deep; lakes.

Cartilaginous Fishes

The cartilaginous fishes have skeletons of somewhat flexible cartilage and several (usually five) pairs of conspicuous external gill slits. This group includes, in waters off the Mid-Atlantic region, sharks, skates, and rays. Sharks typically have an elongated shape that tapers toward each end; one or two triangular dorsal fins, sometimes with a fin spine on the leading edge; two large pectoral fins; two smaller pelvic fins; a tail fin of which the upper lobe is usually larger than the lower; and sometimes an anal fin and a pair of horizontal keels at the base

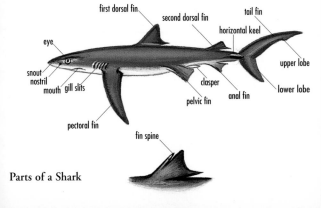

Parts of a Shark

of the tail. The skates and rays have flattened bodies, usually round or diamond-shaped, with greatly enlarged pectoral fins attached to the sides of the head, forming "wings" with which they "fly" through the water. The mouth is located on the underside of the head. Sharks have several rows of sharply pointed teeth; when a tooth breaks off or is worn down, a new tooth takes its place. The skin is rough and sandpapery, studded with tiny tooth-like scales called denticles.

Because cartilaginous fishes lack the swim bladder that keeps the bony fishes buoyant, and the efficient "gill pump" of bony fishes that keeps water moving over their gills, many sharks must swim constantly. Most live in ocean waters, though a few may enter large rivers. The male has a pair of external copulatory organs called claspers, modifications of the pelvic fins that are used to internally fertilize the female. Depending on the species, the female lays eggs enclosed in a horny case, retains the eggs internally until they hatch, or gives birth to live young.

SHORTFIN MAKO
Isurus oxyrinchus
MACKEREL SHARK FAMILY

5–10′. Long and slender; snout pointed. Blue-gray to deep blue above, white below. 1st dorsal fin large, rounded. Teeth large, slender, smooth-edged, pointed backward. Very fast swimmer; often leaps out of water. **CAUTION** Bites; may follow boats. **HABITAT** May–Oct.: surface of open sea; rare near shore.

SMOOTH DOGFISH
Mustelus canis
REQUIEM SHARK FAMILY

3′–4′6″. Snout small, long, pointed. Grayish olive above, whitish below. 2 dorsal fins large, rounded, nearly equal in size; pectoral fins long, wide. Tail fin's upper lobe notched, elongated; lower lobe very short, rounded. Eyes bulge at top of head. Teeth small. **HABITAT** Bottoms to 60′ deep or more; enters bays, river mouths to feed. **RANGE** May–Oct.: entire coast, s Ches. Bay.

BLUE SHARK
Prionace glauca
REQUIEM SHARK FAMILY

7–10′. Very slender; snout pointed. Dark blue above, sides light blue, white below. 1st dorsal fin relatively small, rounded; crescent-shaped pectoral fins long, flexible; tail fin's upper lobe long, very swept-back. Teeth curved, triangular. Follows boats, waiting for offal. Most frequently seen large shark at sea's surface. **CAUTION** Rarely bites beachgoers, but has attacked people swimming off boats at sea. **HABITAT** Near or at surface of open sea; occ. near shore.

SPINY DOGFISH
Squalus acanthias
REQUIEM SHARK FAMILY

24–42″. Snout blunt. Slaty brown above, shading to dirty white below. 2 pointed dorsal fins, 1st larger, each with a spine in front; trailing edge of pectoral fins notched. Upper lobe of tail fin long, without notch. Teeth small, sharp. Imm. has conspicuous white spots above. May swarm in large schools. **CAUTION** Spines are slightly poisonous. **HABITAT** Surf zone to deep water. **RANGE** Mainly cooler waters off Long Is. and NJ.

CLEARNOSE SKATE
Raja eglanteria
SKATE FAMILY

18–30″. Body disk flattened, kite-shaped; pectoral fins enlarged, wing-like. Brown with blackish spots and dashes above, white below. Eyes on top of head. Tail as long as body, tubular, spiny. Spends day half-buried in bottom sediments. Undulates "wings" to "fly" over bottom at night searching for shellfish. Harmless, unobtrusive. Empty egg case, black with curled extensions, called mermaid's purse; often found on beaches. **HABITAT** Sandy bottoms to 200′ deep. Summer: inshore. Winter: offshore.

COWNOSE RAY
Rhinoptera bonasus
EAGLE RAY FAMILY

L 4–7′; W 24–36″. Body disk wider than long. Front of head concave; snout deeply indented; eyes on outer sides of head. Dark brown above, creamy below. Wing-like pectoral fins narrow toward tip; 1 venomous spine at base of long, whip-like tail. Schools "fly" gracefully just below surface. Bears live young; powerful teeth crush mollusks. **HABITAT** Shallow bays, inshore waters; present in warmer months.

SOUTHERN STINGRAY
Dasyatis americana
STINGRAY FAMILY

L 4′–5′6″; W 30–36″. Body disk flattened, kite-shaped. Back color matches local sea bottom: light brown, gray, or olive; whitish below. Lacks dorsal fin, but has irreg. row of short spines along midback ridge. Tail very long, whip-like, with rigid, barbed, venomous spine near base. Mouth on underside; teeth flat, powerful for crunching mollusks, crustaceans. Undulates "wings" when swimming. Often rests half-buried in sand in shallow water. **CAUTION** Tail spine can cause serious wound. **HABITAT** Inshore; shallow sand and mud bottoms. **RANGE** s NJ to s Ches. Bay.

Bony Fishes

Bony fishes normally have harder, less flexible bony skeletons than cartilaginous fishes, as well as a gas- or fat-filled swim bladder that keeps them buoyant. Most bony fishes have overlapping scales embedded in flexible connective tissue, though some lack scales entirely. There is a single gill opening on each side protected by a hard gill cover.

More than 99 percent of all living fishes are ray-finned bony fishes; a few bony fishes (none of which occur in Mid-Atlantic waters) are classified as lobe-finned fishes. The fins of ray-finned bony fishes consist of a web of skin supported by bony rays (either segmented soft rays or stiffer spines), each moved by a set of muscles, which makes the fins very flexible. The tail fin is typically symmetrical.

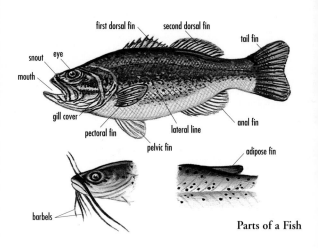

Parts of a Fish

Most bony fishes reproduce by spawning: males directly fertilize eggs after the females release them from their bodies into the water. The eggs may float at mid-levels, rise to the surface, or sink to the bottom. A few fish species guard nests or incubate eggs in a pouch or the mouth. Newborn fish are called larvae; within a few weeks or months, a larva develops to resemble a miniature adult, and is called a juvenile or fry.

This section is presented in two categories: saltwater fishes (starting on page 241) and freshwater fishes (starting on page 250). Most fish species live strictly in either salt water or fresh water. Other species are frequently found in brackish water, where fresh and salt water mix, and some primarily saltwater species breed in fresh water but return to spend most of their lives at sea. Species are placed in the category where they spend most of their time or are most likely to be seen. The icon ![icon] denotes those that live in both types of water (see box, page 248).

ATLANTIC STURGEON
Acipenser oxyrhynchus
STURGEON FAMILY

6–8′. Snout long. 5 rows of bony plates on back, sides, and belly. Bluish black above, silvery below. Fleshy barbels hang from snout. Cruises bottom looking for fish, crustaceans, mollusks. Threatened. **HABITAT** Coasts, brackish estuaries. Spring: enters large rivers to spawn. **RANGE** Entire coast, Ches. Bay.

ATLANTIC MENHADEN
"Mossbunker"
Brevoortia tyrannus
HERRING FAMILY

10–18″. Head scaleless; mouth large. Back pale blue, with 1 small dorsal fin; midback has fatty ridge with modified scales. Sides silvery, washed yellow. Often in vast schools. **HABITAT** Near ocean surface. Apr.–Oct.: also inlets, estuaries, bays. **RANGE** Entire coast, Ches. Bay.

POLLOCK
Pollachius virens
COD FAMILY

24–36″. Brownish green or dark gray above, silvery below. 3 dorsal fins and pelvic and anal fins wide-based. Lower jaw has tiny barbel. Runs in schools. **HABITAT** Surface to 600′ deep. **RANGE** Long Is. to c NJ; rarer south to VA. **Atlantic Cod** (*Gadus morhua*) more spotted, with fan-shaped tail fin; occurs off Long Is.

WHITE HAKE
Urophycis tenuis
COD FAMILY

28″. Cylindrical in front, compressed toward back. Brown with white blotches. 1st dorsal fin short; 2nd runs length of back; anal fin runs along rear half of body; pelvic fin "feelers" hang below gills, in front of pectoral fins; tail fin small. Small chin barbel. **HABITAT** Muddy or silty bottoms 40–360′ deep.

GOOSEFISH
"Monkfish"
Lophius americanus
GOOSEFISH FAMILY

24″. Body horizontally flattened as in flatfish; head broad, large. Brown. 1st dorsal fin spine forward-arching, modified into "fishing pole" with dangling lure; other dorsal fins short; pectoral fins wide, rounded; tail fin small, fan-shaped. Mouth

enormous, upward-angled, lined with about 100 long sharp teeth. Lies on bottom ambushing large fish and sea ducks attracted to waving lure. **HABITAT** Muddy shallows, bottoms to 1,200′ deep.

ATLANTIC NEEDLEFISH
Strongylura marina
NEEDLEFISH FAMILY

12–24". Long, pencil-shaped; jaws needle-like. Greenish blue above; lateral line blue. Single dorsal and anal fins far back. Chases small fish at night. **HABITAT** Coastal, brackish, and nearby fresh waters; occ. seen at surface. Spawns in salt and fresh water; follows prey into rivers. **RANGE** Entire coast, Ches. Bay.

MUMMICHOG
Fundulus heteroclitus
KILLIFISH FAMILY

3–4". Stocky, with rounded back and wide base of tail; head blunt. Dark green, with blackish and silvery bars on sides. Single spineless dorsal fin set far back; tail fin large, rounded. Feeds at surface on small invertebrates and insect larvae. **HABITAT** Estuaries, tidal creeks, salt marshes, nearby fresh waters. **RANGE** Entire coast, Ches. Bay.

ATLANTIC SILVERSIDE
Menidia menidia
SILVERSIDE FAMILY

3½". Silversides: small, long schooling fish with large eyes, silver side stripe. This species: gray-green above, whitish below. 1st dorsal fin small, with 4 spiny rays; anal fin long, straight-edged. Food fish for terns. **HABITAT** Off sandy beaches; shallow bays; estuaries. **RANGE** Entire coast, Ches. Bay.

THREESPINE STICKLEBACK
Gasterosteus aculeatus
STICKLEBACK FAMILY

3". Tapered at ends; sides have bony plates. Olive-brown above, silver below (breeding male red below). 3 stout, widely separated spines on back before dorsal fin. Apr.–July: male builds nest from water plants. **HABITAT** Grassy shallows, estuaries. Spawns in freshwater streams. **RANGE** Entire coast, Ches. Bay.

LINED SEAHORSE
Hippocampus erectus
PIPEFISH FAMILY

4". Elongated; head and tubular snout angle downward; swims upright with head above body, tail dangling below. Armored with lines and ridges. Color varies with background: gray, brown, or dull red. Dorsal fin fan-shaped; tail prehensile, finless, curls around vegetation. Swims (weakly) by rapid vibration of dorsal fin. When mating, pair makes musical sounds; female lays eggs in male's pouch; young hatch and are expelled by male several weeks later. **HABITAT** Eelgrass beds in shallow water with tidal currents. **RANGE** Entire coast, s Ches. Bay.

NORTHERN PIPEFISH
Syngnathus fuscus
PIPEFISH FAMILY

4–8″. Pencil-like, horizontal; head narrow; snout tubular. Flexible body has rings of bony scales. Yellow-green or brown. 1 rectangular dorsal fin. Tail long; fin tiny. Male has brood pouch on underside. **HABITAT** Sea-grass beds in bays, inlets; occ. enters fresh water near coast. **RANGE** Entire coast, c and s Ches. Bay.

NORTHERN SEAROBIN
Prionotus carolinus
SEAROBIN FAMILY

10–15″. Head has bony plate with short spines; eyes on brow ridge. Grayish or rufous above with darker mottling. 1st dorsal fin spiny, with black spot; pectoral fins have 3 "walking" rays. Makes noises out of water. **HABITAT** Summer: shallow inshore waters and bay bottoms. Winter: deeper southern waters.

LONGHORN SCULPIN
Myoxocephalus octodecemspinosus
SCULPIN FAMILY

8–14″. Head and eyes large; long sharp spines on head and gill covers; rear body narrow. Mottled shades of brown; color varies to match bottom color. All fins spiny, fan-like, mottled. Raised scales along lateral line. **CAUTION** Beware of sharp spines.

HABITAT Summer: shoals, harbor bottoms. Winter: deeper waters.

Overfishing off the Mid-Atlantic Coast

While the rich fisheries of the estuaries, shallows, and deep water of the Mid-Atlantic region have been exploited for human food for centuries, fish populations held their own until the middle of the 20th century. Foreign fleets harvested unlimited catches until 1977, when the United States imposed a 200-mile territorial boundary. American fleets then expanded in size and armed themselves with ever-increasing fish-finding technology, and soon exceeded the catch of the Europeans, forcing an array of regulations on total catch, net mesh size, and minimum fish size per species.

Current ecological research focuses on the habitat requirements of fish fry. Trawling operations have ruined large areas of the sea bottom, a major habitat for adult bottom fish and the fry of other species. Because of degradation of the sea bottom, as well as harvesting before fish are sexually mature, Summer Flounder populations have crashed. Agricultural and urban runoff have added large doses of new chemicals and pollutants into once highly productive waters, and longline fisheries have decimated Tilefish and Swordfish populations. A concerned citizenry is working with fish biologists to restore fish habitats. One success story is the rebound of Striped Bass populations after careful management.

WHITE PERCH
Morone americana
TEMPERATE BASS FAMILY

7–12″. Oblong; back rounded; head small; very scaly. Blackish below dorsal fins; rest of body silvery, often with indistinct stripes. 1st dorsal fin has indented strong spines; 2nd dorsal fin triangular; tail fin slightly forked. **HABITAT** Bays (incl. Ches. Bay), brackish estuaries, freshwater rivers, lakes; spawns in fresh water. Some introduced pops. landlocked.

STRIPED BASS
Morone saxatilis
TEMPERATE BASS FAMILY

20–48″. Pale; olive or slaty blue above; sides silvery, with blackish stripes; belly white. 2 dorsal fins triangular; tail fin notched. Numbers are rebounding. **HABITAT** Shallow coastal waters, incl. surf. Spring: spawns in freshwater rivers, esp. off Ches. Bay. **RANGE** Summer–fall: entire coast. Winter: deep inshore channels, offshore depths.

BLACK SEA BASS
Centropristis striata
SEA BASS FAMILY

12–24″. Head large, blackish. Old male dark bluish black with paler blotches, speckling. Female paler brown with darker brown stripes. Whitish blotches on back. Dorsal fin spiny, banded black and white; tail fin 3-lobed, upper lobe often has long ray. **HABITAT** Harbors, jetties, over rough bottoms of continental shelf. **RANGE** Entire coast, Ches. Bay.

BLUEFISH
Pomatomus saltatrix
BLUEFISH FAMILY

12–36″. Head large; teeth prominent. Blue-green above, shading to silvery below. 1st dorsal fin short, with 7 projecting spines; tail fin deeply forked. Attacks smaller fish and squid; often kills more than it can eat. Travels in schools. **CAUTION** May bite. **HABITAT** Apr.–Oct.: inshore and offshore surface waters. **RANGE** Entire coast, s Ches. Bay.

COBIA
Rachycentron canadum
COBIA FAMILY

12–60″. Head long, flat. Adult body has 3 dark brown and 2 buffy stripes. Young striped black and white. Fins blackish; 1st dorsal fin is 8 very short, detached spines; 2nd is long, higher in front. Fast swimmer; often with whales, larger fish; under boats, buoys. **HABITAT** Open sea near surface, waters around piers. **RANGE** Summer: entire coast, Ches. Bay.

CREVALLE JACK
"Jack Crevalle"
Caranx hippos
JACK FAMILY
18–30". Robust. Dark blue-green above; sides and belly yellowish silver. 1st dorsal fin short. 2nd dorsal and yellow anal fin long; pectoral fins have black spot at base; tail fin deeply forked. Eyes large. Fast, powerful swimmer. **HABITAT** River mouths and bays to deep waters. **RANGE** Entire coast, s Ches. Bay.

SHEEPSHEAD
Archosargus probatocephalus
PORGY FAMILY
24–36". Head profile very steep; broad incisor teeth protrude. Iridescent silvery with 5–7 vertical bars. Dorsal fin continuous; rays of dorsal and anal fins have stout sharp spines; tail fin forked. Usu. a solitary, wary bottom dweller. **HABITAT** Muddy shallows, under piers. **RANGE** Entire coast, s Ches. Bay.

SCUP
"Porgy"
Stenotomus chrysops
PORGY FAMILY

8–16". Head profile steep. Brownish above, sides silvery, with many indistinct, brown bars that fade out of water. Continuous spiny dorsal fin; tail fin deeply forked. A schooling bottom feeder. **HABITAT** Mainly May–Oct.: inshore bottoms to continental shelf; estuaries, jetties, piers. **RANGE** Entire coast, Ches. Bay.

SOUTHERN KINGFISH
Menticirrhus americanus
DRUM FAMILY
10–15". Back and sides dull grayish; dark, back-slanted bands or blotches along sides; belly very pale. Tip of 1st dorsal fin black. Short, stout barbel on chin. **HABITAT** Sandy bottoms, 60' and deeper; occasionally muddy bottoms.

ATLANTIC CROAKER
Micropogonias undulatus
DRUM FAMILY
8–15". Front-heavy; snout rounded; mouth small; tiny barbels on chin. Pale blue to olive above, with interrupted bars of dark brown spots; pale gray below. Dorsal fins low, joined. Numbers fluctuate from year to year. **HABITAT** Sandy bottoms and sea-grass beds in shallow waters, bays. **RANGE** Mainly NJ and south; Ches. Bay.

RED DRUM
"Channel Bass"
Sciaenops ocellatus
DRUM FAMILY

24–48″. Rounded above, straight below; snout conical, extends over mouth. Color iridescent, variable: reddish, yellowish brown, or gray; paler below. Dorsal fins joined; black spot on tail before squarish tail fin. HABITAT Surf zone, piers, to open sea; sometimes in fresh water. RANGE Entire coast, s Ches. Bay.

STRIPED MULLET
Mugil cephalus
MULLET FAMILY

10–18″. Head and mouth small; scales large. Back olive green; sides silvery with faint horizontal stripes; belly whitish. Dorsal fins small, triangular; tail fin large, forked. Feeds on algae on muddy bottoms; runs in large schools; often leaps out of water. HABITAT Shallow ocean waters, bays; enters rivers. RANGE Mainly NJ and south; s Ches. Bay.

TAUTOG
Tautoga onitis
WRASSE FAMILY

10–20″. Stout; head rounded, blunt; scales small. Blackish above. Male mottled black and brown on sides. Female and young black and buff. Dorsal fin long, with rounded bump at rear; tail fin rounded. Thick lips. HABITAT Summer: coastal waters to 600′ deep; rocky areas, docks in estuaries, mussel beds. Winter: deep waters. RANGE Entire coast, s Ches. Bay.

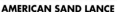

AMERICAN SAND LANCE
Ammodytes americanus
SAND LANCE FAMILY

6″. Blue-green to brownish above, silvery on sides and below. Dorsal fin long, low; lacks pelvic fins; tail fin small, forked. Burrows rapidly in soft bottoms (incl. above low-tide line), swims near surface in schools; undulates like a swimming snake. Major prey for whales, seabirds, terns, larger fish. HABITAT Surface to 120′ deep, esp. offshore banks.

LITTLE TUNNY
"False Albacore"
Euthynnus alletteratus
MACKEREL FAMILY

18–36″. Metallic shiny blue above, with wavy black stripes; whitish below, with black spots forward. Dorsal fins triangular; base of tail has horizontal keel. Runs in schools; common. HABITAT Near surface of open sea; smaller groups near shore. RANGE Entire coast, s Ches. Bay.

ATLANTIC BONITO
Sarda sarda
MACKEREL FAMILY

20–30″. Head and eyes large; snout pointed; jaws up-slanted. Steel blue above, with 7–11 slanted blackish stripes; silvery below. Dorsal fins triangular. Base of tail has horizontal keel; tail fin crescent-like. Travels in large schools. **HABITAT** Mainly summer: near sea surface in warm waters, usu. well offshore. **RANGE** Entire coast, s Ches. Bay.

ATLANTIC MACKEREL
Scomber scombrus
MACKEREL FAMILY

12–16″. Streamlined; head pointed; scales minute. Blue-green above, with about 20 black, wavy, vertical bands; plain silvery below. 1st dorsal fin triangular; 2nd dorsal fin concave; 5 finlets above and 5 below on narrow tail before forked tail fin. Swift swimmer; occurs in schools. **HABITAT** Open sea over continental shelf. Mar.–May: schools move northward near shore.

SPANISH MACKEREL
Scomberomorus maculatus
MACKEREL FAMILY

10–30″. Shiny metallic blue above, silvery below, large golden spots on sides. 1st dorsal fin low, black foreward, pale to rear; 2nd dorsal fin triangular; 8–9 finlets before keeled, deeply forked tail fin. Often in schools. **HABITAT** Warm surface waters of open sea, bays; some to surf line of beaches. **RANGE** Summer: mainly south of c NJ.

BLUEFIN TUNA
Thunnus thynnus
MACKEREL FAMILY

5–7′. Head massive, pointed; mouth large. Dark blue-black above, silvery white below, yellowish stripe on side. 1st dorsal fin triangular; 2nd dorsal fin and anal fins scythe-shaped; base of tail has 8–10 dorsal and 7–9 anal finlets; tail fin crescent-shaped. Very fast swimmer; one of sea's top predators. Numbers declining fast. **HABITAT** Late summer: surface of open sea.

SWORDFISH
"Broadbill Swordfish"
Xiphias gladius
SWORDFISH FAMILY

4–10′. Spindle-shaped; upper jaw very long, ⅓ body length, pointed and flattened. Dark brown above, sides yellowish gray. Dorsal fin extremely large, swept-back, begins just behind head; lacks pelvic fins; tail fin crescent-shaped. Eyes large, above corners of mouth. Fast swimmer, reaches 60 mph; feeds on schooling fish; overharvested. **HABITAT** Warm open sea from surface (often basks there) to 200′ deep; usu. well offshore.

Flatfishes

Flatfish is the group name for three fish families (lefteye flounders, righteye flounders, and soles) with an unusual body form adapted to life on the seafloor. The larval fish starts life swimming normally, with an eye on each side. Soon one eye "migrates" to join the other on one side (right or left, depending on the species). The spineless, continuous dorsal fin and anal fins shift 90 degrees to become fringing horizontal fins, and for the rest of the fish's life, it swims on one side. Flatfishes can change color and pattern, like chameleons, to match their backgrounds; their undersides are normally white. They usually lie partially buried in soft mud or sand bottoms, and dart quickly upward to seize passing small fish, crustaceans, and squid.

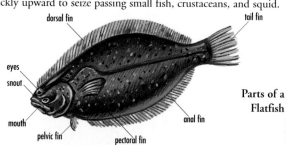

Parts of a Flatfish

HOGCHOKER
"American Sole"
Trinectes maculatus
SOLE FAMILY

5–7". Flat, more rounded than flounders; mouth very small; eyes small, on right side. Dark brown with thin black bars. Continuous dorsal and anal fins fringe body edge; no pectoral fins. Imm. travels to 150 miles up major rivers to feed; spawns in salt water. **HABITAT** Muddy, silty, and sandy bottoms in coastal bays (incl. Ches. Bay), estuaries, rivers.

 Fishes That Live in Both Fresh and Salt Water

Scores of Mid-Atlantic fish species spend occasional to great parts of their lives moving between salt and fresh water. Freshwater fishes such as Brook Trout, Chain Pickerel, and Largemouth Bass may visit brackish estuaries; marine fishes such as Scup and Summer Flounder may regularly move quite far up an estuary; and many other species occasionally cross the boundaries between salt and fresh waters.

Two categories of fishes notable for their mass journeys between marine and freshwater environments are the anadromous and catadromous species. An anadromous fish lives the greater part of its life in salt water but spawns in fresh water. Catadromous fishes reverse this process, spawning in salt water and living the greater part

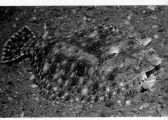

WINTER FLOUNDER
Pleuronectes americanus
RIGHTEYE FLOUNDER FAMILY

12–18″. Flat, oval, with rounded tail fin. Varies in color: usu. brownish, often mottled with dark spots; lateral line straight. Continuous dorsal and anal fins fringe sides of body. Head and mouth small; eyes bulbous. **HABITAT** Muddy and sandy bottoms to more than 100′ deep. **RANGE** Summer: deep water. Fall–spring: entire coast, c and s Ches. Bay.

SUMMER FLOUNDER
"Fluke"
Paralichthys dentatus
LEFTEYE FLOUNDER FAMILY

15–30″. Flat, oval; wedge-shaped tail fin. Brownish above, with dark spots. Dorsal and anal fins fringe body edge. Head and mouth small; eyes bulbous. Buries itself in sand; swims fast to pursue prey. **HABITAT** Summer: sandy or muddy bottoms in bays, estuaries, shallow ocean waters. Winter: ocean to 650′ deep. **RANGE** Entire coast, s Ches. Bay.

OCEAN SUNFISH
Mola mola
MOLA FAMILY

3–8′. Round, massive, compressed; rear end has rounded, flap-like tail fin that looks cut off; scaleless. Mirror-image single dorsal fin and anal fin huge, pointed, placed far back on body; no pelvic fins. Back gray-blue, sides and belly silvery. Eyes large, well back from mouth. Strong swimmer, but often lies on side at surface, waving dorsal fin. Feeds on jellyfish, squid, fish larvae. This uncommon giant is not related to freshwater sunfish. **HABITAT** Warm ocean surface waters in late summer, early fall.

of their lives in fresh water. Mid-Atlantic anadromous species include the Sea Lamprey, American Shad, Rainbow Smelt, Striped Bass, and the now rare Atlantic Salmon. The American Eel is the sole catadromous fish in the Mid-Atlantic region.

Although river pollution, river damming, and overfishing have drastically reduced anadromous and catadromous species from the population levels of colonial days, several rivers in Pennsylvania and Virginia have large annual shad runs, and rivers flowing into Chesapeake Bay are major spawning areas for Striped Bass. The catadromous American Eels can be difficult to observe as they usually migrate at night on their journeys to and from the Sargasso Sea, northeast of the West Indies.

AMERICAN EEL
Anguilla rostrata
FRESHWATER EEL FAMILY
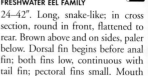

24–42″. Long, snake-like; in cross section, round in front, flattened to rear. Brown above and on sides, paler below. Dorsal fin begins before anal fin; both fins low, continuous with tail fin; pectoral fins small. Mouth large; lower jaw protrudes slightly. Male prefers brackish waters; female swims far up rivers for 8–20 years before trip back to spawn and die. **HABITAT** Rivers, lakes, estuaries. Spawns in open ocean northeast of West Indies; larvae spend 1–3 years at sea becoming elvers (young eels), then enter rivers. **RANGE** Mainland NY to c VA.

LONGNOSE GAR
Lepisosteus osseus
GAR FAMILY

24–42″. Long, slim; slender snout twice length of head. Olive-brown with black spots above, white below. Single dorsal fin and anal fin far back near rounded tail fin; all fins have dark spots. **HABITAT** Rivers, lakes, weedy ponds, reservoirs; enters brackish water. **RANGE** Most of region, ex. se NY and most of NJ.

BOWFIN
Amia calva
BOWFIN FAMILY

15–25″. Bony plates encase head. Olive-brown with speckles above, yellowish below. Long, low, wavy dorsal fin. Male has black eyespot at base of tail fin. Skeleton is bone and cartilage. Can breathe air, gulped at surface. **HABITAT** Quiet vegetated ponds, slow rivers. **RANGE** n and w NY, e MD, e VA.

ALEWIFE
Alosa pseudoharengus
HERRING FAMILY

10–15″. Herring family: silvery schooling fishes that filter plankton. This species: head scaleless; eyes large. Silvery blue-green above, silvery below. Dorsal fin triangular; tail fin deeply forked. **HABITAT** Most of year: Great Lakes, bays, estuaries. Spring: spawning runs in rivers (earlier than shad). **RANGE** Entire coast, Great Lakes, rivers (ex. WV).

AMERICAN SHAD
Alosa sapidissima
HERRING FAMILY

15–25″. Back rounded. Dark blue-green above; sides silvery with 6–10 small black spots, largest one above gills; belly whitish. Single dorsal fin small, triangular; tail fin deeply forked. Head scaleless; eyes yellow. **HABITAT** Most of year: bays, estuaries. Spring: spawning runs in rivers. **RANGE** e NY and e PA to sc VA; Great Lakes.

COMMON CARP
Cyprinus carpio
CARP AND MINNOW FAMILY

10–30″. Oval; back rounded. Dark olive above, shading to yellowish gray below. Dorsal fin long, begins at back's high point, has thick forward spine; tail fin forked, lobes round. 2 pairs of barbels on upper lip. In spring, males thrash about in surface waters in spawning frenzy. Native to Asia; destroys bottom plants needed by native fish as cover for eggs, young. **HABITAT** Clear or turbid rivers, lakes, reservoirs; sometimes brackish waters. Goldfish (*Carassius auratus*; 4½–9″), familiar aquarium fish from China, often released into ponds.

CUTLIPS MINNOW
Exoglossum maxillingua
CARP AND MINNOW FAMILY

2–6″. Stout. Olive-brown above, creamy below. Single dorsal fin; tail fin has 2 rounded lobes; all fins unmarked. Head broad; snout blunt; lower jaw cut into 3 lobes. Male builds raised 15″-wide circular stone nest; defends eggs. **HABITAT** Clear stony streams, esp. in pools. **RANGE** e NY southwest to c VA in hills.

GOLDEN SHINER
Notemigonus crysoleucas
CARP AND MINNOW FAMILY

4–8″. Body deeper, more compressed than most minnow species; scales large. Shining gold when breeding, greenish or pale silver at other times. Single dorsal fin; tail fin forked. Mouth tiny. Usu. occurs in schools near surface. **HABITAT** Near surface of shallow weedy lakes, ponds, streams.

BLACKNOSE DACE
Rhinichthys atratulus
CARP AND MINNOW FAMILY

2–3″. Yellowish olive with heavy black spots above, sides brownish; lateral line thick, black, extends from nose to tail. Single dorsal fin triangular; tail fin forked, lobes rounded. **HABITAT** Springs; cool fast streams. **RANGE** Entire region, ex. Long Is., Delmarva Peninsula, se VA.

FALLFISH
Semotilus corporalis
CARP AND MINNOW FAMILY

4–10″. Elongated; snout overhangs large mouth; scales large, darkly outlined. Olive above, sides silvery. Single dorsal fin triangular; tail fin forked. Eyes large. Region's largest native true minnow; "minnow" is often used in error to describe small fish of many other families. **HABITAT** Clear fast streams, gravel-bottomed lakes. **RANGE** n NY to c DE, c VA.

WHITE SUCKER
Catostomus commersoni
SUCKER FAMILY

12–20″. Cylindrical. Back olive; sides silvery yellow; spawning male darker brown, with red fins. Single dorsal fin triangular; ventral fins often yellow; tail fin forked. Mouth protruding, toothless, adapted for sucking worms and insect larvae off bottom; no barbels. **HABITAT** Cool streams, lakes; sometimes brackish waters. **RANGE** Entire region, ex. Long Is., s Delmarva Peninsula, se VA.

WHITE CATFISH
Ameiurus (Ictalurus) catus
BULLHEAD CATFISH FAMILY

6–18″. Deep, often pot-bellied; lacks scales. Plain (or finely mottled) pale blue-gray above, silver below. Tall dorsal fin at high point of back; rounded adipose fin; tail fin forked with rounded lobes. Head flattened on top; long black whiskers on upper jaw; chin barbels white. **HABITAT** Fresh and brackish streams; ponds, reservoirs. **RANGE** Native from s NY and e PA south; introduced to west.

CHANNEL CATFISH
"Spotted Catfish"
Ictalurus punctatus
BULLHEAD CATFISH FAMILY

14–24″. Fairly slender. Back blue-gray, sides tan or silvery blue with scattered black spots, belly white. Single dorsal fin high, rounded; rounded adipose fin; anal fin long, with rounded outer edge; tail fin deeply forked. Head long; upper jaw overhangs lower; 4 pairs of barbels, upper 2 black, lower ones white. **HABITAT** Flowing rivers with clear bottoms; lakes, reservoirs. **RANGE** n NY to w VA.

BROWN BULLHEAD
Ameiurus (Ictalurus) nebulosus
BULLHEAD CATFISH FAMILY

6–12″. Robust. Back and sides brown, heavily mottled, with darker brown blotches; belly whitish. Fins dusky; 1st dorsal fin narrow, high, rounded; rounded adipose fin; anal fin long, rounded; tail fin square or notched. 4 pairs of barbels flank mouth. **HABITAT** Ponds; vegetated pools in rivers and sluggish streams (common); brackish waters (rare).

CHAIN PICKEREL
Esox niger
PIKE FAMILY

11–25". Moderately compressed; snout long, concave above. Olive to yellowish brown; sides covered with dark markings resembling interlocking chains. Fins plain dusky; single dorsal fin and anal fin both placed far back; tail fin deeply forked. Mouth wide; dark vertical bar under yellow eye. Common. **HABITAT** Grassy lakes, swamps, vegetated stream pools; brackish waters (rare). **RANGE** NY (incl. Long Is.) to sc VA.

REDFIN PICKEREL
"Barred Pickerel"
Esox americanus americanus
PIKE FAMILY

6–12". Cylindrical in cross section; scales tiny. Back dark brown or olive, sides pale yellow with several dozen forward-leaning dark brown bars, belly white. Fins reddish; single dorsal fin far back above anal fin; tail fin slightly forked. Snout pointed; lips wide. Ambush hunter from dense vegetation. **HABITAT** Slow-moving streams, tea-colored acidic ponds. **RANGE** Lake Champlain, Hudson Valley, Long Is.; NY to e VA.

NORTHERN PIKE
Esox lucius
PIKE FAMILY

10–30". Long, cylindrical; head large; snout long, wide, rounded; lower jaw protrudes; teeth fine. Olive green, camouflaged with numerous large yellow spots; whitish below. Fins have dark mottling; single rounded dorsal fin and anal fin set far back on body; tail fin forked. **HABITAT** Cold lakes, slow rivers with heavy vegetation. **RANGE** w, n, and c NY, n PA.

MUSKELLUNGE
Esox masquinongy
PIKE FAMILY

24–60". Somewhat compressed; head concave; lower cheeks and gill covers lack scales (unlike Northern Pike). Back brown or dark green, sides pale olive with many camouflaging brown spots, belly creamy. Fins spotted; single dorsal fin far back above anal fin; tail fin forked. Ambushes fish and aquatic amphibians, reptiles, birds, muskrats. **HABITAT** Well-vegetated lakes, slow rivers. Summer: deep water. **RANGE** Great Lakes south locally to VA.

RAINBOW SMELT
Osmerus mordax
SMELT FAMILY

6–10″. Slender, compressed. Back greenish, sides and belly silvery. Single central dorsal fin triangular; adipose fin smaller, rounded; tail fin forked. Jaws and roof of mouth have strong teeth. **HABITAT** Inshore coastal waters, lakes, estuaries. Spring: spawns in gravelly streams. **RANGE** Lakes Erie and Ontario, inland NY, coast from Long Is. to e MD.

ATLANTIC SALMON
Salmo salar
TROUT FAMILY

24–36″. Dark bluish above in salt water, brownish in fresh, with small black spots; silvery below. Dorsal fin triangular. Breeding male has red spots on sides; lower jaw longer, upward-hooked. Rare today; stocked in lakes where not native. **HABITAT** Rivers, streams, lakes; few in ocean off NY. **RANGE** Finger Lakes, lakes in Adirondacks, Lake Champlain.

RAINBOW TROUT
Oncorhynchus mykiss
(Salmo gairdneri)
TROUT FAMILY

6–20″. Metallic green to brown above, silvery white below; black dots on body and fins. Stream fish have larger spots. Lake fish larger, lighter in color; called "steelheads." Introduced from w N. Amer. **HABITAT** Inshore ocean waters, streams, rivers; some landlocked in lakes. **RANGE** Hill country NY to w VA.

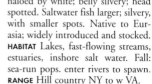

BROWN TROUT
Salmo trutta
TROUT FAMILY

6–20″. Brown above; sides olive with dark brown and red spots haloed by white; belly silvery; head spotted. Saltwater fish larger; silvery, with smaller spots. Native to Eurasia; widely introduced and stocked. **HABITAT** Lakes, fast-flowing streams, estuaries, inshore salt water. Fall: sea-run pops. enter rivers to spawn. **RANGE** Hill country NY to w VA.

BROOK TROUT
Salvelinus fontinalis
TROUT FAMILY

8–16″. Olive green with wavy lines above; sides olive with large yellowish spots and few small red spots with blue halos; belly white (reddish in adult male). Dorsal fin spotted; ventral fins reddish with white and black leading edges. Region's only native trout. **HABITAT** Cold clear streams, cold lakes, tidal streams. Winter: some enter ocean to feed.

BURBOT
Lota lota
COD FAMILY

21″. Eel-like; in cross section, circular in front, compressed toward rear; head flattened. Dark brown with pale brown wavy lines and spots. 1st dorsal fin short; 2nd dorsal fin and anal fin long-based. Mouth wide; barbel on chin. Only freshwater cod. HABITAT Deep cold lakes, streams, rivers. Winter: spawns under ice. RANGE w and n NY, n PA.

MOTTLED SCULPIN
Cottus bairdi
SCULPIN FAMILY

3–4″. Robust; heavier toward front, base of tail fairly deep; head broad, concave between eyes. Brown with large blackish mottling and fine pale flecking above; white below. Fins rounded, serrated at tips, banded. 1st dorsal fin of male black, tipped orange. Eats aquatic insects. HABITAT Lakes, rivers, clear gravelly mtn. streams. RANGE n and w NY to w VA.

RED-BREASTED SUNFISH
Lepomis auritus
SUNFISH FAMILY

5–7″. Oval, compressed. Back dark green, sides pale yellow-green flecked with red spots, belly orange-red; squiggly bright blue lines on face; eyes red; gill cover long, rounded, black. Single dorsal fin rounded at rear; tail fin notched. HABITAT Streams, ponds, rivers, lakes. RANGE East of mtns. from ec NY to s VA.

PUMPKINSEED
Lepomis gibbosus
SUNFISH FAMILY

6–8″. Golden green above, shading to orangy yellow below, usu. with dark speckles; cheeks striped reddish and bright blue; gill cover rounded, black with red tip, outlined in white. Single dorsal fin, notched tail fin, and anal fin all spotted; pectoral fins pointed. HABITAT Ponds, streams, marshes; brackish waters. RANGE Entire region, ex. w VA, w WV.

BLUEGILL
Lepomis macrochirus
SUNFISH FAMILY

6–8″. Olive above, with vertical dusky green bands; male orange below; female whitish below; gills bluish, with broad, untrimmed black cover. Dark spot on rear of dorsal fin. Native west of Appalachians; introduced elsewhere. HABITAT Shallow vegetated lakeshores, stream pools; some in brackish waters.

SMALLMOUTH BASS
Micropterus dolomieu
SUNFISH FAMILY

6–18″. Dark bronzy brown above; sides greenish yellow with vertical brownish bands; belly whitish. 1st dorsal fin joined to 2nd dorsal fin. Native to n and w NY and areas west of Appalachians; introduced elsewhere. **HABITAT** Deep lakes, cool clear streams over rocks. **RANGE** Entire region, ex. coastal plain from Long Is. to c VA.

LARGEMOUTH BASS
Micropterus salmoides
SUNFISH FAMILY

8–18″. Dark green above; sides olive green with brownish mottling; belly whitish. 1st dorsal fin separate from 2nd dorsal fin (unlike Smallmouth); tail fin notched. Mouth extends to point below rear of eye. Native to w NY, w PA, WV; introduced elsewhere. **HABITAT** Warm shallow waters with vegetation, sluggish river backwaters; some in brackish waters.

BLACK CRAPPIE
Pomoxis nigromaculatus
SUNFISH FAMILY

4–12″. Dark olive-brown mottled with dark brown spots. Most fins spotted; single dorsal fin and anal fin rounded. Native to n and w NY, w PA, WV; introduced elsewhere. **HABITAT** Ponds, warm streams; brackish waters. **White Crappie** *(P. annularis)* paler, barred, longer-bodied; found in schools in siltier water.

YELLOW PERCH
Perca flavescens
PERCH FAMILY

4–10″. Olive green, brownish, or yellowish, with 5–8 broad, blackish, vertical bars on sides. 2 separated dorsal fins dusky; ventral fins usu. reddish; 1st dorsal fin and first 2 rays of anal fin have sharp spines. **HABITAT** Clear streams, ponds and lakes with vegetation; some in brackish waters.

WALLEYE
Stizostedion vitreum
PERCH FAMILY

10–20″. Head small, pointed; eyes glassy, reflective. Olive green or brownish, with irreg. blackish vertical bars on back and sides. 2 separated dorsal fins; 1st dorsal fin and first 2 rays of anal fin have sharp spines. Native west of Appalachians; introduced elsewhere. **HABITAT** Clear streams, deep lakes with vegetation. **RANGE** Entire region, ex. coastal plain.

Amphibians

The ancestors of today's amphibians began evolving from fish about 300 million years ago. Members of the class Amphibia typically start life in fresh water and later live on land. Most undergo metamorphosis (a series of developmental stages) from aquatic, water-breathing larvae to terrestrial or partly terrestrial, air-breathing adults. The most primitive of terrestrial vertebrates, amphibians lack claws and external ear openings. They have thin, moist, scaleless skin and are cold-blooded; their body temperature varies with that of their surroundings. In winter, they burrow deep into leaf litter, soft soils, and the mud of ponds, and maintain an inactive state. Unlike reptiles, amphibians can become dehydrated in dry environments and must live near water at least part of the year and for breeding. Their eggs lack shells, and most are laid in water.

Salamanders

Salamanders, members of the order Caudata, have blunt rounded heads, long slender bodies, short legs, and long tails. Salamanders differ from lizards (which are reptiles) in having thin moist skin (lizards have scales) and four toes on the front feet (lizards have five), and in their lack of claws and external ear openings. Most lay eggs in fresh water that hatch into four-legged larvae with tufted external gills; after several months or years, the larvae typically lose their gills and go ashore. Exceptions include the Mudpuppy *(Necturus maculosus)* of northern and western New York, western Pennsylvania, and West Virginia, which retains its gills and is aquatic its entire life; and some salamanders that lay eggs on land and skip the gilled larval stage. Members of the newt family (Salamandridae) start out as aquatic larvae; most then transform into terrestrial subadults (the "eft" stage) and in one to three years change again into an aquatic life form. Hellbenders (Cryptobranchidae) are very large, completely aquatic salamanders that lack external gills; they have gill openings on the neck. Adult lungless salamanders (Plethodontidae) lack lungs and breathe through their thin moist skin; mostly terrestrial, they live under bark, wood, or stones, sometimes near streams. Mole salamanders (Ambystomatidae), which breathe through lungs, burrow into soft soil.

During all life stages, salamanders eat small animal life. They are generally voiceless and hard to see, as they feed under wet leaves and logs; they are easiest to see at night in early spring, when they congregate to mate and lay eggs at temporary pools of fresh water created by the spring thaw and rains (vernal pools). In winter, they become inactive, residing in decaying logs, between the roots of trees, and in soil. There are more than 50 salamander species in eastern North America, more than anywhere else in the world. However, like frogs, salamanders are fast declining in number worldwide, due to habitat destruction and perhaps acid rain, pesticides, and increasing ultraviolet light.

The size given for adult salamanders is the typical length from the tip of the nose to the end of the tail.

EASTERN NEWT
"Red-spotted Newt"
Notophthalmus viridescens
NEWT FAMILY

aquatic adult form (left), eft (right)

Eft 2½"; newt 3½". Newts have 3 forms: a legless larval aquatic form, followed by an imm. land form called an eft, and finally a legged aquatic adult form. This species: bodies of all forms have 10–12 red spots ringed in black, many small black dots. Land form, called red eft, smaller, bright orange. In 1–3 years, becomes larger, aquatic newt: olive above, yellow below; paddle-shaped tail has high keel (esp. male). **HABITAT** Woods (eft); stream pools, ponds, lakes (newt). **ACTIVITY** By day, Mar.–Oct.

HELLBENDER
Cryptobranchus alleganiensis
HELLBENDER FAMILY

16". Stocky, flattened; folds of skin on sides. Uses thick tail to swim. Head flat, wide. Round gill opening on neck; no external gills in adult. Gray to olive-brown; some black-spotted. Aquatic; eats worms, snails, crayfish. **HABITAT** Under logs, boulders in rivers, large streams. **ACTIVITY** Day and night. **RANGE** sw NY, w PA, WV, w VA, Susquehanna Valley.

BLUE-SPOTTED SALAMANDER
Ambystoma laterale
MOLE SALAMANDER FAMILY

4½". Slender; eyes bulbous. Glossy black with hundreds of tiny pale blue dots on body and tail; pale gray below. Seldom seen; lives under logs and rocks, and in burrows. **HABITAT** Broadleaf woods. **ACTIVITY** Day and night, Mar.–Oct. **RANGE** n NY, Hudson Valley, e Long Is.

SPOTTED SALAMANDER
Ambystoma maculatum
MOLE SALAMANDER FAMILY

7". Stocky; snout broad. Black or dark gray with 2 irreg. head-to-tail rows of large yellow (rarely orange) spots. Usu. underground or under logs, rocks. **HABITAT** Broadleaf woods. **ACTIVITY** Day and night, Feb.–Nov. **RANGE** Entire region, ex. s NJ, s Delmarva Peninsula.

EASTERN TIGER SALAMANDER
Ambystoma tigrinum
MOLE SALAMANDER FAMILY

9". Stout; head broad; snout rounded. Eastern race: back and sides dark brown with many irreg. yellowish spots; belly olive-yellow. Lives in mammal and crayfish burrows, under waterside debris. **HABITAT** Sandy pine barrens; breeds in shallow ponds. **ACTIVITY** Underground most of year. **RANGE** Long Is., s NJ, DE, e and c MD, e VA.

NORTHERN TWO-LINED SALAMANDER
Eurycea bislineata
LUNGLESS SALAMANDER FAMILY

3½". Slender. Wide yellow stripe on back, some with tiny black spots on yellow; black side stripe continues to tip of long tail; yellow below. Legs tiny. Runs and swims well. **HABITAT** Brooks, brooksides, moist woodland floors; to 5,000' and higher in mtns. **ACTIVITY** Nights and wet days. **RANGE** Entire region, ex. s NJ.

NORTHERN DUSKY SALAMANDER
Desmognathus fuscus
LUNGLESS SALAMANDER FAMILY

3½". Stout; snout broad. Buffy "tear" line runs from below eye to base of mouth; back brown, bordered on sides by wavy dark stripes; sides gray or buff. Hind legs larger than forelegs. Tail shortish, keeled; triangular in cross section. **HABITAT** Borders of rocky creeks, springs. **ACTIVITY** Day and night, Apr.–Oct.

FOUR-TOED SALAMANDER
Hemidactylium scutatum
LUNGLESS SALAMANDER FAMILY

3". Slender. Reddish brown above, sides grayish, belly white with bold black spots. 4 toes on all feet (most other salamanders have 5 toes on hindfeet). Base of tail narrow; if severed, tail wiggles. Lives under stones, leaf litter. **HABITAT** Floodplains, sphagnum bogs. **ACTIVITY** Nights and wet days, Mar.–Nov. **RANGE** Entire region, ex. n NY.

LONG-TAILED SALAMANDER
Eurycea longicauda
LUNGLESS SALAMANDER FAMILY

5". Slender. Yellow to orange, with small black spots that merge into vertical bands on tail. Three-lined race of e VA: tan above, with median black stripe; sides black with white spots. **HABITAT** Streamsides, cave mouths. **ACTIVITY** Nights and wet days. **RANGE** NY from Catskills southwest, n NJ, PA, n MD, WV, VA.

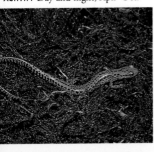

NORTHERN RED-BACKED SALAMANDER
Plethodon cinereus
LUNGLESS SALAMANDER FAMILY

4″. Wide orange-red to brick-red stripe on back, bordered by black; sides gray with white flecks. Lead-backed form lacks reddish stripe. Both forms have black-and-white-mottled belly. **HABITAT** Under logs, rocks in woods, urban parks, often far from water. **ACTIVITY** Nocturnal; may be active during winter thaws.

RED SALAMANDER
Pseudotriton ruber
LUNGLESS SALAMANDER FAMILY

5½″. Stout, with blunt head, compressed tail. Reddish orange; heavily black-spotted above, few spots below. Some adults bronzy above, orange below, with spots. Eats earthworms. **HABITAT** Springs, brooks, rotten logs, leaf litter of woods, often far from water. **ACTIVITY** Nights and wet days. **RANGE** se NY west of Hudson River, and south to VA.

NORTHERN SLIMY SALAMANDER
Plethodon glutinosus
LUNGLESS SALAMANDER FAMILY

6″. Slender; tail cylindrical. Shiny black with white or brassy spots, small on back, larger on sides; throat and belly slaty. Skin sticky-slimy. **HABITAT** Wooded ravines and floodplains to 5,000′ and up, in logs and under rocks. **ACTIVITY** Nights and wet days. **RANGE** NY from Catskills southwest, n NJ, PA, w MD, VA.

Frogs

Adult frogs and toads (order Anura) have large heads and eyes, and wide, usually toothless mouths; they appear neckless, and most lack tails. Many can rapidly extend a long tongue for capturing insects. They have two long muscular hindlegs and two smaller front legs. All must keep their skin moist and avoid drying out in the sun. All frogs in the Mid-Atlantic region pass the winter in a state of torpor, burying themselves in mud at the edge of a pond or crawling between the bark and trunk of a large tree. In the spring, the male vocalizes to attract the larger female, and clings to her while fertilizing eggs as she lays them, usually in water. The eggs hatch into round-bodied, long-tailed aquatic larvae called tadpoles or pollywogs, which begin life with external gills that are soon covered with skin. The tadpole later transforms into a tail-less ground-, tree-, or marsh-dwelling adult with air-breathing lungs.

Toads are a family (Bufonidae) of frogs that have shorter legs for terrestrial hopping and warty skin, which secretes poisons that cause irritations; they have swollen paratoid glands (raised areas behind the eyes). In the treefrog family (Hylidae), tadpoles live in water, and adults live in trees and have disks on their toes for clinging. The true frogs (Ranidae) are large, with slim waists, long legs, pointed toes, and webs on their hindfeet; most live in or near water and are good jumpers. Like salamanders, frogs and toads are declining in number worldwide, partly because of environmental pollutants and atmospheric alterations.

Life Cycle of a Frog

Frogs and toads have excellent hearing and vocal capabilities. Their well-developed ears feature a conspicuous external eardrum (the tympanum), a round disk located behind the eye. In spring or summer, most male frogs and toads announce their presence with loud vocalizations that vary strikingly from species to species. When calling, the animals rapidly inflate and deflate balloon-like vocal sacs on the center or sides of the throat that amplify the sound. Calls are primarily used during the breeding season to attract mates; some species, like the Green Frog, give calls to defend feeding territories long after breeding.

With the first late-winter thaw, Wood Frogs and Spring Peepers open the breeding season by gathering in large, noisy groups that vocalize at dusk near water. Throughout spring and summer in the Mid-Atlantic region, mainly at night, one can often hear a chorus of fascinating sounds made by several species of frogs. Bullfrogs, American Toads, and others also call in the daytime.

The size given for frogs is the typical length from the tip of the nose to the end of the body (not including the hindlegs).

AMERICAN TOAD
Bufo americanus
TOAD FAMILY

3″. Gray-brown; brown spots on back have 1–2 rusty warts. Paratoid glands do not touch cranial bulge. Common toad of upland areas. **VOICE** Lengthy musical trill, often by day, in chorus. **CAUTION** Contact may irritate skin. **HABITAT** Fields, woods. **ACTIVITY** Day and night, Mar.–Oct. **RANGE** Entire region, ex. Long Is., s NJ, e MD, DE, se VA.

WOODHOUSE'S TOAD
Bufo woodhousii
TOAD FAMILY

2½″. Fowler's race: gray-brown; brown spots on back have 3 or more rusty warts. Paratoid glands touch cranial bulge. Common toad of coastal plain. **VOICE** Plaintive, descending *wraah*. **CAUTION** Contact may irritate skin. **HABITAT** Sandy areas near water. **ACTIVITY** Day and night, Apr.–Oct. **RANGE** Hudson Valley, Long Is., s PA, NJ to VA.

PINE BARRENS TREEFROG
Hyla andersoni
TREEFROG FAMILY

1½". Bright green above and on top sides of legs; distinct lavender line through eye and side; concealed portion of legs orange. Toe pads large. Rarely seen. **VOICE** Nasal *quonk*, given 1 per second on warm nights. **HABITAT** Bogs and swamps in pine barrens. **ACTIVITY** Nocturnal; calls Apr.–Aug. **RANGE** c and s NJ.

SPRING PEEPER
Pseudacris (Hyla) crucifer
TREEFROG FAMILY

1". Pale brown or rusty; darker X on back and bar on crown between eyes. Din of hundreds calling, usu. in evening, is early sign of spring; some males also call on warm autumn days. **VOICE** High, up-slurred *preep*. **HABITAT** Swamps, marshes, moist thickets. **ACTIVITY** Occ. seen by day; feeds at dusk and at night, Feb.–Nov.

GREEN TREEFROG
Hyla cinerea
TREEFROG FAMILY

1½". Skin smooth; usu. bright green above; creamy white or pale yellow stripe under eye and along sides; some lack side stripe or have golden flecks above. In cooler months, color may be gray or dull green. Pale cream below. **VOICE** Nasal *queenk*. **HABITAT** Swamps. **ACTIVITY** Nocturnal. **RANGE** DE, e and s MD, e VA.

GRAY TREEFROG
Hyla versicolor (chrysoscelis)
TREEFROG FAMILY

1¾". Skin rough; to match surroundings, quickly changes color from green to brown to gray. Whitish "teardrop" below eye. Region's common larger treefrog. **VOICE** Fluttery, musical trill, often from high in trees. **HABITAT** Lowland trees near water. **ACTIVITY** Rarely seen by day; feeds at night, Apr.–Oct.

BULLFROG
Rana catesbeiana
TRUE FROG FAMILY

5". Ridge from eye to large eardrum; midback bulge. Yellowish green with dark mottling above, pale yellow below; legs dark-banded. Feet mainly webbed. Female lays up to 20,000 eggs; tadpoles become adults in 1–3 years. Region's largest frog. **VOICE** Deep, resonant *jug-o-rum*, day or night. **HABITAT** Marshes, ponds, slow rivers. **ACTIVITY** Day and night, feeds mainly at night, Apr.–Oct.

GREEN FROG
Rana clamitans
TRUE FROG FAMILY

3″. Green to brown above, with few dark spots on lower back and sides; raised ridges on sides of back to midback bulge; legs have blackish bands. If cornered, stands tall, gives high *eek* before leaping. **VOICE** 1 note, like plucked banjo string. **HABITAT** Swamps, brooks, pond shallows. **ACTIVITY** Day and night, Apr.–Oct.

PICKEREL FROG
Rana palustris
TRUE FROG FAMILY

2½″. Pale buffy brown; rectangular, dark brown spots on back (in 2 parallel rows) and legs; sides and belly yellow; round black spots on sides; white stripe on side of upper lip. Nose pointed. **VOICE** Low steady croak or "snore." **HABITAT** Vegetated streams, swamps, moist meadows. **ACTIVITY** Day and night, Apr.–Oct.

WOOD FROG
Rana sylvatica
TRUE FROG FAMILY

2¼″. Unspotted dull brown to rufous (occ. pale); blackish-brown mask from eye past eardrum; whitish on upper lip; legs banded. Breeds at vernal pools. **VOICE** Short raspy *craw-aw-ock*. **HABITAT** Moist woods, often far from water. **ACTIVITY** Mainly by day, Feb.–Oct. **RANGE** Entire region, ex. c and e VA.

SOUTHERN LEOPARD FROG
Rana sphenocephala (utricularia)
TRUE FROG FAMILY

3½″. Green to brown above; dark brown spots; whitish ridge along back behind each eye; white stripe below eye; white spot in eardrum. **VOICE** Short trills. **HABITAT** Ponds, moist woods, waterside grasses, fresh and brackish marshes. **ACTIVITY** Mainly nocturnal. **RANGE** s NY and Long Is. to e VA; not in mtns.

CARPENTER FROG
Rana virgatipes
TRUE FROG FAMLY

2″. Dark brown above; lacks ridges and folds; 4 buffy stripes, 2 on sides of back, 1 on each side; creamy below, often mottled with black. Usu. difficult to see. **VOICE** Loud *pa-TUNK*, like carpenters hitting nails. **HABITAT** Sphagnum bogs, pine barrens ponds, in and near tea-colored waterways. **ACTIVITY** Mainly nocturnal, Apr.–Oct. **RANGE** s NJ, s DE, se MD, se VA.

Reptiles

Members of the class Reptilia are cold-blooded, like amphibians. Their body temperature varies with that of their surroundings; reptilian activities come to a halt in cold weather, when they hibernate alone or in communal dens. Of the four orders of living reptiles, the Mid-Atlantic region has two: turtles and scaled reptiles; the latter order includes both snakes and lizards. The typical reptilian body is low-slung and has a long tail and, except for the snakes, four short legs. Unlike the thin-skinned amphibians, reptiles are covered with protective scales (some are modified into plates in turtles) that waterproof their bodies and help keep them from becoming dehydrated. They breathe via lungs. All breed on land and mate by internal fertilization. Their eggs have brittle or leathery shells; some give birth to live young.

Turtles

Members of the order Testudines, turtles are the oldest living group of reptiles, dating back to the time of the earliest dinosaurs. The upper part of their characteristic bony shell is the carapace, the lower part the plastron; both parts are covered with hard plates called scutes. Some species have ridges, called keels, on the carapace and tail. The exposed skin of turtles is scaly and dry. Most can withdraw the head and legs inside the shell for protection. Aquatic species have flipper-like legs. Turtles are toothless, but their horny beaks have sharp biting edges. Some are vegetarian, some are carnivorous, and others are omnivorous. Most spend hours basking in the sun. From October or November to March or April, turtles

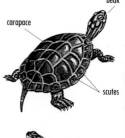
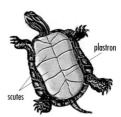

Parts of a Turtle

in the Mid-Atlantic region hibernate. All turtles lay eggs; most dig a hollow, lay the eggs, cover them up, and leave them alone. When the eggs hatch, the young claw their way to the surface and fend for themselves. Lengths given are for the carapace of a typical adult.

EASTERN MUD TURTLE
Kinosternon subrubrum
MUD TURTLE FAMILY
3½". Carapace smooth, domed, keel-less; plain olive to dark brown. Plastron orange to pale yellow, double-hinged. Male has blunt spine at tip of tail. **HABITAT** Shallow ponds, ditches, fresh and brackish marshes, islands; wanders far from water. **ACTIVITY** Day and night, Apr.–Oct. **RANGE** Long Is. to c and e VA.

COMMON SNAPPING TURTLE
Chelydra serpentina
SNAPPING TURTLE FAMILY

15". Carapace oval, smooth or with 3 rows of keels; black or dark brown. Plastron rather small, cross-shaped, yellowish. In spring, female lays eggs in open areas far from water. Otherwise aquatic; seldom basks. Region's largest freshwater turtle. **CAUTION** Powerful jaws can give serious bite. **HABITAT** Fresh waters with mucky bottoms. **ACTIVITY** Day and night.

PAINTED TURTLE
Chrysemys picta
POND AND BOX TURTLE FAMILY

5¼". Carapace oval, smooth, keel-less; has 3 rows of smooth olive-brown to black scutes with pale yellow edges; scutes at carapace edge have red lines. Plastron yellow or orange. Head, neck, legs lined with yellow and red. Most commonly seen turtle. **HABITAT** Ponds, swamps, rivers, lakes. **ACTIVITY** On sunny days, basks in groups on logs, boulders.

SPOTTED TURTLE
Clemmys guttata
POND AND BOX TURTLE FAMILY

4". Carapace oval, smooth and smooth-edged, keel-less; black, smooth, with yellow spots. Plastron yellow with black center and border. Head, neck, and limbs have yellow or orange spots. **HABITAT** Marshy meadows, small ponds, bogs. **ACTIVITY** Basks in spring, hard to find in summer, fall. **RANGE** Entire region, ex. n NY, most of WV, w VA.

WOOD TURTLE
Clemmys insculpta
POND AND BOX TURTLE FAMILY

6½". Carapace rectangular, brownish; centers of scutes raised, with concentric and radiating grooves. Plastron yellow; black smudge on each scute. Head black; neck, forelegs orangish. Becoming rare. **HABITAT** Swamps, woods, meadows, often far from water. **ACTIVITY** Mainly by day, Apr.–Oct. **RANGE** NY (ex. Adirondacks), n NJ, PA to e WV, n MD.

DIAMONDBACK TERRAPIN
Malaclemys terrapin
POND AND BOX TURTLE FAMILY

Female 8"; male 5". Carapace oval, keeled, brown; rings on each scute. Plastron creamy; black circles on scutes. Head, jaws, neck pale gray with black spots. Region's common saltwater turtle. **HABITAT** Salt marshes, estuaries, coastal mudflats, waterways. **ACTIVITY** Day and night in warmer months. **RANGE** Coastal NY to VA.

EASTERN RED-BELLIED TURTLE
Pseudemys (Chrysemys) rubriventris
POND AND BOX TURTLE FAMILY
11″. Carapace round, somewhat domed, black; female has red lines along side scutes; male has reddish wash at center of scutes. Plastron reddish. Basks on sunny days, esp. in spring, beside notably smaller Painted Turtles. **HABITAT** Deep ponds, lakes, rivers, brackish marshes. **ACTIVITY** Mainly by day in warmer months. **RANGE** s NJ and far e WV to e VA.

EASTERN BOX TURTLE
Terrapene carolina
POND AND BOX TURTLE FAMILY
5¼″. Carapace oval, high-domed; dark brown with intricate, variable, orange or yellow patterning. Plastron often yellowish, mottled; transverse hinge allows turtle to completely hide inside shell. Mainly terrestrial; will soak in mud or very shallow water. Declining due to pet trade, cars. **HABITAT** Woods, roadsides, pastures, meadows, sometimes gardens. **ACTIVITY** By day, usu. in morning and after rains. **RANGE** From se NY and c PA south.

LOGGERHEAD
Caretta caretta
SEA TURTLE FAMILY
3′. Carapace elongated, fairly flat; reddish brown. Plastron creamy yellow. Head large, with dark brown scales on top; beak pointed. Skin light yellow. Most frequently seen inshore sea turtle. **HABITAT** Ocean, bays, estuaries. **RANGE** Breeds in s U.S.; wanders northward offshore June–Sept.

Lizards
Lizards (suborder Sauria of the scaled reptile order, Squamata) generally have long tails; most species have legs and are capable of running, climbing, and clinging, though in some the legs are tiny or lacking. Typical lizards resemble salamanders but can be distinguished from them by their dry scaly skin, clawed feet, and external ear openings. Lizard species vary greatly in size, shape, and color; in many, color and patterns differ among adult males, adult females, and young. Most lizards are active by day, and many are particularly active in the midday heat. Most do not swim in water. Fertilization is internal; most lay eggs rather than give birth to live young.

The size given for lizards is the length from the tip of the snout to the end of the tail.

EASTERN FENCE LIZARD
Sceloporus undulatus
IGUANID LIZARD FAMILY

male (left), female (right)

5½". Snout wedge-shaped; tail thin, equal to body length. Male brown above, with gray line on side; black-bordered, bright blue patches on side of belly and base of throat. Female more ornate, with wavy dark and light banding; grayish below. Only lizard in region with rough, scaly appearance. Suns itself on stumps, slabs, wooden fences. HABITAT On ground and on tree trunks in fields, woods, esp. open pinewoods. ACTIVITY By day in warmer months. RANGE c PA and c NJ to WV, s VA.

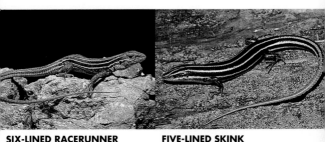

SIX-LINED RACERUNNER
Cnemidophorus sexlineatus
WHIPTAIL FAMILY

8". Slender; tail long, thin, whip-like. Dark unglossy brown above, with 6–7 thin yellow stripes; throat and belly blue-green in male, white in female. Active; very fast runner. HABITAT Well-drained, open, sandy soil in fields, open woods. ACTIVITY By day in warmer months. RANGE West of Ches. Bay in s MD, c and e VA.

FIVE-LINED SKINK
Eumeces fasciatus
SKINK FAMILY

6½". Scales smooth, shiny. Adult slaty with 5 distinct light stripes; tail blue-gray. Older adult male unstriped brown above; snout and throat rufous. Juv. has bright blue tail. HABITAT Leaf litter of woods, rock piles, gardens. ACTIVITY By day in warmer months. RANGE Hudson Valley and from NJ and c PA south.

BROAD-HEADED SKINK
Eumeces laticeps
SKINK FAMILY

9". Very similar to smaller Five-lined Skink. Adult male has broad reddish head. More arboreal than Five-lined: often feeds high in trees; eats wasp pupae; lives in tree holes. HABITAT Woods, rubble piles in open areas. ACTIVITY By day in warmer months. RANGE se PA, DE, c and e MD, s WV, VA.

Snakes

Snakes (suborder Serpentes of the scaled reptile order, Squamata) have elongated scaly bodies without limbs, eyelids, or external ear openings. They grow throughout their lives, shedding their skin from snout to tail every year or so. Carnivorous, snakes swallow their prey whole. The flicking, forked tongue serves as a sensory organ, collecting information on potential prey and dangers. Snakes

RACER
"Black Racer"
Coluber constrictor
COLUBRID SNAKE FAMILY

4'. Medium girth; scales smooth, glossy. Black ex. for white chin and throat. Young grayish, with black-edged brown spots. Holds head high while moving forward. Region's fastest snake. Bites small rodents, frogs, snakes, birds; does not constrict. **CAUTION** Not poisonous, but will bite if cornered. **HABITAT** Fields, open woods. **ACTIVITY** Day and night. **RANGE** Entire region, ex. n NY.

RING-NECKED SNAKE
Diadophis punctatus
COLUBRID SNAKE FAMILY

20". Very slender; smooth-scaled. Slaty or blue-gray above; bright yellow-orange below; head black with golden-orange collar. Rarely bites when handled. Constricts salamanders, frogs, earthworms. **HABITAT** Rocky woods and hillsides, usu. with fallen trunks. **ACTIVITY** Secretive; hides under rocks, logs, stone walls.

CORN SNAKE
Elaphe guttata
COLUBRID SNAKE FAMILY

4'. Slender. Eastern race: orange to gray, with reddish-brown blotches ringed in black, stripe through eye, spear-point pattern on crown. Eats mice, rats, occ. birds. **CAUTION** May coil like rattler when cornered; will bite. **HABITAT** Woods and open areas (esp. pine flatlands), farms, old buildings, trash piles. **RANGE** sc NJ (rare), s DE, se MD, VA.

RAT SNAKE
"Black Rat Snake"
Elaphe obsoleta
COLUBRID SNAKE FAMILY

5'. Long, slender; head wider than body; eyes smaller than in similar Racer; scales keeled. Plain black; throat white. Young strongly patterned (resembles Milk Snake): gray with large black spots. Swims well; often climbs trees. Constricts birds, rodents. **HABITAT** Wood and woodland edges, buildings, roadsides. **RANGE** Entire region, ex. n NY.

in the Mid-Atlantic region mate in the fall, before their winter hibernation, which usually begins in November and ends in March or April. Most species lay eggs in June that hatch in September; a few give birth to live young in September. Snakes in the Mid-Atlantic region are nonpoisonous except for four localized species (see the Copperhead and Timber Rattlesnake accounts, and the box on snakebite). The size given for snakes is the length of a typical adult.

EASTERN HOGNOSE SNAKE
Heterodon platyrhinos
COLUBRID SNAKE FAMILY

27″. Stout; snout up-turned, pointed. Color variable: often yellowish with dark and light brown blotches; some plain slaty with white lower jaw; underside of tail lighter than belly. When threatened, expands neck like a cobra and hisses, then rolls over and plays dead. Toads are main prey. **HABITAT** Sandy fields, open dry woods. **ACTIVITY** By day in warmer months. **RANGE** From se NY and c PA south.

COMMON KINGSNAKE
Lampropeltis getula
COLUBRID SNAKE FAMILY

3′6″. Shiny black with thin white bands in chain-link pattern; scales smooth. Bites snakes and lizards behind head, then coils around them. Secretive; often under boards or logs. **HABITAT** Swamp borders, streamsides in woods; grassy pinelands. **ACTIVITY** Day and night. **RANGE** From s NJ and MD south, ex. Allegheny Mtns.

MILK SNAKE
Lampropeltis triangulum
COLUBRID SNAKE FAMILY

30″. Medium girth; scales smooth. Ground color pale gray to yellowish; red or reddish-brown patches outlined in black along entire body; Y- or V-shaped patch on nape. Constricts rodents and other snakes. Similar, poisonous Copperhead has larger, unmarked head and nape. **HABITAT** Barns, woodpiles, open woods, fields. **ACTIVITY** Secretive; usu. under boards, stones, etc.

NORTHERN WATER SNAKE
Nerodia sipedon
COLUBRID SNAKE FAMILY

3′. Robust; head broad; scales ridged. Gray-brown or yellow-brown with reddish-brown, black-edged bands, wider on back, narrower on sides. Older adult all dark brown or black. Adept swimmer; basks on shores, limbs. **CAUTION** Nonpoisonous, but bites when handled. **HABITAT** Ponds, streams, swamps—most bodies of fresh water. **ACTIVITY** Day and night.

EASTERN PINE SNAKE
Pituophis melanoleucus
COLUBRID SNAKE FAMILY
5′. Robust; head small, pointed; scales keeled. Pale gray, yellowish, or white, with large dark brown spots on back, smaller spots on sides. Constricts small mammals, birds, lizards. When cornered, hisses loudly, vibrates tail. **HABITAT** Sandy pine-oak barrens (NJ); dry upland woods (VA). **RANGE** s NJ, mtns. of VA.

BROWN SNAKE
Storeria dekayi
COLUBRID SNAKE FAMILY
11″. Nondescript: dull brown with grayish dorsal stripe flanked by 2 rows of dark brown spots; black cap on head, with black downward streak behind eye; belly pale brown or yellowish. Scales keeled. **HABITAT** Woods, swamp and creek borders, waste lots in urban parks. **Red-bellied Snake** (*S. occipitomaculata*) of region's upland woods is gray or brown above; has slaty head, large yellow nape spots, red belly. **ACTIVITY** Secretive; common under rubble of vacant lots.

Poisonous Snakes and Snakebite

The Mid-Atlantic region has four poisonous snake species—the Copperhead and the Timber Rattlesnake (see page 271); the Cottonmouth (*Agkistrodon piscivorus*), which lives only in far southeastern Virginia, and the Massasauga (*Sistrurus catenatus*), restricted to western New York and northwestern Pennsylvania. As snake populations have been decimated by automobiles, hunters, and loss of habitat, most people who hike frequently in the region's woods and fields will never see a poisonous snake. Yet on very warm April days, a local herpetologist could find dozens at favorite denning sites on southern and southwestern slopes of rocky hills from New York to Virginia. All poisonous Mid-Atlantic species have retractable fangs that can deliver blood-destroying venom, but most snakes will flee from footsteps. If you encounter a snake, freeze to let it withdraw, then step away. For any poisonous snakebite, the best course of action is to get to medical care as soon as possible, with the dead snake or positive identification of the species, so the proper antivenin can be administered. Meanwhile, the victim should avoid moving, as movement helps the venom spread through the system, and keep the injured body part motionless just below heart level. The victim should be kept warm, calm, and at rest while on the way to medical care. If you are alone and on foot, start walking slowly toward help, exerting the injured area as little as possible. If you run or if the bite has delivered a large amount of venom, you may collapse, but a snakebite seldom results in death.

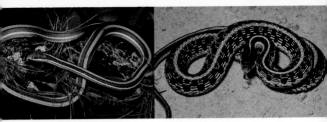

EASTERN RIBBON SNAKE
Thamnophis sauritus
COLUBRID SNAKE FAMILY

28″. Slender; scales keeled. Blackish brown with 3 yellow stripes. Differs from Common Garter Snake in being slimmer (with long, tapering tail) and less spotted, and having dark stripe along margins of belly scales. Found in or near water, where it swims on surface; flees rapidly through shoreline grasses. HABITAT Swamps, freshwater marshes, moist meadows, streamsides.

COMMON GARTER SNAKE
Thamnophis sirtalis
COLUBRID SNAKE FAMILY

22″. Slender. Variable in color and pattern; narrow yellowish stripe along entire midback; rest of back solid blackish or pale brown (some gray), with 2 rows of blackish spots; sides and belly pale buffy or gray. Region's most common striped snake. HABITAT Woods, fields, scrub, waste lots in urban areas, gardens.

COPPERHEAD
Agkistrodon contortrix
PIT VIPER FAMILY

3′. Body fairly thick; scales weakly keeled. Dull orange with rich brown, hourglass-shaped bands that are wide on sides, narrow on back. Head large, triangular, unmarked coppery red. Usu. lethargic; eats mainly rodents. Hibernates in dens with rattlers, other snakes. Hard to see in leaf litter. CAUTION Poisonous—can strike vigorously. HABITAT Wooded hills with rocky outcrops; coastal woods; swamp edges in south. ACTIVITY Apr.–Oct. RANGE From se NY, n NJ, and c PA south.

TIMBER RATTLESNAKE
Crotalus horridus
PIT VIPER FAMILY

4′. Body thick; head thick, triangular, unmarked. Tail has silvery rattle. Dark phase has black head, dark gray body with black blotches edged in white, black tail. Pale phase yellowish brown, incl. head, with dark brown blotches, black tail. Canebrake race of se VA has dark stripe behind eye, narrower crossbands. Pop. greatly reduced in most areas. CAUTION Poisonous; coils before striking; vibrates rattle in warning. HABITAT Wooded hills with rocky outcrops, pine-oak barrens in s NJ, swampy areas in south. ACTIVITY Apr.–Oct. RANGE Locally from Finger Lakes and Lake Champlain south through c PA to WV and w VA; also se VA (Canebrake race).

Birds

Members of the class Aves, birds are the only animals that have feathers, and most are capable of flight. Like their reptile ancestors, they lay eggs; like mammals, they are warm-blooded. They generally have excellent sight and hearing, but few have a good sense of smell. The bird skeleton is adapted for flight: the bones are lightweight, with a sponge-like interior. The forelimbs have become wings, with strong pectoral muscles attached to a keeled breastbone, and the hindlimbs are modified for running, grasping, or perching. Wing shapes vary among types of birds, ranging, for example, from the long broad wings of the soaring raptors to the narrow, fast-moving wings of hummingbirds.

While all Blue Jays look the same regardless of their gender or the time of year, this is not the case for most North American birds. Plumages may vary from immature to adult, from male to female, and from breeding to nonbreeding seasons (summer and winter, respectively). (If both sexes have a summer plumage distinct from nonbreeding plumage, we note this as "summer adult." If only the male has such a summer plumage, we note "summer male.") In some species, groups living in different geographic areas (subspecies, or races) have slightly or distinctly different plumages. Some birds within a given species have different colorations (called morphs or phases) that have nothing to do with where they live. Some birds have ornamental plumes, often developed in the breeding season. This guide describes the plumages most often seen in the Mid-Atlantic region. The photograph shows the male or the adult (if adults look alike), usually in its most distinctive plumage unless otherwise noted.

Flight allows birds to migrate great distances, though some are resident year-round in some or all of the region. Many birds that spend the winter in warmer, southern climes migrate north to breed, taking advantage of the abundant animal life here in the summer. Other birds breed to the north, in Canada or New England, and pass through the Mid-Atlantic states only in migration. Cold and snow rarely kill birds directly but may reduce the amount of food (insects, animals, fruits) they can obtain to maintain their ideal body temperature. Most of our breeding species winter in the southern United States or the tropics of Latin America. Most individuals return to the same breeding and wintering grounds throughout their lives.

Northbound migration occurs from March to early June, southbound from July into December. Migrants often wait until the wind is at their backs before setting off. In spring, warm southwesterly winds help bring migrants northeastward from the southern United States. In autumn, winds from the north aid southbound migrants on their journey south; a strong cold front with northwesterly winds at times floods our coastal points and islands with migrants returning to the nearest point of land after being blown out to sea, often in great numbers. For more about bird migration, see the essay on bird-watching on page 274.

Parts of a Bird

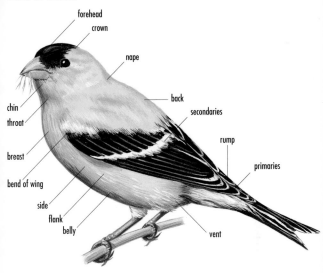

forehead
crown
nape
back
secondaries
rump
primaries
chin
throat
breast
bend of wing
side
flank
belly
vent

In bird species that do not nest in colonies, a male who is ready to breed stakes out and defends a nesting territory from other males. The female chooses a male in part on the quality and size of his territory, the presence of a secure nest site, and the quality of his plumage and song. The avian life cycle typically starts with the female laying one or more eggs in a nest, which, depending on the species, may be a scrape in the sand, a cup of rootlets and fibers, a woven basket, a stick platform, or another type of structure. After an incubation period of roughly two to four weeks, the young are hatched and fed by their parents for a period varying from a few days (shorebirds) to many weeks (most species) to many months (raptors). Smaller birds tend to breed the year following their birth, while many larger birds remain immature for several years before breeding. During the breeding season, many male birds exhibit more colorful and elaborate plumages and courtship displays and rituals in order to attract a mate. Most species mate in solitary pairs, the males competing for breeding territories; other species nest colonially. In this section of the guide, assume a bird is a solitary nester unless the description notes that it nests in colonies. Space limitations prevent us from giving descriptions of nests.

Birds use their voices in many ways. In many species, contact and alarm call notes are given year-round by both sexes. The more musical songs, usually given only in spring and summer by the male, attract mates and define territory. Once the young are born, many birds stop singing. Mid-Atlantic woodlands and shrublands are much quieter in August than in June.

This section's descriptions give the average length of the adult bird from the tip of the beak to the end of the tail. For some large species, both length and wingspan are given.

Bird-watching

Bird-watching, or birding, as it is often termed, can be a casual activity, develop into a hobby, or become a passion. It's fairly easy to see 200 species a year in the Mid-Atlantic region, and possible, with diligence, to see 300 species.

In breeding season, many birds tend to live in only one habitat and are active at certain times of day. Freshwater marsh birds (rails, bitterns, marsh songbirds) are most often calling and active at dawn and dusk, and on rainy days. Until mid-morning on hot days, songbirds search woodlands, fields, and thickets for food; from mid-morning to late afternoon, they tend to be quiet, and forage again late in the day. Birds that live near beaches, lakes, and other aquatic habitats (herons, cormorants, ducks, sandpipers) may be active all day; the activities of seaside species are dictated by the tides. Make an after-dark visit to a forest or swamp to find owls, which may respond to imitated calls, and can be viewed with spotlights.

The greatest variety of birds can be seen during the migration seasons. In early spring (March and April), larger birds such as hawks and waterfowl migrate through the Mid-Atlantic states, while many wintering birds return northward. Most songbirds migrate north to the region during April and May; males arrive a week or so before females in order to stake out territories. When the land bird migration tapers off in late May, sandpipers and plovers are still flying through. While larger birds migrate by day, most species, especially smaller, insect-eating ones, fly at night, resting and feeding during the day, tending to gather in quiet places where food is easy to find. In a light woodland along a stream, where there are newly opened leaves and plenty of small insects, it is possible to see a dozen or

COMMON LOON
Gavia immer
LOON FAMILY

winter (left), summer (right)

32″. Body stout, duck-like. Summer: back black with large white spots; head and neck black; white bands on neck; eyes red. Winter: slaty above, white below. Bill heavy, pointed. In flight, legs extend beyond tail. **VOICE** Quavering laughter, yodeling; heard mainly around northern lakes on summer nights. **HABITAT** Summer and migration: lakes, coast. Winter: coastal bays, ocean. **RANGE** Apr.–May, Oct.: entire region (local); breeds in n NY. Oct.–Apr.: entire coast. **Red-throated Loon** (*G. stellata; 25″*) has similar winter plumage (Nov.–Apr., chiefly on coast); neck snakier; bill thinner, upturned.

more species of warblers in a single spring morning. Migrating songbirds also concentrate in isolated groves of trees along the coast and in city parks.

Fall migration is under way by July, when the first southbound sandpipers and plovers reappear; adults in these groups migrate a week to a month or more before their offspring. From August into October, most of the songbirds pass through; if winds are strong from the northwest, large numbers will be blown toward the coast and islands. The migration of ducks, geese, and raptors starts in September and continues well into early December.

For the serious birder, at least one good field guide is essential; many excellent ones are available, including the *National Audubon Society Field Guide to North American Birds (Eastern Region)*. Binoculars (7-, 8-, 9-, or 10-power) are a must; a close-focusing pair is especially helpful. A 15-, 20-, or 30-power telescope with a wide field of view, mounted on a sturdy, collapsible tripod, is invaluable for viewing waterfowl, shorebirds, and raptors.

While many species are rather tame, others are shy or secretive. Learn to move slowly and quietly, and avoid wearing brightly colored or patterned clothing and making loud noises. Please respect local laws, do not unduly frighten birds, and take great care not to disrupt nesting or resting birds.

For suggestions on attracting birds to your yard, see page 316. In this section, the icon ✲ denotes species that will come into a yard to a feeder. The icon ⬠ indicates species that might use a nest box in a yard.

PIED-BILLED GREBE
Podilymbus podiceps
GREBE FAMILY
13″. Body duck-like. Bill short, thick. Summer: body brown; chin black; black ring on silver bill. Winter: body brown; chin white; bill pale, no ring. Dives for small fish and invertebrates. **VOICE** Series of 8 *cow* notes. **HABITAT** Summer: marshes with open water. Migration, winter: ponds, rivers. **RANGE** Apr.–Oct.: entire region (uncommon migrant, rare breeder). Nov.–Apr.: coastal plain.

HORNED GREBE
Podiceps auritus
GREBE FAMILY
14″. Body duck-like. Winter: back and hindneck slaty; crown black; throat and foreneck white. Neck thin; bill slender; eyes red. Rarely seen flying; migrates at night. **VOICE** Quiet at sea. **HABITAT** Coastal waters, estuaries. **RANGE** Apr., Oct.: larger inland lakes (uncommon). Nov.–Apr.: entire coast.

NORTHERN GANNET
Morus bassanus
BOOBY AND GANNET FAMILY

3'2". Adult mostly white; primaries pointed, black; yellow wash on head. Bill silver, long and pointed; neck longish; tail wedge-shaped. Dives from on high; in migration, flies in lines low to water or high above. **VOICE** Quiet at sea. **HABITAT** Open sea; seen from beaches during migration, storms. **RANGE** Oct.–May: off entire coast.

SOOTY SHEARWATER
Puffinus griseus
SHEARWATER FAMILY

17". Entirely sooty brown above and below; contrasting silvery-white underwing linings. Bill narrow, black. Flies near surface on very stiff wings with fast flaps, long glides. **VOICE** Quiet at sea. **HABITAT** Open sea; rarely seen from shore. **RANGE** Late May–Aug.: off entire coast.

WILSON'S STORM-PETREL
Oceanites oceanicus
STORM-PETREL FAMILY

7". Swallow-like. Black with white rump. Bill short, black. Long legs extend beyond tail in flight. Patters and hops over surface on fluttering wings. **VOICE** Quiet at sea. **HABITAT** Open sea. **RANGE** Late May–mid-Sept.: off entire coast, usu. well offshore.

BROWN PELICAN
Pelecanus occidentalis
PELICAN FAMILY

summer adult (left), winter adult (right)

L 4'2"; WS 7'6". Adult body and wings grayish brown; head white, with yellowish wash on crown. Neck long, chestnut brown in summer, all white in winter; bill long, with pouch. Legs short; feet webbed. Imm. (to 4 years) brown with white belly. Feeds on fish; dives bill-first into water. Rests on pilings, beaches. Flies with slow, regular wingbeats in V formation, glides long distances skimming tops of waves. **VOICE** Usu. silent. **HABITAT** Ocean, bays, estuaries. **RANGE** Apr.–Oct.: nonbreeders from s NJ to VA.

DOUBLE-CRESTED CORMORANT

immature (left), adult (right)

Phalacrocorax auritus
CORMORANT FAMILY

33". Adult black with greenish cast; breeding crest (2 small tufts) hard to see. Bill hooked; orange skin on throat. Imm. brownish, whitish from throat to breast. Swims low in water with bill angled upward; flocks often fly in V; at rest, spreads wings to dry. Nests in colonies. Rapidly increasing. **VOICE** Usu. silent; croaks at nest. **HABITAT** Coasts; larger inland waters. **RANGE** Resident on coast (local breeder). Apr.–Oct.: inland lakes, Great Lakes, rivers.

Herons

Members of the heron family (Ardeidae)—herons, egrets, and bitterns—are large, long-legged, long-necked birds up to 4 feet long. They wade in shallows and marshes, where they use their longish, dagger-like bills to seize slippery fish and aquatic frogs, snakes, and invertebrates. While storks, ibises, spoonbills, and cranes fly with outstretched necks, herons normally fold theirs in an S shape when airborne. During courtship (two to four weeks a year), adults of many of these species have ornamental plumes and bright facial colors. Their nests are usually large platforms of sticks, often in large colonies. Predominantly white heron species are called egrets. Bitterns are shy denizens of marshes with distinct voices.

GREAT BLUE HERON

breeding (left), in flight (right)

Ardea herodias
HERON FAMILY

L 4'; WS 6'. Back and wings blue-gray; shoulder black; crown black with white center; short black plumes from back of head; face white; most of neck buffy gray; foreneck striped black and white; belly blackish. Legs long, dark; bill yellow. Imm. duller; crown slaty. Nests in colonies. **VOICE** Deep squawk. **HABITAT** Marshes, watersides. **RANGE** Apr.–Nov.: entire region, inland and coast; breeds in inland NY and PA, and on much of coast; nests early, disperses widely by July. Dec.–Mar.: coastal plain; fewer inland.

GREAT EGRET
Ardea alba
HERON FAMILY

L 3′3″; WS 4′3″. Largest all-white heron. Neck long, thin. Bill long, yellow; feet and long legs black. During courtship, long, lacy white plumes on back; facial skin green. Nests in colonies, with other species. Symbol of the National Audubon Society. **VOICE** Deep croak. **HABITAT** Marshes. **RANGE** Apr.–Oct.: breeds along entire coast; disperses widely after breeding. Nov.–Mar.: a few from s NJ to e VA.

CATTLE EGRET
Bubulcus ibis
HERON FAMILY

20″. All white; bill yellow; legs and feet usu. dark. Bill and legs shortish for a heron. During courtship, buffy plumes on back, chest, and crown; bill, legs, and feet orange. Social flocks feed together, return to communal roosts each night; nests in large colonies, sometimes with other species. Chases large insects and frogs disturbed by feeding cattle, horses. Self-introduced from Africa via S Amer. **VOICE** Hoarse croaks; usu. silent. **HABITAT** Meadows, lawns, crop fields, marshes. **RANGE** Apr.–Oct. coastal plain.

LITTLE BLUE HERON
Egretta caerulea
HERON FAMILY

adult (left), immature (right)

27″. Neck and legs long; bill gray at base, black-tipped. Adult body and wing slate-blue; head and neck dull dark purple. During courtship, long purplish back and head plumes. Imm. all white; legs and feet dull slaty olive. Feeds on fish in shallow waters; also eats large insects and frogs in meadows. Nests in colonies. **VOICE** Harsh squawk; usu. silent. **HABITAT** Salt- and freshwater marshes; swamps; meadows. **RANGE** Apr.–Oct.: entire coast; some disperse inland in late summer. Nov.–Mar.: a few near coast from s NJ to VA.

SNOWY EGRET
Egretta thula
HERON FAMILY

24″. All white. Neck and legs long; bill slender, black; lores yellow. Adult legs black, feet yellow. During courtship, long, lacy white plumes on back, chest, and crown. Imm. legs dark green. Nests in colonies. **VOICE** Harsh *aah*. **HABITAT** Marshes, ponds. **RANGE** Apr.–Oct.: breeds along entire coast; disperses inland in late summer. Nov.–Mar.: a few from s NJ to e VA.

TRICOLORED HERON
"Louisiana Heron"
Egretta tricolor
HERON FAMILY

26″. Adult back, wings, neck, and head slaty blue; belly and underwings white; white line down entire fore-neck, base of neck purplish. Neck and legs long; bill very long, thin, gray, black-tipped. During courtship, long buffy plumes on back. Imm. neck and shoulders rusty. Fishes by slow stalking and wild running pursuit in shallow water. Nests in colonies, with other species. **VOICE** Guttural squawks; usu. silent. **HABITAT** Salt- and freshwater mudflats and marshes; swamps. **RANGE** Apr.–Oct.: near coast.

BLACK-CROWNED NIGHT-HERON
Nycticorax nycticorax
HERON FAMILY

adult (left), immature (right)

26″. Adult crown and back black; wings gray; forecrown and underparts silvery white; eyes large, red. Neck thick; legs shortish, yellow. Imm. brown, with heavy white streaks and spots. Nests in colonies, esp. on islands. **VOICE** Low *kwock*, often given at dusk. **HABITAT** Ponds, riversides, marshes. **RANGE** Apr.–Oct.: entire coast; inland (local). Nov.–Mar.: a few from Long Is. to VA.

YELLOW-CROWNED NIGHT-HERON
Nyctanassa violacea
HERON FAMILY

26″. Adult body and wings slate gray; head black; cheek and crown white; forecrown yellow; eyes large, red; legs yellow. During breeding, white plumes on nape; legs orange. May appear short-necked; legs longer than those of Black-crowned. Imm. grayish brown, speckled white above. Feeds on crabs, crayfish. **VOICE** Loud *quark*, higher and softer than that of Black-crowned. **HABITAT** Salt marshes, pondsides, rivers. **RANGE** Apr.–Oct.: New York City to e VA; rare inland.

GREEN HERON
Butorides virescens
HERON FAMILY

19″. Adult back and wings dark dull green; cap black; neck chestnut; legs greenish yellow (orange when breeding). Legs shortish; bill dark. Imm. brownish; neck pale with heavy dark brown streaks; legs yellow-green. Often feeds by leaning over water from logs, rocks; also wades. **VOICE** Harsh *keyow*, usu. given in flight. **HABITAT** Ponds, streams, marshes. **RANGE** Apr.–Oct.: entire region.

AMERICAN BITTERN
Botaurus lentiginosus
HERON FAMILY

28″. Adult light brown, with thin white eyebrow, dark brown streaks and black stripe on neck. Legs greenish. **VOICE** Loud *uunk-KA-lunk*. **HABITAT** Freshwater marshes. **RANGE** Apr.–May, Sept.–Oct.: entire region; local breeder in NY and PA to e VA. Nov.–Mar.: a few on coastal plain. **Least Bittern** (*Ixobrychus exilis;* 13″) buffy brown; male has black back and cap. Apr.–Sept.: fresh and brackish marshes.

GLOSSY IBIS
Plegadis falcinellus
IBIS FAMILY

23″. Adult body purplish brown; wings glossy green; appears black in poor light. Neck and legs long; bill extremely long and downcurved. Imm. dull brown. Nests in colonies, with herons. **VOICE** Guttural *ka-onk*. **HABITAT** Saltmarshes, moist meadows. **RANGE** Apr.–Oct.: entire coast; some inland in Apr., late summer.

Waterfowl

The waterfowl family (Anatidae) contains the huge white swans, the large geese, and a wide variety of smaller ducks. All have webbed feet, and thick rounded or pointed bills designed for filtering small organisms in the water or for grasping underwater vegetation and invertebrates. Most waterfowl undergo lengthy migrations between northern or inland breeding areas and southern and/or coastal wintering waters. Their nests, made of grasses and lined with feathers, are usually on the ground, hidden in grass or reeds, and contain many eggs.

Ducks may be split into two main groups. Dabblings ducks upend on the surface of fresh and brackish waters, and can jump up and take flight straight out of the water; some reveal a colorful patch (speculum) on the wings near the body. Swans and geese upend like dabbling ducks, rather than dive for food; most patter across the water to get airborne. Diving ducks dive well under the surface of fresh and salt waters; in taking flight, they run and flap horizontally over the water's surface before gaining altitude. In late summer, male ducks develop a drab eclipse plumage similar to that of females.

Mallard dabbling

Mallard taking off, straight up, from surface of water

Canada Goose taking off by running across water

TUNDRA SWAN
Cygnus columbianus
WATERFOWL FAMILY

L 4′6″; WS 7′. Adult mostly white; head and extremely long neck often stained rusty. Bill thick, black, tapers to eye; may have yellow spot before eye. Feet black; tail short. Imm. light brown; bill pink. Flies with neck outstretched, usu. in flocks. **VOICE** Mellow, high-pitched *hoo-oo-hoo*. **HABITAT** Shallow large lakes, coastal lagoons and bays. **RANGE** Oct.–Nov., Mar.–Apr.: entire region (local). Nov.–Mar.: e MD, DE, and e VA.

MUTE SWAN
Cygnus olor
WATERFOWL FAMILY

L 5′; WS 8′. Adult all white; bill orange with black knob over bill. Legs black. Neck usu. held in S curve at rest. Wing feathers often arched over back while swimming. Imm. pale grayish brown; bill silvery. Flies with whistling wingbeats, neck outstretched. Introduced from Europe. Aggressive to humans and dogs near nest and young. **VOICE** Rarely heard hiss. **HABITAT** Coastal lagoons, ponds. **RANGE** Resident on coastal plain.

BRANT
Branta bernicla
WATERFOWL FAMILY

26″. Head, neck, and chest black; patch of white lines on upper neck (absent in imm.); back and wings dark brown; belly and sides pale brown; rear end mainly white. **VOICE** Throaty *cur-onk*. **HABITAT** Shallow saltwater bays, estuaries, waterside lawns. **RANGE** Nov.–Apr.: entire coast, s Hudson River (common).

CANADA GOOSE
Branta canadensis
WATERFOWL FAMILY

L 3′4″; WS 6′. Adult back and wings dark brown; head and long neck black; large white chinstrap; breast pale brown; vent and rump white; tail short, black. Imm. pale gray; downy young yellow. Often flies in V. **VOICE** Honking *car-uunk*; often calls in flight. **HABITAT** Marshes, ponds, fields, lawns with short grass. **RANGE** Resident in much of region. Mar.–Apr., Oct.–Nov.: some migrate to/from Canada inland, winter on coastal plain.

SNOW GOOSE
Chen caerulescens
WATERFOWL FAMILY

28″. Adult all white with black primaries; bill pink with black "lips"; face often stained rusty; legs pink. Imm. dingy brownish gray; bill, legs, and primaries black. Flies in V high overhead. Dark morph ("Blue Goose") has dark body, white head (uncommon). Numbers increasing. **VOICE** High nasal honks. **HABITAT** Marshes, fields, ponds. **RANGE** Mar.–Apr., Oct.–Nov.: entire region. Nov.–Mar.: some flocks from s NJ to e VA.

WOOD DUCK
Aix sponsa
WATERFOWL FAMILY

19″. Male iridescent; back dark purple; belly white; chest purple with white spots; sides buffy-yellow; head green with laid-back crest; throat and 2-pronged chinstrap white; eye ring and base of bill red. Female mostly grayish-brown with long white eye ring. Region's most colorful inland duck. **VOICE** Male: high whistle when courting. Female: *oo-eek*. **HABITAT** Swamps, ponds, rivers. **RANGE** Mar.–Nov.: entire region. Dec.–Feb.: a few in se VA.

GREEN-WINGED TEAL
Anas crecca
WATERFOWL FAMILY

14″. Dabbler. Male body gray, with vertical white stripe behind chest; head chestnut; bill small, black; green eye patch extends to fluffy nape; vent patch yellow. Female brown. Flight reveals green wing patch. Region's smallest duck. **VOICE** Male: whistled *crick-et*. **HABITAT** Marshes, ponds. **RANGE** Mar.–Apr., Sept.–Nov.: entire region; a few breed in n and w NY, and near coast. Dec.–Feb.: Long Is. to e VA.

AMERICAN BLACK DUCK
Anas rubripes
WATERFOWL FAMILY

23″. Dabbler. Male body and wings dark brown; head and upper neck distinctly paler brown; bill yellow. Female has dark saddle on bill. Legs red-orange. Flight reveals white underwing coverts, purple wing patch. **VOICE** Female: quack. **HABITAT** Ponds, rivers, marshes. **RANGE** Resident from NY, NJ, and n and e PA south to e VA. Oct.–Apr.: entire region, esp. coastal salt marshes.

MALLARD
Anas platyrhynchos
WATERFOWL FAMILY

male (left), female (right)

24″. Dabbler. Male body and wings gray; head and neck glossy green; white ring above purplish chest; rump black; tail white; bill bright yellow. Female buffy brown; bill pale orange with dark saddle. Legs orange. Flight reveals purple wing patch bordered with white. Region's most widespread inland duck. **VOICE** Male: quiet; gives *reeb* call when fighting. Female: quack. **HABITAT** Ponds, rivers, marshes, marinas. **RANGE** Resident in entire region. Sept.–Apr.: influx of migrant winterers from north and west.

NORTHERN PINTAIL
Anas acuta
WATERFOWL FAMILY

26″. Dabbler. Male back, wings, and sides pearly gray; head and hindneck chestnut; foreneck and belly white; very long black central tail feathers. Female smaller, pale brown. Bill long, gray. Neck thin; tail sharp, pointed. **VOICE** Male: wheezy *prip prip*. Female: quack. **HABITAT** Marshes, ponds. **RANGE** Mar.–Apr., Sept.–Nov.: entire region (local). Dec.–Feb.: coastal plain.

BLUE-WINGED TEAL
Anas discors
WATERFOWL FAMILY

15″. Dabbler. Male body pinkish brown with black dots; head slaty blue with white crescent before eye. Female mottled brown. Flight reveals pale chalky blue shoulder. Bill heavier, longer than Green-winged Teal's. **VOICE** Male: peep-like notes. Female: high quack. **HABITAT** Marshes, weedy ponds. **RANGE** Mar.–May, Aug.–Oct.: entire region; breeds in n and w NY, and along coast (rare). Nov.–Feb.: a few from s NJ to e VA.

NORTHERN SHOVELER
Anas clypeata
WATERFOWL FAMILY

18″. Dabbler. Male head glossy dark green; chest white; sides rusty; eyes yellow; bill black. Female brown, speckled; bill often orange. Neck short; bill long and wide, held close to water. Flight reveals chalky blue shoulder. **VOICE** Male: low *took*. Female: quack. **HABITAT** Marshes, ponds, saltwater bays. **RANGE** Mar.–Apr., Sept.–Nov.: entire region; a few breed in w NY. Some winter near coast.

GADWALL
Anas strepera
WATERFOWL FAMILY

20″. Dabbler. Male body and head mostly gray; bill dark gray; rear end mainly black. Female brown; bill black with orange edge. Flight reveals square white wing patch bordered in black, white belly. **VOICE** Male: croaks, whistles. Female: subdued quack. **HABITAT** Lakes, ponds, marshes. **RANGE** Mar.–Apr., Sept.–Nov.: entire region; a few breed in w NY and along coast. Dec.–Feb.: coastal plain.

AMERICAN WIGEON
Anas americana
WATERFOWL FAMILY

21″. Dabbler. Both sexes brownish; sides dull rusty orange; head speckled. Bill short, pale blue with dark tip. Male forehead boldly white; green patch behind eye; vent black and white. Flight reveals white shoulder patch. **VOICE** Male: whistled *whee whee whew*. Female: quack. **HABITAT** Shallow ponds and lakes, esp. near coast. **RANGE** Mar.–Apr., Sept.–Oct.: entire region (local). Nov.–Feb.: coastal plain.

CANVASBACK
Aythya valisineria
WATERFOWL FAMILY

21″. Diver. Male back, wings, and sides silvery white; chest black; head reddish brown; eyes red; tail black. Female back, wings, and sides gray; chest dark brown; head brown. Sloping forehead forms straight line with sloping black bill. Flight reveals plain gray wings. **VOICE** Usu. silent in region. **HABITAT** Lakes, estuaries, coastal bays, large rivers. **RANGE** Oct.–Nov., Mar.–Apr.: entire region (local). Dec.–Feb.: near coast, esp. Ches. Bay.

RING-NECKED DUCK
Aythya collaris
WATERFOWL FAMILY

17″. Diver. Male chest, back, and tail black; sides gray, with white patch at leading edge; head dark purple, with peaked crown. Female brown with pale buffy wash on face, pale eye ring. Bill patterned in both sexes. Flight reveals black shoulder, gray wing stripe. **VOICE** Usu. silent. **HABITAT** Freshwater ponds, lakes, rivers. **RANGE** Mar.–Apr., Oct.–Nov.: entire region; some breed in n NY. Dec.–Feb.: coastal plain.

GREATER SCAUP
Aythya marila
WATERFOWL FAMILY

18″. Diver. Male back gray; sides white; chest and tail area black; head blackish green. Female dark brown, with distinct white face patch. Bill plain gray; eyes yellow. Flight reveals long white stripe on trailing edge of wing. Often form large rafts (flocks). **VOICE** Usu. silent. **HABITAT** Saltwater bays, estuaries; in migration, lakes. **RANGE** Oct.–Apr.: along coast, Great Lakes. **Lesser Scaup** *(A. affinis)* male has dark purple head, shorter stripe on wings; Oct.–Apr.: fresh and brackish waters near coast.

WHITE-WINGED SCOTER
Melanitta fusca
WATERFOWL FAMILY

22″. Diver. Male black; white crescent around eye; bill orange with black knob. Female dark brown with pale face patches. White patch on secondaries. **VOICE** Usu. silent. **HABITAT** Ocean. **RANGE** Oct.–Apr.: off entire coast. Oct., Apr.: also Great Lakes. **Surf Scoter** *(M. perspicillata)* male has white forehead and nape patch; no white on wings. **Black Scoter** *(M. nigra)* male lacks white; has orange knob on bill. Both winter on coast, Oct.–Apr.

COMMON GOLDENEYE
Bucephala clangula
WATERFOWL FAMILY

18″. Diver. Male black and white above; white below; head dark glossy green, fluffed out at rear; large white spot near bill. Female head all dark brown, with white neck ring; body paler grayish. Eyes golden. **VOICE** Quiet; wings whistle in flight. **HABITAT** Summer: northern lakes. Migration, winter: large rivers, coastal bays and ponds. **RANGE** Nov.–Apr.: entire region; a few breed in n NY.

BUFFLEHEAD
Bucephala albeola
WATERFOWL FAMILY

male (left), female (right)

14″. Diver. Male back black; chest and underparts white. Head has greenish-purple gloss, with large white patch on rear half. Female grayish brown, with large white spot behind and under eye. Bill short. Flight reveals extensive white secondaries. **VOICE** Usu. silent. **HABITAT** Coastal bays, estuaries, ponds; in migration, lakes. **RANGE** Oct.–Apr.: entire coast, Great Lakes, inland VA.

HOODED MERGANSER
Lophodytes (Mergus)
cucullatus
WATERFOWL FAMILY

18". Diver. Adult male back, head, and neck black; sides rufous; large white head patch; chest white; eyes yellow. Female gray-brown, with fluffy rusty-brown nape. Crest expandable, fan-like; bill narrow, black. VOICE Low grunts; usu. silent. HABITAT Tree-fringed ponds, lakes, rivers. RANGE Mar.–Apr., Sept.–Nov.: entire region; local breeder inland. Dec.–Feb.: coastal plain.

RED-BREASTED MERGANSER
Mergus serrator
WATERFOWL FAMILY

23". Diver. Male back black; chest rusty; sides gray; neck ring white; head dark green. Female gray; head rusty; throat and foreneck white. Bill long, slender, red; nape crest shaggy. Usually seen in small groups of 6–12. VOICE Usu. silent. HABITAT Inshore ocean and coastal waters, lakes. RANGE Oct.–Apr.: entire coast, Great Lakes. Visits other lakes during migration.

COMMON MERGANSER
Mergus merganser
WATERFOWL FAMILY

25". Diver. Male back black; chest and underparts white; head dark green, with rounded nape. Female body gray; head and neck rusty; chin distinctly white. Bill red, slender. VOICE Usu. silent. HABITAT Lakes, rivers; returns from coastal fresh waters to inland rivers with first thaw. RANGE Nov.–Apr.: entire region; breeds in n NY.

RUDDY DUCK
Oxyura jamaicensis
WATERFOWL FAMILY

16". Diver. Breeding male body ruddy brown; top half of head black, lower half white; bill thick, bright blue. Winter male head as above; body slaty brown; bill gray. Female body and cap brown, with dark line on pale buff cheeks. Tail black, stiff, fan-shaped, often raised. Gathers in small rafts (flocks). VOICE Usu. silent. HABITAT Bays, lakes, ponds, reservoirs. RANGE Oct.–Apr.: coastal Long Is. to c VA. Uncommon migrant, rare breeder inland.

Raptors

The word "raptor" is usually used for birds of prey that are active in the daytime (some experts also use the term for the nocturnal owls, described starting on page 307). Families found in the Mid-Atlantic region include the New World vultures (Carthartidae), the hawks and eagles (Accipitridae), and the falcons (Falconidae). The bills of raptors are strong and sharp for tearing flesh, while the feet (usually yellow) are generally powerful (except in vultures), with curved talons for grasping prey. Immature raptors, often striped below, take a year or more to reach adulthood. Females are 10 to 20 percent larger than males in most species.

The carrion-feeding vultures are black, with broad wings and bare heads. Members of the hawk and eagle family are the very large eagles; the Osprey, a large "fish hawk"; harriers, which fly low over open areas and use their superb hearing as an aid in hunting; and the hawks. There are two types of hawks in this region: the accipiters, bird hunters whose shorter, rounded wings and longer, narrow

Turkey Vulture

Bald Eagle

Flight silhouettes of raptors
(illustrations not to relative scale)

Osprey

BLACK VULTURE
adult (left), in flight (right)
Coragyps atratus
AMERICAN VULTURE FAMILY

L 24"; WS 4'6". Adult all black; head naked, scaly, silvery; bill pale gray. Flight reveals short tail and broad wings; black ex. for whitish patch on outer primaries at wingtips. Soars often; accelerates with 3–5 quick flaps, glides on horizontal wings. Roosts in dead trees. **VOICE** Hisses, grunts; seldom heard. **HABITAT** Fields, woods, watersides, dumps, farms. **RANGE** From NJ and s WV south; a few in s Hudson Valley of NY.

tails allow them to achieve rapid twisting flight, and the broad-winged, soaring buteos. Buteos and eagles ride rising thermals of air on sunny days; acute vision lets them spot unsuspecting prey from great heights. The pointed-winged falcons are fast fliers.

Many raptors migrate to warmer climes in winter, and do so during the day (unlike most songbirds). With the right weather, southbound hawk migrations can be viewed from many hilltops and coastal points in the Mid-Atlantic region. The best spring migration sites are in New York at Derby Hill (north of Syracuse) and Hook Mountain (northwest of Nyack). The best autumn hilltops are Hook Mountain and nearby Mount Peter; Montclair Hawk Lookout and Raccoon Ridge in northern New Jersey; Bake Oven Knob/Bear Rocks, Hawk Mountain, and Wagner's Gap in central Pennsylvania; Monument Knob in western Maryland; Mendota Fire Tower in far western Virginia; and Hanging Rocks Fire Tower in central West Virginia. The best autumn coastal sites are Cape May Point, New Jersey; Assateague Island, Maryland; and Cape Charles, Virginia.

Sharp-shinned Hawk (Accipiter)

American Kestrel (Falcon)

Northern Harrier

Red-tailed Hawk (Buteo)

TURKEY VULTURE
Cathartes aura
AMERICAN VULTURE FAMILY

adult (left), in flight (right)

L 28"; WS 6'. Adult all brownish black; head small, naked, red; bill yellow. Long rounded tail and pale silvery flight feathers seen from below. Soars with wings held at 20 degrees above horizontal; flaps wings less than Black Vulture. Finds carcasses by sight and smell. Gathers at nightly communal roosts in tall trees or towers. Has recently expanded range into Adirondacks. **VOICE** Grunts, hisses, usu. silent. **HABITAT** Over woods, fields, roadsides, dumps. **RANGE** Apr.–Oct.: entire region. Nov.–Mar.: s NJ and se PA south through VA.

OSPREY
Pandion haliaetus
HAWK AND EAGLE FAMILY

immatures (left), adult (right)

L 23"; WS 5'6". The familiar "fish hawk." Adult dark brown above with white crown and dark line through yellow eye; white below; feet gray; flight feathers and tail finely barred. Imm. has buffy crown, pale feather edges on wings and back. Flies with long wings bent at "wrist" like flattened M, often with fish grasped in talons; hovers. Nest is mass of sticks topping dead tree or platform on osprey pole. Devastated by DDT, it has rebounded well since the pesticide was banned. **VOICE** Emphatic *kee-uk* and *cheep*. **HABITAT** Coastal estuaries, rivers, inland lakes. **RANGE** Mar.–Nov.: coastal areas; lakes of n NY.

BALD EAGLE
Haliaeetus leucocephalus
HAWK AND EAGLE FAMILY

adult (left), immature (right)

L 32"; WS 7'. Adult body, wings, and thighs dark chocolate brown (appears black); massive head strikingly white; bill yellow, strongly hooked; eyes, feet, and massive legs yellow; tail white, somewhat rounded. Imm. all dark brown when perched; flight reveals diffuse whitish wing linings and base of tail. Flies with slow deliberate wingbeats, wings held flat, straight out, primaries spread. Perches on tall trees. Numbers increasing, with DDT ban and protection. **VOICE** Piercing scream. Call: loud cackle. **HABITAT** Coastal bays, estuaries, rivers, lakes. **RANGE** Oct.–May: entire region as migrant (uncommon) and winterer (local); some breed in n NY.

NORTHERN HARRIER
adult (left), immature (right)

Circus cyaneus
HAWK AND EAGLE FAMILY

L 22″; WS 4′. Wings and tail long, narrow; rump patch white; head and bill small; owl-like facial disks. Adult male pearly gray above, whiter below, with black wing tips. Adult female brown above, dirty white with brown stripes below. Imm. brown above, solid rusty orange below. Moves in tilting flight low over open areas, wings raised at an angle, listening and watching for rodents, frogs, and baby birds; often hovers and drops. Generally perches near ground, not in trees. **VOICE** Weak *pee*. **HABITAT** Salt- and freshwater marshes, open fields. **RANGE** Mar.–Apr., Sept.–Nov.: entire region; breeds very locally in NY and PA and on coastal plain (rare). Nov.–Mar.: coastal plain; w NY (uncommon).

SHARP-SHINNED HAWK
Accipiter striatus
HAWK AND EAGLE FAMILY

L 12″; WS 21″. Adult upperparts and crown gray; underparts barred rusty. Legs thin, yellow. Imm. brown above, striped below. Flies with fast wingbeats followed by glides; tail square, often notched. Expert at capturing small birds, often at feeders. **VOICE** High *kek* notes. **HABITAT** Woods, shrubby areas. **RANGE** Sept.–Apr.: entire region; uncommon breeder, mainly in hills. Locally common in migration.

COOPER'S HAWK
Accipiter cooperii
HAWK AND EAGLE FAMILY

L 17″; WS 28″. Plumages nearly identical to those of smaller, more common Sharp-shinned Hawk, but head slightly larger and tail longer, distinctly rounded; adult has black cap. Imm. belly whiter, with fewer streaks than Sharp-shinned. **VOICE** High *kek* notes. **HABITAT** Woodlands and borders. **RANGE** Resident in entire region; also spring and fall migrant.

BROAD-WINGED HAWK
Buteo platypterus
HAWK AND EAGLE FAMILY

L 15"; WS 34". Adult head, back, wings plain brown; underparts barred reddish brown on white. Imm. streaked. Flight reveals very white underwing with narrow black borders; adult tail black with 2–3 wide white bands. Thousands pass hawk-watching sites on mtn. ridges in Apr., Sept. **VOICE** High whistled *pee-teee*. **HABITAT** Broadleaf and mixed woods. **RANGE** Apr.–Sept.: entire region.

RED-SHOULDERED HAWK
Buteo lineatus
HAWK AND EAGLE FAMILY

L 20"; WS 3'4". Adult head and back brown; underparts narrowly barred rusty orange; wings barred black and white above; shoulder rufous; tail black with 5 thin white bands. Imm. streaked below, like most buteos. Seen from below, white crescent at base of primaries. **VOICE** Screaming loud *kee yarr*. **HABITAT** Woods, swamps. **RANGE** Mar.–Oct.: entire region. Nov.–Feb.: from se NY, c PA, and WV south.

RED-TAILED HAWK
Buteo jamaicensis
HAWK AND EAGLE FAMILY

immature (left), adult (top and bottom right)

L 22"; WS 4'2". The common large hawk. Head, back, and wings dark brown; upper chest white; lower chest has band of heavy blackish streaks contrasting with white thighs; tail pale orange below, bright rufous above. Seen from below, underwings mainly white, with dark leading edge under shoulder and black crescent beyond wrist. Imm. duller, more streaked; tail barred brown. Perches in open in trees, on poles (often along roadside). Often mobbed by crows, redwings, grackles, kingbirds. **VOICE** Down-slurred squeal: *keee-rrr*. **HABITAT** Woodland edges, isolated trees in fields. **RANGE** Resident in entire region (common).

AMERICAN KESTREL
Falco sparverius
FALCON FAMILY

L 11"; WS 23". Male back rufous; wings blue-gray; chest pale buffy; tail rufous with black band at end. Female rufous above, with fine black bars. 2 thin black sideburns on white face. In flight, pointed wings and long tail obvious. **VOICE** Shrill *killy killy*. **HABITAT** Open fields, towns; often on roadside wires. **RANGE** Resident on coastal plain and in inland valleys; local in summer.

MERLIN
Falco columbarius
FALCON FAMILY

L 12"; WS 25". Adult male blue-gray above, buffy with heavy brown streaks below; tail banded. Female and imm. dark brown above; streaked below; tail finely banded. 1 thin black sideburn. Flies fast and low when chasing small birds. **VOICE** High *ki ki ki ki*. **HABITAT** Coasts: marshes, beaches, open areas. **RANGE** Apr., Sept.–Oct.: entire region, mainly along coast. Nov.–Mar.: some near coast.

immature (left), adult (right)

PEREGRINE FALCON
Falco peregrinus
FALCON FAMILY

L 18"; WS 3'4". Adult upperparts and tail dark slaty gray; underparts and underwing finely gray-barred. Head black above, white below; 1 thick black sideburn. Feet heavy, powerful. Imm. brown above, streaked below. Flight reveals pointed wings, broad at base; tail tapers to squared end. Flies low and high, often surveying bird flocks to spot slow-flying individuals. Nests on ledges of cliffs, high bridges, or tall buildings. Numbers plummeted with DDT; now in assisted recovery. **VOICE** Harsh *kak kak* at nest. **HABITAT** Coasts, marshes, cities. **RANGE** May–Aug.: a few breed on cliff faces of w and n NY. Apr.–May, Sept.–Oct.: entire region, mainly along coast. Introduced urban pairs largely resident.

RING-NECKED PHEASANT
Phasianus colchicus
PARTRIDGE FAMILY

Male 34″; female 22″. Male head and neck iridescent dark green with white necklace and red bare skin around eye; rest of body rufous and bronze, with black-barred tail; wings paler grayish. Female and imm. warm buffy, with black spots above. Tail feathers long, pointed. Flies with rapid wingbeats followed by glides. Introduced from Asia as a game bird; requires repeated restocking in most areas. **VOICE** Male: loud *kaw kawk*. **HABITAT** Lowlands and valleys: farms, meadows, large gardens, overgrown city parks. **RANGE** Resident in NY, PA, NJ.

RUFFED GROUSE
Bonasa umbellus
PARTRIDGE FAMILY

18″. Adult reddish brown or gray, speckled white and black (gray phase more common in NY); head small, slightly crested; neck patch and end of longish tail black. In flight, wings make loud whir. In spring, male "drums" on perch by thumping wings against chest, first slowly, then faster. **VOICE** Alarm call: *quit quit*. **HABITAT** Broadleaf and mixed woods. **RANGE** Resident in entire region, ex. coastal plain.

NORTHERN BOBWHITE
Colinus virginianus
NEW WORLD QUAIL FAMILY

10″. Male chest and upperparts rusty; flanks streaked rusty; belly speckled black and white; brown crown and face patch contrast with white eyebrow and throat. Tail short. Female similar, with buffy eyebrow and throat. Lives in coveys (family groups). **VOICE** Male: loud whistled *bob white*. **HABITAT** Brushy fields and edges. **RANGE** Resident from s PA, n NJ, and Long Is. south; more common southward.

WILD TURKEY
Meleagris gallopavo
PARTRIDGE FAMILY

Male 4′; female 3′. Male body dark brown; looks iridescent coppery green at close range; flight feathers paler gray, banded; tail brown, with terminal black band; head bare, warty, red and/or blue; black "beard" hangs from chest. Female similar, with smaller, duller head. Feeds on ground and visits rural birdfeeders; roosts in trees at night. Once abundant, but extirpated as forests were cleared; with return of forests, has recently been reintroduced successfully. **VOICE** Male: repeated gobble. **HABITAT** Broadleaf woods; agricultural areas in winter. **RANGE** Resident in region.

VIRGINIA RAIL
Rallus limicola
RAIL FAMILY

10″. Adult brown above; chest and wings rufous; flanks barred black and white; cheeks gray; bill long, thin, drooping, orange or red with black tip. Toes long. Tail short. Imm. has blackish chest. Usu. secretive. **VOICE** Repeated *kid ick*, grunting *oink* notes. **HABITAT** Mainly freshwater marshes. **RANGE** Apr.–May, Sept.–Oct.: entire region; breeds along coastal plain and south to PA. Nov.–Mar.: some near coast.

CLAPPER RAIL
Rallus longirostris
RAIL FAMILY

14″. Mottled gray above; flanks dark gray with paler bars; chest and head buffier; bill long, yellowish to orange, droops at tip. Toes long. Tail short. Usu. secretive; runs across low-tide muddy creeks; on high ground during very high tides. **VOICE** Harsh *kek kek kek kek kek*. **HABITAT** Saltwater and brackish marshes. **RANGE** Resident from w Long Is. to e VA; rarer in winter. **King Rail** *(R. elegans)* of freshwater marshes (coastal plain, w NY, w PA) has brown back, rusty orange face and chest.

COMMON MOORHEN
"Common Gallinule"
Gallinula chloropus
RAIL FAMILY

14″. Summer adult brown-backed; underparts, sides, and neck dark slaty; white stripe along side and vent; head black; frontal shield and bill bright red, bill yellow-tipped. Legs mostly yellow-green. Toes very long; feet unwebbed. Numbers declining northward. VOICE Variety of chicken-like clucks, grating notes. HABITAT Cattail marshes with shallow open water. RANGE Apr.–Oct.: entire region (local).

AMERICAN COOT
Fulica americana
RAIL FAMILY

15″. Adult slaty gray; head and neck black; bill thick, white, black near tip; sides of undertail white. Feet not webbed, but long toes lobed. Dives and skitters over water surface to become airborne like a diving duck. Often in rafts (flocks). VOICE Grating *kuk* notes. HABITAT Open marshes, ponds. RANGE Apr.–May, Sept.–Oct.: entire region; breeds locally in w NY, nw PA, and near coast. Nov.–Mar.: coastal plain.

Shorebirds

The term "shorebird" is used for most families of the order Charadriiformes: plovers, oystercatchers, avocets and stilts, and sandpipers, including godwits, dowitchers, yellowlegs, curlews, and the small sandpipers informally known as "peeps." Most shorebirds frequent open muddy, sandy, or rocky shores on the coast and around open inland wetlands. On the coast they tend to roost in moderate to enormous mixed-species flocks at high tide; at low tide they spread out to feed on small invertebrates. Most American shorebirds have a distinct breeding plumage in late spring and early summer; on their southbound migrations from midsummer onward they appear in drabber nonbreeding or juvenile plumages. The majority breed in the Arctic tundra, winter from the southern United States to Tierra del Fuego, Argentina, and are present in the Mid-Atlantic region mainly in migration. The Mid-Atlantic region's greatest shorebird spectacle occurs northwest of Cape May, New Jersey, on the week of the full moon nearest mid-May. Horseshoe Crabs amass to lay eggs on the beaches of Delaware Bay, and swarms of northbound shorebirds, especially Red Knots, stop to feast.

Proportion, shape, bill length, behavior, and voice are more useful in the identification of shorebirds than are colors.

PIPING PLOVER
Charadrius melodus
PLOVER FAMILY

7″. Upperparts pale gray; white below; legs orange. Breeding: partial black collar; base of bill yellow. Non-breeding and imm.: bill black; lacks collar. Appears neck-less; bill short. Endangered, by humans, beach vehicles, dogs. **VOICE** Whistled *peep-lo.* **HABITAT** Barrier beaches. **RANGE** Apr.–Sept.: entire coast (local).

SEMIPALMATED PLOVER
Charadrius semipalmatus
PLOVER FAMILY

7″. Upperparts dark brown; white below. Breeding: base of bill and legs orange; black breast band. Non-breeding and imm.: bill black; breast band brown. Appears neck-less; bill short. **VOICE** Whistled *tu-wheet.* **HABITAT** Beaches, mudflats. **RANGE** May, July–Oct.: entire coast; inland reservoirs (local).

BLACK-BELLIED PLOVER
Pluvialis squatarola
PLOVER FAMILY

breeding (left), nonbreeding (right)

12″. Breeding: back and wings speckled black and white; crown, hindneck, and sides of chest white; face, foreneck, and chest black. Nonbreeding: grayish; back speckled; flight reveals black patch at base of underwing. Bill short, straight; eyes large, black; legs black. **VOICE** Whistled *pee-a-wee.* **HABITAT** Beaches, open mudflats. **RANGE** May, Aug.–Dec.: entire coast; inland (local).

KILLDEER
Charadrius vociferus
PLOVER FAMILY

10″. Adult brown above; white below; 2 black chest bands; pied face with red eye ring; legs pinkish gray. Flight reveals wing stripe, orange rump. Common inland plover in open habitats. Parent feigns broken wing to attract intruders away from nest or chicks. **VOICE** Strident *kill-dee.* **HABITAT** Farms, pastures, muddy fields. **RANGE** Mar.–Oct.: entire region. Oct.–Mar.: s NJ to lowland VA.

BLACK-NECKED STILT
Himantopus mexicanus
STILT FAMILY

14″. Black above, white below; rump and tail white. Head mainly black, with large white spot over eye; bill long, very thin, black. Legs very long, red. Flight reveals wings uniformly blackish above and below. Wades up to its belly, eating aquatic insects, small fish. **VOICE** Sharp *yip yip yip*. **HABITAT** Shallow marshes, sloughs. **RANGE** Late Apr.–Sept.: s NJ and e DE to e VA (uncommon).

AMERICAN OYSTERCATCHER
Haematopus palliatus
OYSTERCATCHER FAMILY

19″. Adult dark brown above, white below; head, neck, and tail black; bill stout, long, straight, red; legs pinkish. Imm. head and bill brown. Flight reveals bold white wing stripe. Feeds on mussels, other shellfish, worms. **VOICE** Loud *kleep*. **HABITAT** Beaches, mudflats; strictly coastal. **RANGE** Mar.–Oct.: entire coast. Some winter in e VA.

GREATER YELLOWLEGS
Tringa melanoleuca
SANDPIPER FAMILY

14″. Breeding: back slaty with white dots; head, neck, and sides speckled dark brown. Nonbreeding: paler; faint brown dots on chest. Neck long; bill 1½ times longer than head, with thicker gray base and thin, black, slightly up-curved tip. Legs long, bright yellow; rump white. Often nods head. **VOICE** Excited *tew tew tew*. **HABITAT** Marshes, mudflats, flooded fields. **RANGE** Apr.–May, July–Nov.: entire coast; inland (local).

LESSER YELLOWLEGS
Tringa flavipes
SANDPIPER FAMILY

11″. Smaller version of Greater Yellowlegs (see at left): plumages similar; legs also bright yellow; bill shorter (equal to length of head), straight, all black. Occurs in tighter flocks and is less wary than Greater Yellowlegs. **VOICE** 1–2 mellow *tew* notes. **HABITAT** Mudflats, marsh pools. **RANGE** Late Apr.–May, July–Oct.: entire coast; inland (local).

SPOTTED SANDPIPER
Actitis macularia
SANDPIPER FAMILY

8″. Breeding: brown above, white with large black spots below. Non-breeding: unspotted; smudge on sides of chest. Often teeters rearparts. Flies on stiff bowed wings. Breeds along many rivers. **VOICE** *Pee-weet-weet.* **HABITAT** Riversides, inland ponds; uncommon on salt water. **RANGE** Late Apr.–Oct.: entire region.

SOLITARY SANDPIPER
Tringa solitaria
SANDPIPER FAMILY

9″. Dark brown with white belly and eye ring; bill greenish at base, black at tip; legs dull greenish. Flight reveals dark wings; outer tail banded white. **VOICE** Strident *peet weet.* **HABITAT** Muddy margins of wooded ponds, ditches, streamsides. **RANGE** Apr.–May, July–Sept.: inland; outer coast (rare).

WILLET
Catoptrophorus semipalmatus
SANDPIPER FAMILY

15″. Breeding: speckled brownish gray. Nonbreeding (pictured): plain gray. Bill thick-based, fairly long, straight; legs blue-gray; tail gray. Flight reveals startling black wings with broad white central stripe. **VOICE** Loud *pill-will-willet.* **HABITAT** Salt marshes, mudflats. **RANGE** Apr.–Oct.: entire coast. Nov.–Mar.: some from s NJ to e VA.

WHIMBREL
Numenius phaeopus
SANDPIPER FAMILY

18″. Neck, chest, and back speckled brown; belly dirty white; 4 dark brown stripes through eye and bordering pale midcrown stripe; legs bluish. Neck thin; bill very long, thin, downcurved. In flight, appears uniformly brown. **VOICE** 5–7 whistled *ti* notes. **HABITAT** Salt marshes, mudflats. **RANGE** Mid-Apr.–May, July–Sept.: entire coast; inland (rare).

RUDDY TURNSTONE
Arenaria interpres
SANDPIPER FAMILY

9″. Breeding: harlequin pattern; back orange and black; head and chest black and white. Nonbreeding: duller; brown chest patch. Bill short, wedge-shaped; legs short, orange. VOICE Rattling *tuk-e-tuk*. HABITAT Pebbly beaches, jetties, mudflats. RANGE May, July–Oct.: entire coast; inland (rare). Nov.–Apr.: s NJ to e VA.

LEAST SANDPIPER
Calidris minutilla
SANDPIPER FAMILY

6″. Breeding: reddish brown above; chest buffy brown, lightly spotted. Nonbreeding: browner than other small sandpipers. Bill short, thin, slightly drooping, black; legs greenish or yellow. Most common inland "peep." VOICE High *kreet*. HABITAT Mudflats, marshes. RANGE Mid-Apr.–May, July–Oct.: entire region.

SANDERLING
Calidris alba
SANDPIPER FAMILY

8″. The familiar "surf beach" sandpiper. Breeding: head and upperparts rusty; belly white. Nonbreeding: gray above; white below; bend of wing black. Imm. crown and back heavily black-spotted. Bill short; legs black. Runs ahead of incoming waves. Usu. in parties of 10–20 or more. VOICE Sharp *plic*. HABITAT Sandy beaches, jetties. RANGE May, July–Nov.: entire coast; many overwinter.

SEMIPALMATED SANDPIPER
Calidris pusilla
SANDPIPER FAMILY

6½". Breeding: spotted dark brown above and on chest; belly white. Nonbreeding: gray-brown above; center of chest and belly white; faint streaking on sides of neck. Bill short, straight, black; legs black. **VOICE** Low *jerk*. **HABITAT** Mudflats, marshy pools. **RANGE** Mid-Apr.–May, July–Oct.: entire coast; inland (local).

DUNLIN
Calidris alpina
SANDPIPER FAMILY

8". Breeding: rusty above, white with fine black dots below; black midbelly patch. Nonbreeding: gray with white belly. Bill rather long, with drooping tip. **VOICE** Soft *krrit*. **HABITAT** Mudflats. **RANGE** May, Sept.–Nov.: entire coast; inland (uncommon). Dec.–Apr.: many on coast from Long Is. to VA.

RED KNOT
Calidris canutus
SANDPIPER FAMILY

11". Breeding: back gray, scaled with black; face and underparts pinkish orange. Nonbreeding: uniformly gray. Bill straight, with thick base; legs short. Flight reveals thin white wing stripe, barred gray rump. Congregates in large flocks at a few sites. Very common in Del. Bay in May. **VOICE** Soft *knut*. **HABITAT** Seaside rocks; beaches, mudflats. **RANGE** May, July–Sept.: entire coast (local).

SHORT-BILLED DOWITCHER
Limnodromus griseus
SANDPIPER FAMILY

12". Breeding: speckled brown above; neck, chest, and sides rusty orange, dotted black; midbelly white. Nonbreeding: gray above, white below. Bill very long, straight. Flight reveals white rump extending up back in wedge. Feeds with rapid sewing-machine motion. **VOICE** Musical *tu tu tu*. **HABITAT** Mudflats, marshy pools. **RANGE** Mid-Apr.–May, mid-July–Sept.: entire coast; inland (rare).

COMMON SNIPE
Gallinago gallinago
SANDPIPER FAMILY

11″. An inland sandpiper. Dark brown above, with few white back stripes; sides barred; midbelly white; head has 4 bold blackish stripes; tail rusty. Bill very long, straight; legs short. Flies in erratic zigzag. **VOICE** Hoarse, rasping *skaip*. **HABITAT** Moist meadows, bogs, freshwater marshes. **RANGE** Mar.–May, Sept.–Oct.: entire region. May–Aug.: local breeder in n NY. Oct.–Mar.: coast, Ches. Bay area (uncommon).

AMERICAN WOODCOCK
"Timberdoodle"
Scolopax minor
SANDPIPER FAMILY

11″. An upland shorebird. Mostly clear buff; back darker, speckled, with gray stripes. Large head; no apparent neck; crown has 3 black patches; eyes large. Bill very long, straight, brownish yellow; legs short. Male's wings make musical twittering in aerial courtship flights. **VOICE** Buzzy *peeent*. **HABITAT** Swampy areas in woods, thickets. **RANGE** Mar.–Nov.: entire region. Dec.–Feb.: some on coastal plain.

Gulls and Terns

All members of the gull family (Laridae)—gulls, jaegers, terns, and skimmers—have webbed feet, and most breed in the open, in colonies, on islands free of predators; their nests are usually mere depressions on the ground. Many people erroneously call gulls "seagulls." However, while gulls are common along the coast, few are found far at sea; in fact, many breed far inland near fresh water. Superb fliers, most adult gulls have wings with white trailing edges and dark tips, and fairly long, strong bills that are slightly hooked at the tip. These generalist feeders and scavengers eat living and dead animal life, and many have adapted to feed on human refuse. Gulls go through a confusing array of plumages and molts until they reach adulthood in two years (small species), three years (medium), or four years (large). For many gull species, this guide describes selected life-stage categories, which may include juvenile (bird's birth summer), first winter, first summer (bird is one year old), second winter, summer adult, or winter adult.

PARASITIC JAEGER
Stercorarius parasiticus
GULL AND TERN FAMILY

L 18″; WS 3′6″. 2 morphs: Typical adult dark brown above; white or light dusky sides and belly; yellowish-white collar; thin brown chestband; tail has 2 longer, pointed central tail feathers. Dark adult all brown. Both have whitish patch at base of primaries. Bill hooked at tip. Chases seabirds; forces them to drop food. **VOICE** Silent at sea. **HABITAT** Open ocean; beaches (rare). **RANGE** May, Aug.–Oct.: off entire coast.

BONAPARTE'S GULL
Larus philadelphia
GULL AND TERN FAMILY

1st winter (left), winter adult (right)

13". Summer adult back and wings silvery gray; neck, underparts, and tail white; head black; white leading edge of wing, narrow black tips on primaries; legs red; bill shortish, black. Winter adult head white; black spot behind eye. 1st winter: head white; tail black-tipped. Often hovers; usu. in flocks. **VOICE** Nasal *cher*. **HABITAT** Estuaries, bays, inlets. **RANGE** Oct.–May: entire coast, Great Lakes; uncommon migrant elsewhere.

LAUGHING GULL
Larus atricilla
GULL AND TERN FAMILY

summer adult (left), juvenile (right)

17". Summer adult back and wings slaty gray; head black; neck, underparts, and tail white; no white on wingtip; eye ring white; bill dark red. Juv. upperparts and chest band unspotted gray-brown; bill black. Nests in colonies on marshy islands. **VOICE** High *haah, haah* notes. **HABITAT** Beaches, estuaries, inshore ocean. **RANGE** Apr.–Nov.: entire coast, Ches. Bay.

RING-BILLED GULL
Larus delawarensis
GULL AND TERN FAMILY

summer adult (left), 1st winter (right)

L 19"; WS 4'. Summer adult head and underparts white; back and wings gray; wingtips black with white spots; bill yellow with black ring near tip. Winter adult head flecked brown. 1st winter: back gray; wing coverts speckled; tail whitish with black band; bill pink with black tip. Juv. pale brown, speckled; bill black; legs gray. **VOICE** High-pitched *high-er*. **HABITAT** Estuaries, lakes, fields, towns. **RANGE** Mar.–May, Aug.–Nov.: entire region; breeds near n NY lakes. Dec.–Feb.: coastal plain, Niagara Falls.

HERRING GULL
Larus argentatus
GULL AND TERN FAMILY

1st winter (left), summer adult (right)

L 25"; WS 4'10". Region's most common large seaside gull. Legs and feet pale pink in all ages. Summer adult back and wings silvery gray; wingtips black with white spots; head and underparts white; bill yellow with red dot. Winter adult head and chest heavily flecked with brown. 1st winter: brown with speckled back; bill black. 2nd winter: pale brown with brown spots; flight feathers and tail black; bill pink with black tip. Eats bivalves, fish, offal, baby terns, garbage; drops clams on rocks or pavement. Nests in colonies on coastal islands. **VOICE** Varied, incl. series of loud *kee-yow* and *gah* notes. **HABITAT** Coasts, ocean, lakes, rivers, towns, dumps. **RANGE** Resident along entire coast, over major inland waters, in cities; inland mainly in winter. Local breeder on coast and in n NY.

GREAT BLACK-BACKED GULL
Larus marinus
GULL AND TERN FAMILY

adult (left), 2nd winter (right)

L 30"; WS 5'5". Adult (summer and winter): back and wings black; head and underparts white; bill heavy, yellow with red dot; legs and feet pink. 1st winter: back and wings speckled blackish brown; head white; bill black. 2nd winter: back black; wings dark brown; bill pink with black tip. Feeds on fish, offal; also kills ducks, terns, other seabirds. Nests in colonies on coastal islands. N. Amer.'s largest gull. **VOICE** Loud, low, repeated *coo-up*. **HABITAT** Coastal waters and shores, inland dumps and lakes. **RANGE** Resident on coast, tidal rivers. Sept.–Apr.: inland lakes, rivers.

COMMON TERN
Sterna hirundo
GULL AND TERN FAMILY

summer adult (left), adult with young (right)

15″. Summer adult back and wings silvery gray, with blackish primaries; white below; cap and hindneck black; bill slender, reddish orange with black tip; legs short, reddish orange; tail deeply forked, outer streamers dusky. Winter adult forehead white; nape black; black shoulder bar. Juv. has scaly brown back. Flight shows primaries blackish above, with wide black trailing edge below. Terns dive headfirst for fish; return to nest with fish in bill. Suitable nesting sites squeezed by large numbers of gulls and humans. Nests in colonies, especially on islands free of land carnivores. **VOICE** Short *kip*, drawn-out *kee-arr*. **HABITAT** Beaches, coastal waters. **RANGE** Apr.–Oct.: entire coast, Ches. Bay, islands.

FORSTER'S TERN
Sterna forsteri
GULL AND TERN FAMILY

15″. Pale silvery gray above, white below; primaries silvery; bill slender; tail forked, long. Summer adult has black cap, red-orange bill with black tip, red legs. Winter adult crown white; long black eye mask; bill black. Feeds on aerial insects; dives for fish. Nests in freshwater marshes. **VOICE** Grating *kay-r-r-r*, repeated *kip*. **HABITAT** Beaches, marshes, lakes. **RANGE** Apr.–Nov.: NJ to e VA; Long Is. (local).

ROYAL TERN
Sterna maxima
GULL AND TERN FAMILY

20″. Pale silvery gray above, white below; primaries tipped blackish; bill orange; legs short, black; tail rather long. Summer adult has black-crested cap. Winter adult forecrown white, rear crown black-crested. Flies high when feeding; dives for fish. Nests in few colonies on shore of Delmarva Peninsula. **VOICE** High harsh *keeeerr*. **HABITAT** Coastal beaches and waters. **RANGE** Apr.–Nov.: coast from s NJ to VA. Aug.–Oct.: wanders in small flocks north to Long Is.

LEAST TERN
Sterna antillarum
GULL AND TERN FAMILY

9″. Summer adult back and wings silvery gray; neck and underparts white; crown black, with white forehead; bill yellow with black tip; legs yellow; tail slightly forked. Juv. pale scaly brown above. Region's smallest tern. Nests in small colonies on beaches and sandbars; do not disturb at nests (scrapes in sand). **VOICE** Repeated *kip*, harsh *chee-eek*. **HABITAT** Ocean beaches, coastal waters. **RANGE** May–mid-Sept.: entire coast.

BLACK TERN
Chlidonias niger
GULL AND TERN FAMILY

10″. Summer: back, wings, and tail uniformly dark gray; head and underparts black; bill and legs black; vent white. Winter: dark gray above; face and underparts white; nape and ear spot black. Tail short, notched. Nests in small colonies on inland marshy lakes. **VOICE** Sharp *kreek*. **HABITAT** Reedy lakes (summer); seacoast (migration). **RANGE** May, July–Sept.: entire coast; inland (uncommon); breeds sparingly in n NY.

BLACK SKIMMER
Rynchops niger
GULL AND TERN FAMILY

18″. Adult black above; forehead and underparts white; legs red, short; tail mainly white, short, notched. Bill long, red and black, lower mandible much longer. Imm. brown above, with white scaly feather edges. Creates ripple in calm waters with lower bill; snaps up fish by touch. **VOICE** Short barks. **HABITAT** Barrier islands, coastal waterways. **RANGE** Mid-Apr.–Oct.: entire coast, s Ches. Bay.

YELLOW-BILLED CUCKOO
Coccyzus americanus
CUCKOO FAMILY

12″. Upperparts gray-brown; primaries rufous; white below. Slender, downcurved bill; black above, yellow below; yellow eye ring. Tail long, with rounded tip, gray above, black below, with 3 wide white bars. Secretive. **VOICE** Song: long, hollow, descending *kuk* notes, ending with drawn-out *kowlp* notes. **HABITAT** Open woodlands and edges, riverside thickets. **RANGE** May–Oct.: entire region, ex. Adirondacks. **Black-billed Cuckoo** *(C. erythropthalmus)* has red eye ring, tail mainly gray below.

ROCK DOVE
"Rock Pigeon"
Columba livia
PIGEON AND DOVE FAMILY

13". Typical: head dark gray; iridescence on neck; body and tail pale gray; white on upper rump; 2 black bars on secondaries; tail tipped black. Variations range from black to pale brown and white. Bill short, black; legs short, red. Powerful flier; flight reveals pointed wings. Common city pigeon, introduced from Europe. **VOICE** Gurgling *coo-cuk-crooo*. **HABITAT** Towns, parks, farms. **RANGE** Resident in entire region, ex. mtns.

MOURNING DOVE
Zenaida macroura
PIGEON AND DOVE FAMILY

12". Back, wings, and tail fawn, with a few brown spots; head and underparts pale buffy. Bill short, black; black spot below eye; legs short, red. Black and white edges on long, pointed, wedge-shaped tail. Wings whistle when taking flight. Has become common in urban areas. **VOICE** Mournful *coo WHO-o coo, coo, coo.* **HABITAT** Fields, towns, sandy scrub. **RANGE** Resident in entire region, ex. mtns.

Owls

Owls are nocturnal birds of prey that range in size in the Mid-Atlantic region from 8 to 23 inches long. They have large heads, with large, forward-facing eyes (yellow in most species). Their eyesight and hearing are both acute. Distinct facial disks conceal large ear openings that provide them with keen hearing, which can pinpoint a squeak or a rustle in the grass in total darkness. The ears are asymmetrically placed on either side of the head, allowing for a greater range of sound and better triangulation for pinpointing sources of sounds. Some owls have tufts of feathers at the corners of the head that look like ears or horns and are called ear tufts. Their fluffy-looking bodies are cryptically colored and patterned to blend with the background of their daytime nests or roosts. Owls are most readily seen in winter in open areas and leafless woodlands. Their bills are short but strongly hooked. The legs are also typically short, and the feet have sharp curved talons. Owls fly silently; their feathers are delicately fringed and very soft. Imitations of their distinctive voices, given at night, bring a response from an owl, which may call or fly in close to the source of the call.

ear tuft

facial disk

Parts of an Owl

BARN OWL
Tyto alba
BARN OWL FAMILY

18″. Pale tawny washed with gray above, white or buffy flecked with black dots below. Head large, round, without ear tufts; white, heart-shaped facial disk; eyes dark. Legs long for an owl. Superb "mouser" with acute hearing. Strictly nocturnal; perches on poles at night. **VOICE** Variety of harsh screams, hisses, clicks. **HABITAT** Old buildings, farms, open fields. **RANGE** Lowlands of entire region.

BARRED OWL
Strix varia
OWL FAMILY

L 21″; WS 3′8″. Dark brownish gray with paler spots above, heavily striped below; dark barring on upper chest; facial disk gray, ringed in black. Eyes brown; no ear tufts. Some males spend winter in urban areas, return to home territories in early spring. Feeds at night; some sit on tree limbs by day. **VOICE** 2 sets of *hoo* notes: *Who cooks for you? Who cooks for you-all?* Caterwauling calls in spring. **HABITAT** Swamps, woods. **RANGE** Resident in entire region.

GREAT HORNED OWL
Bubo virginianus
OWL FAMILY

L 23″; WS 4′7″. Brown with dark brown spots above; paler, with heavy dark brown bars below; dark streaks on upper chest; facial disk rich rusty brown, ringed in black. Eyes yellow; fluffy ear tufts. May be seen in daylight. **VOICE** 3–8 deep hoots, 2nd and 3rd rapid and doubled. **HABITAT** Woods. **RANGE** Resident in entire region.

EASTERN SCREECH-OWL
Otus asio
OWL FAMILY

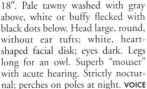

9″. The common small owl. 2 color morphs: gray and rufous. Facial disk pale gray or rufous, ringed in black; dark streaks on breast; row of white spots on shoulder. Eyes yellow; fluffy ear tufts. **VOICE** Mournful whinny rising then falling in pitch; also fast even-pitched series of *hu* notes. **HABITAT** Woods, swamps, cemeteries, towns. **RANGE** Resident in entire region.

COMMON NIGHTHAWK
Chordeiles minor
NIGHTJAR FAMILY

10″. Dark brown, heavily mottled above; throat white; legs very short. Flight reveals long, pointed, black primaries with prominent white bar; long notched tail. Flies high, erratically, mainly at dusk. Hunts at night for insects. Has declined seriously in recent years; formerly common over many towns. **VOICE** Nasal *peeent*. **HABITAT** Fields, towns, parks. **RANGE** May–Sept.: entire region.

WHIP-POOR-WILL
Caprimulgus vociferus
NIGHTJAR FAMILY

10″. Mottled "dead leaf" pattern above; throat dark, with partial white collar below. Flight reveals rounded wings, long rounded tail. Corners of tail white in male, buffy in female. Nocturnal; catches moths on wing. **VOICE** Weak *whip* followed by louder, slurred *poor-weell*. **HABITAT** Open mixed woods. **RANGE** May–Sept.: entire region. **Chuck-will's Widow** (*C. carolinensis;* 12″); voice different: calls its name; May–Sept.: Long Is. to e VA.

RUBY-THROATED HUMMINGBIRD
male (left), young and female (right)
Archilochus colubris
HUMMINGBIRD FAMILY

3½″. Male upperparts, sides, and crown iridescent green; chest and vent white; black line below eye; iridescent "ruby" throat appears black at most angles; tail black, forked. Female green above, white below; tail corners tipped black and white. Bill long, needle-like, black; small white spot behind eye. Imms. resemble adult female. Hovers at hummingbird feeders and flowers, preferring red or orange tubular ones. Beats wings dozens of times a second; male's wings can make humming sound. Hummingbirds are the only birds that can fly backward. **VOICE** High *chip* notes, squeaks. **HABITAT** Woodland edges, clearings, rural gardens. **RANGE** May–Sept.: entire region.

CHIMNEY SWIFT
Chaetura pelagica
SWIFT FAMILY

5½". Sooty gray; bill tiny; wings extend past tail. Flight reveals pale gray throat, long pointed wings; short, squared-off tail. Clings upright with very small feet. Flies fast, fairly high, in arcs. For nest, cements sticks with saliva to vertical spaces in chimneys, buildings, tree hollows. Does not perch; clings upright on vertical surfaces. **VOICE** Rapid *chitter* and *chip* notes, given often in flight. **HABITAT** Over towns and fields. **RANGE** Apr.–mid-Oct.: entire region.

BELTED KINGFISHER
Ceryle alcyon
KINGFISHER FAMILY

female (left), male (right)

13". Male blue-gray above; throat, neck, and belly white; blue-gray belt on chest. Female more colorful; belly has 2nd (rufous) belt extending onto sides. Head large, with ragged fore and rear crests; bill very long, heavy, pointed; white spot before eye. Feet small. Active, calls often; dives headfirst to seize small fish. As nest, excavates tunnel 12–24″ into earthen bank, sometimes far from water. **VOICE** Loud woody rattle. **HABITAT** Rivers, lakes; coasts (winter). **RANGE** Apr.–Oct.: entire region. Nov.–Mar.: restricted to open water on coastal plain.

Woodpeckers

Woodpeckers, which range widely in size, cling to the trunks and large branches of trees with their sharp claws (on short legs) and stiff, spine-tipped tails that help support them in a vertical position. Their rather long pointed bills are like chisels, able to bore into wood. Curled inside the woodpecker head is a narrow tongue twice the length of the bill, tipped with spear-like barbs that impale wood-boring insects. Members of this family laboriously dig out nest holes in living or dead tree trunks and limbs. The sexes are very much alike, but the red (or yellow) patches on the heads of the males are reduced or lacking in females of many species. In spring, males rapidly bang their bills against resonant wood on trees and buildings in a territorial drumming that is louder and more rapid than the tapping made while feeding. Most woodpeckers in the Mid-Atlantic region are year-round residents, but most flickers and all sapsuckers migrate.

RED-HEADED WOODPECKER
Melanerpes erythrocephalus
WOODPECKER FAMILY

9″. Adult back and wings black, ex. for large white wing patch that shows at rest; head and neck all crimson-red; rump white; tail black. Imm. back, much of wings, and head brown. Caches acorns in tree cavities; feeds on ground and in trees; catches large insects in air. **VOICE** Loud high *chuurr*. **HABITAT** Open oak and pine woods. **RANGE** From w NY, PA, and NJ south.

RED-BELLIED WOODPECKER
Melanerpes carolinus
WOODPECKER FAMILY

9″. Back and wings barred black and white; face and underparts pale buffy gray; red on belly hard to see. Male forehead, crown, and hindneck red. Female crown gray; forehead spot and nape red. **VOICE** Rolling *chuurr*, double *chiv chiv*; brief drum. **HABITAT** Open woods, feeders. **RANGE** From sw and se NY south; range expanding northward.

DOWNY WOODPECKER
Picoides pubescens
WOODPECKER FAMILY

6½″. The common small woodpecker. Like Hairy Woodpecker, head boldly pied; back white; wings black, white-spotted; underparts white; male has red nape patch. Downy is smaller than Hairy, with shorter bill and black spots on white outer tail feathers. **VOICE** Rapid descending whinny, flat *pick*; long drum. **HABITAT** Woods, suburbs. **RANGE** Resident in entire region.

HAIRY WOODPECKER
Picoides villosus
WOODPECKER FAMILY

9″. A duplicate of the more common Downy Woodpecker, head boldly pied; back white; wings black, white-spotted; underparts white; male has red nape patch. Hairy is larger, with longer bill and white, unspotted outer tail feathers. **VOICE** Loud rattle (not descending), sharp *peek*; long drum. **HABITAT** Woods, suburbs. **RANGE** Resident in entire region.

YELLOW-BELLIED SAPSUCKER
Sphyrapicus varius
WOODPECKER FAMILY

8″. Adult back and wings speckled, with long white shoulder patch; upper chest black; belly pale yellow; forecrown red; head boldly pied; throat red in male, white in female. Drills rows of holes in thin bark; laps sap; eats insects drawn to sap. **VOICE** Nasal downward *cheerrr*, drum rapid, then slow. **HABITAT** Broadleaf and mixed woods. **RANGE** Apr.–May, Sept.–Oct.: entire region; breeds in hills of NY, PA, e WV, w VA. Oct.–Apr.: NJ and south through most of VA.

NORTHERN FLICKER
Colaptes auratus
WOODPECKER FAMILY

13″. Yellow-shafted race: male back brown with blackish bars; belly pale buff with black spots; crown gray; red nape crescent; face buffy with black "mustache"; black chest crescent. Female lacks "mustache." Shows white rump and golden underwings in flight. **VOICE** Rapid series of *wic* and *woika* (or *flicker*) notes, loud *klee-err;* drums softly. **HABITAT** Open woods, farms. **RANGE** Apr.–Oct.: entire region; abundant fall migrant on coast. Nov.–Mar.: coastal plain, most of VA.

PILEATED WOODPECKER
Dryocopus pileatus
WOODPECKER FAMILY

18″. Black; crest pointed, red; white and black stripes on face and down sides of neck. Male forehead and "mustache" red; female forehead and "mustache" black. Neck thin; bill heavy. Flight reveals bold white underwing linings. A dramatic treat to see. **VOICE** Flicker-like *wucka* notes, but louder, higher, and "wilder." **HABITAT** Woods. **RANGE** Resident in entire region; more common southward.

Songbirds (Passerines)

The birds described from here to the end of the section belong to a single order called Passeriformes. Known as passerines or, more commonly, perching birds or songbirds, they are the most recently evolved of the 25 bird orders; members of this order comprise more than half the world's birds. Their sizes range from 3½-inch kinglets to 24-inch ravens, but they are generally small land birds with pleasing songs; among the finest songsters are the wrens, mockingbirds, and thrushes. Songbirds give call notes year-round, while most sing only during the breeding season (spring and early summer). In some species, the male has a particularly colorful summer breeding plumage that is changed in winter to drabber, female-like coloration. In the spring, migrant males generally arrive in the Mid-Atlantic region seven to ten days before the females and stake out breeding territories, which they defend against neighboring males. After a male shows a female around his territory, she may be satisfied (especially if the vegetation and insect life are plentiful) and stay with him, or search for another singing male whose territory is more to her liking. Most songbirds build open-topped, rounded nests of grasses, sticks, fibers, and rootlets in a tree fork or shrub, or tucked under tall grass. Some eat insects year-round, while others focus on seeds, grains, or fruit; all feed insects to their hatchlings. In the fall, the sexes may migrate south together, the adults often several weeks or more before the young born that year.

EASTERN WOOD-PEWEE
Contopus virens
TYRANT FLYCATCHER FAMILY

6″. Dark grayish brown above, dingy white below; sides of chest gray; 2 narrow white wing bars; head often appears pointed; lower mandible dull orange; lacks eye ring. Late-returning migrant. Stays high in woodland trees, but sallies out to snatch insects in air. **VOICE** Slurred, mournful *pee-ah-weee.* **HABITAT** Broadleaf and mixed woods. **RANGE** May–Sept.: entire region.

ACADIAN FLYCATCHER
Empidonax virescens
TYRANT FLYCATCHER FAMILY

5½″. Back, head, and sides dark olive; 2 buffy wing bars on dark brown wings; belly yellowish white; eye ring white. One of 5 very similar species in this genus, best told apart by distinctive songs and habitats. **VOICE** Song: emphatic *peet-SEET.* **HABITAT** Swamps, riverine woods. **RANGE** May–mid-Sept.: entire region, ex. c and n NY.

EASTERN PHOEBE
Sayornis phoebe
TYRANT FLYCATCHER FAMILY

7″. Above gray-brown; head notably darker; dingy white below (some fall birds show yellowish wash on belly). Bill black; lacks eye ring and wing bars. Pumps tail constantly. Early-returning migrant. Easy to see; usu. perches low. Nests under bridges, building overhangs. VOICE Hoarse *fee-bree.* HABITAT Watersides, edges of woods, suburbs. RANGE Mar.–Oct.: entire region.

GREAT CRESTED FLYCATCHER
Myiarchus crinitus
TYRANT FLYCATCHER FAMILY

8″. Upperparts and crown olive brown; throat and chest pale gray; belly bright yellow; primaries and tail edged rufous; 2 thin white wing bars. Head appears a bit fluffy, but no true crest; bill fairly heavy; tail fairly long. More often heard than seen; stays fairly high in trees. VOICE Loud rising *wheeep.* HABITAT Broadleaf and mixed woods. RANGE Late Apr.–Sept.: entire region.

EASTERN KINGBIRD
Tyrannus tyrannus
TYRANT FLYCATCHER FAMILY

8″. Back and wings slaty; throat and underparts white; head black; tail black with white terminal band. Often flies slowly, with quivering wings; flies fast when attacking crows and hawks that come near its territory. Perches on wires and outer tree branches. VOICE Agitated *kit-kit-kittery,* nasal *tzeer.* HABITAT Trees near fields, waterways, roads. RANGE Late Apr.–Sept.: entire region.

HORNED LARK
Eremophila alpestris
LARK FAMILY

7½″. Fawn brown above and on flanks; belly white; pied head pattern; black crescent on chest; throat white or yellowish. Bill slender, black; legs short. Male has 2 tiny "horns." Flight reveals white underwings, black tail, white outer tail feathers. VOICE Song: high tinkling. HABITAT Fields, airports, dunes. RANGE Resident locally. Oct.–Apr.: coastal plain, inland valleys.

TREE SWALLOW
Tachycineta bicolor
SWALLOW FAMILY

6″. Male dark iridescent green-blue above, snowy white below. Female duller. Imm. all brown above. Tail notched. Slow flier; short flapping circles and a climb. Flocks in spring over ponds, in late summer over salt marshes. **VOICE** Song: *weet-trit-weet*. Call: *cheat cheat*. **HABITAT** Fields, wooded ponds, marshes, waterways. **RANGE** Mar.–May, Aug.–Oct.: entire region; breeds from NY to n WV, e VA. Nov.–Feb.: a few near coast.

PURPLE MARTIN
Progne subis
SWALLOW FAMILY

8″. Male mainly dark iridescent blue-purple. Female upperparts and head dull purplish; nape, throat, and chest dusky gray, with darker fine scales and streaks; belly and vent white. Tail forked. Glides more than other swallows; often circles with short flaps, then a glide. **VOICE** Call: throaty *chew chew*. **HABITAT** Over fields and marshes; nests around towns. **RANGE** Apr.–Aug.: entire region (local).

NORTHERN ROUGH-WINGED SWALLOW
Stelgidopteryx serripennis
SWALLOW FAMILY

5½″. Dull brown above; throat and chest pale ashy brown; breast and vent white. Tail notched. Flies with slow deep wingbeats. Often in solitary pairs. **VOICE** Raspy *brit*. **HABITAT** Ponds, rivers. **RANGE** Apr.–Sept.: entire region (rare in late summer). **Bank Swallow** has sharp dark neck band. **Tree Swallow** imm. brown above, all snowy white below.

BANK SWALLOW
Riparia riparia
SWALLOW FAMILY

5″. Dull brown above, white below, crossed by brown neck band. Flies with rapid wingbeats. Often in flocks. **VOICE** Low flat *chert chert*, buzzy chatter. **HABITAT** Waterways, fields; nests in banks. **RANGE** Mid-Apr.–May, Aug.–Sept.: entire region; breeds from NY south to n WV, e VA. **Northern Rough-winged Swallow** has pale brown throat; lacks neck band.

CLIFF SWALLOW
Hirundo pyrrhonota
SWALLOW FAMILY

6″. Adult back and crown blue; underparts grayish white; forehead buffy or creamy; rump buffy, distinct; tail short, square. Nests in colonies, most often under bridges or eaves. Declining as House Sparrows usurp nests. **VOICE** Call: grating *syrup*. **HABITAT** Farms, fields, waterways. **RANGE** Apr.–May, Aug.–Sept.: entire region; breeds from NY locally south to c NJ, w VA.

BARN SWALLOW
Hirundo rustica
SWALLOW FAMILY

7″. Streamlined. Adult glossy dark blue above; forehead chestnut; throat dark rusty, with thin blue necklace; rest of underparts buffy orange; outer tail streamers very long. Fast flier. Nest is open cup of mud pellets and grass inside or under overhang of barn or bridge. **VOICE** Song: long twittering. Calls: soft *vit vit* and *zee-zay*. **HABITAT** Fields, farms, waterways. **RANGE** Apr.–Sept.: entire region.

Attracting Birds to Your Yard

Many people enjoy attracting birds into their yards, and supplemental feeding helps birds in winter, when naturally occurring foods are covered by snow. Once started, winter feeding should be continued into spring. In the birds section, species that will come into a yard to feed are indicated by the icon 🔾.

Birdfeeders come in many designs. Hanging, clear seed feeders with short perch sticks are popular with goldfinches, siskins, and other finches. Window boxes and platforms on a pole are best for such medium-size birds as Evening Grosbeaks, Northern Cardinals, and Blue Jays, while Dark-eyed Juncos, Mourning Doves, and many sparrows prefer to feed on the ground. Mounting a birdfeeder inevitably means an ongoing struggle with squirrels, who are endlessly resourceful at defeating devices intended to keep them out of the feeders.

Grains and seeds are the best all-purpose fare for feeders. Many species like sunflower seeds, but your local birds may have particular preferences. Thistle seed is popular with goldfinches, white millet seed is a good choice for small species, and cracked corn is appreciated by large, ground-feeding birds. Many seed mixes are available at supermarkets and garden supply stores.

Birds also like fruit. In summer, you can lay out orange slices for Baltimore Orioles; apples, oranges, and grapes can also be put out on a platform or lawn or mounted on feeders. The fat and protein

BLUE JAY
Cyanocitta cristata
CROW AND JAY FAMILY

12″. Back and prominent crest blue; dingy white below; face whitish; black necklace; wings and long rounded tail bright blue, banded black, edged in white. Brash; conspicuous. Roaming flocks in autumn. **VOICE** Noisy; harsh *jaay*, liquid *queedle;* imitates hawks. **HABITAT** Deciduous woods (esp. oaks), towns. **RANGE** Resident in entire region.

FISH CROW
Corvus ossifragus
CROW AND JAY FAMILY

17″. All glossy black; bill heavy, black; wings rounded, wingtips "fingered"; legs black; tail longish, flat. Looks very similar to American Crow, but call sounds different. **VOICE** Hoarse, high, nasal *cah*, double *uh-oh*. **HABITAT** Coasts, major rivers, lakesides, nearby woods, towns. **RANGE** se NY and se PA to e VA.

---

in nuts makes them popular. Suet, in a mesh holder hung from a branch or mounted on a tree trunk, attracts birds such as nuthatches and woodpeckers that feed on insects in tree bark and bushes; it should be discontinued in summer, when it spoils quickly and mats feathers. Hummingbirds and orioles will come to specially designed red plastic dispensers of sugar water.

Water is important, especially during periods when natural water sources dry up or freeze over. Many species are attracted to a bird bath, which should be regularly scrubbed with a brush to rid it of algae and prevent diseases from spreading.

You might want to make or purchase a nest box to attract breeding birds. The most popular—inviting to Tree Swallows, chickadees, nuthatches, wrens, and bluebirds—is an enclosed box with a square floor area 4 to 7 inches wide and long, and about twice as high as it is wide (8 to 12 inches). Specifications vary depending on the species, and include floor area, the size of the entrance hole, height from the base of the box to the hole, and proper siting of the box. Larger boxes of particular dimensions attract Eastern Screech-Owls and Wood Ducks. Other birds will nest in open-fronted shelves or martin houses. Information on building and siting nest boxes and feeders is available from your local Audubon Society or nature center. In the birds section, the icon 🐦 denotes species that have used nest boxes in the right habitat.

AMERICAN CROW
Corvus brachyrhynchos
CROW AND JAY FAMILY

18″. All glossy black; bill heavy, black. Flight reveals rounded wings, "fingered" wingtips, squarish tail with rounded corners. Bold, noisy. Huge night roosts in winter. **VOICE** Loud descending *caw.* **HABITAT** Woods, farms, fields, shores, roadsides, urban areas. **RANGE** Resident in entire region; many shift southward or toward cities in winter.

COMMON RAVEN
"Northern Raven"
Corvus corax
CROW AND JAY FAMILY

24″. All glossy black; bill black, very heavy; throat has long shaggy feathers. Flight reveals long, wedge-shaped tail. Soars frequently. Shy but conspicuous. **VOICE** Very low *croonk.* **HABITAT** Mtns., woods. **RANGE** Resident in n NY; south in mtns. to Shenandoah NP, WV.

RED-BREASTED NUTHATCH
Sitta canadensis
NUTHATCH FAMILY

4½″. Male back blue-gray; chin white; underparts cinnamon; cap black; face white; black line through eye. Female similar: crown gray, underparts buffy. Tail short. Often on conifer cones. **VOICE** High nasal *enk* series. **HABITAT** Coniferous woods. **RANGE** Resident in mtns. from NY to w VA. Sept.–mid-May: entire region; common some autumns.

WHITE-BREASTED NUTHATCH
Sitta carolinensis
NUTHATCH FAMILY

6″. Male back steel blue; wings edged white; face and breast white; narrow black crown; vent and sides washed rusty. Female crown and back grayer. Like Red-breasted Nuthatch, creeps headfirst in all directions on tree trunks. **VOICE** Song: rapid *wer* notes. Call: loud *yank.* **HABITAT** Broadleaf and mixed woods, parks. **RANGE** Resident in entire region.

BROWN CREEPER
Certhia americana
CREEPER FAMILY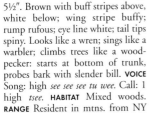

5½". Brown with buff stripes above, white below; wing stripe buffy; rump rufous; eye line white; tail tips spiny. Looks like a wren; sings like a warbler; climbs trees like a woodpecker; starts at bottom of trunk, probes bark with slender bill. **VOICE** Song: high *see see see tu wee.* Call: 1 high *tsee.* **HABITAT** Mixed woods. **RANGE** Resident in mtns. from NY to w VA. Oct.–Apr.: entire region.

TUFTED TITMOUSE
Baeolophus (Parus) bicolor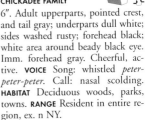
CHICKADEE FAMILY

6". Adult upperparts, pointed crest, and tail gray; underparts dull white; sides washed rusty; forehead black; white area around beady black eye. Imm. forehead gray. Cheerful, active. **VOICE** Song: whistled *peter-peter-peter.* Call: nasal scolding. **HABITAT** Deciduous woods, parks, towns. **RANGE** Resident in entire region, ex. n NY.

BLACK-CAPPED CHICKADEE
Poecile (Parus) atricapillus
CHICKADEE FAMILY

5½". Back, wings, and long narrow tail gray; white below, with light buffy sides; wings edged white; cap and throat black; face white. Friendly, inquisitive; often in family groups. Acrobatic when feeding. **VOICE** Song: clear *fee-bee.* Call: *chick-a-dee-dee-dee.* **HABITAT** Woods, parks, gardens. **RANGE** Resident in NY, n NJ, all PA ex. se, mtns. of WV.

CAROLINA CHICKADEE
Poecile (Parus) carolinensis
CHICKADEE FAMILY

4½". Back, wings, and long narrow tail gray; dusty white below; crown and throat black; cheeks white; bill very short, black. Family parties glean insects off branches. **VOICE** Song: *fee-bee fee-bay.* Call: high fast *chick-a-dee-dee-dee.* **HABITAT** Pine and broadleaf woods, towns. **RANGE** Resident in se PA, s NJ, most of MD, DE, most of WV, VA.

CAROLINA WREN
Thryothorus ludovicianus
WREN FAMILY

6″. Upperparts and crown rufous brown; light cinnamon below; fine black bars on wings and tail; long white eyebrow bordered in black; throat white. Usu. furtive but curious at times. **VOICE** Song: rollicking repeated *tea-kettle*. Call: harsh *jeer*. **HABITAT** Open woodlots, thickets, parks, towns. **RANGE** Resident in entire region, ex. n NY.

HOUSE WREN
Troglodytes aedon
WREN FAMILY

5″. Head and back plain grayish-brown; wings and tail lightly barred black; mainly clear brownish white below; sides finely barred. Tail often cocked. Aggressive to other nearby hole-nesters; destroys their eggs. **VOICE** Song: long, pleasing, descending gurgle. Call: *chuurr*. **HABITAT** Open woodlots, thickets, vines, towns. **RANGE** Mid-Apr.–Oct.: entire region.

WINTER WREN
Troglodytes troglodytes
WREN FAMILY

4″. Dark brown above and below; sides, wings, and tail finely black-barred; indistinct eyebrow and throat buffy. Often cocks very short tail over back. Region's smallest wren. **VOICE** Song: beautiful long series of very high warbles and trills. Call: hard *kip kip*. **HABITAT** Woodland ravines, brush piles, tangled roots. **RANGE** Resident in mtns. from NY to w VA. Oct.–Apr.: entire region, ex. n NY.

MARSH WREN
Cistothorus palustris
WREN FAMILY

5″. Back black with bold white stripes; white below; wings, rump, and tail rufous brown; sides buffy; long white eyebrow under dark brownish crown. Tail usu. cocked. **VOICE** Song: varied gurgling rattle. Call: loud *check*. **HABITAT** Large cattail marshes, phragmites beds. **RANGE** Apr.–Oct.: entire region (local). Nov.–Mar.: a few near coast.

GOLDEN-CROWNED KINGLET
Regulus satrapa
KINGLET FAMILY

3½". Drab olive all over; wings have yellowish edging and narrow wing bars; crown black, with center orange and yellow (male) or yellow (female); eyebrow white; black line through eye. Tail short, notched. **VOICE** Call: 3 high *tsee* notes. Song: same, then chatter. **HABITAT** Spruce and mixed woods. **RANGE** Resident in mtns. from NY to w VA. Oct.–Apr.: entire region.

RUBY-CROWNED KINGLET
Regulus calendula
KINGLET FAMILY

4". Drab olive all over, paler below; wings have yellowish edging and 2 white bars; large white eye ring. Male raises red midcrown patch in display. **VOICE** Song: high warbles ending with 3 *look-at-me's*. Call: scolding *je-dit*. **HABITAT** Summer: conifers. Migration: mixed woods, shrubs. **RANGE** Apr.–mid-May, mid-Sept.–Oct.: entire region. June–Aug.: n NY. Oct.–Apr.: coastal plain from se NY to c VA.

BLUE-GRAY GNATCATCHER
Polioptila caerulea
OLD WORLD WARBLER FAMILY

4½". Blue-gray above, white below; long, narrow tail black with white outer tail feathers; eye ring white. Male has black line over eye in summer. Often wags tail sideways. **VOICE** Song: thin wheezy warble. Call: inquiring *pwee*. **HABITAT** Open woods, waterside trees. **RANGE** Apr.–Sept.: entire region, ex. Adirondacks; more common southward.

EASTERN BLUEBIRD
Sialia sialis
THRUSH FAMILY

7". Male brilliant blue above; throat, chest, and sides rusty orange; midbelly and vent white. Female head and back blue-gray, breast duller. Sits upright on snags and wires. **VOICE** Song: pleasing, down-slurred *cheer cheery charley*. Call: musical *chur-lee*. **HABITAT** Fields, woodland edges, farms. **RANGE** Mar.–Nov.: entire region. Nov.–Mar.: from se NY and c PA south.

SWAINSON'S THRUSH
Catharus ustulatus
THRUSH FAMILY

7″. Olive-brown above; dark brown spots on buffy throat and chest; belly white; lores, and wide eye ring buffy. More arboreal than other thrushes; often feeds on fruit in trees. **VOICE** Song: breezy, up-slurred whistles. Calls: *whit* and *heep*. **HABITAT** Coniferous and mixed woods; thickets (migration). **RANGE** May, Sept.–Oct.: entire region; breeds in Adirondacks and Catskill Mtns. of NY, and higher elevations south to n WV, n VA.

VEERY
Catharus fuscescens
THRUSH FAMILY

7″. Uniformly dull rufous brown above; throat and upper chest buffy with tiny diffuse spots; sides grayish; midbelly and vent white; very thin, pale eye ring. **VOICE** Song: descending spiral of flute-like notes. Call: low *pheeuw*. **HABITAT** Swamps, riverside broadleaf woods. **RANGE** May–Sept.: NY, PA, n NJ, and south in mtns. to w VA; migrant in rest of region.

WOOD THRUSH
Hylocichla mustelina
THRUSH FAMILY

8″. Crown and upper back rich reddish brown; wings, lower back, and tail brown; snowy white with heavy round black spots below; thin white eye ring. Declining due to cowbird parasitism. **VOICE** Song: flute-like *ee-oo-lay?* Call: loud *wit-wit-wit.* **HABITAT** Broadleaf woods. **RANGE** May–Sept.: entire region.

HERMIT THRUSH
Catharus guttatus
THRUSH FAMILY

7″. Head, back, wings brown; sides grayish buff; brown spots on throat and upper chest; center of chest and belly whitish; lower rump, tail rufous brown; pale eye ring. **VOICE** Song: flute-like phrases at different pitches. Call: low *chuck.* **HABITAT** Woods; thickets. **RANGE** Apr., Oct.–Nov.: entire region; breeds from NY south to WV mtns. Nov.–Apr.: Long Is. southwest to all of VA.

AMERICAN ROBIN
Turdus migratorius
THRUSH FAMILY

immature (left), adult (right)

10". Male breast and sides rufous orange; back and wings brownish gray; head blackish; bill yellow; tail black with tiny white corners; vent white. Female head and back duller grayish. Imm. buffy white below with blackish spots; buffy scaling on back. In spring and summer, eats earthworms, fruits. In fall and winter, roams in flocks, roosts communally. **VOICE** Song: rising and falling *cheery-up cheery-me*. Calls: *tut tut tut* and *tseep*. **HABITAT** Woods, towns. **RANGE** Mar.–Nov.: entire region. Dec.–Feb.: mainly coastal plain.

GRAY CATBIRD
Dumetella carolinensis
MOCKINGBIRD FAMILY

9". Entirely slaty gray ex. for black crown and rusty vent. A skulker; often cocks or swings blackish tail. **VOICE** Song: long, rambling series of single phrases; often mimics other birds. Calls: cat-like *meeow*, sharp *check*. **HABITAT** Dense shrubs, woodland edges, gardens. **RANGE** May–Oct.: entire region. Oct.–May: some on coastal plain.

BROWN THRASHER
Toxostoma rufum
MOCKINGBIRD FAMILY

11½". Bright rufous brown above, buffy white with dark brown stripes below; white wing bars; gray cheeks around yellow-orange eyes. Bill sturdy, downcurved; tail very long, rounded. **VOICE** Song: mimics other birds; repeats song twice. Call: loud *chack*. **HABITAT** Thickets, old fields, oak woods. **RANGE** Apr.–Oct.: entire region. A few winter near coast.

NORTHERN MOCKINGBIRD
Mimus polyglottos
MOCKINGBIRD FAMILY

10". Back, head, and rump gray; paler grayish white below; 2 slender wing bars and large wing patch white, conspicuous in flight; tail blackish with white outer tail feathers. Bill small, thin. Sings by day and often at night. **VOICE** Song: often mimics other birds, repeats songs 3–6 times. Calls: loud *chack*, softer *chair*. **HABITAT** Shrubs, fields, towns. **RANGE** Resident in entire region.

EUROPEAN STARLING
Sturnus vulgaris
STARLING FAMILY

summer (left), winter (right)

8″. Summer adult glossy green and purple; back lightly speckled; bill yellow. Winter adult blackish, heavily flecked with white; bill dark. Wings short, pointed, rusty-edged; bill longish, pointed; legs dull pink; tail short, square. Imm. uniformly gray-brown. Usu. in flocks. Very successful species introduced from Europe, but very detrimental to native birds. Boldly takes over most nest holes and birdhouses, occupied or not. Depletes wild and garden fruit stock and feeder suet. **VOICE** Song: mix of whistles, squeals, and chuckles; will mimic other birds. Calls: rising, then falling *hoooeee*, harsh *jeer*. **HABITAT** Towns, cities, farms, fields. **RANGE** Resident in entire region, though few in mtns.

CEDAR WAXWING
Bombycilla cedrorum
WAXWING FAMILY

7″. Adult back and pointed crest brown; fawn-brown chest grades to yellow belly; wings gray, with waxy red tips on secondaries; black eye mask, edged in white. Rump and tail gray, with yellow tip. Usu. in flocks. **VOICE** Call: high thin *zeee*. **HABITAT** Woodland edges, gardens. **RANGE** Aug.–May: entire region; breeds erratically inland, mainly in mtns.

WHITE-EYED VIREO
Vireo griseus
VIREO FAMILY

5″. Vireos have thicker, hooked bills and move more slowly than warblers. This species: olive green above, white below; sides yellowish; 2 pale wing bars; yellow "spectacles" around white eyes. Furtive skulker. **VOICE** Song: enunciated *CHICK-per-wee-o-CHICK*. **HABITAT** Swampy thickets, scrub. **RANGE** Apr.–Sept.: from c PA, NJ, se NY south.

BLUE-HEADED VIREO
"Solitary Vireo"
Vireo solitarius
VIREO FAMILY

5½″. Back olive; sides washed yellow; underparts and wing bars white; head bluish-slaty with white "spectacles." **VOICE** Song: slow, sweet whistled phrases. **HABITAT** Coniferous and mixed woods. **RANGE** Apr.–May, Sept.–Oct.: entire region; breeds in upland NY, PA, n NJ, and south in mtns. to w VA.

YELLOW-THROATED VIREO
Vireo flavifrons
VIREO FAMILY

5½". Upperparts grayish olive; belly and wing bars white; throat, chest, and bold "spectacles" bright yellow. **VOICE** Song: burry *tweoo toowee three-eight*. Longer pauses between songs than Red-eyed and Solitary Vireos. **HABITAT** Broadleaf woodland canopies, swampy woods. **RANGE** May–Sept.: entire region.

WARBLING VIREO
Vireo gilvus
VIREO FAMILY

5". Gray with slight olive cast above, dingy white below; no wing bars; eyebrow white, not outlined in black. Imm. sides washed yellow-green. **VOICE** Song: melodious warbling with an upward inflection at end. Call: wheezy *twee*. **HABITAT** Broadleaf woods, esp. on riversides. **RANGE** May–Sept.: entire region.

RED-EYED VIREO
Vireo olivaceus
VIREO FAMILY

6". Olive green above, dingy white below (yellow wash on belly in fall); no wing bars; crown gray; black line through dark red eye and above white eyebrow. **VOICE** Song: monotonous *cher-eep cher-oop*, repeated up to 40 times a minute, all day long until late July. Call: scolding *meew*. **HABITAT** Broadleaf woodland canopies. **RANGE** Late Apr.–Oct.: entire region.

Wood Warblers

Warblers native to the New World, often called wood warblers, were once dubbed the subfamily Parulinae, part of the warbler, grosbeak, and sparrow family (Emberizidae), but are now considered their own family, Parulidae. In May, 30 species of migrating warblers can flood into a single Mid-Atlantic county, filling the woods with color and song. Spring "warbler waves" occur when overnight winds are from the southwest, especially after several days of contrary winds and/or rains. Many adult males have the same plumage year-round, but some have breeding (summer) and nonbreeding (winter) plumages. Females, fall males, and immature birds usually have a trace of the summer male pattern. Each species has a distinct song, given rarely after June; the warbler call tends to be a simple *chip*. During summer, these birds breed in a variety of woodland and scrub habitats. Most nests are cups on small forks of branches or hidden under bushes. Warblers glean insects from leaves with their thin unhooked bills. In early autumn, nearly all return to tropical forests of Central and South America and the West Indies.

NASHVILLE WARBLER
Vermivora ruficapilla
WOOD WARBLER FAMILY

4¾". Back, wings, and tail olive green; no wing bars; throat and underparts bright yellow; gray head with white eye ring. Female duller. **VOICE** Song: 2-part *see-it see-it see-it titititi.* **HABITAT** Young broadleaf woods, edges. **RANGE** May–Aug.: uplands of n NY to w MD. May, Aug.–Sept.: entire region.

BLUE-WINGED WARBLER
Vermivora pinus
WOOD WARBLER FAMILY

4¾". Back and nape olive; yellow unstriped head and underparts; wings blue-gray, with white wing bars; black line through eye. Female duller. **VOICE** Song: "inhale/exhale" *beee buzz.* **HABITAT** Second-growth broadleaf woods, shrubs, pastures. **RANGE** May–Aug.: c NY to NJ, mtns. of w VA. Late Apr.–May, Sept.: entire region.

NORTHERN PARULA
Parula americana
WOOD WARBLER FAMILY

4½". Male dull blue above; olive back patch; belly white; orange band on yellow throat and upper breast; white wing bars; partial eye ring. Female lacks breast band. **VOICE** Song: rising trill, with lower end: *zeeeeeeee-up.* **HABITAT** Woods, often near water. **RANGE** Mid-Apr.–mid-Oct.: entire region; breeds locally.

YELLOW WARBLER
Dendroica petechia
WOOD WARBLER FAMILY

5". Male olive-yellow above; head, underparts, and wing and tail edging bright yellow; chestnut stripes on chest and sides. Female lacks stripes. **VOICE** Song: cheerful rapid *sweet sweet sweet I'm so sweet.* **HABITAT** Shrubby areas, esp. watersides, overgrown gardens. **RANGE** Mid-Apr.–mid-Sept.: entire region.

CHESTNUT-SIDED WARBLER
Dendroica pensylvanica
WOOD WARBLER FAMILY

5". Olive with black stripes above, gleaming white below; sides chestnut; yellow crown; black "mustache" and line through eye; white cheek and wing bars. **VOICE** Song: slow *pleased pleased pleased to meet you.* **HABITAT** Woodland undergrowth, shrubs. **RANGE** May–Sept.: NY, nw NJ, PA, and south in mtns. to w VA. May, Aug.–Sept.: entire region.

MAGNOLIA WARBLER
Dendroica magnolia
WOOD WARBLER FAMILY

5″. Summer male back black; crown gray; yellow with black streaks below; rump yellow; white line over black mask. Female dull gray above; faint streaking below. **VOICE** Song: musical *weetee weetee weeteo*. **HABITAT** Mixed and young coniferous woods. **RANGE** May–Aug.: upland NY and PA to e WV. May, Aug.–mid-Oct.: entire region.

CAPE MAY WARBLER
Dendroica tigrina
WOOD WARBLER FAMILY

5″. Summer male olive with black stripes above, yellow with black stripes below; yellow rump; chestnut cheek on yellow face. Female greenish brown above; pale neck patch and rump. **VOICE** Song: high *seet seet seet seet*. **HABITAT** Summer: spruces. **RANGE** May–Aug.: n NY (rare). May, Sept.–Oct.: entire region, esp. coastal areas in fall.

BLACK-THROATED BLUE WARBLER
Dendroica caerulescens
WOOD WARBLER FAMILY

5″. Male dark blue above; face, throat, sides black; belly white. Female brownish above, buff below. White wing spot. **VOICE** Song: lazy *sir sir sir please?* **HABITAT** Undergrowth in mixed woods. **RANGE** May–Aug.: upland NY and PA to w VA. May, Sept.–Oct.: entire region.

BLACK-THROATED GREEN WARBLER
Dendroica virens
WOOD WARBLER FAMILY

5″. Male crown and back olive green; face yellow; belly white; throat black; sides white, black-streaked. Female has yellow face and throat. **VOICE** Song: *see see see suz-ee*. **HABITAT** Woods. **RANGE** May–Sept.: NY, PA, and south in mtns. to w VA. Apr.–May, Sept.–Oct.: entire region.

BLACKBURNIAN WARBLER
Dendroica fusca
WOOD WARBLER FAMILY

5″. Summer male black above, whitish below; black side stripes; white shoulder patch; orange throat and head, with black mask. Female duller, striped brown above and on sides; throat orange-yellow. **VOICE** Song: high *sip sip sip titi zeeee*. **HABITAT** Conifers, mixed woods. **RANGE** May–Aug.: upland NY and PA to w VA. May, Sept.: entire region.

YELLOW-RUMPED WARBLER
Dendroica coronata
WOOD WARBLER FAMILY

female (left), summer male (right)

5½". Summer male gray above with black streaks on back, white wing bars; white below; chest patch and side streaks black; yellow patches on crown and sides of chest; black mask. Female and imm. mask and upperparts brown. Rump strikingly yellow. Common early arrival in spring, and abundant fall migrant. **VOICE** Song: musical trill. Call: loud *check*. **HABITAT** Summer and migration: coniferous and mixed woods. Winter: coastal bayberry thickets. **RANGE** May–Sept.: mtns. of NY, e PA. Apr.–May, Sept.–Oct.: entire region. Nov.–Mar.: coastal plain; a few from w NY to w WV.

YELLOW-THROATED WARBLER
Dendroica dominica
WOOD WARBLER FAMILY

5½". Gray above; throat yellow; 2 white wing bars; white sides streaked black; white eyebrow and neck spot; black cheek patch. Forages along trunks and branches. **VOICE** Song: descending *teeeuw teeuw teew-tew-tew-twee*. **HABITAT** Deciduous woods; pine-oak woods. **RANGE** Apr.–Sept.: s NJ, DE, e MD, e VA, w WV.

PINE WARBLER
Dendroica pinus
WOOD WARBLER FAMILY

5½". Male upperparts and cheeks olive green; belly and wing bars white; throat and chest yellow; faint olive stripes on sides. Female duller; imm. more so. **VOICE** Song: slow trill on one pitch. **HABITAT** Pinewoods. **RANGE** Apr.–Oct.: entire region; local in some areas. Nov.–Mar.: some along coast, esp. c NJ to VA.

PRAIRIE WARBLER
Dendroica discolor
WOOD WARBLER FAMILY

4¾". Male olive green above; chestnut stripes on back; underparts and face yellow; black lines on face and sides; pale yellow wing bars. Female duller. Wags tail. **VOICE** Song: 8–10 buzzy *zee* notes, each one higher. **HABITAT** Brushy old fields, pine-oak barrens. **RANGE** May–Sept.: entire region; local in w NY, n PA.

AMERICAN REDSTART

male (left), female (right)

Setophaga ruticilla
WOOD WARBLER FAMILY

5". Adult male mainly black; midbelly white; large orange patches on wings, sides of chest, basal corners of tail. Female olive brown above, whitish below; yellow patches on wings, sides of chest, basal corners of tail; head gray with narrow white "spectacles." Imm. male has yellow-orange patches. Often fans tail. Widespread. **VOICE** Songs variable; one is *teetsa teetsa teetsa teetsa teet;* another is *zee zee zee zee tsee-o.* **HABITAT** Broadleaf woods, shrubs. **RANGE** May–Sept.: entire region.

PALM WARBLER

Dendroica palmarum
WOOD WARBLER FAMILY

5½". Summer: olive above; crown chestnut red; underparts and eyebrow yellow; rusty side stripes. Winter: faintly brown-striped; pale eye line; vent yellow. Wags tail. **VOICE** Song: slow buzzy trill. **HABITAT** Waterside shrubs, brushy fields. **RANGE** Mid-Apr.–mid-May, mid-Sept.–Oct.: entire region. Nov.–Apr.: coast from Long Is. to VA.

BLACKPOLL WARBLER

Dendroica striata
WOOD WARBLER FAMILY

5½". Summer male brownish gray above, white below; black back and side stripes; crown black; cheek and throat white. Summer female grayish with weak stripes. **VOICE** Song: high, on one pitch: *ze ze ze ze ZEE ZEE ZEE ze ze.* **HABITAT** Summer: spruce-fir woods. Migration: mixed woods. **RANGE** May, Sept.–Oct.: entire region. June–Aug.: n NY mtns.

CERULEAN WARBLER

Dendroica caerulea
WOOD WARBLER FAMILY

4¾". Male bright blue above; 2 bold white wing bars; pure white below, with black necklace and side streaks. Female crown and back blue-green; 2 white wing bars; creamy with streaks below. Tail short. Stays high in trees. **VOICE** Song: buzzy trill. **HABITAT** Broadleaf forests. **RANGE** Apr.–Sept.: from w and se NY south.

PROTHONOTARY WARBLER
Protonotaria citrea
WOOD WARBLER FAMILY

5½". Male head and breast orange yellow; back olive; wings, rump, and tail blue-gray; vent white. Female crown olive; breast yellow. Lacks stripes. **VOICE** Song: long series of *sweet* notes. Call: loud *tink*. **HABITAT** Swamps, riversides. **RANGE** Apr.–Sept.: w NY to w WV; NJ south to c and e VA.

BLACK-AND-WHITE WARBLER
Mniotilta varia
WOOD WARBLER FAMILY

5¼". Male body striped black and white; cheeks and throat black; crown black with median white stripe; white eyebrow and "mustache." Female cheeks gray; throat white. Creeps and forages along branches and tree trunks, like nuthatches. Widespread. **VOICE** Song: 6–12 high *wee-zy* notes. **HABITAT** Mixed woods. **RANGE** Apr.–Oct.: entire region.

WORM-EATING WARBLER
Helmitheros vermivorus
WOOD WARBLER FAMILY

5". Upperparts dull grayish brown; head and chest pale fawn buff; bold black lines through eyes and bordering crown. No wing bars. Feeds both high and low; inconspicuous. **VOICE** Song: series of rapid *chip* notes, like Chipping Sparrow. **HABITAT** Broadleaf woods, esp. hillsides and ravines; tangles. **RANGE** Apr.–Sept.: se NY and south; along coast only in migration.

OVENBIRD
Seiurus aurocapillus
WOOD WARBLER FAMILY

6". Upperparts and sides of head brownish olive; white with black stripes below; crown stripe orange bordered by black; eye ring white; legs pink. Walks on forest floor in bobbing, deliberate manner. Widespread. **VOICE** Song: far-reaching *TEACH-er*, repeated 6–8 times, ever louder; commonly heard. **HABITAT** Mixed broadleaf woods; pine-oak woodland on coastal plain. **RANGE** May–Sept.: entire region.

NORTHERN WATERTHRUSH
Seiurus noveboracensis
WOOD WARBLER FAMILY

6″. Upperparts and head plain brown; underparts and eyebrow (tapers to rear) yellowish white; throat dotted; breast striped dark brown; legs pink. Almost always pumps rearparts; walks deliberately on ground. **VOICE** Song: loud rapid *wit wit wit sweet sweet sweet chew chew chew.* **HABITAT** Swamps, bogs, moist woods, watersides. **RANGE** May–Aug.: uplands from NY to e WV. May, Aug.–Sept.: entire region.

LOUISIANA WATERTHRUSH
Seiurus motacilla
WOOD WARBLER FAMILY

6″. Upperparts and head plain brown; underparts and eyebrow (wider at rear) pure white, but buffy under on lower flanks; throat unspotted; breast striped brown; legs pink. Behavior like Northern Waterthrush. **VOICE** Song: 4 slow, up-slurred notes, then fast jumble of high and low notes. **HABITAT** Woods with flowing clear streams or brooks (uplands); swampy woods (southward). **RANGE** Apr.–Aug.: w and se NY to VA.

KENTUCKY WARBLER
Oporornis formosus
WOOD WARBLER FAMILY

5½″. Olive green above, all yellow below; yellow lores and "spectacles"; forecrown and mask-like patch below eye black (slaty in female and imm.). Legs long, flesh-colored. **VOICE** Song: rapid *shur-ree*, repeated 4 times. **HABITAT** Wooded deciduous ravines; bottomland woods. **RANGE** Apr.–Sept.: from se NY and c PA south.

COMMON YELLOWTHROAT
Geothlypis trichas
WOOD WARBLER FAMILY

5″. Male upperparts and sides olive green; throat and chest yellow; midbelly white; prominent black mask over forehead and cheeks; broad white line above mask. Female olive brown above; pale eye ring; throat yellow, belly whitish. Feeds low; often raises tail at angle, like wren. Widespread and common. **VOICE** Song: rollicking *witchity-witchity-witchity-witch*. Call: flat *chep*. **HABITAT** Wooded swamps, wet meadows, thickets, shrubs. **RANGE** May–Oct.: entire region. Oct.–May: some along coast.

HOODED WARBLER
Wilsonia citrina
WOOD WARBLER FAMILY

5½". Male olive green above, clear yellow below; black hood encircles yellow face and beady black eyes. Female olive above, yellow below, with trace of hood. **VOICE** Loud *wee-ta wee-ta wee-tee-oo*. **HABITAT** Shrubs in broad-leaf woods, often with laurels; swampy woodlands southward. **RANGE** Late Apr.–mid-Sept.: w and se NY to VA.

CANADA WARBLER
Wilsonia canadensis
WOOD WARBLER FAMILY

5½". Male upperparts and crown bluish gray; yellow below, with necklace of black stripes on chest; yellow "spectacles"; lores and area below eyes black. Female gray above, yellow below; faint gray necklace. Often forages in understory. **VOICE** Song: musical *CHIP chupedy-swee-ditchedy*. **HABITAT** Mixed woods, waterside shrubs and thickets. **RANGE** May–Aug.: much of NY and PA, and south in mtns. to w VA. May, Aug.–Sept.: entire region.

YELLOW-BREASTED CHAT
Icteria virens
WOOD WARBLER FAMILY

7". Olive green above; throat and breast rich yellow; belly grayish white; white "spectacles"; lores black in male, gray in female. Tail long; bill heavy. Sings from concealed perch or display flight, day or night. Shy. **VOICE** Song: long series of scolds, whistles; also soft crow-like *caw* notes. Call: loud *chack*. **HABITAT** Dense thickets, old fields, riverside woods. **RANGE** Apr.–Sept.: c NY to VA. Oct.–Mar.: a few on coastal plain.

SUMMER TANAGER
Piranga rubra
TANAGER FAMILY

7½". Adult male entirely rosy red, head and underparts brightest. Female and imm. yellowish olive, brighter below, often tinged ochraceous. Bill thick, whitish, conical. Lives in treetops. **VOICE** Song: varied melodious phrases (robin-like), often a repeated *chur wee sue weet*. Call: fast *trickydicky*. **HABITAT** Swamp and upland oak-pine woods. **RANGE** Apr.–Oct.: from s PA and s NJ south.

SCARLET TANAGER
Piranga olivacea
TANAGER FAMILY

female (left), male (right)

7″. Summer male body and head brilliant scarlet red; wings and tail black; no crest or black on face like cardinal. Female and imm. olive green above, yellow below; wings and tail dusky olive. Bill thick, pale, conical. Widespread, common treetop dweller. Migrates to wintering grounds in neotropics; survival linked to fate of Latin American forests. **VOICE** Song: sweet burry *shureet shureer shurooo*, like a hoarse robin. Call: *chip-burr*, 2nd note much lower. **HABITAT** Tall broadleaf woods, esp. oaks. **RANGE** May–mid-Oct.: entire region.

NORTHERN CARDINAL
Cardinalis cardinalis
GROSBEAK FAMILY

male (left), female (right)

9″. Male grayish red above; underparts, crest, and cheeks bright red; black face encircles swollen, pointed, orange-red bill. Female buffy brown; top of crest red; face black; bill red; wings and tail dusky red. Imm. like female, but bill black. Sought-after feeder bird that likes sunflower and safflower seeds, cracked corn. Has spread northward in region due to climatic warming and winter bird-feeding. **VOICE** Song: pleasing clear whistles; variations on *wait wait wait cheer cheer cheer*. Call: short, high, metallic *chip*. **HABITAT** Woodland edges, shrubs, yards, gardens. **RANGE** Resident in entire region, ex. higher mtns.

ROSE-BREASTED GROSBEAK
Pheucticus ludovicianus
GROSBEAK FAMILY

female (left), male (right)

8″. Male back, head, wings, and tail black; large white patches on wings; rosy triangular patch on chest; sides, belly, and rump white. Female and imm. look like large female Purple Finch: dark brown above, buffy white with dark streaks below; wing bars white; most of head solid brown; eyebrow and median crown stripe white. Bill thick, pale. **VOICE** Song: melodious rich warbling; robin-like, but faster. Call: sharp metallic *chink*. **HABITAT** Broadleaf woods (mainly second-growth) and woodland edges. **RANGE** May–Sept.: NY, PA, n NJ, and south in mtns. to w VA. May, Sept.–mid-Oct.: entire region.

INDIGO BUNTING
Passerina cyanea
GROSBEAK FAMILY

female (left), male (right)

5½″. Summer male rich blue all over, deepest on head; wings and tail partly black; often appears all dark, ex. in good light. Female uniformly warm brown above, paler brown below; trace of blue on primaries. Bill less heavy than that of Blue Grosbeak. Male sings from (often exposed) perch. **VOICE** Song: sweet paired *sweet sweet chew chew sweet sweet*. Call: sharp *spit*. **HABITAT** Woodland edges, shrubby old fields, powerline cuts. **RANGE** May–Oct.: entire region.

BLUE GROSBEAK
Guiraca caerulea
GROSBEAK FAMILY

7″. Adult male dark purplish blue above and below; black stripes on back; shoulder and wing bar chestnut; black at base of bill. Female and imm. fawn brown, with 2 cinnamon wing bars. Bill thick, silvery. May feed on ground; often twitches tail; perches on wires. **VOICE** Song: sweet warbled phrases. Call: loud *chink*. **HABITAT** Brushy pastures, thickets. **RANGE** May–Sept.: se PA and c NJ to c and e VA; w WV.

EASTERN TOWHEE
"Rufous-sided Towhee"
Pipilo erythrophthalmus
AMERICAN SPARROW FAMILY

male (left), female (right)

8". Male back, head, chest, and wings black; sides rufous; midbelly white. Female head, throat, upperparts brown; sides rufous; breast and belly white. Juv. streaked. Eyes red; bill conical; white wing patches; tail longish and rounded, outer tail feathers and outer half of undertail white. Kicks around foraging for insects in dead leaves. **VOICE** Song: 2 whistles, followed by high trill: *DRINK your teeeeee*. Call: loud *che-wink* or *tow-whee*. **HABITAT** Brushy areas, pine-oak woods, open second-growth woods. **RANGE** Apr.–Oct.: entire region. Nov.–Mar.: coastal plain, most of VA; scarcer to north.

AMERICAN TREE SPARROW
"Winter Sparrow"
Spizella arborea
AMERICAN SPARROW FAMILY

6". Rufous brown above; black back stripes; unstreaked grayish white below, tinged rusty at sides; white wing bars; rufous eye line and cap; pale gray eyebrow, throat, and chest; black ace on chest. **VOICE** Call: weak *twee-dle eet*. **HABITAT** Fields, thickets. **RANGE** Late Oct.–mid-Apr.: entire region; more scarce to south.

CHIPPING SPARROW
Spizella passerina
AMERICAN SPARROW FAMILY

5½". Summer: brown with black streaks above, pale gray below; white wing bars; rufous cap; white eyebrow; black eye line; bill yellow below; tail notched. Winter: striped brown crown. **VOICE** Song: series of 20 dry *chip* notes. **HABITAT** Woods, fields, towns. **RANGE** Apr.–Oct.: entire region. Nov.–Mar.: NJ, DE, e MD, most of VA; scarcer to north.

FIELD SPARROW
Spizella pusilla
AMERICAN SPARROW FAMILY

5½". Upperparts, crown, and thin eye stripe rufous; black back stripes; white wing bars; breast clear grayish white, tinged rusty at sides; bill pink; narrow eye ring white. **VOICE** Song: series of *teeuw* notes, each one higher in scale. **HABITAT** Old fields, pastures. **RANGE** Apr.–Oct.: entire region. Nov.–Mar.: w and se NY to VA.

SAVANNAH SPARROW
Passerculus sandwichensis
AMERICAN SPARROW FAMILY

5½″. Brown and white–striped above and below; front of and often entire eyebrow yellow; bill and legs pink. Tail short, notched. Ipswich Sparrow race larger, paler; winters in small numbers alongside dark form in coastal dunes. **VOICE** Song: buzzy *zit zit zit zeeee zaaay*. **HABITAT** Grasslands, coastal marshes, sandy areas. **RANGE** Apr.–May, mid-Sept.–Oct.: entire region. May–Sept.: NY, NJ, PA. Nov.–Mar.: coastal plain, most of VA.

FOX SPARROW
Passerella iliaca
AMERICAN SPARROW FAMILY

7″. Upperparts and rump bright rufous, with gray wash on back; white with heavy rufous stripes below; gray eyebrow. Scratches and rustles in dead leaves when feeding. **VOICE** Song: rising clear notes followed by melodious descending whistles. **HABITAT** Mixed woods, dense thickets, brush. **RANGE** Mar.–mid-Apr., mid-Oct.–Nov.: entire region. Dec.–Mar.: se NY and s PA to VA.

SEASIDE SPARROW
Ammodramus maritimus
AMERICAN SPARROW FAMILY

6″. Adult slaty gray above; gray blurry stripes on sides; yellow lores; blackish "mustache"; tail short, pointed. Imm. brown above; brown stripes on sides. Restricted to wetter sections of salt marshes; sings from tall grass; usu. hard to see. **VOICE** Song: *hut-hut hiiiike*. Call: hard *jack*. **HABITAT** Salt marshes. **RANGE** Resident along entire coast.

SWAMP SPARROW
Melospiza georgiana
AMERICAN SPARROW FAMILY

5¼″. Summer: brown above, striped black on back; breast clear gray, with thin stripes on sides; belly whitish; throat white; much of wings and crown rufous; eyebrow gray; thin black "mustache." **VOICE** Song: slow musical trill on one pitch. **HABITAT** Freshwater cattail marshes, swamps and bogs, shrubs. **RANGE** Apr.–Oct.: NY, PA, and NJ to c WV. Nov.–Mar.: w and se NY to VA.

SONG SPARROW
Melospiza melodia
AMERICAN SPARROW FAMILY

6¼". Dark brown stripes on warm brown back and white underparts; grayish-brown eyebrow; large, central, dark brown spot on chest; tail fairly long, unpatterned, rounded. Common and frequently heard from spring through summer. **VOICE** Song: *sweet sweet sweet towhee tritritritri.* **HABITAT** Shrubs, dense thickets, fields, roadsides, watersides. **RANGE** Resident in entire region, ex. higher mtns.

WHITE-THROATED SPARROW
Zonotrichia albicollis
AMERICAN SPARROW FAMILY

6¼". Brown-striped above; throat white; cheeks and breast gray; bold black and white (or dark brown and buff; juvs. and some adults) crown stripes; yellow spot before eye; tail long, notched. **VOICE** Song: whistled *old sam peabody, peabody, peabody.* **HABITAT** Mixed woods (breeding), brush, thickets, overgrown fields (winter). **RANGE** June–Sept.: mtns. of NY and ne PA. Oct.–May: entire region.

WHITE-CROWNED SPARROW
Zonotrichia leucophrys
AMERICAN SPARROW FAMILY

7". Adult back and nape brown with heavy black streaks; gray below; crown striped black and white; bill pink. Imm. crown striped brown and buff. **VOICE** Song: 1–3 clear notes, then a trill. Call: sharp *pink.* **HABITAT** Forest edges, thickets, old fields, coastal scrub. **RANGE** Apr.–May, Oct.: entire region. Nov.–Mar.: NJ to c VA (uncommon).

DARK-EYED JUNCO
"Slate-colored Junco"
Junco hyemalis
AMERICAN SPARROW FAMILY

6". Adult mainly slaty gray; midbelly white; bill pale pink, conical. Flight reveals white outer tail feathers. Imm. gray areas browner. Juv. chest and back striped brown. Travels in flocks. **VOICE** Song: loose musical trill. Call: light *snack.* **HABITAT** Mixed woods, summits (summer); woods, brushy edges, parks (winter). **RANGE** May–Sept.: mtns. of NY south to w VA. Oct.–Apr.: entire region.

SNOW BUNTING
Plectrophenax nivalis
AMERICAN SPARROW FAMILY

6½". Winter (pictured): Mainly white; back overlaid with rusty tinges (more so in female), speckled black; crown buffy. Flight reveals large white wing patch, black primaries. Found in large roving flocks, often with Horned Larks in winter. **VOICE** Calls: whistled *tew*, short buzz, musical rattle. **HABITAT** Vast open fallow farmlands, seaside dunes. **RANGE** Nov.–Mar.: NY, NJ, Delmarva Peninsula.

HOUSE SPARROW
Passer domesticus
OLD WORLD SPARROW FAMILY

6". The familiar street sparrow. Male: back and wings rufous brown; underparts, crown, cheeks, and rump gray; throat and upper chest black (only chin black in winter); wide chestnut stripe behind eye. Female: plain grayish-brown above, ex. for blackish back streaks; pale eyebrow stripe; pale dusky below. Abundant European import. **VOICE** Song: *chereep* notes. Call: *chir-rup*. **HABITAT** Towns, parks, farms. **RANGE** Resident in entire region.

BOBOLINK
Dolichonyx oryzivorus
BLACKBIRD FAMILY

male (left), female (right)

7". Summer male black with large buffy-yellow nape patch; rump and base of wings white. Male from Aug. on, female, and imm.: buffy, sparrow-like; dark brown stripes on head, back, and sides; tail spiky; feet pink. In spring, male flies over meadows in slow circles, singing and with rapidly beating wings. In late summer, birds gather in flocks at marshes at dusk to roost. **VOICE** Song: bubbly, rollicking, repeated *bob-bob-o-lincoln*, often given in flight. Call: clear *pink*. **HABITAT** Hayfields, grasslands; perches on nearby fences, shrubs, trees. **RANGE** May–Sept.: NY to c NJ and c WV. May–Sept.: entire region.

RED-WINGED BLACKBIRD
Agelaius phoeniceus
BLACKBIRD FAMILY

male (left), female (right)

9″. Male all glossy black, with red shoulder epaulets bordered by yellow; epaulets less visible in late summer and fall. Female heavily streaked brown; crown and eye line dark brown; eyebrow buffy. Bill fairly long, pointed. This species, robins, and grackles are earliest returning birds in spring. Frequently in flocks outside breeding season. **VOICE** Song: gurgling *conk-a-ree*. Calls: harsh *check*, high *tee-eek*. Calls from trees, shrubs, tall reeds. **HABITAT** Marshes, swamps, fields. **RANGE** Mar.–Nov.: entire region. Dec.–Feb.: w and se NY to VA.

EASTERN MEADOWLARK
Sturnella magna
BLACKBIRD FAMILY

9″. Speckled brown above and on sides; yellow throat and breast, with black V on chest; dark brown and whitish head stripes. Flight reveals white outer tail feathers on short tail. Bill long, pointed; feet large. Flies with flaps and glides. Numbers declining. **VOICE** Song: slurred, whistled *tee-you tee-yerr*. Call: harsh *serrt*. **HABITAT** Grasslands, pastures; coastal marshes (winter). **RANGE** Breeds locally throughout; in winter, retires to coastal areas and southward.

RUSTY BLACKBIRD
Euphagus carolinus
BLACKBIRD FAMILY

9″. Summer male glossy black. Summer female dull dark gray. Winter (pictured): both sexes blackish or brown with rusty scaling. Bill long, thin; eyes yellow. **VOICE** Song: creaky *cush-a-lee cush-lay*. Call: harsh *shaq*. **HABITAT** Boreal bogs (summer), wooded swamps and watersides, wet thickets (migration). **RANGE** May–Sept.: n NY (rare). Mar.–Apr., Oct.–Nov.: entire region. Dec.–Feb.: a few on coastal plain, most of VA.

BROWN-HEADED COWBIRD
Molothrus ater
BLACKBIRD FAMILY

7″. Adult male glossy greenish black with coffee-brown head. Adult female uniformly dull brownish gray. Imm. changes from drab brown-striped to slate gray. Bill medium-size, conical, gray. Travels in tight flocks outside nesting season. Brood parasite that is causing great losses in numbers of native songbirds; female lays single egg in several nests of native songbirds; baby cowbird pushes out other eggs and babies, and is raised by foster parents. **VOICE** Song: bubbly creaking *bubble-lee come seee*. Flight call: high *weee teetee*. **HABITAT** Open woodlands, fields, farms, lawns. **RANGE** Apr.–Nov.: entire region. Dec.–Mar.: s NY (rarely) to VA.

male (top left), female (top right)
nestling (bottom)

BOAT-TAILED GRACKLE
Quiscalus major
BLACKBIRD FAMILY

male (left), female (right)

Male 16″; female 13″. Adult male black, glossed purple on head, bluish on back and wings; bill long, heavy, pointed, black; eyes yellow; tail very long, with wedge-shaped tip, often carried in V. Female dark brown above; buffy eye line and underparts; eyes dark; tail flat, blackish. Often solitary or in small groups. **VOICE** Song: harsh high *jeep jeep jeep*. Call: harsh *check*. **HABITAT** Salt marshes, beaches. **RANGE** Mainly resident from coastal w Long Is. to e VA; spreading northward.

COMMON GRACKLE
Quiscalus quiscula
BLACKBIRD FAMILY

13″. Male often appears black; has iridescent blue-green head, dark purple wings, bronzy green back and breast; wedge-shaped tail is held flat or carried in V (courtship). Female smaller, duller gray. Bill long, pointed; eyes yellow. In flocks outside breeding season. **VOICE** Song: short high *gurgle-eek*. Call: loud *shack*. **HABITAT** Farms, watersides, gardens, fields. **RANGE** Mar.–Nov.: entire region. Dec.–Feb.: NJ to VA, mostly on coast and in valleys.

ORCHARD ORIOLE
Icterus spurius
BLACKBIRD FAMILY

7¼″. Male mainly black; rump, shoulder, and belly dark chestnut; faint pale wing bar. Female olive above, yellower below; 2 white wing bars. Bill thin, pointed. Imm. male like female but large throat patch black. Somewhat secretive; usu. high in trees. **VOICE** Song: rapid whistles, down-slurred at end. **HABITAT** Orchards, shade trees, tree breaks on farmland, woodland edges. **RANGE** May–July: from se NY and PA south; more common southward.

male (left), female (right)

BALTIMORE ORIOLE
"Northern Oriole"
Icterus galbula
BLACKBIRD FAMILY

8½″. Male back, head, throat, wings, and tail black; underparts and shoulder bright orange; white patches on wing; yellow tail corners. Female brownish or olive-gray above; face, underparts, and rump yellowish, often with orange tinge. Bill fairly thin, pointed. Stays quite high in trees; will visit feeders for fruit and sugar water. Builds woven, hanging, sock-like grass and fiber nest pouch that stays on tree through most winters. **VOICE** Song: 4–8 pleasing whistles. Call: low whistled *tee-tew*. Call of young: plaintive *tee dit-it* from treetops. **HABITAT** Broadleaf woods, shade trees, parks. **RANGE** May–Sept.: entire region (e VA only in migration).

PURPLE FINCH
Carpodacus purpureus
FINCH FAMILY

male (left), female (right)

6″. Male back and wings mixed brown and rose; head, throat, sides of chest and rump rosy; dull brownish-red cheek and "mustache." Female darker brown and more heavily striped than House Finch; head has white eyebrow, dark brown cheek patch, and wide brown "mustache." Tail quite forked. **VOICE** Song: lively complex warbling. Calls: musical *pur-lee*, sharp *chink*. **HABITAT** Coniferous and mixed woods, woodland edges; yards (winter). **RANGE** May–Sept.: NY and mtns. in PA to e WV. Oct.–Apr.: entire region.

HOUSE FINCH
Carpodacus mexicanus
FINCH FAMILY

male (left), female (right)

5½″. Male back, midcrown, wings, and tail brown; sides and belly whitish, streaked brown; wide eyebrow, throat, and chest rosy red. Female upperparts and head plain dull brown; dusky with brown streaks below. Recent introduction from w U.S. and Mexico; now far more common than related Purple Finch, esp. in cities, suburbs, and at feeders. Sings and initiates courtship in early Feb. **VOICE** Song: musical warbling ending with down-slurred *jeer*, heard frequently from building rooftops. **HABITAT** Cities, residential areas, garden trees. **RANGE** Resident in most of region.

PINE SISKIN
Carduelis pinus
FINCH FAMILY

5″. Very heavily striped brown above and below; yellow patch on wing; yellow on basal sides of notched tail. Bill thin, pointed. **VOICE** Calls: loud *clee-up*, rising *shreee*. **HABITAT** Coniferous and mixed woods; yards (winter). **RANGE** Mid-Oct.–mid- May: entire region; breeds in Adirondacks, irregularly south to n NJ.

EVENING GROSBEAK
Coccothraustes vespertinus
FINCH FAMILY

8″. Male foreparts mostly dark brown; rearparts golden-yellow; eyebrow and forehead yellow; wings black with large white secondaries. Female plain grayish, tinged yellow; wings black with large white spots. Head large; bill massive, ivory; tail black, fairly short. **VOICE** Call: ringing *cleeer* (like House Sparrow). **HABITAT** Mixed woods, trees in residential areas. **RANGE** Resident in n NY. Nov.–Apr.: entire region; common some winters, scarce most.

female (left), male (right)

AMERICAN GOLDFINCH
Carduelis tristis
FINCH FAMILY

5″. Summer male brilliant "canary" yellow; cap, wings, and notched tail black; rump white. Summer female olive green above; throat and chest yellow. Winter male brownish above; face and shoulder yellow. Winter female grayish with or without trace of yellow on throat. All have white wing bars on black wings. Slow, undulating flight. Often feeds on thistles. **VOICE** Song: canary-like; long, pleasing, rising and falling twittering. Call: rising *sweeeeat*. Flight call: *per chicory*. **HABITAT** Fields, woodland edges, farms, yards. **RANGE** Resident in entire region.

Mammals

All members of the vertebrate class Mammalia are warm-blooded and able to maintain a near-constant body temperature. Males generally have an external penis for direct internal fertilization of the female's eggs. Almost all mammals are born live rather than hatching from eggs (exceptions are the Platypus and the echidnas of Australia and New Guinea). Mammary glands, unique to mammals, produce milk that is high in nutrients and fat and promotes rapid growth in the young. Mammals have abundant skin glands, used for temperature regulation (sweating), coat maintenance, territory-marking, sex and species recognition, breeding cycle signals, and even defense, as in skunks and others that can repel predators with their powerful secretions.

Nine mammalian orders are represented in the Mid-Atlantic region, including humans (members of the primates order). Opossums (order Didelphimorphia) give birth to young in an embryonic state; they then develop in a separate fur-lined pouch on the mother's belly. The tiny energetic shrews and moles (Insectivora), which eat insects and other invertebrates, have long snouts, short dense fur, and five toes on each foot. Bats (Chiroptera), with their enlarged, membrane-covered forelimbs, are the only mammals that truly fly.

Hares and rabbits (Lagomorpha) resemble large rodents but have four upper incisor teeth—a large front pair and a small pair directly behind them—that grow continuously, and five toes on their front feet and five in back; digits on all feet are very small. Rodents (Rodentia—including chipmunks, marmots, squirrels, mice, rats, muskrats, voles, porcupines, and beavers) have two upper incisor teeth that grow continuously, and most have four toes on their front feet and five in back.

Carnivores (Carnivora)—bears, the Coyote, foxes, weasels, raccoons, cats, and seals—have long canine teeth for stabbing prey, and most have sharp cheek teeth for slicing meat. The even-toed hoofed mammals (Artiodactyla), in the Mid-Atlantic region represented by the deer family, have two or four toes that form a cloven hoof. The whales, dolphins, and porpoises (Cetacea) are hairless; in both seals and cetaceans, the legs have evolved into flippers.

Most mammals have an insulating layer of fur that helps them to maintain a fairly constant body temperature independent of their surroundings, making them among the most successful animals in cold climates. Many molt twice a year and have a noticeably thicker coat in winter. Some, such as certain weasels and hares, change colors, developing a concealing white coat in winter. Sea mammals have thick layers of insulating blubber that help retain body heat.

The body parts and appendages of mammals exhibit a wide and adaptive variety of sizes, shapes, and functions. Most mammals have well-developed eyes, ears, and noses that provide good night vision, hearing, and sense of smell. Mammalian teeth range from fine points for capturing insects (bats and insectivores) to chisel-like gnawing teeth (rabbits and rodents), wide plant-crushing teeth (other rodents and hoofed mammals), and heavy pointed instruments for flesh-ripping (carnivores, including seals). Most large whales have huge brushes (called baleen), composed of a fingernail-like substance called keratin, that are used for straining plankton.

Mammals generally have four limbs. In many rodents, in some carnivores, and in primates, the ends of the forelimbs are modified into complex, manipulative hands. Solid hooves support the heavy weight of deer.

In the species accounts, the typical adult length given is from the tip of the nose to the end of the tail, followed by the tail length; for larger mammals, shoulder height is also given. Wingspan is given for bats.

Mammal Signs and Tracks

The evidence that a particular animal is or has been in a certain area is called its "sign." The sign can be scat (fecal matter), burrow openings, nutshells, tracks, or other evidence. Tracks are a useful aid in confirming the presence of mammal species. Impressions vary depending on the substrate and whether the animal was walking or running. Animals can leave clear tracks in mud, dirt, snow, and sand, usually larger ones in wet mud and snow. Because animals come to ponds or streams to drink or feed, tracks are likely to be found near waterways; damp mud often records tracks in fine detail, sometimes showing claws or webbing. Prints in snow may leave a less clear impression but can often be followed for a long distance, and may show the pattern of the animal's stride. The track drawings below, of selected mammals that live in the Mid-Atlantic region, are not to relative scale.

Virginia Opossum

Eastern Cottontail

Snowshoe Hare

Eastern Gray Squirrel

American Beaver

Common Muskrat

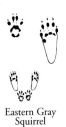

Common Porcupine

Common Raccoon

Coyote

Red Fox

Common Gray Fox

Black Bear

Striped Skunk

Long-tailed Weasel

Mink

Northern River Otter

Bobcat

White-tailed Deer

VIRGINIA OPOSSUM
Didelphis virginiana
OPOSSUM FAMILY

L 28″; T 11″. Grizzled gray, with mix of black underfur and longer white guard hairs. Head pointed; nose long; face white, with long whiskers; ears small, round, black with white tip. Legs short, black; feet have 5 digits; hindfeet have opposable, grasping inner thumbs. Tail long, tapered, naked, pink with black base. Eats fruit, nuts, bird eggs, large insects, carrion. May hang from branches using wraparound, prehensile tail. If surprised at close range, may "play possum" (feign death). **BREEDING** 1–14 (avg. 8) pea-size young attach themselves to nipples in mother's pouch for 2 months; 2–3 litters per year. **SIGN** Tracks: hindprint 2″ wide, 3 middle toes close, outer toes well spread; foreprint slightly smaller, star-like. **HABITAT** Broadleaf woods, watersides, farms. **ACTIVITY** Nocturnal; much less active in winter. **RANGE** Entire region, ex. Adirondacks.

NORTHERN SHORT-TAILED SHREW
Blarina brevicauda
SHREW FAMILY

L 4¾"; T 1". Body and head grayish black. Nose conical; jaws long, open wide. Legs short; 5 toes on each foot. Tail nearly hairless. Heart can beat 700 times a minute. Eats its weight daily. Builds tunnels where it caches food: worms, snails, insects, amphibians, and mice. **CAUTION** Mildly poisonous. **BREEDING** Avg. 5–7 young; several litters per year. **HABITAT** Woods, meadows, watersides, brush. **ACTIVITY** Intensely active day and night, year-round. **RANGE** Entire region, ex. e VA.

LEAST SHREW
Cryptotis parva
SHREW FAMILY

L 3"; T ½". Grayish brown above; paler below. Ears small. Tail shorter than Northern Short-tailed's. Eats invertebrates in leaf litter; called "bee mole" because enters beehives to feed on brood. Nest is ball of grass under rock or stump. Unusually social; up to 30 may live together during breeding season and in winter; may engage in cannibalism if food becomes scarce. **BREEDING** 3–6 young; several litters per year. **HABITAT** Fields, marshy areas, wet woods. **ACTIVITY** Most active at night; year-round. **RANGE** Entire region, ex. n NY.

STAR-NOSED MOLE
Condylura cristata
MOLE FAMILY

L 7"; T 3". Slate-colored, with star-like snout fan of 22 pink tentacles (may be prey-sensing device). Eyes and ears tiny, hidden. Legs very short; feet short, wide, long-clawed, turned outward. Tail long, hairy, wider in middle. Sometimes aboveground. Swims well; often feeds in water. **BREEDING** 3–7 young mid-Apr.–June. **SIGN** Piles of dirt outside 2" burrow openings. **HABITAT** Waterside woods, fields. **ACTIVITY** Day and night, year-round.

EASTERN MOLE
Scalopus aquaticus
MOLE FAMILY

L 7"; T 1". Fur short, velvety, gray to pale brown. Snout long, pink, flexible; eyes and ears not visible. Legs very short; front feet have wide, round, fleshy palms that are turned out, and 5 long white claws. Tail short, with few hairs. Feeds on earthworms and beetle larvae in shallow tunnels under soil surface. **BREEDING** 2–5 young born in tunnels Apr.–May. **SIGN** Low raised ridges on soil surface. **HABITAT** Fields, lawns, well-drained woods. **ACTIVITY** Day and night; peaks near dawn and dusk. Inactive during droughts and freezes. **RANGE** se NY to c and e VA.

Bats

Bats are the only mammals that truly fly (the flying squirrels glide). The bones and muscles in the forelimbs of bats are elongated; thin, usually black wing membranes are attached to four extremely long fingers. When bats are at rest, the wings are folded along the forearm; they use their short, claw-like thumbs for crawling about. Small insectivorous bats beat their wings six to eight times a second.

Bats are mainly nocturnal, though some species are occasionally active in the early morning and late afternoon. Their slender, mouse-like bodies are well furred, and their eyesight, while not excellent, is quite adequate to detect predators and general landscape features. Most use echolocation (sonar) to locate flying insects and avoid obstacles. In flight, they emit 30 to 60 high-frequency calls per second that bounce off objects and return to their large ears. Bats interpret these reflected sounds as they close in on prey or evade an obstacle. Echolocation sounds are mainly inaudible to humans, but bats also give shrill squeaks most humans can hear. By day, most bats hang upside-down from the ceilings of caves, tree hollows, and attics, using one or both hindfeet. Members of solitary species may roost alone under a branch or among the foliage of a tall tree. In other species, large colonies gather in caves and under natural and man-made overhangs.

All bats in the Mid-Atlantic region are insect-eaters. By night, they pursue larger individual insects through the air or glean them from trees, and skim open-mouthed through swarms of midges. A bat will trap a large flying insect in the membrane between its hindlegs, then seize it with its teeth. Bats are the most important predators of night-flying insects; they feed on many serious pest species, consume hundreds of thousands of tons of destructive insects each year, and are essential in maintaining the balance of nature. Because of the lack of insects in winter, bats in the Mid-Atlantic region either hibernate here or migrate south to hibernate or feed in winter. Sheltered hibernation roosts can provide protection from extreme cold.

Watch for bats overhead on warm summer evenings, especially around water, where insects are abundant and where bats may skim the water surface to drink.

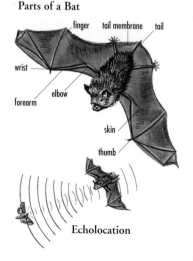

Parts of a Bat

finger   tail membrane   tail

wrist

elbow

forearm

skin

thumb

Echolocation

BIG BROWN BAT
Eptesicus fuscus
VESPERTILIONID BAT FAMILY

L 4½"; WS 12". Dark brown above, pale brown below. Wing and tail membranes furless. Face and ears broad, black. Flight straight, fast. Flies later in autumn, earlier in spring than others. The larger bat most often seen in summer over gardens and adjacent woods. **BREEDING** 2 young in June. **HABITAT** All habitats; roosts and breeds in attics, barns, tree hollows, under bridges; often in cities. **ACTIVITY** Summer: active. Winter: hibernates in region.

LITTLE BROWN MYOTIS
"Little Brown Bat"
Myotis lucifugus
VESPERTILIONID BAT FAMILY

L 3½"; WS 9". Rich glossy brown above, buffy below. Rounded ears short for a bat; face broad, blunt, furry. Often flies before dusk; flight erratic. Squeaks audible. Region's most common bat. **BREEDING** Mates in fall; female stores sperm until spring; 1 young born usu. in June. **HABITAT** Streams, lakes, trees, fields; roosts in trees, caves, mines, barns, attics, dark places. **ACTIVITY** Summer: active. Winter: hibernates in caves.

EASTERN RED BAT
Lasiurus borealis
VESPERTILIONID BAT FAMILY

L 4½"; WS 12". Fur soft, fluffy; body white below. Male head, upperparts rich reddish orange. Female buffy, frosted white, above; head pale buffy orange. Ears short, rounded. Wings long for a bat. Wings and tail pointed. Flight strong, fast. Gives sharp audible chirp. **BREEDING** 1–4 young in June. **HABITAT** Woods, woodland edges; roosts in tree foliage. **ACTIVITY** Summer: active. Winter: most migrate south (migrators may be seen by day along coast in fall).

EASTERN PIPISTRELLE
Pipistrellus subflavus
VESPERTILIONID BAT FAMILY

L 3"; WS 7". Yellowish brown to drab brown. Face usu. has blackish mask. Ears black, short, rounded. Smallest bat in East. Often flies before dusk; flight low, erratic. **BREEDING** 2 young born June–July; carried in air for 1st week by mother. **HABITAT** Roosts in caves, rocky areas, buildings, waterside trees. **ACTIVITY** Nocturnal; in warmer months. Some hibernate in region, others migrate south.

adult (left), young in nest (right)

EASTERN COTTONTAIL
Sylvilagus floridanus
HARE AND RABBIT FAMILY

L 17"; T 1½". Grayish brown, mixed with black hairs; belly white. White eye ring; many have white spot on forehead. Ears to 2½" long, with thin black stripe on upper edges. Rusty wash on nape. Legs buffy; hindlegs heavily muscled. Raises fluffy tail when bounding away, displaying white underside ("cottontail"). **BREEDING** 4–5 young Apr.–May; several litters each year. **SIGN** Clean-cut woody sprigs, stripped bark on young trees above deep snow. Tracks: 3" oblong hindprints in front of smaller, round foreprints. Scat: piles of dark brown, pea-size pellets. **HABITAT** Fields, woodland edges, thickets, gardens, lawns. **ACTIVITY** Late afternoon, night, early morning; spends midday in nest-like "form" in grass, thickets; year-round, ex. in deep snows.

summer (left), winter (right)

SNOWSHOE HARE
"Varying Hare"
Lepus americanus
HARE AND RABBIT FAMILY

L 19"; T 2". Summer: brown; somewhat blackish toward rear; short tail whitish below. Winter: pure white (sometimes mottled with brown), ex. for black ear tips; thick fur on hindfeet creates "snowshoes." Larger than a cottontail, with longer (4") black-tipped ears, notably larger hindfeet. If surprised, may thump hindfeet, then run off at up to 30 mph. **BREEDING** 3 young per litter; alert, furred, able to hop in hours. 1st litter April; 2 more follow. **SIGN** Packed-down trails in snow. Scat: piles of brown pellets a bit larger than cottontails'. Hindprint 4–5", toes widely spread. **HABITAT** Coniferous and mixed woods. **ACTIVITY** Late afternoon, night, early morning; rests by day in nest-like "form" or hollow log. **RANGE** n and c NY south in mtns. to w VA.

Rodents

Rodentia is the world's largest mammalian order; more than half of all mammal species and more than half of all mammal individuals on earth are rodents. In addition to the mice and rats (a family that also includes the mouse-like but chubbier voles and the muskrats), other rodent families in the Mid-Atlantic region are the squirrels (including chipmunks and the Woodchuck), jumping mice, porcupines, and beavers. Mid-Atlantic species range from mice weighing roughly an ounce to the American Beaver, which may weigh up to 66 pounds, but most rodents are relatively small. They are distinguished by having only two pairs of incisors—one upper and one lower—and no canines, leaving a wide gap between incisors and molars. Rodent incisors are enameled on the front only; the working of the upper teeth against the lower ones wears away the softer inner surfaces, producing a short, chisel-like, beveled edge ideal for gnawing. The incisors grow throughout an animal's life (if they did not, they shortly would be worn away), and rodents must gnaw enough to keep the incisors from growing too long. The eyes are bulbous and placed high on the side of the head, enabling the animals to detect danger over a wide arc.

EASTERN CHIPMUNK
Tamias striatus
SQUIRREL FAMILY

L 9"; T 4". Reddish brown above; gray stripe from crown to back; sides have whitish-buff stripe edged with black; belly white. Pale buffy lines above and below eye; ears short. Tail fairly long, slightly fluffy. Calls include loud, bird-like *chip* and soft *cuck-cuck*. Gathers nuts and seeds; usu. forages on ground. **BREEDING** 3–5 young in May. **SIGN** Burrow entrances 2" wide, without dirt piles, on a wooded slope. Tracks: hindprint 1⅞"; foreprint much smaller. **HABITAT** Mixed woods, brush, rock piles. **ACTIVITY** Mar.–Nov.: active. Winter: sleeps in burrows; may surface during thaws.

WOODCHUCK
"Groundhog" "Eastern Marmot"
Marmota monax
SQUIRREL FAMILY

L 21"; T 5". Grizzled brown above, some with blackish or rufous tones; buffy below. Ears short, rounded; face has pale buffy patches. Legs short, powerful. Tail bushy. Gives shrill whistle, followed by *chuck, chuck*. Vegetarian; eats heavily in summer, early fall; does not store food. Sometimes climbs trees; digs burrows. **BREEDING** 4–5 young Apr.–May. **SIGN** 8–12" burrow entrance, with dirt piles on sides. **HABITAT** Fields, woodland edges, farms, highway verges, gardens. **ACTIVITY** Summer: feeds by day. Winter: hibernates early, deeply.

EASTERN GRAY SQUIRREL
Sciurus carolinensis
SQUIRREL FAMILY

common gray coat (left), rarer black coat (right)

L 19"; T 9". Gray above, white below; in summer, head, legs, and sides washed with tawny brown. Eye ring buffy; tail long, bushy, grizzled blackish and white. All-black individuals occur locally, esp. in urban areas. Vocal; gives variety of chattering and clucking calls. Eats nuts, buds, inner bark, fruit on ground and in trees. Region's most commonly seen mammal. **BREEDING** 2 litters of usu. 2–3 young Apr.–May in nest in tree cavity. **SIGN** Summer: stick platform in tree; gnawed nutshells. Winter: spherical leaf nest in tree; holes in snow above nut caches. Tracks: longer hindprints in front of smaller foreprints. **HABITAT** Broadleaf and mixed woods, towns. **ACTIVITY** By day, year-round.

EASTERN FOX SQUIRREL
Sciurus niger
SQUIRREL FAMILY

L 24"; T 11". Color variable: gray or yellow-brown above; legs, feet, underparts, and edges of bushy tail rusty buff (some whitish). Tail proportionally longer than Eastern Gray Squirrel's. Delmarva race: mainly gray; muzzle whitish. Head blackish in s VA race. Caches nuts in tree cavities. Normally uncommon in region. Gives loud *que, que, que*. **BREEDING** 1–2 litters of 2–4 young Mar., July–Aug. Young remain in leaf nest 2 months. **SIGN** Mounds of nutshells under feeding branch, large leaf nests high in trees. **HABITAT** Urban parks, woods. **ACTIVITY** By day, year-round. **RANGE** s and w PA, DE, MD, WV, VA.

RED SQUIRREL
Tamiasciurus hudsonicus
SQUIRREL FAMILY

L 13"; T 5". Underparts white; tail long, bushy, reddish. Summer: dark reddish gray above, with black side stripe; ears rounded. Winter: paler above; no side stripe; ears tufted. Mainly arboreal. Stores seeds, nuts in large caches. Noisy; gives angry, chattering *chick-r-r-r-r*. **BREEDING** 4–5 young Apr.–May and/or Aug.–Sept. in tree cavity or leaf-and-stick nest in treetop. **SIGN** Cones, nuts with ragged hole at one end, often in little piles, on stumps. Tracks: hindprint 1½"; 5 toes print. **HABITAT** Coniferous and mixed woods. **ACTIVITY** Mainly by day, year-round. **RANGE** Entire region, ex. s coastal plain.

SOUTHERN FLYING SQUIRREL
Glaucomys volans
in flight (left), carrying young (right)
SQUIRREL FAMILY

L 9″; T 3″. Brown above: darker, redder in summer, paler fawn in winter; white below. Eyes huge; ears rounded. Tail flat, bushy, narrow-based. Folds of furred skin connect fore- and hindlimbs, allowing glides between trees. May visit birdfeeders at night; mainly eats insects in warmer months. Fairly common but seldom seen. **BREEDING** 3–4 blind, naked young in spring, late summer. Nests in tree cavities, attics, birdhouses. **HABITAT** Broadleaf and mixed woods. **ACTIVITY** Strictly nocturnal. Winter: enters state of torpor in cold spells; active during thaws. **Northern Flying Squirrel** (*G. sabrinus*) larger (11″), somewhat richer brown; in mtns. from NY to w VA.

AMERICAN BEAVER
Castor canadensis
gnawed tree (bottom left), lodge (right)
BEAVER FAMILY

L 3′4″; T 16″. Rich dark brown. Back high, rounded. Eyes and ears small. Legs short; feet webbed. Paddle-shaped tail black, scaly, flattened horizontally. Eats bark, twigs of broadleaf trees; stashes branches underwater for winter use. Swims with only head above water. Slaps tail on water loudly to warn family of danger. Fells trees by gnawing trunk down to a "waist" that finally cannot support the tree. Dams small streams with sticks, reeds, saplings caulked with mud. Builds dome-like lodge up to 6′ high and 20′ wide in newly created pond; underwater tunnels reach up to dry chambers, hidden from view, above water level. Ponds formed by dams promote growth of habitat (broadleaf trees) favored by beavers; dams also help form marshes for other wildlife. N. Amer.'s largest rodent. **BREEDING** Usu. 3–5 young born May–July, inside lodge. **SIGN** Dams, lodges, cone-shaped tree stumps. 12″ territorial scent mounds of mud and grass. Tracks: 4–6″, 5-toed hindprint covers smaller foreprint. **HABITAT** Ponds, lakes, rivers, adjacent woods. **ACTIVITY** Mainly at dusk and night, year-round; active by day where not persecuted.

HOUSE MOUSE
Mus musculus
MOUSE AND RAT FAMILY

L 7″; T 3″. Gray or brownish tan above, gray or buffy below. Tail long, naked, with ring-like scales. This common house pest was introduced to N. Amer. from Eurasia. **BREEDING** 2–5 litters of 3–11 young Mar.–Oct.; year-round indoors. **SIGN** Small dark droppings, musky odor, damaged materials. **HABITAT** Buildings, towns, farms. **ACTIVITY** Mainly nocturnal, year-round.

WHITE-FOOTED MOUSE
Peromyscus leucopus
MOUSE AND RAT FAMILY

L 7″; T 3″. Reddish brown; middle of back blackish; underparts and feet white. Ears and eyes large. Tail finely haired. With White-tailed Deer, host of Lyme disease tick and bacterium. **BREEDING** Many litters; usu. 5 young Apr.–Nov. in tree nest. **SIGN** Piles of small nuts, each with 2–3 small openings. Tracks: hindprint ⅝″; narrow heel, 5 splayed toes. **HABITAT** Dry pine-oak woods, field edges. **ACTIVITY** Nocturnal, year-round, ex. in extreme weather. **Deer Mouse** *(P. maniculatus)*, of uplands, is nearly identical; has fainter midback stripe.

SOUTHERN RED-BACKED VOLE
Clethrionomys gapperi
MOUSE AND RAT FAMILY

L 5″; T 1½″. Reddish brown; wide chestnut stripe along upper back; grayish below. Ears small. Tail shorter than body. Its color pattern makes this one of the region's most easily identifiable small mammals. **BREEDING** Several litters of 2–8 young Mar.–Dec. **SIGN** Runways and burrows on forest floor. **HABITAT** Coniferous and mixed woods, rock piles. **ACTIVITY** Mainly nocturnal, year-round. **RANGE** NY, NJ, PA; in mtns. from w MD to w VA.

MEADOW VOLE
Microtus pennsylvanicus
MOUSE AND RAT FAMILY

L 7″; T 2″. Dark brown in summer, grayish brown in winter. Ears small. Tail much shorter than body. Major prey of foxes, owls, hawks. **BREEDING** 6–17 litters of 1–9 young per year. The common short-tailed, dark brown "mouse" seen in fields and meadows. **SIGN** Summer: piles of grass cuttings along runways. Winter: runways in snow and underground. Nests under boards, grass clumps. Tracks: hindprint ⅝″; 5 widely splayed toes. **HABITAT** Marshes, fields, farms, roadside edges. **ACTIVITY** Day and night, year-round.

BROWN RAT
"Norway Rat"
Rattus norvegicus
MOUSE AND RAT FAMILY

L 15"; T 7". Grayish brown above, gray below. Ears partly hidden in fur. Tail long, scaly, pale. Digs network of tunnels 2–3" wide in ground. Eats insects, stored grain, garbage. Introduced from Eurasia. **BREEDING** 6 litters of 6–8 young a year. **SIGN** Holes in walls, paths to food supplies. Tracks: long 5-toed hindprint in front of rounder foreprint. **HABITAT** Cities, farms. **ACTIVITY** Mostly nocturnal, year-round. **Black Rat** *(R. rattus)* of seaport cities is darker, with longer, dark tail.

MEADOW JUMPING MOUSE
Zapus hudsonius
JUMPING MOUSE FAMILY

L 9"; T 5". Dark brown on back, pale yellowish on sides, white below. Head small, rounded. Large hindfeet and thighs allow hops of up to 3'. Tail thin, much longer than body. **BREEDING** 2 litters of 2–8 young June–Oct. **SIGN** 1–1½" cuttings of grass. **HABITAT** Meadows, marshes, brush. **ACTIVITY** Summer: day and (esp.) night. Winter: hibernates for long period.

COMMON MUSKRAT
Ondatra zibethicus
MOUSE AND RAT FAMILY

L 23"; T 10". Fur rich brown, dense, glossy; belly silver. Tail long, scaly, blackish, vertically flattened, tapering to a point. Hindfeet partially webbed, larger than forefeet. Eyes and ears small. Excellent, steady swimmer, with head, back, and sculling tail visible. Mainly eats aquatic vegetation. **BREEDING** 2–3 litters of usu. 6–7 young a year Apr.–Sept. **SIGN** Conspicuous "lodge" of cattails, roots, and mud floats in marsh or other body of water; rises up to 3' above surface of water. Burrows in stream banks. Tracks: 2–3" narrow hindprint (5 toes print); smaller round foreprint; often with tail drag mark. **HABITAT** Fresh and salt marshes, ponds (even in urban areas), rivers, canals. **ACTIVITY** Day and night; lodge-bound on coldest days.

COMMON PORCUPINE
Erethizon dorsatum
NEW WORLD PORCUPINE FAMILY

L 33"; T 8". Blackish; fur often has "frosted" look. Long wiry guard hairs on front half of body; up to 30,000 shorter, heavier, paler quills (hairs modified into sharp, mostly hollow spines) on front of body but mainly on rump and longish, rounded tail; underfur long, soft, wooly. Back high-arching. Legs short; soles of feet knobbed; claws long, curved. Walks pigeon-toed on ground. Makes squeals and grunts. Eats green plants, and twigs, buds, and bark of trees; sometimes damages wooden buildings and poles. **CAUTION** May lash out with spiny tail if approached too closely. **BREEDING** 1 young Apr.–June. **SIGN** Tooth marks on bark; irreg. patches of bark stripped from tree trunks and limbs. Tracks: inward-facing, up to 3" long; claw tips well forward. Scat: piles of variable-shaped pellets near crevice or base of feeding tree. **HABITAT** Woods, esp. spruce, hemlock, birch. **ACTIVITY** Mainly nocturnal, year-round. **RANGE** Uplands of NY and PA.

Carnivores

Members of the order Carnivora mainly eat meat, though many also eat a variety of fruit, berries, and vegetation. Carnivores vary greatly in size, from tiny weasels to massive bears. They have long canine teeth for stabbing prey, and most have sharp cheek teeth for slicing meat. None truly hibernates, but several den up in well-insulated logs and burrows, and sleep soundly during colder parts of the winter. Most live on land, although otters spend most of their time in water, and seals (introduced on page 365 with other marine mammals) haul out on land mainly for mating and giving birth. Most carnivores have a single yearly litter of offspring, which are born blind and receive many months, sometimes even a year or more, of parental care. Carnivore families in the Mid-Atlantic region include the bears, dogs (Coyote and foxes), weasels (Mink, skunks, and otters), raccoons, cats, and seals.

COMMON RACCOON
Procyon lotor
RACCOON FAMILY

L 32″; T 9″. Coat long and thick, grizzled grayish brown. Black mask below white eyebrow. Legs medium-length; paws buffy; flexible toes used for climbing trees and washing food. Tail ⅓ body length, thick, banded with black rings. Swims well; can run up to 15 mph. Omnivorous; feeds in upland and aquatic habitats; raids trash bins. **BREEDING** Usu. 4 young Apr.–May. **SIGN** Den in hollow tree or crevice. Tracks: flat-footed; hindprint much longer than wide, 4″; foreprint rounded, 3″; claws show on all 5 toes. **HABITAT** Woods and scrub near water; towns. **ACTIVITY** Mainly nocturnal, but sometimes seen in daytime. Winter: dens up; active in milder periods.

COYOTE
Canis latrans
DOG FAMILY

H 25″; L 4′; T 13″. Coat long, coarse; grizzled gray, buffy, and black. Muzzle long, narrow; ears rufous. Tail bushy, black-tipped. Runs up to 40 mph. Eats small mammals, birds, frogs, snakes. 20th-century invader from w U.S. Usually not dangerous to humans, but known to attack pets. **VOICE** Barks, howls, series of *yip* notes followed by wavering howl. **BREEDING** 4–8 pups in Apr. **SIGN** 24″ den mouths on slopes. Tracks: in nearly straight line; foreprint larger, 2⅜″ long. Scat: dog-like, usu. full of hair. **HABITAT** Woods, brushy fields, edges of towns. **ACTIVITY** Mainly nocturnal, year-round.

RED FOX
Vulpes vulpes
DOG FAMILY

H 15″; L 3′2″; T 14″. Rusty orange above, whitish below; lower legs black. Muzzle narrow; large ears pointed, black. Tail bushy, white-tipped. Eats rodents, rabbits, birds, insects, berries, fruit. Has strong scent. Native and introduced English stock now intermixed. Numbers increasing. **VOICE** Short yap, long howls. **BREEDING** 1–10 young Mar.–Apr. **SIGN** Den often a Woodchuck burrow on a rise, entrance enlarged to 3′. Tracks: slightly larger foreprint 2⅛″ long; 4 toe pads. **HABITAT** Brushy and open areas. **ACTIVITY** Mainly nocturnal, year-round; often also by day in winter.

COMMON GRAY FOX
Urocyon cinereoargenteus
DOG FAMILY

H 14″; L 3′; T 13″. Grizzled silvery gray above; throat, midbelly white; collar, lower sides, legs, sides of tail rusty; top and tip of tail black. Eats rabbits, rodents, birds, grasshoppers, fruit, berries. Climbs trees. Declining; being replaced by more adaptable Red Fox in many areas. **BREEDING** 2–7 young in summer. **SIGN** Den hidden in natural crevice in woods; often has snagged hair, bone scraps near entrance. Tracks: foreprint 1½″ long; hindprint slightly narrower. **HABITAT** Wooded and brushy areas. **ACTIVITY** Day or night, but secretive; year-round.

BLACK BEAR
Ursus americanus
BEAR FAMILY

waking from winter sleep

H 3′4″; L 5′; T 4″; male much larger than female. Black, long-haired; some have white patch on chest. Muzzle long, brownish; ears short, rounded. Eats more vegetation than most carnivores; eats inner layer of tree bark, fruit, plants, fish, honeycombs, insects in rotten logs, and vertebrates, incl. small mammals. Powerful swimmer and climber; can run up to 30 mph. Region's largest carnivore. Numbers increasing; spreading closer to suburbs. **CAUTION** Do not feed, approach, or get between one and its food or cubs; will usu. flee, but can cause serious injury. Campers must firmly seal up food. **BREEDING** Usu. 2 cubs, about ½ lb at birth, born in den Jan.–Feb. **SIGN** Torn-apart stumps, turned-over boulders, torn-up burrows, hair caught on shaggy-barked trees. Tracks: foreprints 5″ wide; hindprints to 9″ long. Scat: dog-like. **HABITAT** Upland woods, swamps, dumps. **ACTIVITY** Mainly nocturnal, but often out in daytime; semi-hibernates in colder regions. **RANGE** e NY, nw NJ, most of PA, w MD, e WV, w VA; also Dismal Swamp of se VA.

female with cub

STRIPED SKUNK
Mephitis mephitis
WEASEL FAMILY

L 24″; T 9″. Coat thick, fluffy, mainly black; large white nape patch continues as 2 stripes along sides of back, usu. reaching tail (occ. mostly white above); narrow white forehead stripe. Head pointed; ears and eyes small. Legs short; tail long, very bushy. Eats insects, rodents, bird and turtle eggs, fruit, roadkills, garbage. **CAUTION** If threatened, raises tail, backs up, may stomp ground; may very quickly emit foul-smelling, sulphurous spray that travels to 15′, stings eyes of predators, pets, humans. **BREEDING** 6–7 young in May. **SIGN** Strong musky odor if one has sprayed or been run over recently, scratched-up lawns and garbage bags. Tracks: round 1″ foreprint; hindprint broader at front, flat-footed, 1½″. **HABITAT** Woods, fields, farmlands, towns. **ACTIVITY** Dusk to dawn; dens up and sleeps much of winter in colder areas.

Rabies
Rabies is a serious viral disease that is carried and can be transmitted by some bats, foxes, raccoons, and skunks, as well as domestic animals; it can make humans deathly ill. Infected animals may be agitated and aggressive, or fearless and lethargic; nocturnal animals who are diseased may roam about fearlessly in daytime. As the disease drives infected individuals to try to bite others, rabid animals must be avoided. Stay away from any animal that is acting strangely, and report it to animal-control officers. The disease, which attacks the central nervous system, has an incubation period of 10 days to a year. If you are bitten by a possibly rabid animal, you must immediately consult a doctor for a series of injections that will save your life. There is no cure once symptoms emerge.

SHORT-TAILED WEASEL
"Ermine"
Mustela erminea
WEASEL FAMILY

L 11"; T 3"; female much smaller. Summer: brown above; underparts, insides of legs, feet white; tail has black tip. Winter: white, with black tail tip. Tail fairly long but not bushy. Expert mouser; also takes rabbits, birds, frogs, insects. Tireless, active hunter. Less common in region than Long-tailed Weasel. **BREEDING** 4–9 young in Apr. **SIGN** Spiral scat along trails. Tracks: similar to Long-tailed Weasel's, but slightly smaller. **HABITAT** Woods, brush, fields, wetlands. **ACTIVITY** Day and night, year-round. **RANGE** NY, PA, n NJ, n MD.

LONG-TAILED WEASEL
Mustela frenata
WEASEL FAMILY

L 16"; T 5"; female much smaller. Brown above, white below; feet and outside of legs brown. Tail has black tip; slightly longer than Short-tailed Weasel's. Many northern and montane individuals develop white winter coat Nov.–Mar., but retain black tail tip. Wraps sinewy body around prey; kills by biting base of skull. Good swimmer, climber. **BREEDING** 6–8 young Apr.–May. **SIGN** Cache of dead rodents under log; drag marks in snow. Tracks: hindprint ¾" wide, 1" long; foreprint a bit wider, about half as long. **HABITAT** Woods, brush, fields. **ACTIVITY** Day and night, year-round.

MINK
Mustela vison
WEASEL FAMILY

L 21″; T 7″; female smaller. Lustrous blackish brown above and below; chin white. Muzzle pointed; ears tiny. Tail fairly long, bushy. (Weasels are smaller, paler, white below; have thinner tails.) Swims often; eats fish, birds, rodents, frogs; often travels far in search of food. **BREEDING** 3–4 young Apr.–May. **SIGN** Holes in snow, where mink has pounced on vole; 4″ burrow entrance in stream bank. Tracks: round, 2″, in snow. **HABITAT** Freshwater ponds and shores, woodlots, coastal marshes. **ACTIVITY** Late afternoon to morning, year-round; dens up in coldest, stormiest periods. **Fisher** *(Martes pennanti)* is larger (L 3′; T 12″), bulkier, warmer brown, with bushier tail; mainly eats porcupines (rarely fish).

NORTHERN RIVER OTTER
Lutra canadensis
WEASEL FAMILY

L 3′ 7″; T 16″. Fur dense, dark brown, often silvery on chin and chest. Ears and eyes small. Legs short; feet webbed. Tail long, thick-based, tapering to a point. Swims rapidly, stops with head raised out of water. Eats fish, frogs, turtles, and muskrats. Runs well on land; loves to exercise and play; wanders widely. **BREEDING** Mates in water; 2–3 young born blind but furred in Apr. **SIGN** 12″-wide slides on sloping, muddy riverbanks in flat areas; vegetation flattened in large patch for rolling, feeding, defecating; trails between bodies of water. Tracks: 3¼″ wide, toes fanned. **HABITAT** Clean rivers, wood-edged ponds, lakes; occ. coastal estuaries. **ACTIVITY** Day and night, year-round.

BOBCAT
Lynx rufus
CAT FAMILY

H 20"; L 3'; T 5". Orange-brown in summer, paler grayish in winter; underparts and insides of long legs white; all variably spotted and barred with black. Face wide and flat; black lines radiate onto facial ruff; ears slightly tufted, backsides black. Very short (bobbed) tail. Stalks and ambushes mammals and birds at night. **VOICE** Yowls and screams, though mostly silent. **BREEDING** Usu. 2 young in May. **SIGN** Tracks in snow at scent posts and scratching trees. Tracks: like domestic cats, but 2" vs. 1". **HABITAT** Woods, swamps. **ACTIVITY** Mainly nocturnal, year-round. **RANGE** Entire region, ex. s coastal plain; rare.

Hoofed Mammals

Most hoofed mammals worldwide are in the order Artiodactyla, the even-toed ungulates. (Ungulates are mammals that have hooves, an adaptation for running. The order Perissodactyla—the odd-toed ungulates: horses, zebras, rhinos, tapirs—has no extant native species in the United States.) Even-toed ungulates have a split, two-part hoof (actually two modified toes) and two small dewclaws (vestigial toes) above the hoof on the rear of the leg. Their lower incisors are adapted for nipping or tearing off vegetation, their molars for grinding it. Most hastily swallow their food, which is stored temporarily in the first, largest compartment of their four-chambered stomachs; the food then passes to the second stomach, where it is shaped into small pellets of partly digested plant fiber (the cud). While the animal is at rest, the cud is returned to the mouth, slowly chewed to pulp, and swallowed; it then passes through all four chambers of the stomach. This process allows an animal to feed quickly, reducing its exposure to predators, and afterward chew its cud in a concealed spot.

The deer family (Cervidae) is the only family of wild hoofed mammals extant in the Mid-Atlantic region. Members of the cattle family (Bovidae), which includes domestic cows, goats, and sheep, have permanent horns that stay on and grow continuously. Those in the deer family have paired bony antlers that grow, usually only on males, during the summer, at which time they are soft and tender, and covered with a fine-haired skin ("velvet") containing a network of blood vessels that nourishes the growing bone beneath. By late summer, the antlers reach full size, and the velvety skin dries up, loosens, and peels off. The bare antlers then serve as sexual ornaments; rival males may use them as weapons in courtship battles in fall. During winter, the antlers fall off; the animal grows a new pair the next summer. As long as an individual has an adequate diet, its antlers become larger and have more points each year until it reaches maturity.

female and fawns (top), male (bottom)

WHITE-TAILED DEER
Odocoileus virginianus
DEER FAMILY

H 3′3″; L 6′; T 12″; male ⅓ heavier than female. Rich reddish brown in summer, gray-brown in winter. Ring around nose, eye ring, throat, mid-belly, and underside of tail white. Ears large; nose and hooves black. Summer male develops antlers with main beam curving out and up, points issuing from it. Fawn reddish orange, with many white spots. Communicates danger by loud whistling snort; flees with white undertail prominently erected. Can run 35 mph, clear 8′ tall obstacles, leap 30′. Host, with White-footed Mouse, of Lyme disease tick and bacterium. Wipes out many native plants (and their butterflies) when allowed to overpopulate in areas free of predators and hunting. **BREEDING** Mates Oct.–Nov.; bucks with swollen necks wander widely to find receptive does. Usu. 1–2 fawns in late spring; nibble greens at 2–3 weeks; weaned at 4 months. **SIGN** Raggedly browsed vegetation along well-worn trails; "buck rubs" where male rubs bark off trees with antlers; flattened beds in grass or snow. Tracks: "split hearts," with narrow, pointed end forward, 2–3″ long; dots of dewclaws behind. Scat: ¾″ cylindrical dark pellets. **HABITAT** Broadleaf and mixed woods and woodland edges, fields, watersides, gardens, coastal scrub. **ACTIVITY** Day and night, year-round.

Marine Mammals

North American marine mammals—the seals, sea lions, and Walrus of the order Carnivora, and the whales, porpoises, and dolphins of the order Cetacea—mainly live in ocean waters, although a few species enter estuaries.

Seals are covered with fine dense fur and insulating layers of fat; their legs have been modified into front and rear flippers. The only common seal in the Mid-Atlantic region belongs to the hair seal family (Phocidae), whose members have no external ear flaps, only small orifices, and rear flippers that are permanently turned backward; their fore and rear flippers have "fingernails." Fast swimmers, they move in a slow, clumsy fashion on land, propelled solely by muscular contractions of the body and dragging their rear flippers; whenever possible, they roll or slide on ice. Seals spend weeks at sea, but haul out when near shore or when tending young. In the species accounts that follow, lengths given are from the tip of the snout to the tip of the tail.

Cetaceans (dolphins, porpoises, and whales) have thick hairless skin and insulating layers of blubber. Their front legs have been modified into flippers. The tail ends in wide, horizontally flattened flukes, used for propulsion. They breathe through one or two nostrils (blowholes) on the top of the head; the cloud of vapor exhaled is called a spout or a blow. In some species, the shape, size, or pattern of the blow is an identifying characteristic. Cetaceans can dive deep and swim fast; larger species can remain submerged for lengthy periods—sperm whales can stay under for more than an hour. Most smaller species prey on large fish, while many of the larger whales instead use broom-like structures (called baleen) in the mouth to strain the water for schools of smaller fish and shrimp-like krill. The baleen whales have throat grooves (pleats) that expand when the animal takes in a vast amount of water and prey, and contract as water strains out. Cetaceans never haul out on land, except when ill or dying; young are born live in the water. In the species accounts, lengths given are from the tip of the snout to the end of the tail flukes.

Most cetacean species occur in waters off the Mid-Atlantic region somewhat erratically; their presence depends on the availability of food. In summer, some Humpback, Fin, and Minke Whales may be seen well offshore. These species pass through these waters in April and May and between October and December as they migrate between their New England and eastern Canadian feeding grounds and their tropical calving waters.

Party fishing boats and whale-watching boats (departing from ports on Long Island, the New Jersey shore, the Delmarva Peninsula, and lower Chesapeake Bay) offer opportunities for spotting whales and dolphins as well as various seabirds and other surface marine life, such as seals, sharks, Ocean Sunfish, and marine turtles.

HARBOR SEAL
Phoca vitulina
HAIR SEAL FAMILY

5′. Heavy; appears neck-less. Yellowish gray mottled with dark spots and whitish rings; pale silvery when dry; enormous individual color variation. Short, dog-like muzzle on wide face; V-shaped nostrils; large, round, black eyes; no external ear flaps. When in water, can be noisy (snorts, growls, barks, grunts), playful, shy but curious. Feeds in incoming and high tides on fishes, crustaceans, mollusks; may follow fish runs up to 10 miles inland on major rivers. **HABITAT** Coastal waters, rivers near sea. Hauls out at low tide on rocks, jetties, beaches, mudflats, ice. **RANGE** Winter: off Long Is. Late winter, early spring: some southward to waters off e VA.

SADDLE-BACKED DOLPHIN
"Common Dolphin"
Delphinus delphis
OCEAN DOLPHIN FAMILY

8′. Back and flippers black; flanks gray or pale yellow in hourglass pattern; belly white. 2 white lines on forehead. Beak long, pointed. Dorsal fin swept-back, pointed. Travels in large parties; some jump high out of water; rides bow waves. **BREEDING** 1 young every 2–3 years. 3′ long at birth; family helpers push newborn to surface for first breath of air. **HABITAT** Open ocean. **RANGE** Mar.–Oct.: entire coast.

BOTTLE-NOSED DOLPHIN
Tursiops truncatus
OCEAN DOLPHIN FAMILY

10'. Gray above, paler on sides, whitish gray on throat and belly. Bump on forehead; beak fairly long and broad. Dorsal fin large, swept-back, pointed. Travels in small parties; curious, often friendly, very intelligent. Interacts with humans in wild; will ride ship's bow waves. In captivity, performs in aquarium shows. Feeds on fish, sometimes chases them onto shoreline. **BREEDING** 1 young every 2–3 years. 3' long at birth; family helpers push newborn to surface for first breath of air. **HABITAT** Shallow brackish inshore waters as well as open ocean. **RANGE** Warmer months: mainly south of c NJ.

LONG-FINNED PILOT WHALE
"Blackfish" "Common Pilot Whale"
Globicephala melas
OCEAN DOLPHIN FAMILY

20'; male much larger than female. All shiny black, with white chest patch. High bulging forehead above short protruding beak. Prominent, swept-back dorsal fin forward of body center. Flippers long, narrow, pointed. Tail fluke black, narrow. Strong herd instinct; often touches other individuals; entire pod (group) occ. follows leader blindly onto shallow beaches, with dozens or more becoming stranded and dying as tide goes out. Migrates north and south with seasons, feeding mainly on squid. **BREEDING** Mates May–Nov.; gestation 16 months; 1 young 6' at birth; nurses for 22 months. **HABITAT** Ocean, usu. well offshore. **RANGE** Apr.–Nov.: entire coast (uncommon).

FIN WHALE
Balaenoptera physalus
RORQUAL FAMILY

70'. Relatively slender; head flat. Brownish black above; white below. Dorsal fin small, swept-back, located ⁴/₅ of way back on body. Lower jaw white on right, blackish on left. Baleen plates unusually colored: all on left side and rear of right side dark; those on front of right side yellowish white. Has 50–80 throat grooves. Flippers fairly small. Tail fluke rarely seen. Swims on side when feeding. Fast swimmer. Does not breach like a Humpback. 2nd largest mammal on earth (after Blue Whale). **SIGN** Spout rises as 20' column; expands into ellipse. **HABITAT** Ocean, mainly offshore. **RANGE** Mainly Mar.–Nov.: entire coast. **Black (Northern) Right Whale** *(Balaena glacialis)*, 40', lacks dorsal fin; migrates well offshore between N. Engl. and Caribbean.

MINKE WHALE
Balaenoptera acutorostrata
RORQUAL FAMILY

25'. Streamlined, slender; head fairly small; snout pointed. Dark blue-gray above, white below. Baleen plates yellowish white; has about 50 throat grooves. Flippers pointed, fairly small; white central band above, white below. Dorsal fin located ⅔ of way back on body; broad-based; swept-back, with pointed, curved tip. Follows and swims under boats and ships, lifting head to look around. The smallest baleen whale. **SIGN** Spout single, short, with rounded vapor cloud. **HABITAT** Inshore and deep sea waters. **RANGE** Mainly Apr.–Dec.: entire coast.

mother and calf

HUMPBACK WHALE
Megaptera novaeangliae
RORQUAL FAMILY

40'. Blackish above, white below. Head adorned with fleshy bumps and barnacles; throat has about 25 massive grooves. Small hump just in front of leading edge of rounded dorsal fin; when diving, back angles down sharply after dorsal fin. Extremely long 15' white flippers with fleshy knobs along leading edge. Tail variously patterned, with white below; variations help researchers identify individuals (hundreds have been catalogued). Sometimes playful and active. Only large whale that regularly breaches (jumps clear out of water), rolls, then comes crashing down. Also rolls on surface from side to side, slapping long flippers, and performs head-down "lobtail," slapping flukes down. Creates cylindrical "net" of rising air bubbles deep down that confuses and walls in schools of small fish; whale then rises up with mouth open inside "net." Most popular target of whale-watching boats. **BREEDING** Gestation 1 year; 1 young, 16' at birth, born in tropics; stays with mother 1 year. **SIGN** Spout is expanding column up to 20' high. **HABITAT** Ocean, inshore and offshore. **RANGE** Apr.–Nov.: off Long Is.; migrates off rest of coast.

breaching

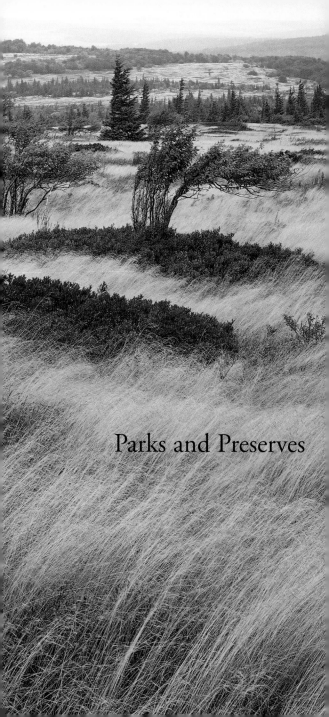

Parks and Preserves

Introduction

The Mid-Atlantic region is an area of outstanding beauty, enormous geographical and biological contrasts, and such North American superlatives as the largest waterfall (Niagara), biggest estuary (Chesapeake Bay), oldest river (New River), largest park not owned by the federal government (Adirondack), and most famous of

America's hiking trails (Appalachian). Home at various times to some of the world's outstanding naturalists—John Burroughs, Roger Tory Peterson, John James Audubon—this region boasts such superb scenic areas as Watkins Glen and Shenandoah Valley, such migratory bird hotspots as Hawk Mountain and Cape May, and such varied landscapes as the alpine summit of Mount Marcy and the mossdraped Bald Cypresses of the Great Dismal Swamp.

High Peaks from Mount Jo, Adirondack Park, New York

Hundreds of state forests, parks, wildlife management areas, and other designated natural areas, as well as municipal and privately owned preserves, combine with the federally managed national forests, recreation areas, wildlife refuges, parks, and seashores of the region to offer an enormous wealth of wildlife habitats.

This section provides introductions to 50 of the most important natural parks and preserves in the Mid-Atlantic region, plus annotated listings of dozens more. Mailing addresses and telephone numbers are given for all sites (most will send brochures and other information), and the general location is given for each of the 50 featured areas. Since fees and exact hours of operation change frequently, they are not included in the listings. Access to the areas is year-round, unless otherwise noted.

This guide highlights some of the most noteworthy plants and animals you may see as you visit parks and preserves throughout the region, but always ask if local lists of flora and fauna are available, as these can help verify identifications.

Important Bird Areas (IBAs) are sites where a significant population or exceptional diversity of birds occurs. IBAs are the focus of conservation strategies of National Audubon Society, working with other conservation groups, including American Bird Conservancy, and as a member of Partners in Flight. In the descriptions that follow, IBAs are noted.

Delaware

I-95 between Newark and Wilmington, at the northern end of the state, divides Delaware into its two main physiographic regions—the rolling hills of the piedmont to the north and the broad lowlands of the Atlantic coastal plain to the south. It is an uneven distribution of geography, as the piedmont barely has a foothold in the state; at its greatest breadth, the Delaware piedmont is a mere 10 miles wide. While much of northernmost Delaware is well populated, cultivated, and urbanized, there are corners of fine scenic splendor in the hills and parklands; Brandywine Creek State Park is an exceptional example. Pea Patch Island, near Wilmington, has the largest breeding colony of herons and egrets north of Florida.

The coastal plain of the Delmarva Peninsula comprises, in its northeastern quadrant, the rest of the 2,057 square miles of the state. This almost ubiquitous low relief is the backdrop for some of the state's most delightful natural areas, including the Delaware Bay wildlife sanctuaries at Bombay Hook, Little Creek, and Prime Hook, and 25 miles of Atlantic beaches, more than half the length of which are protected by Delaware Seashore and Cape Henlopen State Parks. Great masses of migrating and wintering swans, geese, and ducks descend upon the marshes, ponds, and agricultural lands of coastal Delaware in a yearly phenomenon that is much anticipated by birdwatchers and hunters alike. Surfcasters, sun lovers, sailors, and seafood fanciers keep the waters of Rehoboth, Indian River, and Assawoman Bays, as well as the sandy Atlantic beaches, well populated most of the year. Storm tides cast up Atlantic Surf Clams, sand dollars, and sea glass in varied hues.

Aside from the majestic Delaware River, which forms the state's northeastern boundary, and the Indian River, which drains a sizeable portion of its southeastern regions, Delaware's waterways tend to be small to medium-size. From north to south, they include the Christina, Appoquinimink, Leipsic, St. Jones, Mispillion, Broadkill, and Indian flowing eastward, and the Chester, Choptank, Marshyhope Creek, and Nanticoke running toward Chesapeake Bay in the west.

Delaware has two national wildlife refuges, 10 state parks, three state forests, and a number of other state-protected wild lands.

BRANDYWINE CREEK STATE PARK   Wilmington

This charming 1,000-acre park in Delaware's northernmost corner is in the lower reaches of the piedmont and has the region's characteristic rolling hills. The preserve takes up a tiny fraction of 1 percent of the Mid-Atlantic piedmont, yet Albert Radford, the renowned American botanist, called the forest here "the most beautiful high-canopied woody community in the entire Piedmont." Tulip Tree Trail wanders through this magnificent woodland, which supports the state's finest assemblage of upland bird species. In spring and fall, there are large numbers of warblers, flycatchers, grosbeaks, vireos, and other songbirds; watch for Eastern Bluebirds in open areas, migrant raptors from the hawk-watch area. The secretive Bog Turtle is sometimes seen along the freshwater marsh boardwalk in the park's southeastern corner. More than 300 wildflower species grow here in habitats ranging from marsh to meadow to tall broadleaf woods. Twelve miles of trails traverse the property.

LOCATION 3 miles north of Wilmington, at intersection of Rtes. 100 and 92. **CONTACT** Brandywine Creek S.P., Delaware Div. of Parks and Recreation, P.O. Box 3782, Wilmington, DE 19807; 302-577-3534. **VISITOR CENTER** Nature Center ⅔ mile past park entrance.

BOMBAY HOOK
NATIONAL WILDLIFE REFUGE   Smyrna

If you are not a birder when you arrive in early morning at Bombay Hook National Wildlife Refuge, you may well be by noon. More than 300 species of birds have been seen here. This remarkable refuge provides fine access to its 16,000 acres of marshland, tidal flats, impoundments, crop-

lands, and woods. A 12-mile round-trip auto tour on dirt roads and dikes passes alongside or through the sanctuary's varied habitats. Three large impoundments—Bear Swamp, Shearness Pool, and Raymond Pool, totaling 1,200 acres—have nature trails and observation towers. From fall through spring, expect to see thousands of Snow and Canada Geese, teals, American Wigeons, mergansers, scaups, and just about every other duck. In winter, Rough-legged Hawks and Short-eared Owls fly over the marshes. Summer brings shorebirds (most southbound migrants) and lots of mosquitoes. In June, Diamondback Terrapins lay eggs on the dikes.

LOCATION Whitehall Neck Rd., off Rte. 9, 6 miles north of Leipsic. **CONTACT** Bombay Hook N.W.R., U.S. Fish and Wildlife Svc., RD 1, Box 147, Smyrna, DE 19977; 302-653-9345. **VISITOR CENTER** On Whitehall Neck Rd., near refuge entrance.

LITTLE CREEK WILDLIFE AREA — Little Creek

Black-necked Stilts

Visitors will want to explore all three of this 4,500-acre preserve's roads. Less than a mile east of Route 9, along Port Mahon Road, turn right on the gravel road to the north impoundment and its wealth of birdlife: terns, herons, egrets, and Black-necked Stilts in summer, Northern Harriers, falcons, ducks, and geese from fall to spring. The main entrance road leads to a boardwalk and observation tower overlooking the south impoundment; at migration times, especially early spring, waterfowl concentrations here can be impressive. Pickering Beach Road provides another access point for overlooking the south impoundment; at its terminus there are often good numbers of bay ducks and gulls in season. Little Creek is 8 miles south of Bombay Hook National Wildlife Refuge (see opposite). The two locales complement each other: each has its own mix of species, and while Bombay Hook has optimal lighting conditions in the morning, at Little Creek the light is best in the afternoon.

LOCATION 3 access roads off Rte. 9: Port Mahon Rd., the main entrance, and Pickering Beach Rd. **CONTACT** Little Creek W.A., Delaware Div. of Fish and Wildlife, 89 Kings Hwy., Dover, DE 19901; 302-739-5297.

DELAWARE SEASHORE AND CAPE HENLOPEN STATE PARKS — Rehoboth Beach and Lewes

These parks, which protect seaside lagoons, flats, thickets, dunes, and beaches, are at their natural best from fall through spring. In autumn, watch for flights of songbirds and hawks; the great autumn concentrations that build up at Cape May, New Jersey, make their first landfall after crossing Delaware Bay in the Virginia Pines and bayberries here. Winter brings Yellow-rumped Warblers, Savannah Sparrows, Snow Buntings, and Lapland Longspurs along the dunes and open scrubby areas. Oldsquaws, Greater Scaups, Common Goldeneyes, Brants, and Great and Double-crested Cormorants fly offshore. The fishing pier at Cape Henlopen is excellent for sea casting and birdwatching. In spring, watch for arriving breeding birds—Common and Least Terns and Piping Plovers—and migrating shorebirds.

LOCATION Delaware Seashore S.P.: off Rte. 1, 2 miles south of Rehoboth Beach. Cape Henlopen S.P.: east of Lewes on Rte. 9. **CONTACT** Delaware Seashore S.P., Delaware Div. of Parks and Recreation, Inlet 850, Rehoboth Beach, DE 19971; 302-227-2800. Cape Henlopen S.P., 42 Cape Henlopen Dr., Lewes, DE 19958; 302-645-8983. **VISITOR CENTER** At Cape Henlopen Seaside Nature Center on main park road.

GREAT CYPRESS SWAMP   Selbyville

Located along the Delaware–Maryland border, this 11,000-acre swampland (known as Pocomoke Swamp in Maryland) is truly southern in nature, with Barred Owls and elusive Swainson's Warblers. **CONTACT** Great Cypress Swamp, Delaware Div. of Fish and Wildlife, 4876 Hay Point Landing, Smyrna, DE 19977; 302-653-2880.

KILLENS POND STATE PARK   Felton

The 2.5-mile Pondside Nature Trail traverses tall woodlands of Yellow Poplar and Loblolly Pine. The millpond itself has Northern River Otters and many Pickerel and Largemouth Bass. **CONTACT** Killens Pond S.P., 525 Killens Pond Rd., Felton, DE 19943; 302-284-4526.

LUMS POND STATE PARK   Bear

Some 1,200 acres of woodlands, lake, and fields, with resident raccoons, beavers, and woodchucks, are accessible via uncrowded footpaths and an equestrian trail. **CONTACT** Lums Pond S.P., Delaware Div. of Parks and Recreation, 1068 Howell School Rd., Bear, DE 19701; 302-368-6989.

Lums Pond State Park

ROBERT L. GRAHAM/NANTICOKE WILDLIFE AREA   Laurel

The Nanticoke River, running southwest from Delaware to the Chesapeake Bay, is a canoeist's delight, with fine Loblolly and Virginia Pines and great beds of Wild Rice and its attendant bird life. The wildlife area has 2,500 acres. **CONTACT** Robert L. Graham/Nanticoke W.A., Delaware Div. of Fish and Wildlife, P.O. Box 1401, Dover, DE 19903; 302-739-5297.

NORMAN G. WILDER WILDLIFE AREA   Viola

This area of upland forest and dense shrub growth has lofty oaks of several species and fine stands of American Holly. **CONTACT** Norman G. Wilder W.A., Delaware Div. of Fish and Wildlife, P.O. Box 1401, Dover, DE 19903; 302-739-5297.

PEA PATCH ISLAND   Delaware City

Weekend ferries serve this 161-acre park, summer home to thousands of breeding herons, egrets, and ibises in one of the country's largest rookeries. **CONTACT** Pea Patch Is., Ft. Delaware State Park, Delaware Div. of Parks and Recreation, P.O. Box 170, Delaware City, DE 19706; 302-834-7941.

PRIME HOOK NATIONAL WILDLIFE REFUGE   Milford

You have to try a little harder at this 88,000-acre refuge, which has no developed loop roads for automobiles, but the rare birds, such as Sedge Wrens and Black Rails, as well as thousands of Snow Geese, compensate your efforts. **CONTACT** Prime Hook N.W.R., U.S. Fish and Wildlife Svc., RD 3, Box 195, Milton, DE 19968; 302-684-8419.

TRAP POND STATE PARK   Laurel

Twelve species of oaks and one of the northernmost stands of Bald Cypress add to the outstanding variety of trees in this 2,300-acre park. Small mammals (foxes, otters, beavers) and amphibians and reptiles (salamanders, treefrogs, chorus frogs, bog turtles) are common. You may also see rare wood warblers here. **CONTACT** Trap Pond S.P., Delaware Div. of Parks and Recreation, Rte. 2, Box 331, Laurel, DE 19956; 302-875-5153.

Trap Pond State Park

Maryland

Straight along some borders and a cartographer's nightmare along others, Maryland is not large (10,460 square miles) but exhibits great geographic contrast. Beginning in the westernmost panhandle, the highest of Maryland's provinces is the Allegheny Plateau, which averages 2,500 feet and tops off at 3,360-foot Backbone Mountain, within hollering distance of West Virginia; state parks and forests protect much of the picturesque land here. The North Branch Potomac and the wild Youghiogheny are the region's main rivers. To the east is the ridge and valley province, with narrow valleys, oak-hickory forests, and elevations up to about 2,000 feet. To the east again, and spreading southward to the fall line, which ranges from Elkton through Baltimore to Washington, D.C., is Maryland's piedmont area, where pine-oak woodlands and farmlands are commonplace, as is suburban and commercial development. The Susquehanna, Patuxent, and Potomac Rivers run northwest to southeast across the province toward Chesapeake Bay.

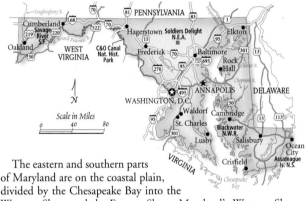

The eastern and southern parts of Maryland are on the coastal plain, divided by the Chesapeake Bay into the Western Shore and the Eastern Shore. Maryland's Western Shore (of the bay) is moderately elevated and around Calvert Cliffs a good place for fossil hunting. The Eastern Shore makes up much of the Delmarva Peninsula and has 31 miles of Atlantic shoreline, blackwater swamps, national wildlife refuges, and scenic rivers—the Elk, Chester, Choptank, Nanticoke, and Pocomoke—flowing southwest into the bay.

Chesapeake Bay has 4,000 miles of shoreline. The freshwater and salt marshes and shallow waters of the Chesapeake's 150 tributaries pour forth their biological richness into the Bay, which in turn nurtures and supports myriad animals. As a coastal fishery the Chesapeake Bay knows no equal—more than half of the Soft-shelled Clams and Blue Crabs, as well as a fifth of the oysters, harvested in the nation come from these waters. Millions of birds winter here, where the feeding is great and waters remain ice-free.

Maryland has four national wildlife refuges, 37 wildlife management areas, 38 state parks, and six state forests.

BLACKWATER
NATIONAL WILDLIFE REFUGE   Cambridge

Blackwater National Wildlife Refuge, in common with all of the prominent coastal reserves in the Mid-Atlantic region, is a superb place to see bird life. On the refuge's more than 20,000 acres, plus surrounding marshlands, pinewoods, and islands, visitors are sure to see great numbers of birds from fall to spring. Even in summer, this can be a birdwatcher's delight—more than 20 pairs of Bald Eagles nest in the vicinity, and perhaps 10 inhabit the refuge proper.

The magnificent sprawling freshwater to brackish marshes of this Eastern Shore locale are home to skulking rails and furtive sparrows that determined long-time birders seek out at special times of the year, but the main attraction for nature lovers of all ages and experience is the concentration of waterfowl during the cooler months. From mid-October to late November and again from mid-February to late March, the refuge is flooded with thousands upon thousands of ducks and geese. The greatest numbers are in large flocks of Canada Geese, Mallards, American Black Ducks, American Wigeons, and Green-winged Teals, but also expect to see Northern Shovelers, Gadwalls, and Northern Pintails. Dabbling or "puddle" ducks and geese are much more frequent here than diving ducks.

Visit the Wildlife Interpretive Center to get oriented before setting out on 5-mile Wildlife Drive. Every pond and trail along the way is likely to have much of interest. The very first pond along the drive is often as good as any on the refuge for a diversity of waterfowl, while the nature trail just beyond the pond leads to Loblolly Pine woods, home to noisy, nervous Brown-headed Nuthatches. In all of the sanctuary's woodlands, watch for endangered Delmarva Peninsula Fox Squirrels, which have their largest population here. Muskrats and Nutrias are common in the marshes.

Canada Geese

Watch low over the marshes and overhead, as well as on snags, for avian predators—this is an outstanding raptor refuge. Expect to see Ospreys, Turkey Vultures, Northern Harriers, Cooper's and Sharp-shinned Hawks, Bald Eagles, and Short-eared Owls. Golden Eagles and Black Vultures occur regularly. Shorter's Wharf Road, immediately east of Blackwater, and the Hooper's Island complex to the southwest are both outstanding for varied bird life.

LOCATION 12 miles south of Cambridge on Key Wallace Dr. CONTACT Blackwater N.W.R., 2145 Key Wallace Dr., Cambridge, MD 21613; 410-228-2677. VISITOR CENTER Wildlife Interpretive Center.

ASSATEAGUE ISLAND NATIONAL SEASHORE

Berlin

Barrier islands are reconfigured by the powerful Atlantic Ocean on an unfathomable time schedule. Hurricanes, winter and spring storms, and the daily flow of the tides combine through the days, months, and years to move sand with dramatic surges or minute pulses. This unpredictable dynamism makes these islands fascinating to revisit again and again.

Assateague Island, at 37 miles, is the longest barrier island on the Delmarva Peninsula. Its miles of uninhabited beaches, dense bayberry and wax-myrtle thickets, dunes, and broad salt marshes make it one of the region's most desirable natural destinations.

The northern two-thirds of the island, including Assateague Island State Park near the northern end, are in Maryland, while the southern third of Assateague belongs to Virginia. (The Virginia portion of the island is featured in the description of Chincoteague National Wildlife Refuge on page 416.) It is a 55-mile drive on the mainland from one end of the island to the other. Here we concentrate on the northern sections.

Upon crossing the Sinepuxent Bay bridge, your first decision will be whether to drive straight ahead to the state park (from which it is a 6-mile walk north along the beautiful beach to Ocean City Inlet) or to drive south along Bayberry Drive to the National Seashore parking area, campground, and ranger station. From this spot, there is a wooden walkway across the dunes to the ocean strand. Scan the ocean for Bottle-nosed Dolphins, Brown Pelicans, and, in winter, Northern Gannets and other seabirds. Shell collecting and beachcombing are good at the seashore, and sometimes excellent after a heavy blow. Birdwatching is invariably rewarding, perhaps best in fall; the falcon migration can be particularly good.

Many seashore visitors come to see the island's wild ponies, which roam freely and often prefer the breezy, mosquito-free open beaches in summer. Fishermen will find Striped and Channel Bass, White Perch, Atlantic Croaker, and Black Drum.

Canoeing is a wonderful way to explore the leeward side of Assateague, and many visitors enjoy wilderness camping, but you must make plans in advance. Contact seashore officials about boating and camping regulations, suggestions, and precautions. (Mosquitoes, in particular, can be horrendous in the marshes.) Rangers lead daily nature walks during the summer months and regularly give campfire talks and slide programs for evening and overnight visitors.

LOCATION Rte. 611, 8 miles south of Ocean City. **CONTACT** Assateague Is. N.S., National Park Svc., 7206 National Seashore Lane, Berlin, MD 21811; 410-641-1441. **VISITOR CENTER** On mainland side of Rte. 611.

SAVAGE RIVER STATE FOREST   Grantsville

In far western Maryland—where the terrain rises in great folds and the land is forested and, in places, quite rugged and challenging—lie the 53,000 acres of Savage River State Forest, which includes two state parks, New Germany and Big Run. The parks offer picnicking, boating, camping, and other activities. The state forest lands outside the parks, much less used by humans, range in elevation from 1,300 to 3,075 feet and are covered with a beautiful forest of deciduous oaks, hickories, birches, and maples, as well as evergreen hemlocks and pines. Turkeys, grouse, deer, raccoons, beavers, and Bobcats are a few of the larger woodland denizens. Hiking trails include Meadow Mountain Overlook, a 1½-mile round-trip stroll for families and picnickers; 6-mile-long Monroe Run, connecting New Germany Road to Big Run State Park; and Big Savage Trail, 17 miles long and with challenging stretches.

LOCATION South of Interstate 68 on New Germany Rd. **CONTACT** Savage River S.F., Dept. of Natural Resources, Maryland Forest, Park, and Wildlife Svc., 349 Headquarters La., Grantsville, MD 21536; 301-895-5759.

CHESAPEAKE AND OHIO CANAL   Cumberland, MD,
NATIONAL HISTORICAL PARK   to Washington, D.C.

From the Maryland panhandle mountains of Cumberland south and east to the tidewater landscape of Washington, D.C., the 184-mile cartpath paralleling the Chesapeake and Ohio Canal constitutes one of the finest strolling and bicycling trails in the nation. In the late 1800s this park was a vital working canal; some 50,000 tons of coal, grain, and lumber moved through the locks daily. Today most of the canal is filled with vegetation, and the 12-foot-wide, packed-dirt towpath is the main attraction. Naturalists will have to share the park with bicyclists, joggers, and rollerbladers, but there are enough miles of quiet pathway to satisfy most photographers, botanists, and birdwatchers. The area around Great Falls Tavern, about 10 miles northwest of Washington, is the most heavily utilized. If your tastes run to larkspurs, orioles, and Zebra Swallowtails, try a more serene section, such as south toward Old Angler's Inn and beyond to Carderock.

LOCATION Many access points between Cumberland, MD, (north) and Washington, DC (south). **CONTACT** Chesapeake and Ohio Canal N.H.P., National Park Svc., P.O. Box 4, Sharpsburg, MD 21782; 301-739-4200. **VISITOR CENTERS** At Cumberland, MD; Hancock, MD; Great Falls Tavern, Potomac, MD; Williamsport, MD; and Georgetown, in Washington, DC.

SOLDIERS DELIGHT NATURAL ENVIRONMENT AREA — Owings Mills

Botanists have long been fascinated by the small, isolated habitats known as serpentine barrens. The critical element of a serpentine barren is the soil, which contains high levels of magnesium, nickel, and the greenish mineral serpentine. Where moisture levels are low, these soils present a harsh living environment for most plants; only species adapted to barren life can survive. Maryland has four serpentine barrens, and Soldiers Delight is the largest. Although the flora of these barrens appears relatively impoverished, the plant life here comprises a number of interesting and rare species. Virginia Pine and Blackjack and Post Oaks are common trees on these 2,000 acres, which may be traversed on several miles of hiking trails. Look for the flowers of Serpentine Aster, Sandplain Gerardia, Appalachian Fameflower, and Blazing Star, as well as such grasses as Little Bluestem and Tufted Hairgrass. Raccoons, opossums, and foxes are sometimes seen.

LOCATION Deer Park Rd. in Owings Mills, northwest of Baltimore. **CONTACT** Soldiers Delight N.E.A., 5100 Deer Park Rd., Owings Mills, MD 21117; 410-922-3044. **VISITOR CENTER** On Deer Park Rd.

ROCK CREEK PARK — Washington, D.C.

First in the nation to be established by Congress (in 1890), this urban natural park contains the largest forested area in Washington, D.C. Its 2,100 acres, together with 4,400 additional acres in adjacent Rock Creek Regional Park in Maryland, feature steep ravines, fields, valleys, and ridgetops. The mature woodlands of Black Cherry, Northern Red Oak, White Oak, Yellow Poplar, and other tree species have been fragmented over the years, but still provide habitat for  a good variety of mammals and such impressive birds as Red-shouldered Hawks, Barred Owls, and Pileated Woodpeckers. During May, the ridge on the west side of Rock Creek between Military and Broad Branch Roads can be aswarm with wood warblers of two dozen species. There are any number of ways to explore Rock Creek. Ten miles of roads are driveable, but most of the wildlife and plant life is best appreciated outside an automobile. The park maintains 13 miles of hiking trails and 10 miles of bridal trails.

LOCATION Military Rd., off 16th St. NW. **CONTACT** Rock Creek Park, National Park Svc., 3545 Williamsburg La. NW, Washington, DC 20008; 202-282-1063. **VISITOR CENTERS** Visitor Information Center and Rock Creek Nature Center, both off Military Rd.

CALVERT CLIFFS STATE PARK
Lusby

Northward from Point Lookout, fossil hunting is very productive at this 1,300-acre park. Calvert Cliffs is perhaps the best spot, with 15-million-year-old sharks' teeth, seashells, and brachiopods. **CONTACT** Calvert Cliffs S.P., P.O. Box 48, Scotland, MD 20687; 301-872-5688.

CATOCTIN MOUNTAIN PARK
Hagerstown

Sharing 50 miles of beautiful hiking trails with neighboring Cunningham Falls State Park, this 5,770-acre tract features tall Chestnut Oaks and hickories and outcrops of Catoctin greenstone. **CONTACT** Catoctin Mtn. Park, National Park Svc., 6602 Foxville Rd., Thurmount, MD 21788; 301-663-9388.

Catoctin Mountain Park

CEDARVILLE STATE FOREST
Waldorf

The forest, with more than 20 miles of equestrian and hiking trails through woodlands and beside streams and bogs, is a nice introduction to the natural communities of immense Zekiah Swamp, the largest freshwater swamp in the state. **CONTACT** Cedarville S.F., 11704 Fenno Rd., Upper Marlboro, MD 20772; 301-888-1410.

EASTERN NECK NATIONAL WILDLIFE REFUGE
Rock Hall

Resident Delmarva Peninsula Fox Squirrels, fall migrant hawks and butterflies, and flocks of wintering Tundra Swans highlight the natural year at this 2,300-acre island refuge. **CONTACT** Eastern Neck N.W.R., 1730 Eastern Neck Rd., Rock Hall, MD 21661; 410-639-7056.

GREEN RIDGE STATE FOREST
Cumberland

Visit one of the region's unique shale barrens, with its unusual plant life, or hike some of the 27-mile Green Ridge Trail, linking Pennsylvania and Virginia across Maryland's narrow panhandle. **CONTACT** Green Ridge S.F., HCR 13, Box 50, Flintstone, MD 21530-9525; 301-478-3124.

JANES ISLAND STATE PARK
Crisfield

The summertime ferry *Osprey* carries you to this 3,000-acre, undeveloped island of sweeping marsh grasses, bountiful seashells, and perhaps a glimpse of a Diamondback Terrapin. **CONTACT** Janes Island S.P., 26280 Alfred Lawson Dr., Crisfield, MD 21817; 410-968-1565.

SANDY POINT STATE PARK
Annapolis

A variety of habitats in a compact 800 acres supports diverse animal life, especially birds. Spring and fall hawk flights can be exceptional, and the spring flocks of up to 10,000 gulls have considerable variety. **CONTACT** Sandy Point S.P., 800 Revell Hwy., Annapolis, MD 21401; 410-974-2149.

SWALLOW FALLS STATE PARK
Oakland

Breathtaking mountain scenery, fine old hemlocks and pines, and the swirling, plunging Youghiogheny River make for an outstanding 300-acre natural area. **CONTACT** Swallow Falls S.P., Rte. 5, Box 2180, Oakland, MD 21550; 301-387-6938.

Swallow Falls State Park

New Jersey

There are three reasons why the World Series of Birding is held each May in New Jersey. First, the state attracts both southern and northern species of birds (as well as other animals and plants). Second, New Jersey's range of elevational and vegetational zones provides a variety of niches for migrants and breeding species. Third, the Garden Staters thought it up, so they get to be hosts. Even if this international competition had never existed, naturalists would flock to the bird migrations at Cape May, the horseshoe crab spectacle on Delaware Bay, the rare flowers, butterflies, reptiles, and amphibians of the Pine Barrens, the blizzards of Snow Geese at Brigantine, and the scenic Delaware Water Gap. While New Jersey is the nation's most densely populated and industrialized state, beyond the metropolitan areas are some of the region's choicest natural destinations.

About 20 percent of New Jersey, in the northwest, is highlands, with elevations ranging up to 1,803 feet at High Point. In this re-

gion are several series of ridges and valleys, and many glacial lakes and ponds. Northern butterflies and birds, such as the Arctic Skipper and Black-capped Chickadee, live here. To the southeast, in elevations ranging from several hundred feet to sea level, and north of a line that stretches from Trenton to Newark, is the New Jersey piedmont, another 20 percent of the state's land area; the Raritan River and its tributaries run through this part of the state.

Below the piedmont and comprising all of southern New Jersey is the coastal plain. The state's Pitch Pine–oak woodlands are not as extensive as they once were, nor are its coastal salt marshes, but the lowlands still hold large tracts of important habitats. Some of the most vital are protected in the Pine Barrens, a vast, sandy semiwilderness in south-central New Jersey, where, among 800 plant species, 100 have reached their northern range limits. Reptiles and amphibians occur here in outstanding variety. Coastal plain rivers include the Manasquan, Metedecank, Toms, Mullica, and Maurice.

Within New Jersey's 7,836 square miles are one national recreation area, four national wildlife refuges, 11 state forests, 37 state parks, 42 state natural areas, and 65 wildlife management areas.

CAPE MAY

A naturalist's mecca, Cape May is one of the outstanding birding areas in North America. What lures so many nature lovers to these 6 square miles? The answer has a great deal to do with geography. From July through November, hundreds of millions of birds stream south across North America. The migratory journeys of many species cover thousands of miles, with shorebirds, such as the familiar Sanderling, often flying south as far as the uttermost shorelines of Patagonia. Connecticut Warblers spend their winters in the Amazon rain forest, Wood Thrushes in Central American jungles, American Robins in South Carolina crab apple trees. While birds may pass over any spot on the map, North America's greatest migratory concentrations tend to follow geographical landmarks such as coastlines, mountain ridges, and major river valleys. For southbound avian travelers, the Atlantic coastline is a wonderful visual guidepost.

Along the Mid-Atlantic coast there are two long, prominent southward-pointing peninsulas—Cape May, New Jersey, and Cape Charles, Virginia. As birds fly south in late summer and fall, following the eastern and western shorelines of New Jersey and the Delmarva Peninsula, the land constricts and focuses their flight paths. Eventually the funneling action of the convergent coastlines brings vast numbers of birds over the southernmost points of the two peninsulas. Cape May, because of its more varied habitats and history of migratory studies, has many more devotees than Cape Charles, at least for now.

Cape Island, which includes Cape May town, West Cape May, Lower Township, and Cape May Point, is commonly known as just Cape May. This southern tip of New Jersey is separated from the mainland by the Intracoastal Waterway. While any place in the area can have a sky full of Blue Jays, flickers, or hawks from before sunrise to dusk, there are four areas no naturalist should miss:

SOUTH CAPE MAY MEADOWS, located on the south side of Sunset Boulevard west of the town of Cape May, is a 180-acre preserve of the Nature Conservancy that protects open pasture land and dune vegetation. It is a fine area for shorebirds in late summer and fall, with unusual species such as Baird's and Buff-breasted Sandpipers and Lesser Golden-Plovers. The wet spots attract herons, egrets, and ibises, and year-round this is a good roosting area for gulls.

CAPE MAY POINT STATE PARK, 190 acres in extent, is the premier gathering place for hawks, hawk watchers, and all visitors to Cape May Point. Travel west on Sunset Boulevard from the meadows to Lighthouse Avenue, which leads to the park. The large parking area has an elevated hawk-watching platform at its east end; this  is where the official hawk counters sit, tallying up the daily, weekly, and seasonal totals of accipiters, buteos, falcons, vultures, Ospreys, and eagles. This is also where everyone else sits or stands and gazes at the vast numbers of birds of prey soaring, swooping, chasing, hovering, and gliding over the meadows and passing overhead or, in some cases, almost alongside the observers. As many as 89,000 raptors have been seen here in a single fall season. Ornithologists who operate an ongoing banding program between South Cape May Meadows and the state park give regular banding demonstrations and natural history talks, all with live birds of prey, near the hawk-watching platform. While at the park, take in the trails that lead through the marsh and out to the open beach.

CAPE MAY BIRD OBSERVATORY (NORTHWOOD CENTER), on East Lake Drive just north of the state park, offers outstanding natural history programs in botany, ornithology, insect study, and much more throughout the year.

HIGBEE BEACH WILDLIFE MANAGEMENT AREA, reached via Bayshore Road (across from the Meadows) and then left on New England Road, encompasses 416 acres and is a gem of a nature preserve. The fields, dunes, and woodlands here provide food and harbor for multitudes of migrant cuckoos, woodpeckers, flycatchers, thrushes, vireos, warblers, blackbirds, finches, and sparrows from late August into November. The raptor show is also exceptional. Butterfly populations are varied and exciting from spring though fall. Tiger Salamanders breed in a few shallow ponds, and American Woodcocks occur in large numbers late in the fall.

Higbee Beach

This description emphasizes fall attractions, but Cape May is a marvelous place for nature study year-round.

LOCATION New Jersey's southernmost tip. **CONTACT** Cape May Point S.P., P.O. Box 107, Cape May Point, NJ 08212; 609-884-2159. Cape May Bird Observatory, Northwood Ctr., 701 E. Lake Dr., Cape May Point, NJ 08212; 609-884-2736. **VISITOR CENTER** In Cape May Point S.P., in hdqtrs. bldg. at west side of parking lot.

EDWIN B. FORSYTHE NATIONAL WILDLIFE REFUGE, BRIGANTINE DIVISION

Oceanville

More than 40,000 acres of salt marsh, upland fields, woodlands, islands, ponds, and huge impoundments (pools) draw wildlife to this outstanding sanctuary, known as Brigantine. An 8-mile auto tour winds through the sanctuary's habitats and permits panoramic viewing of the salt marshes and pools. As you pass along the elevated dikes, look into the roadside channels, which harbor Green-winged and Blue-winged Teals, Northern Shovelers, Northern Pintails, Gadwalls, and other ducks from fall through spring. Check out the dikes themselves for Woolly Bear Caterpillars, which are on the march in mid-fall. The flowers along the dike edges, as well as elsewhere in the refuge, attract Black Swallowtails, Common Buckeyes, Red Admirals, American and Painted Ladies, and Monarchs.

A telescope is useful but not essential for exploring the vast expanses of Brigantine's marshes and pools. Binoculars alone can provide great looks at many shorebirds, including yellowlegs, Dunlins, dowitchers, and plovers; Forster's Terns and Black Skimmers; huge flocks of Snow and Canada Geese; Mute and Tundra Swans; Glossy Ibises; Little Blue and Tricolored Herons; Black-crowned Night-Herons; and swirling flocks of ducks and swallows, depending on the season. There are resident Peregrine Falcons, and the refuge is known as New Jersey's finest spot for wintering birds of prey.

After passing the large pools, watch for deer, hawks, and turtles along the edges of the roads and woods. The woods can be good for migrant songbirds and a few breeding species, such as the Eastern Towhee and Northern Cardinal. Wood Ducks, Pied-billed Grebes, and other fowl can be seen on the lily ponds near the refuge entrance. In a building at the first parking area is a book for recording interesting wildlife observations.

LOCATION East of Oceanville, on Great Creek Rd. **CONTACT** Edwin B. Forsythe N.W.R., Brigantine Div., Great Creek Rd., P.O. Box 72, Oceanville, NJ 08231-0072; 609-652-1665. **VISITOR CENTER** In hdqtrs. building.

GREAT SWAMP
NATIONAL WILDLIFE REFUGE   **Basking Ridge**

The Great Swamp is 7,355 acres of wilderness in the heart of America's densest metropolitan area. The eastern two-thirds of the refuge is a wilderness area, with no development except trails; the western portion is more carefully managed for plant and animal life. The area is mainly wetlands—swamps, ponds, and marshes—though there are also smaller sections of upland hardwood forest and pasturelands. A series of color-coded trails provides access to wildlife. The Orange Trail may be best for breeding birds, while the Red Trail is home to Pileated Woodpeckers and Eastern Bluebirds. Among the thickets, woodlands, and damp places, watch for muskrats, Striped Skunks, and the occasional river otter and Long-tailed Weasel. Herpetologists may see a Blue-spotted Salamander or Bog Turtle. Everyone should see Wood Ducks—there are more than 500 breeding pairs at Great Swamp.

LOCATION Pleasant Plains Rd., south of exit 26 of the Garden State Parkway. **CONTACT** Great Swamp N.W.R., R.D. 1, Box 152, Basking Ridge, NJ 07920; 973-425-1222. **VISITOR CENTER** Wildlife Observation Center, on Long Hill–New Vernon Rd.

WHARTON STATE FOREST   **Batsto**

The New Jersey Pine Barrens, of which 110,000-acre Wharton State Forest is a representative portion, is one of the East's great wilderness areas, a habitat for rare and familiar plants and animals. The soils are sandy and acidic, the dark streams acidic as well; the flora and fauna are species that have adapted to this relatively sterile environment. Before exploring the sandy back roads, check road conditions with the rangers in Batsto and get a map. Hikers can explore 50-mile Batona Trail, and four major canoe trails exist in the park. A patient observer might see some of 18 species of snakes. The region's best-known amphibian, the Pine Barrens Treefrog, is more often heard than seen, as is the more abundant Carpenter Frog. Over 90 species of butterflies inhabit the Pine Barrens. Spring is the prime season. Botanists may seek out 10 species of carnivorous plants, including three sundews, as well as Arethusa, Rose Pogonia, and other bog-loving orchids. Minks, beavers, and Northern River Otters are common in places.

LOCATION Off Rte. 542. **CONTACT** Wharton S.F., New Jersey State Park Svc., Batsto, R.D. 9, Hammonton, NJ 08037; 609-561-0024. **VISITOR CENTER** In historic Batsto Village; 609-561-3262.

GREAT BAY
WILDLIFE MANAGEMENT AREA   Tuckerton

The 4,000-acre Great Bay Wildlife Management Area comprises most of the area also known as the Tuckerton Marshes. From spring to fall this area is worth exploring. For botanists, there are saltmarsh asters, fleabanes, rushes and grasses, and Sea Lavender. Mammal watchers sometimes see red bats roosting in shrubbery or trying to avoid a Merlin in flight. Butterfliers find American Ladies and Juniper Hairstreaks along the 5-mile drive from the first bridge to the end of Great Bay Boulevard, but the most visible wildlife may be the wading birds and shorebirds that probe among the marsh grasses for invertebrates. Great Blue, Little Blue, Green, and Tricolored Herons, Black-crowned Night-Herons, Glossy Ibises, and Great and Snowy Egrets live here. Shorebirds include Willets, American Oystercatchers, sandpipers, dowitchers, yellowlegs, and plovers, and rarer species in late summer and fall.

LOCATION Great Bay Blvd. **CONTACT** Great Bay W.M.A., N.J. Div. of Fish, Game, and Wildlife, P.O. Box 400, Trenton, NJ 08625; 609-259-2132.

REED'S BEACH   Dennisville

Twice-daily high tides are strengthened twice a month by the moon's pull into "spring tides," the month's highest, which once a year carry ashore an amazing spectacle on Reed's Beach. Atlantic Horseshoe Crabs spend most of their lives in deep waters along the coast; during the second half of May, when tides are fullest, they migrate into shal-

Atlantic Horseshoe Crabs and gulls

low water in a few areas. Males, much smaller than females, cling to the latters' shells, and thousands upon thousands of these duos scuttle onto the beach and lay tens of millions of tiny green eggs before returning to the ocean. Great flocks of Ruddy Turnstones, Red Knots, Sanderlings, Semipalmated Sandpipers, and Laughing Gulls descend upon this buffet and gorge themselves, the shorebirds doubling their weight in two weeks' time. Reed's Beach, Moore's Beach (near Delmont), and the beach at Port Mahon Road (near Little Creek, Delaware) are all excellent places to see the horseshoe crab spectacle, as are four beaches south of Reed's Beach: Cook's Beach, Kimble's Beach, Pierce's Point, and Norbury's Landing.

LOCATION South of Dennisville, on Beach Ave. **CONTACT** Reed's Beach, N.J. Div. of Fish, Game, and Wildlife, 2201 County Rte. 631, Woodbine, NJ 08270; 609-628-2103.

ASSUNPINK WILDLIFE MANAGEMENT AREA   Hightstown
This 5,400-acre refuge is excellent for ducks in spring and fall. The fields are good for butterflies; the hedgerows are home to Blue Grosbeaks in summer. **CONTACT** Assunpink W.M.A., New Jersey Div. of Fish, Game, and Wildlife, 386 Clarksburg–Robbinsville Rd., Robbinsville, NJ 08691; 609-259-2132.

BENNETT BOGS PRESERVE   Lower Township, Cape May County
Bennett Bogs is an outstanding refuge for rare coastal plain pond flora. More than 250 species of plants have been found on these 25 acres, including the Pine Barren Gentian. **CONTACT** Nature Conservancy, Elizabeth D. Kay Environmental Ctr., 200 Pottersville Rd., Chester, NJ 07930; 908-879-7262.

GATEWAY NATIONAL RECREATION AREA, SANDY HOOK UNIT   Highlands
The 1,665 acres of "the Hook" are best visited outside the beach-going season. Visit for the American Holly forest, miles of beautiful beaches, and hordes of migrating birds. **CONTACT** Gateway N.R.A., Sandy Hook Unit, National Park Svc., P.O. Box 530, Sandy Hook, NJ 17732; 732-872-5970.

HIGH POINT STATE PARK   Sussex
At the state's northern tip, contiguous with Stokes State Forest (see below), these 13,400 wooded acres are home to beavers, warblers, and the state's highest peak (High Point) at 1,803 feet. **CONTACT** High Point S.P., New Jersey State Park Svc., 1480 Rte. 23, Sussex, NJ 07461; 201-825-4800.

High Point State Park

INSTITUTE WOODS/ROGERS REFUGE   Princeton
For May songbird-watching, there is no better area in New Jersey than these 550 acres. Warblers and other northbound migrants flow through in great variety and numbers. **CONTACT** Institute Woods/Rogers Refuge, Institute for Advanced Studies, Olden Lane, Princeton, NJ 08540; 609-734-8000.

KEARNY MARSH   Kearny
These 342 acres host the state's largest breeding populations of Least Bitterns, Pied-billed Grebes, and Ruddy Ducks. **CONTACT** Not a protected area; information available from Hackensack Meadowlands Commission, 1 DeKorte Park Plaza, Lyndhurst, NJ 07071; 201-460-1700.

MCNAMARA WILDLIFE MANAGEMENT AREA   Marmora
Locally known as Tuckahoe, this 13,300-acre site comprises fresh- and saltwater marshes, impoundments, and upland forest. See herons, shorebirds, and turtles here. **CONTACT** New Jersey Dept. of Fish and Wildlife, Land Mgmt. Div., P.O. Box 400, Trenton, NJ 08625; 609-292-2965.

PARVIN STATE PARK   Vineland
One of the state's loveliest parks, Parvin (1,135 acres) is great for botanizing and birdwatching. Look for Prothonotary Warblers in warmer months. **CONTACT** Parvin S.P., R.D. 1, Box 374, Elmer, NJ 08318; 609-358-8616.

STOKES STATE FOREST   Newton
Mosses, rhododendrons, and hemlocks adorn stunning Tillman Ravine, and Sunrise Mountain is another popular site at this 15,000-acre forest, contiguous with High Point State Park (above). **CONTACT** Stokes S.F., New Jersey State Park Svc., 1 Coursen Rd., Branchville, NJ 07826; 201-948-3820.

WEBB'S MILL BOG   Whiting
Botanizing is marvelous at this small preserve. Carnivorous plants include bladderworts and sundews. Orchids and the rare Bog Asphodel also grow here. Listen for the Pine Barrens Treefrog. **CONTACT** Webb's Mill Bog, Div. of Fish, Game, and Wildlife, CN 400, Trenton, NJ 08625; 609-292-2965.

New York

The Empire State has a superb variety of natural areas within its 49,576 square miles. Geology and geography have combined to produce 120-mile-long Long Island, the alpine summits of the Adirondacks, the mystical glens of the Finger Lakes, the cataracts of Niagara, the sleepy hollows of the Catskills, and the great basins and winding shorelines of two Great Lakes, Erie and Ontario.

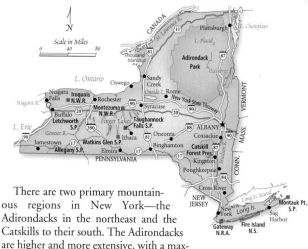

There are two primary mountainous regions in New York—the Adirondacks in the northeast and the Catskills to their south. The Adirondacks are higher and more extensive, with a maximum elevation of 5,344 feet atop Mount Marcy. The Catskills have an average elevation of 3,500 feet. Stretching west across most of the southern half of the state is the Allegheny Plateau, an upland region of rich forests, hills, and deep valleys. The other highland area of note is the Tug Hill Plateau, just west of the Adirondacks.

New York's lowlands are dominated by its major river valleys, the Great Lakes shorelines, and Long Island. Along the Canadian border, the St. Lawrence River runs northeast past the Thousand Islands to the corner of Lake Ontario. Along the state's eastern edge, the Lake Champlain and Hudson River valleys run from Quebec to New York Harbor, Champlain's low valleys in the north giving way to the Hudson Highlands and the palisades in the Hudson's lower reaches. The Mohawk River Valley lies between the Adirondacks and the Catskills before joining the Hudson Valley. In western New York, narrow plains extend landward from the shores of Lake Erie and Lake Ontario. The Great Lakes and the Lake Champlain–Hudson River valleys are the state's most important bird migration corridors. Long Island has New York's mildest year-round climate and almost all of its Atlantic coastline.

New York has one national seashore, one national recreation area, 11 national wildlife refuges, one national forest, 400 state forests, and the most acreage of natural areas of any state in the East.

CATSKILL FOREST PRESERVE   Kingston

Located about halfway between New York City and the southern edge of the Adirondacks, Catskill Forest Preserve is one of the region's most-visited natural areas, yet many places within its nearly 300,000 acres offer tranquillity and fine nature viewing, including four wilderness areas totaling more than 90,000 acres.

The Catskills are a range of highly dissected 2,000- to 4,000-foot mountains, with 98 peaks over 3,000 feet. There are very few valleys in the region, and the range as a whole has more a rough than a grand outward appearance. Slide Mountain, the region's tallest at 4,204 feet, attracts the greatest attention and can be quite crowded on fine weekends. An alternate trek might be up Balsam Lake Mountain, to the west; the peak rises to 3,723 feet, there is a bog among the Balsam Firs just off the trail near the summit, and

Sugar Maple in autumn

the crowds are mainly elsewhere. More than 300 miles of trails are maintained in the preserve.

The Catskills have some of the purest waters anywhere; the streams and reservoirs are famous for their populations of trout, bass, and other fishes. More than 500 miles of trout streams criss-cross the area. The Ashokan, Cannonsville, Neversink, Pepacton, Rondout, and Schoharie Reservoirs, which serve as New York City's water supply, harbor good numbers of waterfowl in autumn. Look for Canada Geese, American Wigeons, Green-winged Teals, Buffleheads, Common Goldeneyes, and Hooded Mergansers; Common Loons and grebes also are often seen. In winter 30 or more Bald Eagles may linger in the vicinity of Rondout Reservoir, in the southern Catskills, feeding on fish in the partially open waters.

The entire Catskill region is good for birds (several subalpine areas are Important Bird Areas), with breeding Red-tailed and Broad-winged Hawks, Yellow-bellied Sapsuckers, Cliff Swallows, Winter Wrens, Cedar Waxwings, Swainson's, Wood, Hermit, and Bicknell's Thrushes, Canada Warblers, American Redstarts, and Scarlet Tanagers along the woodland trails. For those who prefer fur to feathers, there is a healthy and burgeoning Black Bear population in the Catskills, as well as large numbers of Red, gray, and flying squirrels, Striped Skunks, raccoons, and White-tailed Deer.

LOCATION Off Interstate 87 (New York Thruway), exits 19 and 20. **CONTACT** Catskill Forest Preserve, New York State D.E.C., Div. of Lands and Forests, 21 S. Putts Corners Rd., New Paltz, NY 12561-1696 (park maps available); 914-256-3000. **VISITOR CENTER** Near exit 19.

ADIRONDACK PARK

McKenzie Mountain Wilderness and Whiteface Mountain

The great 10,000-square-mile oval of the Adirondack Mountain range dominates northeastern New York. These are mountains unto themselves, unrelated to the Appalachians to the east and the sprawling Allegheny Plateau to the southwest. First and foremost a land of forests, the Adirondacks include huge acreages of rich northern hardwood forests, dominated by American Beeches, Sugar Maples, and Yellow Birches; mixed woodlands of Red Maple, Black Cherry, Eastern White and Red Pines, and Eastern Hemlock; and northern coniferous woods fragrant with Balsam Fir and Red Spruce.

Of the nearly 1 million acres of wetlands in the Adirondacks, 95 percent are of the wooded variety known as swamps, many dominated by deciduous Red Maple and Black Ash and coniferous Tamarack, Black Spruce, and Balsam Fir. There are 100,000 acres of old-growth, near-virgin forest here, most in designated wilderness areas, but whether old growth or second growth, upland or wetland, deciduous or evergreen, these forests can overwhelm visiting campers, hikers, boaters, botanists, birders, cross-country skiers, and fishermen with their magnificence.

High Peaks from Mount Jo

Almost 300 species of birds have been recorded in Adirondack Park, a great many of them breeding species. Waterfowl are conspicuous spring through fall, while hawks of every description, from bird-hunting, resident Northern Goshawks to summering, insect- and rodent-feeding Broad-winged Hawks inhabit the woodlands and their edges. Eight species of woodpeckers, nine flycatchers, and an incredible 35 wood warblers have been observed here. The Adirondack High Peaks Wilderness Area is an Important Bird Area.

Mammal lovers also have a lot to be watchful for. This was once prime country for Moose, Lynx, and Gray Wolf, and perhaps they will return some day, but for now the park is home to 52 species, including such minuscule creatures as the Water Shrew and Southern Red-backed Vole, as well as lumbering Black Bears, tree-climbing Porcupines, and a panoply of weasels, from Ermine to Fisher.

At almost 6 million acres, Adirondack Park is the single largest park of any kind in the United States outside Alaska. The park's vastness comprises 46 mountain peaks topping 4,000 feet, including Mount Marcy, New York's tallest, at 5,344 feet; some 2,200 ponds and lakes, with 50 lakes 1 square mile or more in area; 1,200

Heart Lake at sunrise

miles of rivers; 30,000 miles of streams; and more than 1,000 miles of billboard-free roadways. Not all of the land is publicly owned; in fact, 62 percent of the holdings are private. Nevertheless, there are mountains, lakes, streams, and woodlands galore for everyone.

While not the geographic center of the park, Lake Placid is the perfect base area for exploring many of the park's northern sectors. The village of Lake Placid has hosted two winter Olympics and so is geared up for cold-weather activities. Whiteface Mountain, to the north of town, is the tallest ski mountain in the East. At any season its summit affords awesome views of Lake Champlain and the peaks of the Adirondacks and the more distant Green Mountains. To the southeast, trails lead up Mount Marcy, a popular if strenuous peak to conquer. The highest reaches of Marcy and 10 other Adirondack mountains have the region's only alpine zone vegetation.

Northwest of Lake Placid is the Visitor Interpretive Center at Paul Smiths. Among the attractions at this 3,000-acre facility are six loop trails, including Barnum Brook Trail (an easy-access trail for the handicapped), the Forest Ecology Trail, and the Boreal Life Trail. Beavers and Closed Gentians are highlights. West of Lake Placid are Tupper Lake and the Saranac Lakes, prime canoeing country. Northeast are the tall sandstone cliffs of Ausable Chasm and the waters of Lake Champlain beyond.

LOCATION Interstate 87 (New York State Thruway) runs north–south through eastern part of park. **CONTACT** Adirondack Park Agency, P.O. Box 99, Ray Brook, NY 12977; 518-891-4050. **VISITOR CENTERS** Two Visitor Interpretive Centers, open daily ex. Thanksgiving and Christmas: Paul Smiths is on Rte. 30, 12 miles north of Saranac Lake. Newcomb is on Rte. 28N, 14 miles east of Long Lake.

NIAGARA FALLS

Whether viewing the American or the Canadian Falls, one is left in awe of the cacophonous, plunging cascades of water at Niagara Falls. There are any number of breathtaking overlooks; some of the most thrilling are the view from the top of Goat Island, which divides the Niagara River and is one of the island units of Niagara Reservation State Park; those from Queen Victoria Park in Canada; and the surreal visions of the falls available at the New York State Observation Tower and elevator at Prospect Park.

Here *Maid of the Mist* boats take passengers into the river and under the mist that envelops the falls. For geologists, the falls alone are reason enough to visit this area. Birdwatchers come to see thousands of gulls and waterfowl over and in the turbulent waters, especially above Horseshoe Falls. Strong currents keep the Niagara River ice free in winter; the place is a birder's paradise from fall to early spring. The gull watching is excellent, and rarities turn up routinely. The Niagara River corridor is an IBA.

LOCATION Off Interstate 90. **CONTACT** Niagara Reservation S.P., NYSO-PRHP Western District, Niagara Region, P.O. Box 1132, Niagara Falls, NY 14303-0132; 716-278-1770. **VISITOR CENTER** Off Prospect St.

ALLEGANY STATE PARK

Salamanca

Over 60,000 acres in the southwestern part of the state, Allegany State Park (an IBA) combines with Pennsylvania's Allegheny National Forest to form one of the East's largest and most beautiful forest preserves. Fertile soils support tall second-growth woodlands of Sugar Maple, American Beech, and Yellow Birch. To walk among the lush car-

Mouth of Quaker Run

pet of ferns and wildflowers and marvel at the echoing carols of Swainson's, Hermit, and Wood Thrushes is an early summer delight. In winter, you might spook a Snowshoe Hare or Ruffed Grouse from a hemlock grove. Big Basin Trail, south of Red House Lake, has 300-year-old northern hardwoods. State Park Route 1 bisects the Big Basin area, providing access to the area's less-traveled trails. For a different atmosphere, explore the aspen woods and fields of Quaker Run. Firetower, Three Sisters, and Bear Caves trails are good choices.

LOCATION Off State Rte. 17, exits 18–20. **CONTACT** Allegany S.P., Western District, Allegany Region, 2372 ASP Rte. 1, Suite 3, Salamanca, NY 14779; 716-354-9101.

MONTEZUMA
NATIONAL WILDLIFE REFUGE Seneca Falls

Montezuma National Wildlife Refuge (an IBA) lies at the shallow northern end of Cayuga Lake, along the New York State Thruway. The almost 7,000 acres here are managed especially for migrant waterfowl, and someone is doing a very good job: this a waterfowl paradise in fall and spring. At peak seasons (mid-March and mid-October) some 100,000 ducks and geese of two dozen species mill about the marshes, ponds, and grain fields. Twelve thousand or more Snow Geese may highlight the spring migration, while fall numbers of Canada Geese, Mallards, and black ducks are in the tens of thousands. Summer wildlife watchers can find nesting Ospreys, resident Bald Eagles, numbers of handsome Black Terns, and various rails, bitterns, and herons.

LOCATION 5 miles northeast of Seneca Falls, on Rtes. 20/5. **CONTACT** Montezuma N.W.R., U.S. Fish and Wildlife Svc., 3395 Rtes. 20/5 East, Seneca Falls, NY 13148; 315-568-5987. **VISITOR CENTER** At southeastern corner of refuge.

WATKINS GLEN STATE PARK
AND THE FINGER LAKES
Watkins Glen

New York's Finger Lakes and the area's exquisite waterfalls, hanging valleys, and shadowy glens must be seen to be appreciated. The 11 Finger Lakes span west-central New York State and are a powerful reminder of the force of the glaciers that carved them. State parks abound here, with seven in the Cayuga Lake Valley and five around Seneca Lake. Taughannock Falls, Robert H. Treman, Stony Brook, Buttermilk Falls, and Fillmore Glen State Parks offer some of the finest scenery and waterfalls. Woodlands of oaks and other northern hardwoods alternate with vineyards and fields. Watkins Glen is the region's premier spectacle. Nineteen waterfalls and a remarkable chasm provide splendid scenery along Glen's Gorge Trail, which parallels Glen Creek; open from mid-May to early November, the trail has more than 800 stone steps. Watkins Glen State Park preserves about 1,000 acres. Access is year-round at Watkins Glen; many other glens are closed in winter. Cayuga, Seneca, and Canandaigua Lakes are IBAs.

LOCATION Rte. 14, Watkins Glen. **CONTACT** Watkins Glen S.P., P.O. Box 304, Watkins Glen, NY 14891; 607-535-4511. **VISITOR CENTER** Inside east (main) entrance.

CENTRAL PARK   **New York City (Manhattan)**

Central Park's 843 acres provide a green and scenic respite from city life. The park is a favored destination for exercisers, photographers, sweethearts, and springtime birders, who flock here by the hundreds from April though early June. Over the course of a typical spring, 140 to 150 avian species pass through the groves of oak, cherry, willow, and other deciduous species. The single most frequented birding locale is the 33 acres in the south-central area known as the Ramble; here warblers can be fabulous on a May morning, with Yellow, Magnolia, Black-throated Blue, Yellow-rumped, Black-throated Green, Blackpoll, Black-and-white, and Canada among the most numerous. The Point, a peninsula in Rowboat Lake, can also be wonderfully birdy in the spring.

LOCATION. Bounded by Fifth Ave., Central Park South, Central Park West, and West 110th St. **CONTACT** Central Park Conservancy, The Arsenal, Central Park, New York, NY 10021; 212-360-3444. **VISITOR CENTERS** The Dairy: mid-park at 65th St.; Belvedere Castle: mid-park at 79th St.; Charles A. Dane Discovery Center: 110th St. near Fifth Ave.

GATEWAY NATIONAL RECREATION AREA, JAMAICA BAY UNIT   **New York City (Queens)**

There are three units of Gateway National Recreation Area (an IBA), but the Jamaica Bay–Breezy Point unit, which comprises 9,155-acre Jamaica Bay Wildlife Refuge, Floyd Bennett Field, Jacob Riis Park, Breezy Point, and other sections of Queens and Brooklyn, is the most diversified. The combination of salt marsh, shallow bay, tidal flats, freshwater

Lesser Yellowlegs

impoundments, and grasslands attracts a diversity of wildlife species that would be the envy of most wildlife refuges. More than 340 species of birds have been recorded; many nest here, including Ospreys, Glossy Ibises, and Clapper Rails. Families of Barn Owls are raised in special nest boxes. Jamaica Bay is also a great marine-life and butterfly study area. The 2-mile path along the West Pond dike is one of the easiest and most productive.

LOCATION Off Cross Bay Blvd., in Queens. **CONTACT** Gateway N.R.A., Jamaica Bay Unit, National Park Svc., Floyd Bennett Field, Brooklyn, NY 11234; 718-318-4340. **VISITOR CENTER** Near the Cross Bay Blvd. entrance.

LONG POND GREENBELT   Sag Harbor

On the South Fork of Long Island are a series of glacial kettleholes—with names like Crooked Pond, Lily Pond, Otter Pond, and Long Pond—stretching in a north-south corridor from Sag Harbor to Bridgehampton and surrounded by mixed woodlands of oak, pine, Sassafras, hickory, and beech. Beneath the trees grow a spectrum of heaths—azaleas, blueberries, laurels, and Trailing Arbutus. Hike among the ponds and along the woodland trails, and you may find all of the area's seven turtles, seven snakes, and seven frogs and toads. Common and rare butterflies, dragonflies, and birds occur in plenty. This site—637 acres of the most diverse habitat on the South Fork—may have the highest concentration of rare animals and plants in New York.

LOCATION Between the north end of Sag Harbor and the Atlantic Ocean. CONTACT Nature Conservancy, 250 Lawrence Hill Rd., Cold Spring Harbor, NY 11724; 516-367-3225.

FIRE ISLAND NATIONAL SEASHORE   Patchogue

With a state park, a national seashore (an IBA), and the state's only federally designated wilderness, Fire Island has a lot to offer. Lying across Great South Bay off Long Island's south shore, it is a classic barrier island: 32 miles long by a half mile wide by 30 feet tall. Its swales, dunes, and wide-open expanses are replete with Northern Bayberry thickets, cranberry bogs, mudflats, shell-strewn sandy beaches, salt marshes, and maritime woodlands. The best-known of the woods is the Sunken Forest, which huddles down behind the high dunes west of Sailors Haven. Gray Catbirds mew from the low branches of American Holly, Sassafras, Red Maple, and shadbush. Yellow Warblers, Eastern Towhees, and Brown Thrashers add their voices to the morning chorus from late April to September. Birding can be superb in autumn, especially at the island's western end at Robert Moses State Park. Watch for migrating falcons and accipiters.

LOCATION From Rte. 27, Robert Moses Causeway leads to the island's western end, William Floyd Parkway to the eastern end. Ferry service May–Oct. from Bay Shore, Sayville, and Patchogue. CONTACT Fire Island N.S., National Park Svc., 120 Laurel St., Patchogue, NY 11772; 516-289-4810. VISITOR CENTERS Four, from west to east: Fire Island Lighthouse, Sailors Haven, Watch Hill, and Smith Point.

ALBANY PINE BUSH PRESERVE   Albany
These 2,300 acres are the last remnants of the vast Pitch Pine–Scrub Oak barrens that once covered most of the upper Hudson River Valley. In areas where Wild Lupine grows, watch in late May–early June and late July–early August for the endangered Karner Blue butterfly. **CONTACT** Albany Pine Bush Preserve, 1653 Central Ave., Albany, NY 12205; 518-464-6496.

BRADDOCK BAY PARK   Rochester
On southwest winds in mid- to late April, thousands and thousands of migrating hawks ride the northbound breezes past this 440-acre park (an IBA). Raptor enthusiasts also search for roosting owls. **CONTACT** Braddock Bay Park, 199 E. Manitow Rd., Hilton, NY 14468; 716-663-0200.

CORNELL LABORATORY OF ORNITHOLOGY   Ithaca
Part outdoor bird sanctuary, part indoor research center, the Laboratory of Ornithology at Sapsucker Woods presents a fine opportunity to get involved in the lives of birds. **CONTACT** Cornell Laboratory of Ornithology, 159 Sapsucker Woods Rd., Ithaca, NY 14851; 607-254-2425.

COXSACKIE AND ATHENS FLATS   Coxsackie
The 10 square miles of fields and hedgerows in the Athens–Coxsackie areas are marvelous for wintering raptors, including Barn, Snowy, and Short-eared Owls, Northern Harriers, Rough-legged and Red-tailed Hawks. **CONTACT** None; not a protected area.

HIGHLAND PARK   Rochester
This 100-acre urban park is one of Rochester's favorite birding areas. A May visitor can enjoy the blossoms of 1,600 lilacs and the fluting of Baltimore Orioles. **CONTACT** Highland Park, 171 Reservoir Ave., Rochester, NY; 716-234-4769.

IROQUOIS NATIONAL WILDLIFE REFUGE   Medina
Almost 11,000 acres of meadow, marsh, and woodland support populations of pheasant, grouse, and Great Blue Herons, and attract teeming flocks of waterfowl of many species at this IBA. **CONTACT** Iroquois N.W.R., U.S. Fish and Wildlife Svc., P.O. Box 51, Alabama, NY 14003; 716-948-5445.

JOHN BURROUGHS SANCTUARY   Kingston
World-famous naturalist-writer and conservationist Burroughs lived at this 175-acre site for the last 25 years of his life. Trails lead through oak-hickory and northern hardwood woodlands. **CONTACT** John Burroughs Sanct., John Burroughs Memorial Association, 261 Floyd Ackert Rd., West Park, NY 12493; 914-384-6320.

LETCHWORTH STATE PARK
Geneseo
The Genesee River Gorge along this 17-mile-long park (an IBA) is awe-inspiring, with dramatic waterfalls, centuries-old cedars and hemlocks, and a score of breeding wood warblers. **CONTACT** Letchworth S.P., New York State Office of Parks, Recreation, and Historic Preservation, Western District, Genesee Region 1 LSP, Castile, NY 14427; 716-493-3600.

Letchworth State Park

MENDON PONDS COUNTY PARK   Rochester
Glacial eskers and potholes make this 2,500-acre landscape enchanting. Watch for large Pileated Woodpeckers as well as diminutive chickadees begging for a handout along Birdsong Trail. **CONTACT** Mendon Ponds C.P., Parks Dept., 171 Reservoir Rd., Bedford, NY 14620; 716-256-4950.

MONTAUK POINT STATE PARK
Montauk

In fall and winter, the windswept moorlands and bluffs at this 720-acre site (an IBA) are excellent for sea-watching: Look for Northern Gannets, mergansers, scoters, Common Eiders, and Harbor Seals. Nearby Montauk County Park has interesting flora and Blue-spotted and Four-toed Salamanders. **CONTACT** Montauk Point S.P., Long Island Region, R.R. 2, Box 206A, South Fairview Ave., Montauk, NY 11954; 516-668-3781.

Montauk Point State Park

OSWEGO HARBOR AREA
Oswego

Bordered by two lengthy breakwaters, Oswego Harbor shelters enormous numbers of wintering Red-breasted, Common, and Hooded Mergansers, scaups, Ruddy Ducks, and gulls on the southeastern shore of Lake Ontario. **CONTACT** None; not a protected area.

ROGER TORY PETERSON INSTITUTE OF NATURAL HISTORY
Jamestown

Roger Tory Peterson was one of our greatest naturalists. His dream of educating children and teachers about the glories of nature lives on in this important organization. Displays of Peterson's paintings and ornithological collections are ongoing at the 27-acre site, which includes walking trails. **CONTACT** Roger Tory Peterson Institute of Natural History, 311 Curtis St., Jamestown, NY 14701-9620; 716-665-2473 and 800-758-6841.

SANDY POND
Sandy Creek

Dragonfly skimmers and darners, butterfly checkerspots and coppers, avian turnstones and dowitchers—watch for all in the wonderful mosaic of habitats at this pond on the eastern shore of Lake Ontario, southwest of Sackets Harbor. Sandy Pond is an IBA. **CONTACT** None; not a protected area.

TAUGHANNOCK FALLS STATE PARK
Trumansburg

A springtime visit to photograph or simply gaze at the highest waterfall east of the Rockies will undoubtedly coincide with some very good birding at this 780-acre park, especially from the Taughannock Park Road overlook. **CONTACT** Taughannock Falls S.P., Finger Lakes Region, P.O. Box 1055, Trumansburg, NY 14886; 607-387-6739.

THOUSAND ISLANDS
Alexandria Bay

Tour boats ferry visitors among the 1,700 islands in this stretch of the St. Lawrence River; the area is an IBA. Wellesley Island State Park (2,600 acres) has excellent trails. **CONTACT** Thousand Islands S.P. Region, P.O. Box 247, Alexandria Bay, NY 13607; 315-482-2593.

VERONA BEACH STATE PARK AND SYLVAN BEACH, ONEIDA LAKE
Rome

The beaches at Oneida Lake attract late-summer shorebirds, while the state park offers varied woodlands. **CONTACT** Verona Beach S.P. and Sylvan Beach, Oneida Lake, P.O. Box 245, Verona Beach, NY 13162; 315-762-4463.

WARD POUND RIDGE RESERVATION
Cross River

Habitat variety makes this 6-square-mile reservation one of the finest butterfly watching areas in the East—81 species have been tallied here. The area is excellent for wildflowers and dragonflies as well, and it is an IBA. **CONTACT** Ward Pound Ridge Res., Cross River, NY 10518; 914-763-3993.

WEST BRANCH NATURE PRESERVE
Oneonta

The 20-acre grove of immense Eastern White Pines is the most impressive feature of this 445-acre site, but don't neglect the fine surrounding deciduous woodlands, rich in plants and birds. **CONTACT** West Branch N.P., Nature Conservancy, 200 Broadway, 3rd floor, Troy, NY 12180; 914-244-3271.

Pennsylvania

Almost 60 percent of Pennsylvania is wooded; one researcher estimated that there are more than 8 billion trees in the Keystone State. The Pennsylvania woodlands are 92 percent deciduous and 8 percent coniferous. In its 45,333 square miles, stretching from Lake Erie to the Delaware River, Pennsylvania covers several major physiographic provinces, including the lowlands of the Lake Erie coastal plain in the northwest, the plateaus and highlands of the Appalachians dominating the greater part of the state, the piedmont to the north and west, and the Atlantic coastal plain in the southeast.

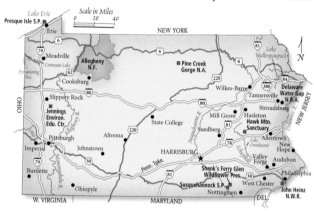

The major rivers are the Schuylkill, Delaware, and Susquehanna, which flow through eastern Pennsylvania and into its coastal plain, and the Monongahela, Allegheny, and Ohio, which drain large watersheds in western Pennsylvania. The valleys of the Ohio, Delaware, and Susquehanna are of primary importance to vast numbers of migratory birds. There are tens of thousands of miles of flowing water in the state but few natural lakes and ponds; the largest is Conneaut Lake in the northwest, with about 2½ square miles of surface area. Various large reservoirs, including Pymatuning in the northwest, Lake Wallenpaupack in the northeast, and Lake Ontelaunee in the southeast are good nature-viewing areas.

Mammal watchers know that Pennsylvania is White-tailed Deer country. Not as well known are the Little Brown Myotis bats that are a nightly feature at Canoe Creek State Park, and the Elk that live in Elk and Cameron Counties. There are 37 reptiles and 36 amphibians on the state lists, while bird species number in the high 300s. Hawk Mountain Sanctuary on the Kittatinny Ridge is one of the world's foremost hawk-watching sites. For botanizers, Pennsylvania has more than 2,800 herbaceous plants and 186 tree species, and many fine sanctuaries.

Pennsylvania has two national wildlife refuges, a national recreation area, a beautiful national forest, several huge state forests, and 114 state parks.

ALLEGHENY NATIONAL FOREST

Warren

At the Tracy Ridge Campground along Route 321, one finds the trailhead for the Land of Many Uses Interpretive Trail. This trail and its message personify the management practices of the Allegheny National Forest. In common with many other such forests across the region, Allegheny provides ample opportunities for fishing, birdwatching, botanizing, and other outdoor pursuits. What sets this land apart, however, are the thousands of active oil and gas wells within the forest's boundaries. The multiple-use land management concept is fully embraced on the more than one-half million acres of Allegheny National Forest.

With 194 miles of hiking trails, 17 campgrounds that run the gamut from primitive to full-amenity, numerous boat launches, picnic areas, and beaches, the forest is an inviting place to explore year-round. Take pains to avoid areas where well digging and timber harvesting are ongoing, however, as these tend to be very noisy operations. Winter activities include ice fishing and cross-country skiing. There are three district offices within the national forest; each can provide maps and helpful advice:

BRADFORD (IN THE NORTH) Don't miss the trail that meanders through the 122-acre Hearts Content Scenic Area, which shelters mature and centuries-old hemlocks, as well as Eastern White Pines, American Beeches, and Sugar Maples. Also visit the Campbell Mill Interpretive Trail, which begins at the Dewdrop Campground.

MARIENVILLE (SOUTHWEST) The Songbird Sojourn Trail is a 1.6-mile interpretive trail through parts of Buzzard Swamp Wildlife Management Area. The region is renowned for its varied bird life.

RIDGWAY (SOUTHEAST) The 35-acre Twin Lakes Recreation Area is a good place for fishing and bird and plant watching.

Other notable features of the forest include the 8,663-acre Hickory Creek Federal Wilderness Area, accessible by foot and essentially unaltered by the hand of man; the 368-acre Allegheny Islands Wilderness; and the 27-mile long Allegheny Reservoir, also known as Kinzua Dam, located at the northern end of the park and a center of activity for fishermen, Ospreys, and Bald Eagles.

LOCATION Off U.S. Rtes. 6 and 62. **CONTACT** Allegheny N.F., U.S. Forest Svc., 222 Liberty St., Warren, PA 16365; 814-723-5150. **VISITOR CENTER** Kinzua Point Information Center is 9 miles east of Warren, where Rte. 59 and Longhouse Scenic Drive intersect. Tionesta Visitor Center is on Rtes. 62 and 36 in Tionesta.

PRESQUE ISLE STATE PARK   Erie

Presque Isle peninsula, on Lake Erie in northwestern Pennsylvania, is a most rewarding natural history destination. If your trips are timed to miss the bulk of the 4 million annual human visitors (summer) and to hit the times of greatest avian activity (spring and fall, plus early mornings year-round), you will be amply rewarded. The 3,202 acres of Presque Isle State Park (an IBA) protect a lagoon, sand dunes, ponds, marshes, and an oak-maple forest. More than 500 species of plants thrive here, including 55 designated as threatened or "special concern" species in the state. Numerous trails (13 miles in total) cross the park's habitats. Sample the forest animal and plant life along Fox Trail, Cranberry Pond along the Marsh Trail, flowering shrubs along the Sidewalk Trail, and perhaps a sky full of springtime raptors along the Thompson Circle–Dead Pond Trail. In spring the park attracts weary northbound birds, which stop in the shrubby thickets and woods to rest and refuel. The sheer numbers of songbirds may be overwhelming at the peak of migration or in inclement weather.

LOCATION Rte. 832, north of Alt. Rte. 5. **CONTACT** Presque Isle S.P., P.O. Box 8510, Erie, PA 16505; 814-833-7424. **VISITOR CENTER** Stull Interpretive/Visitor Center, just inside the park's entrance.

JENNINGS ENVIRONMENTAL EDUCATION CENTER   Slippery Rock

Few species garner enough support to have a nature preserve developed with their particular needs in mind, but the Northern Blazing Star is such a species and Jennings Environmental Education Center is such a place. The relict prairie ecosystem here protects the dazzling Northern Blazing Star, as well as Bowman's-Root, purple fringed orchids, and other showy species that bloom alongside it in late summer. The greenish-yellow blossoms of the tall American Columbo can be seen earlier in the year. There are 8 miles of trails through the fields and woodlands of this 300-acre preserve. When walking on the Blazing Star, Prairie Loop, and Massasauga Trails, be watchful for the rare, state-endangered snake for which the last trail is named. Eastern Bluebirds, Wild Turkeys, and American Woodcocks haunt the fields and edges.

LOCATION Western Pennsylvania, east of Rte. 79. **CONTACT** Jennings Environmental Education Ctr., R.D. 1, Slippery Rock, PA 16057; 412-794-6011. **VISITOR CENTER** At main parking area.

PINE CREEK GORGE NATURAL AREA   Wellsboro

Leonard Harrison State Park

Also known as the Grand Canyon of Pennsylvania, Pine Creek Gorge is an area of outstanding scenic and geologic interest, and an IBA. Over its 18 miles, the gorge plummets to depths of more than 1,000 feet; the canyon walls are more than a mile wide at points. Wonderful views of some of the grandest scenery in these Tioga State Forest lands are visible from Colton Point and Leonard Harrison State Parks, which lie on opposite sides of the gorge. The 25-mile West Rim Trail traverses meadows, steep hillsides, shady glens, and rocky ridges, and a new rail-trail offers means of seeing the gorge by bicycle or horseback. Perhaps the most majestic views of the canyon walls are from Pine Creek itself. On a canoe or rafting adventure, watch the spectacular geology unfold and keep an eye out for water-loving creatures such as raccoons, Minks, and Great Blue Herons. A large shadow on the water may be cast by one of the park's resident Bald Eagles.

LOCATION 10 miles west of Wellsboro on U.S. Rte. 6. **CONTACT** Pine Creek Gorge N.A., Tioga State Forest, District Forester, P.O. Box 94, Rte. 287 South, Wellsboro, PA 16901; 717-724-2868. **VISITOR CENTER** Small visitor center at Leonard Harrison S.P.

LOWER SUSQUEHANNA RIVER   Lancaster County

River valleys are good sites for viewing a region's fishes, birds, and geologic history. Year-round, visitors to the Lower Susquehanna River Valley have excellent opportunities for observing these aspects of southeastern Pennsylvania's natural heritage. Fishermen angle for the river's

88 species of fishes, while rockhounds admire the Wissahickon Schist at Susquehannock State Park and the Chickies Quartzite at Chickies Rock. Conowingo Fisherman Park, south of Conowingo Dam, is a great place to see the Bald Eagles that winter in the vicinity. The low islands at Conejohela Flats are excellent in summer for shorebirds, night-herons, egrets, and other long-legged waders; up to 10,000 Tundra Swans and thousands of Snow Geese may be here in March. The farmlands around the river valley are wintering grounds for Snow Buntings, Horned Larks, hawks, and owls.

LOCATION Access near towns of Drumore, Holtwood, and Bethesda. **CONTACT** Susquehannock State Park, 1880 Park Dr., Drumore, PA 17518; 717-432-5011.

SHENK'S FERRY GLEN WILDFLOWER PRESERVE

Pequea

Blue Phlox

Spring blossoms are the center of attention at this sanctuary. Part of 5,000-acre Holtwood Recreation Area, Shenk's Ferry Glen is a vernal delight, with more than 70 species of herbaceous wildflowers in lush bloom along Grubb Run stream. Expect to see Bloodroot, Blue Phlox, Celandine, Coltsfoot, False Solomon's Seal, Miterwort, Dutchman's Breeches, Purple Trillium (white phase), Squirrel Corn, Virginia Bluebell, White Trout Lily, Wild Columbine, Wood Betony, and yellow Trout Lily. (White trilliums and trout lilies are uncommon elsewhere.) Picking wildflowers is prohibited.

LOCATION Along River Hill Rd., north of Pequea. **CONTACT** Shenk's Ferry Glen Wildflower Pres., Pennsylvania Power and Light Company, 9 New Village Rd., Holtwood, PA 17532; 717-284-2278.

DELAWARE WATER GAP NATIONAL RECREATION AREA

East Stroudsburg

Some 38 miles of the Delaware River tumble and wind through the 70,000-acre Delaware Water Gap National Recreation Area. Anglers come to land a few of the river's 55 fish species, river rafters and canoeists for the exhilaration of the ride. Scenery is superb on both the Pennsylvania and New Jersey sides of the river, with shady

gorges cloaked in ancient Eastern Hemlocks and sprawling Great Laurels. Among the 60 miles of hiking trails winding through the gap are some 25 miles of the Appalachian Trail; Dingmans Falls Trail, where naturalists lead weekend walks; and Tumbling Waters and Fossil Trails at the

excellent Pocono Environmental Education Center. Spring wildflowers are best along trails at Adam's Creek, Tom's Creek, Hornback's Creek, and Dingmans Falls. Turn over a few stones in the woods and at river's edge to uncover the hiding places of the region's salamanders. Birdwatchers come here at all seasons, for the breeding birds, migrants, and wintering species. The Gap is also home to several bat species, Common Porcupines, Northern River Otters, Star-nosed Moles, and Black Bears.

LOCATION Off Rte. 209, between Interstates 80 and 84. **CONTACT** Delaware Water Gap N.R.A., National Park Svc., Bushkill, PA 18324; 717-588-2435. **VISITOR CENTERS** Kittatinny Point Visitor Center at the park's southern end (in Columbia, NJ, off I-80). Dingmans Falls Visitor Center (May–Oct.) in the northern half, at Dingmans Falls, PA, off U.S. Rte. 209.

HAWK MOUNTAIN SANCTUARY   Kempton

The Kittatinny Ridge is a series of low mountains running northeast to southwest across eastern Pennsylvania and northern New Jersey. Every fall hawks, eagles, and other birds of prey by the thousands ride the updrafts of warm air from the ridge on their long southward migrations. Hawk-watchers perch themselves at various lookouts to delight in the spectacle. Nowhere along the ridge front are the raptors and views greater than at Hawk Mountain (an IBA). A great deal of avian and ecological research takes place on the sanctuary's 2,226 acres, but most people come to just watch raptors—in September, Broadwings, American Kestrels, and Bald Eagles; in October, Red-shouldered, Red-tailed, Cooper's, and Sharp-shinned Hawks; in November, Rough-legged Hawks, Northern Goshawks, and Golden Eagles. The South Lookout, 300 yards from the main parking area, is easiest to reach; the North Lookout is ¾ miles away via a more strenuous path. Closed Thanksgiving and Christmas.

LOCATION West of Allentown, on Rte. 895 in Drehersville. **CONTACT** Hawk Mountain Sanct., 1700 Hawk Mtn. Rd., Kempton, PA 19529; 610-756-6961. **VISITOR CENTER** At main parking area.

JOHN HEINZ NATIONAL WILDLIFE REFUGE AT TINICUM   Philadelphia

Scarcely a mile from the Philadelphia airport, this refuge is an important preserve for reptiles and amphibians, a fine bird sanctuary (an IBA), and an excellent spot to study wildflowers and other plants. These 1,200 acres include a large freshwater tidal marsh, ponds, streams, and woodlands. There are wildlife blinds, a boardwalk, and a two-tiered observation platform. The 3-mile-long Impoundment Trail gets one close to King Rails, Marsh Wrens, and seasonally abundant waterfowl and shorebirds. Northern Diamondback Terrapins

wander into tidal waters here, and Eastern Red-bellied Turtles and Red-eared Sliders may be glimpsed in the impounded areas. Marsh Marigolds (Cowslips) brighten the wetlands in spring, while Marsh Mallows add their color in late summer.

LOCATION 86th St. and Lindbergh Blvd., north of Rte. 291. **CONTACT** John Heinz N.W.R., U.S. Fish and Wildlife Svc., International Plaza II, Suite 104, Philadelphia, PA 19113; 215-365-3118. **VISITOR CENTER** At Lindbergh Blvd. parking area.

AUDUBON WILDLIFE SANCTUARY   Mill Grove
On these 175 acres, John James Audubon began his studies of American bird life. Over 175 birds and 400 flowering plants have been seen here. **CONTACT** Audubon W.S., P.O. Box 7125, Audubon, PA 19047; 610-666-5593.

BLUE KNOB STATE PARK   Johnstown
These 5,614 acres are among the state's most scenic. Miles of trails and fine trout streams, including Bob's Creek, await exploration. **CONTACT** Blue Knob S.P., R.D. 1, Box 449, Imler, PA 16655-9407; 814-276-3576.

BOWMAN'S HILL WILDFLOWER PRESERVE   New Hope
Twenty-six trails cross 80 acres of wildflowers. More than 1,000 species, including 800 natives, are protected here. **CONTACT** Bowman's Hill Wildflower Preserve, P.O. Box 103, Washington Crossing, PA 18977; 215-862-2924.

CANOE CREEK STATE PARK   Altoona
Up to 15,000 bats stream forth nightly from their summer roost at this 950-acre park. On a spring day, see a thousand Yellow Lady's Slippers. **CONTACT** Canoe Creek S.P., R.D. 2, Box 560, Hollidaysburg, PA 16648; 814-695-6807.

COOK FOREST STATE PARK   Cooksburg
On these 6,400 acres, check towering Eastern Hemlocks and White Pines for Great Horned, Barred, and other owls. When Red and White-winged Crossbills visit Pennsylvania in winter, this is a favorite spot. **CONTACT** Cook Forest S.P., P.O. Box 120, Cooksburg, PA 16217; 814-744-8407.

ENLOW FORK NATURAL AREA   Burdette
The carpet of May wildflowers at 914-acre Enlow Fork is simply breathtaking. The local Blue-eyed Mary is the show-stopper; there are also outstanding populations of larkspur, phlox, and many other species. **CONTACT** Enlow Fork N.A., Pennsylvania Game Commission, Southwest Region, P.O. Box A, Ligonier, PA 15658; 412-238-9523.

ERIE NATIONAL WILDLIFE REFUGE
Meadville
With 2,500 of its 8,750 acres as wetlands, this refuge is excellent for viewing waterfowl, marsh birds, amphibians, reptiles, and beavers. **CONTACT** Erie N.W.R., R.D. 1, Wood Duck Lane, Guys Mills, PA 16327; 814-789-3585.

HICKORY RUN STATE PARK   Hazleton
For geologist and nature lover alike, the 60-acre glacial boulder field here is unique. The park's other 15,000 acres have 36 miles of hiking trails through hardwood forests. **CONTACT** Hickory Run S.P., R.D. 1, Box 81, White Haven, PA 18661; 717-443-0400.

Hickory Run State Park

HONEY HOLLOW ENVIRONMENTAL
EDUCATION CENTER   New Hope
The comprehensive programs offered at this 700-acre site, which encompasses fields, marshes, forests, streams, and ponds, are designed to instill an understanding and respect for the natural world. The Center's water, soil, and wildlife conservation practices encourage productive farming as well as healthy populations of local plants and animals. (See also page 48.) **CONTACT** Honey Hollow Environmental Education Center, Bucks County Audubon Society, 6324 Upper York Rd., New Hope, PA 18938; 215-297-5880.

LONG POND NATURE PRESERVE   Stroudsburg
Best explored by canoe (bring your own), this 15,000-acre preserve is a biological gem, with several dozen rare or threatened species. **CONTACT** Long Pond Nature Pres., Nature Conservancy, Pocono Mountains Office, P.O. Box 211, Bakeslee, PA 18610-0211; 717-643-7922.

NOTTINGHAM COUNTY PARK   Nottingham
These 651 acres protect one of the finest serpentine barrens in the Northeast. Rare plants thrive in the metallic soils. Butterfly specialties include the Mottled Duskywing. **CONTACT** Nottingham C.P., 150 Park Rd., Nottingham, PA 19362; 610-932-2589.

OHIOPYLE STATE PARK AND FERNCLIFF
PENINSULA NATIONAL NATURAL LANDMARK   Ohiopyle
This park of 18,719 acres encompasses 14 miles of wild whitewater rapids in the Youghiogheny River and the nationally recognized Ferncliff Peninsula botanical area. **CONTACT** Ohiopyle State Park, P.O. Box 105, Ohiopyle, PA 15470; 412-329-8591.

PYMATUNING RESERVOIR   Meadville
Created in the 1930s, this 16-mile-long lake attracts migrating loons, swans, and ducks by the tens of thousands in spring and fall. **CONTACT** Pymatuning State Park, P.O. Box 425, Jamestown, PA 16134; 412-932-3141.

RACCOON CREEK STATE PARK   Imperial
Wander the 7,323 acres here, but don't miss the park's 314-acre Wildflower Preserve, with 500 species. **CONTACT** Raccoon Creek S.P., Pennsylvania Bureau of State Parks, 3000 SR 18, Hookstown, PA 15050; 412-899-2200.

RICKETTS GLEN STATE PARK
Wilkes-Barre
Known for its 22 waterfalls, Ricketts Glen has 13,050 acres, including the Glens Natural Area, with outstanding trails, wildflowers, and geology, and towering hemlocks in the Boston Run Natural Area. **CONTACT** Ricketts Glen S.P., RD2, Box 130, Benton, PA 17814-8905; 717-477-5675.

Ricketts Glen State Park

RIDLEY CREEK STATE PARK   West Chester
Walkers in this 2,600-acre park should see many birds and wildflowers, including the Kentucky Warbler and Showy Orchis. **CONTACT** Ridley Creek S.P., Sycamore Mills Rd., Media, PA 19063-4398; 610-892-3900.

SWATARA STATE PARK   Suedberg
Collecting is allowed at two fossil beds, with trilobites, cephalopods, and brachiopods more than 400 million years old quite common. The park has 3,300 woodland acres. **CONTACT** Swatara S.P., c/o Memorial Lake State Park, R.R.1, Box 7045, Grantville, PA 17028; 717-865-6470.

TANNERSVILLE CRANBERRY BOG PRESERVE   Tannersville
Contact the Nature Conservancy for permission to visit this Tamarack–Black Spruce bog and swamp, with 1,000 acres of northern-affinity species, including Snowshoe Hares and boreal conifers. **CONTACT** Tannersville Cranberry Bog Preserve, Nature Conservancy, Monroe County Conservation District, 8050 Running Valley Rd., Stroudsburg, PA 18360; 717-629-3061.

VALLEY FORGE NATIONAL HISTORICAL PARK   Valley Forge
The history resonates, the pace is easy, and the setting is lovely. This 3,500-acre park is a good place for bird and White-tailed Deer watching. **CONTACT** Valley Forge N.H.P., P.O. Box 953, Valley Forge, PA 19481-0953; 610-783-1000.

WOLF CREEK NARROWS NATURAL AREA   Slippery Rock
During spring wildflower season, see Large-flowered Trilliums, Dutchman's Breeches, Virginia Bluebells, and foamflowers along the 1½-mile trail. **CONTACT** Wolf Creek Narrows N.A., Western Pennsylvania Conservancy, 316 Fourth Ave., Pittsburgh, PA 15222-2075; 412-288-2777.

Virginia

More than 600 miles from west to east, with 40,767 square miles, elevations ranging from sea level in the tidewater to 5,729 feet at the top of Mount Rogers, and with a diversity of fauna and flora said to exceed that of any comparably sized temperate region anywhere, Virginia is a naturalist's paradise.

In the eastern quarter of the state, the coastal plain includes the southern third of the Delmarva Peninsula, known locally as the Eastern Shore, the lower end of the Chesapeake Bay, the three great

peninsulas on the western shore of the Chesapeake—Northern Neck, Middle, and Virginia—and the Great Dismal Swamp and coastal lowlands of southeasternmost Virginia. To the west, above the fall line that demarcates the western edge of the coastal plain, is the Virginian Piedmont Plateau. The Piedmont is a huge triangular province, narrowest in the north and widest along the North Carolina border; it is about two-thirds forested, and ranges in elevation from some 300 feet above sea level in the east to 1,000-plus feet in the Appalachian foothills.

Rising above the piedmont to the west are the Blue Ridge Mountains. The Blue Ridge province is narrowest at its northern end. As it spreads south, it gradually widens (from 10 miles to 70 miles) and gains height (from 4,000 feet to more than 5,700 feet). Paralleling the Blue Ridge Mountains, again to the west, is the Great Valley of Virginia, which comprises three separate named valleys—from north to south, the Shenandoah, the Valley of the James, and the Roanoke. The western frontier of Virginia, at the Kentucky and West Virginia borders, is part of the Allegheny Mountains. Jefferson and George Washington National Forests spread across almost all of this expansive western boundary.

Virginia is home to several National Park Service properties, including the southern third of Assateague Island National Seashore, Shenandoah National Park, the Blue Ridge Parkway, and Mount Rogers National Recreation Area. The state's conservation lands are made up of seven national wildlife refuges, two national forests, 28 state parks, 18 state natural areas, 25 Nature Conservancy preserves, 545 miles of the Appalachian National Scenic Trail, and many other reserves and trail systems.

GREAT DISMAL SWAMP
NATIONAL WILDLIFE REFUGE Suffolk

The Great Dismal Swamp was hacked away at for some 200 years, and the draining, lumbering, and development schemes perpetrated here have left their marks. This is a marvelous refuge, but a lot of the "great" has long since been removed from the swamp. Still, with more than 100,000 acres of Red Maple-Black Gum swamp, marsh and bog lands, handsome stands of Bald Cypress and Atlantic White Cedar, and 3,100-acre Lake Drummond, this refuge holds natural secrets that can take a lifetime of exploration to uncover. Some 40 miles of dirt roads pass through the habitats; although generally not open to motorized vehicles, they are perfect for foot and bicycle travel, and usually give visitors a multitude of wildlife-viewing opportunities, for this sanctuary is full of creatures great and small.

Lying at the northeastern periphery of the truly southern forest types, Great Dismal Swamp National Wildlife Refuge is home to great numbers of animals that barely reach north into the geographical area covered by this guide. Nearly 80 species of reptiles and amphibians, including snakes, lizards, turtles, salamanders, frogs, and toads, have been observed here—an extraordinary diversity. Various turtles, such as the Spotted and the Yellow-bellied, are conspicuous in the roadside canals and ponds, sunning themselves on logs and cypress stumps. Other amphibians and reptiles are easily recognized by their voices—the "clink" of the Green Treefrog and the "plink plink" of the Carpenter Frog. Three poisonous snake species, the Timber Rattlesnake, Copperhead, and Cottonmouth, live here.

Other wildlife includes birds—210 species recorded. Breeding wood warblers, among the most colorful avian residents from spring to fall, include Prothonotary, Yellow-throated, Kentucky, Hooded, and the extremely local Swainson's Warblers. Mammal watchers, as usual, will have to work a lot harder to build a long sightings list, but their efforts may lead to looks at Black Bears, White-tailed Deer, beavers, gray squirrels, Red and gray foxes, Eastern Cottontails, Marsh Rabbits, muskrats, Minks, Northern River Otters, and Bobcats. Great Purple Hairstreak and Palamedes Swallowtail are two of the many beautiful butterflies here.

The road at the Washington Ditch entrance leads to Lake Drummond, one of only two natural lakes in the state. It also accesses the ¾-mile Boardwalk Trail, which hints at some of the swamp's natural treasures.

LOCATION South of Suffolk, on Rte. 32. **CONTACT** Great Dismal Swamp N.W.R., P.O. Box 349, Suffolk, VA 23434; 757-986-3705.

SHENANDOAH NATIONAL PARK

Front Royal through Waynesboro

At the north end of the Blue Ridge, between the Virginian pied-mont hills to the east and the Great Valley of Virginia (known in this part of the state as Shenandoah Valley) to the west, lie the 300 square miles of Shenandoah National Park. The beauty of the park's woodlands—mountain spruce-fir ridges and low-country dogwood-redbud slopes—makes Shenandoah a natural marvel.

The park has more than 500 miles of hiking trails in pristine woodlands. The Potomac Appalachian Trail Club (703-242-0315) publishes trail maps, maintains huts and cabins for overnight hik-ers, leads hiking trips, and provides assistance to those who want to get into the Shenandoah backcountry. Park rangers also offer a wealth of information on hiking opportunities. (Bicycles, not per-mitted on national park trails, are welcome on park roadways.).

For those who most enjoy nature from the roadside or car window, spectacular Skyline Drive winds through the park for 105 miles, providing great views of and access to many of the park's highlights. Shenan-doah is known for its spec-tacular fall foliage, but at any season one can enjoy beautiful scenery, waterfalls, and interesting wildlife from a large number of roadside pull-offs.

Woodland in spring

Along the paths and roadways, watch for some of the park's 205 species of birds, 40 mammals, 50 amphibians and reptiles, 47 ferns and allies, 100 trees, and 1,100 wildflowers and shrubs. Some 600 Black Bears live here, and ten times as many White-tailed Deer.

The text below surveys Skyline Drive; the numbers are distances, in miles, from its northern terminus. The park entrance is at Front Royal, 0.6 mile from the start of the drive. Since many park services are closed in winter (the drive itself may close in bad weather), we concentrate on some of the best natural areas from spring to fall.

22.2 MATHEWS ARM Family campgrounds are located here and at Big Meadows (mile 51.3), Lewis Mountain (57.5), and Loft Mountain (79.5). Reservations are recommended for all campsites, especially during the busy summer season (800-999-4714).

43.0 LIMBERLOST TRAIL The 1½-mile round-trip trail traverses a fine stand of Eastern Hemlocks. Here and in other hemlock groves in Shenandoah, listen for the high, thin, upwardly slurred call of the Blackburnian Warbler. The glowing orange throat of the male shines like a beacon from the dark hemlock boughs. Red Squirrels add their own color and calls to this evergreen surrounding.

46.7 HAWKSBILL MOUNTAIN TRAIL This moderately strenuous 2-mile trail leads to the highest peak in the park and the best hawk-watching area. The 360-degree views from 4,051-foot Hawksbill Mountain are superb on a clear day. If the day is also windy and your visit coincides with the hawk migration season (September–November), expect to see a nice variety of raptors. The best hawk-watching is on days with northerly winds.

View from top of Hawksbill Mountain

51.3 BIG MEADOWS WAYSIDE Aptly named Big Meadows is the best place along Skyline Drive to appreciate the park's meadow flora and fauna. Naturalists consider this one of the prime areas in the Mid-Atlantic region for viewing White-tailed Deer, which are most likely to visit woodland openings early or late in the day. Eastern Meadowlarks, Eastern Bluebirds, and Barn Swallows are conspicuous in summer, as are Woodchucks and Eastern Cottontails. Wildflower enthusiasts will find sun-loving blueberries, buttercups, irises, Black-eyed Susans, Golden Alexanders, goldenrods, asters, and grasses galore through the warmer months. Big Meadows has one of three park gas stations and a 227-site campground.

51.7–53.0 TANNERS RIDGE OVERLOOK TO MILAM GAP In spring and fall (May and September are prime months), this stretch of Skyline Drive is inundated with migrant songbirds. The Appalachian Trail parallels Skyline Drive here and is a logical, off-road birding choice.

62.8 SOUTH RIVER FALLS AND PICNIC AREA The varied woodlands along the trails here, in conjunction with the trail design, which cuts across the slope of the hillside and makes canopy viewing relatively easy, combine to make this the premier place in Shenandoah for breeding birds. The variety of woodpeckers, flycatchers, thrushes, vireos, and warblers is astonishing. Listen for the conversational calls of Blue-headed, Red-eyed, and Yellow-throated Vireos, the buzzy songs of Black-throated Blue and Cerulean Warblers, and the robin-like song of the brilliant Scarlet Tanager. This is the perfect spot for hearing and seeing songbirds.

79.5 LOFT MOUNTAIN CAMPGROUND This facility has all the campground amenities, as well as a self-guiding nature trail and various ranger-conducted campfire programs and hikes during the summer.

LOCATION 4 main access points: Rte. 340 at Front Royal; Rte. 211 at Thornton Gap; Rte. 33 at Swift Run Gap; Rte. 64 at Rockfish Gap. **CONTACT** Shenandoah N.P., Rte. 4, Box 348, Luray, VA 22835; 703-999-2266. **VISITOR CENTERS** At Dickey Ridge (mile 4.6), Harry F. Byrd, Sr. (51), and Loft Mountain (79.5).

GEORGE WASHINGTON NATIONAL FOREST

Western Virginia has two huge national forests protecting 1.8 million acres of some of the loveliest mountain forest and valley landscapes in the world. George Washington National Forest, with slightly more than 1 million acres, is the larger of the two. It includes a wide, continuous swath of forest along the West Virginia border (and into West Virginia in places), as well as large holdings to the west and south of Shenandoah National Park.

All of the national forest lands run, like the Appalachians themselves, in a northeast-southwest orientation, spreading out over a tremendous latitudinal range. Do not try to take in this forest in a weekend; it is just too big.

Rhododendrons along Blue Ridge Parkway

Because of its expanse and the great variety of habitats included within its boundaries, George Washington National Forest contains, in one corner or another, virtually all of the animals and plants known from the Virginian Appalachians. Snowshoe Hares, Fishers, and Red Spruces co-mingle at high elevations; local salamanders hide under wet rocks and vegetation at various elevations; Black Bears pursue blueberries on open hillside patches and in the valleys. The forest has 950 miles of maintained hiking trails leading through and into its various habitats.

There are a number of ranger districts within the forest. They are presented below (with telephone numbers) in geographic order, from north to south.

LEE DISTRICT (540-984-4101) The Massanutten Mountain and Fort Valley region, between the North and South Forks of the Shenandoah River, is a welcome change of pace from Interstate 81, which runs just to its west. Massanutten Visitor Center, some 3 miles east of New Market, has information on caverns and other local attractions. The Kennedy Peak Loop is a moderately steep 5.4-mile loop that climbs to an observation tower with excellent views of Page Valley. The Signal Knob Loop is a steeper and longer hike composed of four trails.

DRY RIVER DISTRICT (540-828-2591) The North River Gorge Trail offers beautiful streamside scenery, interesting geology, and a chance to fish or view wildlife; as it requires fording the North River nine times, it should be hiked during periods of low water. The Reddish Knob area has Shenandoah Mountain, which at 4,397 feet, allows spectacular views of the Shenandoah Valley to the east.

DEERFIELD DISTRICT (540-885-8028) The North Mountain Trail is a 14-mile hiking trail that winds along mountain crests, providing excellent panoramic views of the forest. Elliot Knob, at 4,463 feet the forest's highest peak, lies just off the trail. Ramseys Draft Wilderness Area, a 6,500-acre mountainous area within the Deerfield District, is accessed by seven trails.

WARM SPRINGS DISTRICT (540-839-2521) Hidden Valley, a peaceful vale of farms and meadows, and Laurel Fork, a mountain ridge high on the West Virginia border, present the extremes of George Washington National Forest landscapes; both are spectacular. The Bolar Mountain area has 11 miles of trails that offer scenic overlooks and provide nice loop hikes.

Lower Crabtree Falls

JAMES RIVER DISTRICT (540-962-2214) The Highlands Scenic Tour is a 20-mile automobile roadway looping through parts of Allegheny and Rockbridge Counties. The thoroughfare, paved in places and gravel in places, with unforgettable scenery and more than a few sharp turns, is best negotiated and appreciated in summer and fall. For hikers, 8-mile North Mountain Trail winds up the crest of North Mountain past stream habitats, interesting rock formations, varied forest types, opportunities for wildlife viewing, and panoramic views as it rises in elevation from 1,700 to 3,200 feet.

PEDLAR DISTRICT (540-291-2188) Crabtree Falls is a series of brilliant waterfalls tumbling more than 1,200 feet. If you are in the vicinity, do not miss them. However, please take the cautionary signs to heart and do not wander too close to the falls' edge—more than a score of people have lost their lives doing this. After the steep trails at Crabtree, explore Sherando Lake in the Big Levels Wildlife Management Area, where there are a variety of woodland trails for birdwatching and botanizing, as well as swimming and boating facilities.

LOCATION Western Virginia. **CONTACT** George Washington N.F., Harrison Plaza, Harrisonburg, VA 22801; 888-265-0019. **VISITOR CENTER** Massanutten Visitor Information Center on Rte. 211, 3 miles east of New Market (Apr.–Oct.).

JEFFERSON NATIONAL FOREST

Stretching generally south and west from the George Washington National Forest, Jefferson National Forest comprises 710,000 awe-inspiring acres. The National Forest Service allows camping anywhere; there are 16 campgrounds throughout the forest, but unless an area is specifically posted with "No Camping" signs, one is free to stop for the evening at any site. Elevations range from 600 feet at the James River to 5,729 feet atop Mount Rogers, Virginia's highest peak, so there is plenty of habitat to enjoy.

Red-tailed Hawks, at home in a wide variety of places, sail over the highland ridges and hunt the river valleys. Most animals and

plants, however, prefer one or a few chosen habitats, and to find a goodly range of the floral and faunal species in the forest it is necessary to visit the forest types they inhabit. Hiking and horse trails and roadways get naturalists into these areas, some outlined below. Sites are grouped by the ranger district that administers them.

Eastern Redbuds in bloom

BLACKSBURG DISTRICT (540-552-4641) Cascades National Recreation Trail, which leads to a 66-foot-tall waterfall, and the Mountain Lake Wilderness Area, at 11,113 acres the largest in the forest, are two of the district's premier natural attractions. White Rocks Campground provides access to many of Blacksburg's best trails.

CLINCH DISTRICT (540-328-2931) Home to the Mount Rogers National Recreation Area (see the briefer listings on page 419), Clinch has other fine natural areas, including Little Stony National Recreation Trail, with superb hemlocks and rhododendrons, and Hanging Rock Picnic Area; the observation tower atop High Knob, where one can look out over five states; and Lake Keokee, with an easy 4-mile loop trail through hardwood forest.

GLENWOOD DISTRICT (540-291-2188) The wilderness areas of Thunder Ridge and James River Face provide 11,500 acres of challenging backcountry. Don't miss the 215-foot-tall Natural Bridge.

NEW CASTLE DISTRICT (540-864-5195) Roaring Run National Recreation Trail loops through a marvelous shaded gorge, while the Barbours Creek Wilderness Area offers 5,700 acres of prime mountain scenery.

WYTHE DISTRICT (540-228-5551) Four-mile-long Seven Sisters Trail will test your endurance. If you can easily hike it, perhaps you are up for a trek through the Beartown Wilderness Area. Its 5,600 remote acres include beaver ponds and steep mountain trails.

LOCATION Western Virginia. **CONTACT** Jefferson N.F., USDA Forest Svc., 5162 Valleypointe Pkwy., Roanoke, VA 24019; 888-265-0019. **VISITOR CENTER** Highland Gateway Visitor Center, Factory Merchants Mall, exit 80 off I-81.

BLUE RIDGE PARKWAY
Roanoke

The Blue Ridge Parkway and its northern extension, Skyline Drive (see page 410), wind for 469 gorgeous miles along the Blue Ridge Mountains, providing unequaled scenic viewing from Rockfish Gap, Virginia, to Great Smoky Mountains National Park (along the Tennessee–North Carolina border). Described here are some of the most interesting stops along the 216 miles of the Blue Ridge Parkway in Virginia. The numbers are mileposts, from Rockfish Gap south.

0.0 ROCKFISH GAP The luxurious hawk-watch on the deck of the inn here is worth a stop from September to November, especially when the wind is out of the north.

5.8 HUMPBACK ROCKS VISITORS CENTER A late-19th-century homestead gives visitors a taste of life in the beautiful, rugged Blue Ridge. There are a log cabin, barn, and other structures, as well as a museum of pioneer implements. The site is surrounded by Yellow Poplar-hickory-oak woodlands, home to woodland salamanders, Wild Turkeys, Veeries, and Dark-eyed Juncos.

Patrick County, Virginia

63.6 JAMES RIVER VISITORS CENTER Here at 646 feet, the parkway's lowest elevation, are a mixture of plant and animal life unlike that typically associated with more montane areas. Two trails—Otter Creek Trail and Trail of the Trees—run through bottomland and upland forests and along waterways, where Belted Kingfishers, Baltimore Orioles, and Rose-breasted Grosbeaks may be seen.

78.4 SUNSET FIELD OVERLOOK In the 14 miles from the James River cut, the road has climbed more than 3,500 feet to this spot, the highest on the parkway at 4,225 feet. Along the dirt road that ascends Apple Orchard Mountain, the rhododendron display, as elsewhere at many places along the parkway, is very fine.

80.4 FLOYD FIELDS Mountain Laurels, rhododendrons, and handsome oaks and hemlocks make this a good place for a stroll.

86.0 PEAKS OF OTTER RECREATION AREA This destination has motel, campground, restaurant, picnic area, hiking trails, and bus service to Sharp Top, which has good views, as does Flat Top.

169.0 ROCKY KNOB RECREATION AREA The demanding 10.8-mile loop of the Rock Castle Gorge National Recreation Trail traverses Appalachian cove forests and other woodlands. Easy and moderate trails and other amenities are also available at this 4,800-acre site.

Most facilities along Blue Ridge Parkway close between November and April. Sections may close in bad winter weather.

LOCATION South of Shenandoah National Park. **CONTACT** Blue Ridge Parkway, National Park Svc., 400 BB&T Bldg., 1 Pack Sq., Asheville, NC 28801. **VISITOR CENTERS** At mileposts 5.8, 63.6, 86, and 169 in Virginia.

CHINCOTEAGUE
NATIONAL WILDLIFE REFUGE   Assateague Island

The Native American name Chincoteague (pronounced SHIN-co-teeg) means "beautiful land across the waters." Here at the southern end of Assateague Island, the 13,682 acres of Chincoteague National Wildlife Reserve are home to dramatic coastal vistas, great surf, huge concentrations of bird life, and the famous wild ponies. Nature lovers find the area fascinating.

Sleeping, eating, and bicycle rental establishments are located in the town of Chincoteague, on the island of the same name between the mainland and Assateague. Cross the bridge onto the barrier island and in half a mile, pull into the visitor center on the left. This is the epicenter of wildlife-viewing activities at the refuge; indoor and outdoor programs and escorted walks are offered. Two of the most popular are the "Family Fishing" outing aboard the *Osprey* (summer) and the "Wildlife Safari" tour through the refuge (daily in summer; weekends spring and fall). Reserve in advance.

Just beyond the visitor center is Wildlife Drive, one of the island's premier wildlife viewing spots and, despite its name, a "drive" only from 3:00 P.M. to dusk; at all other times, it is a wildlife walk. This 4-mile loop road curves around Snow Goose Pool and through maritime woodlands, providing great views of the seasonal cavalcade of bird life. From November to April, watch for Snow and Canada Geese, Mute and Tundra Swans, and dabbling ducks of many species. During the summer months, the wetlands along Wildlife Drive are excellent resting and feeding areas for gulls, terns, Black Skimmers, shorebirds, herons, and egrets, while in fall the trees and shrubs are frequently flooded with migrating songbirds and the Sharp-shinned Hawks and Merlins that follow them south. At all seasons, be alert for Northern River Otters in open water and the endangered Delmarva Peninsula Fox Squirrel in wooded areas.

Much of the rest of the refuge, stretching north of Snow Goose Pool, may be explored on foot. Just east of the refuge is the southern visitor center for Assateague Island National Seashore (see page 379 section). Here, at Toms Cove, is the jumping-off point for the Hook, a great sandy spit that extends south and west around the cove and ends at Fishing Point. Much of this area is closed from mid-March to late August to protect breeding birds. Trek down the beach at other seasons, watching for migrant and wintering raptors, the odd Red Fox, or whelks, jingle shells, and moon snails.

LOCATION Rte. 175, east of Rte. 13. **CONTACT** Chincoteague N.W.R., P.O. Box 62, Chincoteague, VA 23336; 757-336-6122. **VISITOR CENTER** On west side of Snow Goose Pool.

VIRGINIA COAST RESERVE   **Exmore**

The Atlantic coast barrier islands and their marshes and protected lagoons are fascinating, but many are overrun with people in warm weather. At this 50-mile-long site, however, access is limited, making the barrier islands of the Virginia Coast Reserve the least altered of their kind on the eastern seaboard. Perhaps the best way to enjoy some of the 45,000 acres of this island chain is to reserve a spot on one of the regularly scheduled tours provided by the Nature Conservancy. For six or seven hours, you will cruise past salt marshes filled with fiddler crabs and Clapper Rails, walk uninhabited shores and tidal inlets, and learn about the ecology, biology, and geology of the islands. Birds are the conspicuous life-form; many choose these relatively isolated shorelines and dunes for nesting. Populations of seven tern species are high. Never visit in summer without a guide, as you may wander into a colony of nesting terns or gulls; call for tour schedules.

LOCATION Along outer and southern coast of Delmarva Peninsula. **CONTACT** Virginia Coast Reserve, P.O. Box 158, Nassawadox, VA 23413; 757-442-3049.

KIPTOPEKE STATE PARK   **Cape Charles**

There's a fishing pier, cottontails populate the meadows, and Bottle-nosed Dolphins cavort offshore, but for the naturalist, 375-acre Kiptopeke is a quintessential birdwatcher's paradise. Come in the fall, when the place is mobbed with birds. Kiptopeke is at the terminus of the long, narrow southern third of the Delmarva Peninsula. Huge numbers of birds from many families follow a coastal path in their autumnal journeys, concentrating at narrow capes. From early August into November, birdwatchers, bird banders, and bird migration

specialists gather here at the state park to witness the great southern passage. Merlins and Peregrine Falcons dash about after shorebirds and songbirds, to the thrill of onlookers who sometimes see life-and-death chases played out only feet away. Hawks, Ospreys, flickers, swallows, thrushes, kinglets, vireos, and warblers can fill the skies and bushes. The nearby Eastern Shore of the Virginia National Wildlife Refuge is equally great for birds.

LOCATION Off Rte. 13, 3 miles north of Chesapeake Bay Bridge-Tunnel. **CONTACT** Kiptopeke S.P., 3540 Kiptopeke Dr., Cape Charles, VA 23310; 757-331-2267.

BACK BAY NATIONAL WILDLIFE REFUGE   Virginia Beach
An outstanding wildlife area of 7,700 acres, the refuge protects up to 10,000 wintering Snow Geese, nesting Loggerhead turtles, Brown Pelicans, and myriad other species. **CONTACT** Back Bay N.W.R., P.O. Box 6286, Virginia Beach, VA 23456; 757-721-2412.

BREAKS INTERSTATE PARK
Breaks
Through the millennia, the Russell Fork River carved out the longest (5 miles) and deepest (1,600 feet) canyon east of the Mississippi in this 4,500-acre park spanning the Virginia–Kentucky border. **CONTACT** Breaks Interstate Park, P.O. Box 100, Breaks, VA 24607-0100; 540-865-4413.

Breaks Interstate Park

CALEDON NATURAL AREA   Fredericksburg
Up to 60 Bald Eagles summer here, often roosting in the 100-year-old hardwoods that populate about a third of the area's 2,600 acres. Guided eagle tours are available. **CONTACT** Caledon N.A., 11617 Caledon Rd., King George, VA 22485; 540-663-3861.

CHESAPEAKE BAY BRIDGE AND TUNNEL   Norfolk
First write and get permission to stop along the way. Then, from fall through spring, be amazed at the bird life that drifts by and rests at the manmade CBB&T islands—everything from storm-petrels to meadowlarks. **CONTACT** Chesapeake Bay Bridge and Tunnel, P.O. Box 111, Cape Charles, VA 23310-0111; 757-331-2960.

CUMBERLAND STATE FOREST   Farmville
With Bear Creek Lake State Park and the 16-mile riparian Willis River Trail included in its 16,500 acres, Cumberland is home to White-tailed Deer, Northern Pike, and impressive Yellow Poplars. **CONTACT** Cumberland S.F., Virginia Dept. of Conservation and Recreation, Rte. 1, Box 250, Cumberland, VA 23040; 804-492-4121.

FAIRY STONE STATE PARK   Bassett
This park and surrounding Fairystone Farms Wildlife Management Area combine for 10,000 acres of hilly woodlands, replete with miles of hiking trails and fairy stones, staurolite crystals in the shape of crosses. **CONTACT** Fairy Stone S.P., Rte. 2, Box 723, Stuart, VA 24171; 540-930-2424.

HUNTLEY MEADOWS PARK   Alexandria
Amid the sea of suburbia and freeways, the 1,261 acres here are a jewel. A long boardwalk into the marsh and wide level paths afford excellent looks at beavers, King Rails (this is the best place to see them on the East Coast), and fine marsh and woodland flora. In May hundreds of Northern Water Snakes mate and bask in the sun here. **CONTACT** Huntley Meadows Park, Fairfax Co. Park Authority, 3701 Lockheed Blvd., Alexandria, VA 22306; 703-768-2525.

JAMES RIVER PARK   Richmond
A patchwork park of various parcels of bottomland in the west end of the city, this 450-acre park is the area's best birding site and one of the state's best spots for Smallmouth Bass. **CONTACT** James River Park, City of Richmond, 700 Blanton Ave., Richmond, VA 23221; 804-780-5311.

JOHN H. KERR RESERVOIR (BUGGS ISLAND LAKE)   Boynton
More than 800 miles of shoreline provide access to this 50,000-acre lake, known for its Largemouth Bass, Striped Bass, and Crappie. Bald Eagles should be watched for. **CONTACT** Kerr Reservoir (Buggs Island Lake), U.S. Army Corps of Engineers, 1930 Mays Chapel Rd., Boynton, VA 23917; 804-738-6143.

LAKE ANNA — Mineral

With a telescope or boat or both, a birdwatcher can find loons, grebes, ducks, terns, and shorebirds in great numbers and variety on this popular 7,000-acre lake. **CONTACT** Lake Anna State Park, 6800 Lawyers Rd., Spotsylvania, VA 22553; 540-854-5503.

MASON NECK NATIONAL WILDLIFE REFUGE — Lorton

The refuge land was protected and is managed for Bald Eagles, and the 2,000 acres here are a prime wintering area, with 50 or more eagles most years. Wild Rice marshes entice great numbers of waterfowl. **CONTACT** Mason Neck N.W.R., U.S. Fish and Wildlife Svc., 14416 Jefferson Davis Hwy., Suite 20A, Woodbridge, VA 22191; 703-690-1297.

MOUNT ROGERS NATIONAL RECREATION AREA — Marion

Fraser Fir, Flame Azalea, and blueberries cloak the slopes of Mount Rogers (5,729 feet) and nearby Whitetop Mountain (5,520 feet), Virginia's two highest peaks, at this picturesque and wild 120,000-acre site in Jefferson National Forest. **CONTACT** Mount Rogers N.R.A., USDA Forest Svc., Rte. 1, Box 303, Marion, VA 24354; 540-783-5196.

MOUNT VERNON TRAIL — Mount Vernon to Roosevelt Island

Avoid mid-morning and late afternoon bicyclists and joggers to take best advantage of the natural highlights, including well-known Dyke Marsh, along this 17-mile pathway. **CONTACT** Mt. Vernon Trail, George Washington Memorial Parkway, Turkey Run Park, McLean, VA 22101; 703-285-2600.

POCAHONTAS STATE PARK — Richmond

The amusing whistles of the Yellow-breasted Chat and the powerful crescendo of the Ovenbird are but two of the summer songs heard in this largest (7,600 acres) of Virginia's state parks. **CONTACT** Pocahontas S.P., 10300 Park Road, Chesterfield, VA 23832; 804-796-4255.

SCOTTS RUN NATURE PRESERVE — McLean

Described as the piedmont's most diverse forest from a plant community and species standpoint (it's great for spring ephemerals), Scotts Run comprises 340 acres along the Potomac. **CONTACT** Scotts Run N.P., 7400 Georgetown Pike, McLean, VA 22102; 703-759-9018.

SEASHORE STATE PARK AND NATURAL AREA
Virginia Beach

It may be the state's most visited park, but Seashore has quiet areas away from beachgoing crowds in its 2,900 acres. Numerous amphibians and reptiles include several colorful turtle species, including the Chicken and the Eastern Red-bellied. **CONTACT** Seashore S.P. and N.A., 2500 Shore Dr., Virginia Beach, VA 23451; 804-481-2131.

Seashore State Park and Natural Area

G. R. THOMPSON WILDLIFE MANAGEMENT AREA — Front Royal

Most visitors come to this 4,500-acre site to revel in the spring trillium blossoms, estimated at 18 million. Hawk-watchers also love this spot in fall. **CONTACT** G. R. Thompson W.M.A., Virginia Wildlife Division, 1320 Belman Rd., Fredericksburg, VA 22401; 540-899-4169.

TUSCARORA TRAIL

A 220-mile-long western loop of the Appalachian Trail, with 112 miles in Virginia, Tuscarora can provide weeks or a lifetime of fabulous hiking and scenery. **CONTACT** Tuscarora Trail, Potomac Appalachian Trail Club, 118 Park St., S.E., Vienna, VA 22180; 703-242-0315.

West Virginia

West Virginia has a unique geographic position. With an eastern panhandle that pushes into the Shenandoah Valley, a northern arm that stretches halfway up the western side of Pennsylvania, and a southwestern mountainous bulge that extends as far south as Roanoke, West Virginia is a mixing ground for species from throughout the East.

West Virginia is the highest state east of the Mississippi, with a mean elevation of 1,500 feet. The highest mountain is Spruce Knob, at 4,861 feet. The two major mountain systems are the Appalachians in the eastern quarter of the state and the Alleghenies in the broad central and western sectors. The great bisecting ridge of the Allegheny Backbone divides West Virginia from southwest to northeast and determines the flow of the state's major river systems. Flowing toward the northwest and draining about 80 percent of West Virginia's 24,181 square miles are the Big Sandy, Little Kanawha, and Monongahela Rivers, which roll into the Ohio. The Potomac and Greenbrier are two of the East's important rivers. Other West Virginia rivers have some of the best white water in the East.

West Virginia has exceptional hiking trails. The Appalachian Trail has its national headquarters in Harper's Ferry. The American Discovery Trail travels 276 miles from Tygart Lake State Park to Monongahela National Forest; the Greenbrier River Trail covers 80 miles from North Caldwell to Cass; and the 234-mile Allegheny Trail runs north from Peters Mountain in Monroe County to the Pennsylvania line near Morgantown.

West Virginia misses out on some of the spectacular flights of waterfowl seen farther west and east, but the state has Red Spruces, Sugar Maples, Black Oaks, and American Sycamores enough to attract a variety of breeding birds from mountain ridge to river bottom. Species whose ranges extend well north into Canada, such as Blue-headed Vireos and Northern Saw-whet Owls, inhabit the highlands, while more southern birds, including Yellow-billed Cuckoos and Carolina Wrens, call the lowlands home.

There are one national forest, one national wildlife refuge, nine state forests, and 36 state parks in West Virginia.

OHIO RIVER ISLANDS
NATIONAL WILDLIFE REFUGE

Common Muskrat

The 38 islands that dot the Ohio River for 362 miles along the northwest boundary of West Virginia have always been known for their wildlife. The back channels near the islands provide nursery and feeding grounds for more than 50 species of warm-water fishes. These shallow waters also harbor one of the finest assemblages of freshwater mussels in North America; the bivalves, wonderfully varied in form, have names like Ohio River Pig-toe and Pink Mucket Pearly Mussel. Common mammals include muskrat, Virginia Opossum, Mink, American Beaver, Woodchuck, and White-tailed Deer. Waterfowl are numerous. Great Blue Herons nest on a few of the islands, and in general the river islands are great for birdwatching. Since 1990, when the refuge was established, efforts have been underway to protect all of the Ohio River islands. Thus far 19 are part of the refuge, with more than 1,100 total acres.

LOCATION Two islands in Pennsylvania, 15 in West Virginia, two in Kentucky; many north of Parkersburg, WV, with seven clustered near Sistersville. **CONTACT** Ohio River Islands N.W.R., 3004 7th St., P.O. Box 1811, Parkersburg, WV 26102; 304-422-0752.

KANAWHA STATE FOREST   **Charleston**

Just south of the capital city of Charleston is the beautiful, 9,302-acre expanse of Kanawha State Forest. This is the picnic spot of choice for Charlestonians. But if you hanker for some hiking, botanizing, and birdwatching to make your visit complete, Kanawha will also fit the bill very nicely. For hik-

ers and walkers there are 19 trails, ranging in length from ¼ to 2½ miles. Alligator Rock, Hemlock Falls, Johnson Hollow, Mossy Rock, and Spotted Salamander are but a few of the interesting trails within the forest. Spotted Salamander Trail is specially designed for wheelchair-bound and blind people. Budding and seasoned botanists can search out some of the 1,000 species of plants here, among them some 23 species of orchids, including Yellow-fringed Orchis and Showy Orchis. Birdwatchers will find the Appalachian cove forest breeding-bird populations outstanding; colorful wood warblers alone number 19 species.

LOCATION South of Charleston, off Rte. 119, exit 58A. **CONTACT** Kanawha S.F., Rte. 2, Box 285, Charleston, WV 25314; 304-558-3500.

MONONGAHELA NATIONAL FOREST

Monongahela National Forest, more than 900,000 acres of wild mountain and forest landscapes in eastern West Virginia, is the state's largest parcel of land preserved under one agency. Within its borders, Monongahela has extensive rich northern hardwood forests of beech, maple, and birch; luxurious stands of Red Spruce; splendid waterfalls; and various physical features whose names need a bit of translation. In West Virginia, a bog is known as a "glade," and mountain peaks are referred to as "knobs"; a West Virginia Appalachian mountain bald is called a "sod." The national forest has its share of all three.

The forest's diverse ecosystem—elevations from 1,000 to 4,861 feet, a variety of tree types and ages, plus wetlands, cliffs, grassy meadows, and cascading streams—provides a multitude of habitats for 70 species of resident birds, 89 breeding migrants, and 71 non-breeding migratory bird species.

Every region of the forest has its highlights, but the northern district of Monongahela has perhaps the greatest abundance of noteworthy sites. Gaudineer Scenic Area has the largest tract (140 acres) of virgin Red Spruce in the state. If you are herpetologically inclined, search for the Cheat Mountain Salamander, which lives here and nowhere else on earth. Three designated wilderness areas—Otter Creek, Laurel Fork North, and Laurel

North Fork Mountain

Fork South—offer more than 32,000 acres of unmanaged forests and rivers to explore. The very local and endangered West Virginia Northern Flying Squirrel inhabits Otter Creek woodlands. Look throughout these regions for signs of Black Bears and other mammals, whose tracks are often easier to find than the creatures themselves. The endearingly spritely Golden-crowned Kinglet is quite common in coniferous settings.

Spruce Knob/Seneca Rocks National Recreation Area has the highest peak in the state, as well as several fine hiking trails, ranging from the 1-mile Big Bend Loop Trail to the 24-mile North Fork Mountain Trail. Unique to this forest—in fact, unique to West Virginia—are the so-called cedar glades at Smoke Hole, in the northeasternmost part of the national forest. Here, in the mountains' rain shadow, dry limestone and shale barrens, as well as the

Big Run Beaver Pond

glades themselves, support a mixture of plants, including dwarf pines, quite unlike that found anywhere else in the region. Visit two nearby state parks, both within the forest's boundaries: Canaan Valley (see page 428) is the highest major river valley in the East, and Blackwater Falls has a marvelously photogenic river that drops 560 feet within the parks' 1,700 acres.

In the southern part of the national forest, check out the trails of Seneca State Forest, West Virginia's oldest, and Watoga State Park, the state's largest. Both provide access to 80-mile-long Greenbrier River Trail while offering many miles of trails of their own—23 in Seneca and 30 in Watoga. The Brooks Arboretum at Watoga contains mature Yellow Poplars, Ohio Buckeyes, cottonwoods, and scores of other native species.

In the beautiful mountain valley known as the Lake Sherwood Recreation Area, choose from a variety of trails that include Upper Meadow Trail (1.2 miles), which is lined with pines, rhododendrons, and hardwoods; Meadow Creek Trail (2.7 miles), which has good opportunities to see wildlife; and Meadow Mountain Trail (3.5 miles), which provides panoramic views of Meadow Creek Valley and Lake Sherwood.

The Highland Scenic Highway, extending 43 miles from Richwood to U.S. Route 219, about 7 miles north of Marlinton, is a beautiful corridor through Monongahela National Forest. The highway traverses the mountainous terrain of the Allegheny Plateau and rises from an elevation of 2,325 feet at Richwood to more than 4,500 feet along its route. Six miles west of the Cranberry Mountain Visitor Center, a ¾-mile trail provides access to three waterfalls cascading over rock layers of sandstone and shale at Falls of Hills Creek.

LOCATION Eastern West Virginia. CONTACT Monongahela N.F., USDA Forest Svc., 200 Sycamore St., Elkins, WV 26241; 304-636-1800. VISITOR CENTERS Cranberry Mountain Visitor Ctr., on Rte. 39 in the southern part of the forest, and Seneca Rocks Visitor Ctr. in the north, at intersection of Rtes. 28 and 33.

BLUESTONE STATE PARK **Hinton**

In southeastern West Virginia, near the confluence of the Bluestone River (a National Scenic River) and the New River (despite its name, America's oldest river) lie two fine state parks, with 6,000 acres of mountain peaks, waterfalls, gorges, steep hillsides, open water, and fine forests between them. Bluestone State Park, with 2,155 acres,

Falls feeding Bluestone Lake

showcases glistening Bluestone Lake and a surrounding woodland with good populations of Bobcats and Wild Turkeys. All variety of boats are available for rental. The Bluestone River has an abundance of aquatic life that attracts kingfishers and Great Blue Herons. The river and its gorge support a variety of mammals, including American Beavers, foxes, Bobcats, and White-tailed Deer. Mushrooms and wildflowers thrive throughout the park. Hikers will enjoy the 2-mile Boundary Trail, which leads to a forest cave site.

LOCATION Off State Rte. 20. **CONTACT** Bluestone S.P., HC 78, Box 3, Hinton, WV 25951; 304-466-2805. **VISITOR CENTER** 2 miles from park entrance.

PIPESTEM RESORT STATE PARK **Pipestem**

Located south of Bluestone State Park, Pipestem is named for a flowering shrub (also known as Meadowsweet) that is common in the area. The Bluestone River has gouged out a 1,200-foot-deep gorge; hike the Canyon Rim Trail to Heritage Point for spectacular views of the gorge. Pipestem's 4,023 acres harbor 19 species of salamanders and a great fall hawk-watching vantage point atop Pipestem Knob. Year-round nature programs are offered by park personnel.

LOCATION Off State Rte. 20. **CONTACT** Pipestem Res. S.P., Box 150, Pipestem, WV; 25550; 304-466-1800. **VISITOR CENTER** 1½ miles from park entrance.

CRANBERRY GLADES BOTANICAL AREA Marlinton

Sheltered in a 3,400-foot-high bowl at the foot of Cranberry, Kennison, and Black Mountains, 750-acre Cranberry Glades Botanical Area is remarkable in many respects. It is widely held to be the finest gladed (bog) area in West Virginia, and is often mentioned as one of the most outstanding in the East.

From the visitor center, a half-mile boardwalk crosses through one of the otherwise virtually impenetrable alder and shrub thickets and across two of the area's four glades. The botanical richness of these bogs includes Bog Rosemary, at its southernmost limit, Cotton Grass, two species of cranberries, sphagnum mosses and lichens, sparkling if diminutive sundews, and a number of dazzling orchids.

Bogs are acidic wetlands more commonly found in the northern areas of the United States and in Canada. The bog forest in Cranberry Glades is made up of Red Spruce, hemlock, and Yellow Birch, trees that have the shallow roots needed to survive in this wet area. Round Glade affords a close look at the bog's vegetative structure; sphagnum moss grows on the surface, while dead and decaying moss, called peat, extends below the surface several feet. These layers of moss and peat give the areas its "sponginess." Also in Round Glade, look for the tiny Cranberry vine, which grows in the sphagnum moss.

Orchids grow in Flag Glade. Both the Snake-mouth and the Grass Pink orchid can be seen here in late June and early July. Tiny sundews, carnivorous plants with leaves smaller than a fingernail, can be seen on the left side of the walk in Flag Glade.

At least five species of birds—Swainson's and Hermit Thrushes, Mourning Warbler, Northern Waterthrush, and Purple Finch—are at their southernmost breeding limits in the eastern U.S. here. Among the mammals that have been sighted are White-tailed Deer, Mink, Bobcat, Snowshoe Hare, and Eastern Cottontail. Local roads may not be plowed in winter.

LOCATION Along Rte. 39/55, west of Marlinton. **CONTACT** Cranberry Glades Botanical Area, U.S. Forest Svc., P.O. Box 110, Richwood, WV 26261; summer: 304-653-4826, winter: 304-846-2695. **VISITOR CENTER** Cranberry Mountain Visitor Ctr., on Rte. 39 in the southern part of the forest.

CRANESVILLE SWAMP
NATURE PRESERVE
Terra Alta

Southeast of Morgantown, near the Maryland border, lie two fascinating, yet very different natural areas. Combine them for a full day's nature experience. Cranesville Swamp Nature Preserve, a Nature Conservancy property, has as the highlight of its 1,200 acres an extraordinary mountain bog, with a 2,500-foot boardwalk to allow visiting naturalists to explore in comfort. Cranesville Swamp is a peatland bog, a permanently wet area where partially decomposed plant debris has collected and compacted into acidic and nutrient-poor peat. Cotton Grass and various carnivorous plants, including sundews and pitcher plants, are some of the more than 200 plant species that also thrive here. As most trees are unable to survive in these harsh conditions, the dominant plants are sedges, cranberry, and sphagnum moss. Around the bog is an extensive woodland of Red Spruce, Yellow Birch, Quaking Aspen, and the southernmost stands of Tamarack.

LOCATION Cranesville–Terra Alta Rd., off Rte. 7 in Terra Alta. CONTACT Cranesville Swamp N.P., Nature Conservancy of WV, P.O. Box 3754, Charleston, WV 25337; 304-637-0160.

CATHEDRAL STATE PARK
Aurora

From Cranesville Swamp Nature Preserve (above), head south to Cathedral State Park, one of the last living commemorations of the vast virgin hemlock forest that once flourished in the Appalachian highlands, and home to the Centennial Hemlock—123 feet tall, 18 feet around, and 500 years old, and only one of hundreds of virgin Eastern Hemlocks found in this 133-acre park. Meandering paths wind through the towering columns of hemlocks and past fine beeches, oaks, spruces, and rhododendrons. Trailing Arbutus, Jack-in-

Jack-in-the-Pulpit

the-Pulpit, and Canada Violet brighten the forest floor with delightful springtime blossoms. Road conditions may become difficult in winter.

LOCATION Along Rte. 50 in Aurora. CONTACT Cathedral S.P., Rte. 1, Box 370, Aurora, WV 26705; 304-735-3771. VISITOR CENTER Maps available at park entrance.

DOLLY SODS WILDERNESS AND SCENIC AREA

Laneville

A visit to the Dolly Sods, an area of high-elevation, windswept plains on the Allegheny Plateau, is an otherworldly experience. At 2,600 to 4,000 feet above sea level, this ridgetop preserve, 13 miles long and between 2 and 4 miles wide, is often enveloped in a cool, misty shroud. The land is a mosaic of mountain streams, grassy balds, sphagnum bogs, and scattered Red Spruces that flag all of their branches to the east because of the prevailing and persistent west winds. The area is named for the Dahle family, who once raised livestock on the grassy sods here. In winter 12 feet or more of snow can fall on the Dolly Sods, and a few drifts persist into May, so most visitors plan their explorations for the warmer months. Fourteen trails run for 45 miles across this wilderness, and hikers soon discover that the trails come with outstanding scenery but without bridges through and over wetland areas. Thin, acidic soils such as

those of the Dolly Sods are perfect for ericaceous (heath) plant growth; the entire area is overrun with rhododendrons, azaleas, Trailing Arbutus, blueberries, and huckleberries. Bleeding Heart blooms beneath dwarf birches and maples in early May, while Mountain Laurels flower in full splendor the first two weeks of June. About 100 species of birds are known from here; there is a large bird-banding operation in the fall. As the main access road to the area is not paved, winter visits are not recommended.

LOCATION Within Monongahela National Forest, between Rtes. 32 and 4, on Forest Rd. 19. **CONTACT** Dolly Sods Wilderness and Scenic Area, District Ranger, Potomac Ranger District, U.S. Forest Svc., Rte. 3, Box 240, Petersburg, WV 26847; 304-257-4488.

ALTONA PIEDMONT MARSH
Charles Town

Rails and Red-winged Blackbirds inhabit the extensive acreage here at this noteworthy Shenandoah Valley marshland. Wintering populations of American Woodcocks may be large. **CONTACT** West Virginia Nature Conservancy, P.O. Box 3754, Charleston, WV 25337; 304-345-4350.

Babcock State Park

BABCOCK STATE PARK
Clifftop

Twenty miles of hiking trails cross this 4,127-acre park, past spring and summer floral displays of Mountain Rosebay and Great Laurel. **CONTACT** Babcock S.P., HC 35, Box 150, Clifftop, WV 25831; 304-438-3004.

CABWAYLINGO STATE FOREST
Dunlow

These 8,123 acres may be enjoyed along hiking trails ranging from 1 to 3 miles in length. Twelvepole Creek offers good trout fishing and a fine scenic corridor through the forest. **CONTACT** Cabwaylingo S.F., W.V. Division of Natural Resources, Rte. 1, Box 85, Dunlow, WV 25511; 304-385-4255.

CACAPON RESORT STATE PARK
Berkeley Springs

Cacapon has 6,000 acres—more than 20 miles of hiking and bridle trails through mixed hardwood forests and scenic sandstone outcrops. **CONTACT** Cacapon Resort S.P., Rte. 1, Box 304, Berkeley Springs, WV 25411; 304-258-1022.

CANAAN VALLEY NATIONAL WILDLIFE REFUGE
Tucker County

High elevation (average 3,200 feet) and a cool, moist climate have created a unique wetland and northern forest in Canaan Valley, which is 14 miles long and 5 miles wide. This boreal ecosystem—plants (580 species) and vertebrates (290 species) usually found much farther north—has been called a little bit of Canada gone astray. **CONTACT** Canaan Valley N.W.R., P.O. Box 1278, Rte. 250 South, Elkins, WV 26241; 304-637-7312.

COOPERS ROCK STATE FOREST
Morgantown

The state's largest state forest (17,713 acres) offers spectacular views 1,200 feet above the Cheat River, and 50 miles of hiking and cross-country ski trails—ideal territory for year-round nature exploration. **CONTACT** Coopers Rock S.F., Rte. 1, Box 270, Bruceton Mills, WV 26525; 304-594-1561.

FORK CREEK WILDLIFE MANAGEMENT AREA
Charleston

With 9,000 acres and fine populations of raccoons, foxes, Virginia Opossums, and Striped Skunks, as well as excellent wildflowers and butterflies, this is a perfect day trip from Charleston. **CONTACT** Fork Creek W.M.A., Rte. 1, Box 484, Point Pleasant, WV 25550; 304-675-0871.

LARENIM PARK
Burlington

West Virginia has a lot of butterflies. The beautiful Olympia Marble, very local in distribution, is a highlight of this 365-acre shale-barren park. **CONTACT** Larenim Park, 150 Armstrong St., Kaiser, WV 26726; 304-788-5732.

MOUNTWOOD COUNTY PARK
Parkersburg

With 2,600 acres of woodlands and 9 miles of streamside creeks, this park offers great birding—up to 20 nesting wood warblers. **CONTACT** Mountwood C.P., Rte. 2, Box 56, Waverly, WV 26184; 304-679-3611.

TOMLINSON RUN STATE PARK
New Manchester

With 1,400 acres of northern hardwoods, lofty sandstone and shale cliffs, and the steep gorge of Tomlinson Run itself, this park is a beautiful wilderness spot. **CONTACT** Tomlinson Run S.P., P.O. Box 97, New Manchester, WV 26056; 304-564-3651.

The Authors

Peter Alden, principal author of this series, is a birder, naturalist, author, and lecturer. He has led nature tours to over 100 countries for the Massachusetts Audubon Society, Lindblad Travel, Friends of the Harvard Museum of Natural History, and cruises on all the world's oceans. Author of books on North American, Latin American, and African wildlife, Peter organized an event called Biodiversity Day in his hometown of Concord, Massachusetts.

Brian Cassie, author of the habitats, parks and preserves, and other sections of this guide, writes and teaches about natural history. He is the co-author of the *National Audubon Society Field Guide to New England*. Brian lives with his family in Foxboro, Massachusetts.

Jonathan D. W. Kahl, Ph.D., co-wrote the weather section of this book. He teaches and researches meteorology, air pollution, and climate at the University of Wisconsin in Milwaukee. Jon has published professional articles and children's books on atmospheric science and weather, including the *National Audubon Society First Field Guide: Weather*.

Eric A. Oches, Ph.D., author of the topography and geology section of this guide, is an assistant professor in the Department of Geology and Environmental Science and Policy Program at the University of South Florida. He has also written on geology for other guides in this series.

Harry Zirlin co-wrote the invertebrates section of this book. Harry travels extensively in the United States, studying and photographing insects, and his photographs and writings have been featured in numerous publications, including *American Butterflies*.

Wendy B. Zomlefer, Ph.D., co-author and consultant of the flora section of this guide, is a post-doctoral associate in the botany department at the University of Florida in Gainesville and courtesy assistant curator of the University of Florida Herbarium.

Acknowledgments

The authors collectively thank the many botanists, zoologists, geologists, artists, photographers, and naturalists we have worked with over the years and whose books and papers provided a wealth of information for this book. The following organizations were especially helpful: National Audubon Society, Massachusetts and New Jersey Audubon Societies, Audubon Naturalist Society of the Central Atlantic States, Harvard Museum of Natural History, Nature Conservancy, American Museum of Natural History, Academy of Natural Sciences of Philadelphia, Smithsonian Institution, Linnaean Society of New York, American Birding Association, North American Butterfly Association, and Roger Tory Peterson Institute. We also thank the staffs of the many federal and state land, game, and fish departments.

We thank the following experts for their help in writing and reviewing various sections of this guide: Rudolf Arndt (fishes); John L. Behler (amphibians and reptiles); Richard Keene (weather and night sky); Amy Leventer (topography and geology); Gary Mechler (weather and night sky); Jeffrey Ryan (topography and geology); Stephen Sharnoff and Sylvia Sharnoff (lichens); Ernie Brodo, Jonathan Dey, Elizabeth Kneiper, and Bruce Ryan (lichens selections). Guy Tudor, the regional consultant, reviewed several sections of the book.

Special thanks go to Paul Boccardi, Bill and Peggy Brace, Richard Carey, Sarah Jane Cassie, Rick Cech, Tom Davis, Sidney Dunkle, Pete Dunne, Michael Fahey, John Flicker, the late Richard Forster, Frank Gill, Karsten Hartel, Fred Heath, Boris Kondratieff, Vernon Laux, Paul Opler, Dennis Paulson, Simon Perkins, Wayne Petersen, the late Roger Tory Peterson, Virginia Peterson, Noble Proctor, Bob Ridgely, Judy Schwenk, Jeff Stone, Richard Walton, and Edward O. Wilson.

We are grateful to Andrew Stewart for his vision of a regional field guide encompassing the vast mosaic of the Mid-Atlantic region's topography, habitats, and wildlife, and to the staff of Chanticleer Press for producing a book of such excellence. Editor-in-chief Amy Hughes provided conceptual guidance as well as constant encouragement and supervision. Series and project editor Patricia Fogarty was the project's guiding light, and the success of the book is due largely to her expertise. Senior editor Miriam Harris and editors Pamela Nelson and Holly Thompson thoroughly examined and refined the invertebrates and flora sections. Managing editor George Scott shepherded the book through the editorial process. Associate editor Michelle Bredeson fact checked, copyedited, and proofread the book through all stages. Assistant editor Elizabeth Wright and editorial interns Samten Chhosphel, Abby Gordon, and Morisa Kessler-Zacharias offered much assistance and support. Editorial freelancers Jennifer Dixon, Lisa Lester, Lisa Leventer, and Mike Stanzilis (aka Mike Taylor), made many valuable contributions. Art director Drew Stevens and designers Vincent Mejia and Anthony Liptak took 1,500 images and tens of thousands of words of text and created a book that is both visually beautiful and eminently usable. Patricia Harris assisted in the layout of the book. Howard S. Friedman created the beautiful and informative color illustrations. Wil Tirion produced the stunning night sky maps. Ortelius Design made the many detailed maps that appear throughout the book, and the mammal tracks illustrations were contributed by Dot Barlowe. Photo director Zan Carter and her staff sifted through thousands of photographs in their search for the stunning images that contribute so much to the beauty and usefulness of this guide. They carefully chose images that best represented each subject, and worked patiently with the authors, consultants, and natural history experts. Photo editors Jennifer McClanaghan and Christine Heslin researched and edited the photos used in the parks and preserves and overview sections, respectively. Linda Patterson Eger and Lois Safrani of Artemis Picture Research Group, Inc., brought considerable skills and experience to the research and editing of many of the species photographs. Permissions manager Alyssa Sachar facilitated the acquisition of photographs and ensured that all photo credits were accurate. Photo editor Ruth Jeyaveeran and photo assistants Karin Murphy, Leslie Fink, and Marie Buendia offered endless support. Dan Hugos's database kept track of hundreds of photographers and thousands of photographs. Director of production Alicia Mills and production manager Philip Pfeifer saw the book through the complicated production and printing processes. They worked closely with Dai Nippon Printing to ensure the excellent quality of these books. Office manager Raquel Penzo offered much support.

In addition, we thank all of the photographers who gathered and submitted the gorgeous pictures that make this book a delight to view.

—Peter Alden, Brian Cassie,
Jonathan D. W. Kahl, Eric A. Oches,
Harry Zirlin, Wendy B. Zomlefer

Picture Credits

The credits are listed alphabetically by photographer. Each photograph is listed by the number of the page on which it appears, followed by a letter indicating its position on the page (the letters follow a sequence from top left to bottom right).

Kevin Adams 136f, 147a & c, 160e, 162d, 163a, 167a, 171b & e, 173c, 178a, 179a, 181a & b
Gene Ahrens 34b
Frederick D. Atwood 19a
Ron Austing 225e, 262b, 282d, 286c, 289a, 292a & c, 302b, 304a, 308d, 309b, c & d, 310a, 311a, b & d, 312c, 313b, 321b, 325c, 326a, 328b, 334a, 336d, 339c, 340d, 355a
Robert E. Barber 361b
R. D. Bartlett 259d
Bill Beatty 108c, 112a, 113e, 114e, 116e, 117b, 131e, 137b, 140c, 161f, 165e, 187b, 214e, 259b & e, 425
Lance Beeny 232d
Steve Bentsen 295a, 310c
Bio-Photo Services
Jeanne Apelseth 110c
Kerry Dressler 89d, 112d, 116a, 120d, 121a & b, 163c, 181c
Kit Breen 378
Bruce Coleman, Inc.
Phyllis Betow 215d
Michael H. Black 117c
Robert P. Carr 131f
E. R. Degginger 251c
Michael P. Gadomski 117a
Keith Gunnar 123f
Hans Reinhard 119c
John Shaw 123e
Joy Spurr 116d
Norman Owen Tomalin 244c
L. West 60b
Fred Bruemmer 304b
Bucks County Audubon Society 48b
Sonja Bullaty & Angelo Lomeo 102c, 103c, 105a, c & d, 107b, 109a, 113a & b, 116c, 120b, 122c, 123d
Gay Bumgarner 308b, 337d, 341d, 342b
Joyce Burek 179b
George H. Burgess 246e, 247e
The Caddisfly Handbook* 212c
Scott Camazine 214c
David Cavagnaro 96d, 105e, 111e, 114b, 122f, 129a, 155a & e, 169b, 177a
Rick Cech 122a, 162e, 165b, 205a, 222a, 223b & d, 224c & d, 225c, 226a, b & c, 227a & e, 228b, d & e, 229a, d & e, 230a, b, d & e
Kathy Adams Clark/ KAC Productions 228c
Herbert Clarke 276b, 295b, 303a, 306b & d, 316a, 322a, 325b, 327a, 329c, 331d
Willard Clay 424a & b
CNAAR
Suzanne L. Collins 268d
Suzanne L. & Joseph T. Collins 266a
John M. Coffman 36, 80a, 99e, 209b, 211e
Eliot Cohen 156b
Color-Pic, Inc.
E. R. Degginger 15a, 20a, 23a & c, 26b, 31b, 80b, 83c, 87c, 90d, 91c, 92a, 93c, 97a, c & d, 98e, 99a, b, c & f, 112c, 115a, 120a, 126e, 128c, 129d, 136c, 139b, 140e, 141b, 146c, 157d, 158c, 159e, 160c, 164c, 168d, 170d, 173e, 176d, 185c, 191d, 192, 193d & e, 195a, 196b, 197d, 199a, 200c, 205d, 208a, b & e, 211d, 212b, e & f, 214a, 215a, 216b & c,
220b, c, d & e, 221a, 222b, 224e, 227d, 229b, 231e, 233d, 234a & c, 243a, 253a, 254e, 255d, 258b, 262c, 269c, 270b, 271d, 303f, 340c
Phil Degginger 37b, 252d, 256b
Gerald & Buff Corsi/ Focus on Nature, Inc. 318b
Daniel J. Cox/Natural Exposures, Inc. 358b, 359b, 364b
Bob Cranston 249c
Sharon Cummings 300c, 339a, 352d
Rob Curtis/The Early Birder 80d, 150d, 172b, 207e, 211b, 214d, 223e, 233c, 315c, 318c, 319a, 321a, 328c, 336b, 337a, 338a
Jaret C. Daniels 225d
Rameshwar Das 397a
Grace Davies 385a
Richard Day/Daybreak Imagery 265a
Larry Dech 86a, 89c, 92d, 93b
Dembinsky Photo Associates
Gary Meszaros 244a, 250c, 347c
Carl E. Sams 351a
David M. Dennis 258a & c, 259a, 267a
Jack Dermid 154a, 185d, 262a, 267d, 289b, 346, 350b
Alan & Linda Detrick 125e & f, 145b, 166b
Larry Ditto 283b, 339d
Christine M. Douglas 90b, 91b, 109b, 128d, 159c, 169d, 172d
Sidney W. Dunkle 203d & f, 204b, 206d, 207b
David Dvorak, Jr. 155d
Harry Ellis 153d
A. Murray Evans**

The Caddisfly Handbook: An Orvis Guide. The Lyons Press, New York, NY, 1999.
**From *A Field Manual of Ferns and Fern Allies of the United States and Canada* by D. B. Lellinger. Smithsonian Institution Press, Wash., DC, 1985.

Front Cover: Youghiogheny River, Pennsylvania, by Ed King

Spine: Higbee Beach, Cape May, New Jersey, by Jonathan Wallen

Back Cover: Pekka Parvianen/Science Photo Library/Photo Researchers, Inc. (a), Jack Dermid (b), Arthur Morris/BIRDS AS ART (c), Charles Gurche (d)

Index

Converting to Metric

Limited space makes it impossible for us to give measurements expressed as metrics. Here is a simplified chart for converting standard measurements to their metric equivalents:

	MULTIPLY BY
inches to millimeters	25
inches to centimeters	2.5
feet to meters	0.3
yards to meters	0.9
miles to kilometers	1.6
square miles to square kilometers	2.6
acres to hectares	.40
ounces to grams	28.3
pounds to kilograms	.45
Fahrenheit to Centigrade	subtract 32 and multiply by .55

Prepared and produced by Chanticleer Press, Inc.

Founder: Paul Steiner
Publisher: Andrew Stewart

Staff for this book:

Editor-in-Chief: Amy K. Hughes
Managing Editor: George Scott
Senior Editor: Miriam Harris
Series Editor: Patricia Fogarty
Contributing Editors: Pamela Nelson, Holly Thompson
Associate Editor: Michelle Bredeson
Assistant Editor: Elizabeth Wright
Photo Director: Zan Carter
Photo Editor: Ruth Jeyaveeran
Associate Photo Editor: Jennifer McClanaghan
Photo Research and Editing: Christine Heslin, Artemis Picture
Research Group, Inc.
Rights and Permissions Manager: Alyssa Sachar
Art Director: Drew Stevens
Designers: Vincent Mejia, Anthony Liptak
Director of Production: Alicia Mills
Production Manager: Philip Pfeifer
Office Manager: Raquel Penzo
Illustrations: Howard S. Friedman
Maps: Ortelius Design
Night Sky Maps: Wil Tirion

Series design by Drew Stevens and Vincent Mejia

All editorial inquiries should be addressed to:

Chanticleer Press
665 Broadway, Suite 1001
New York, NY 10012

To purchase this book or other National Audubon Society Field
Guides and Pocket Guides, please contact:

Alfred A. Knopf
201 East 50th Street
New York, NY 10022
(800) 733-3000
www.randomhouse.com